Cases and Materials in Banking Law

Cases and Materials in Banking Law

A. Arora

Senior Lecturer in Law,
Faculty of Law,
University of Liverpool

To Nikki

Pitman Publishing
128 Long Acre, London WC2E 9AN

A Division of Longman Group UK Limited

© Longman UK 1993

British Library cataloguing in Publication Data
A CIP catalogue record for this book is available from the British Library.

ISBN 0 273 03739 0

Typset by PanTek Arts, Maidstone, printed and bound in Great Britain
by Bell and Bain Ltd., Glasgow

Contents

Preface   vii

Table of Cases   ix

Table of Statutes   xxi

1 Parties to the banker–customer relationship   1

What is a bank or bank institution? Early attempts to define the term bank;
The Banking Act 1987; Other methods of regulation through the Banking
Act; Has regulation under the Banking Act 1987 been successful? The
influence of the European Community; Other reforms in banking law and
practice; The UK banking structure; Who is a customer? Capacity to contract
and types of customer

2 The bank account   53

Types of bank account; Obtaining services; Nature of an overdraft;
Repayment of an overdraft; Interest

3 The banker–customer relationship   60

The debtor–creditor relationship; Customer's right to recover credit balances;
Right to recover balances; Appropriation; The default rule case; Consolidation
of accounts (banker's set-off); The Banking and Building Societies'
Ombudsmen

4 The banking contract   77

Duties owed by the bank to its customers; Duty to account; Duties owed by
the customer to the bank; Duty of the bank in tort; Bankers' liability for
advice in respect of currency transactions

5 Termination of the banker–customer relationship   107

Termination by the customer; Termination by the bank; Termination by
operation of law; Outbreak of war; Liquidation of the bank

6 Negotiable instruments   122

What is a negotiable instrument? Payment by letter of credit; Payment by charge card; Payment equivalent to cash

7 Bills of exchange   132

Definitions and conditions for incurring liability; Parties to the instrument and conditions for incurring liability; Forged signatures and forgery of the instrument; Consideration on a bill of exchange; The holder in due course; Bill must be regular on the face of it; Good faith requirement; Estoppel and bills of exchange; Payment and discharge of a negotiable instrument; Alteration of a bill of exchange; Dishonour of a negotiable instrument

8 Cheques   162

Crossings on cheques; Restriction of the payment instruction; Recovery of amounts incorrectly paid; Liability of the paying and collecting banks in negligence; Further recommendations of the Jack Committee

9 Bank finance   189

Bank overdraft and term loans; Commercial documentary credits; Performance guarantees and performance bonds

10 Security for bankers' advances and enforcing the security   218

Factors affecting the validity of a security contract; Types of security; Can a bank be held liable in the insolvency of a company? Retention of title clauses

Appendix – The recommendations of the Bingham Report   253

Preface

This book has been written at a time of considerable change in the law and practice of banking. Although changes in the common law are to be expected in any area of law, the field of banking law has undergone substantial judicial scrutiny. The book aims to explain and deal with the established case law and to explain and illustrate recent judicial developments in their context. For example, the *Re Charge Card Ltd* case deals with the nature of a payment made by a debit card and the basis of the banker–customer relationship, and the duties and obligations owed under the banking contract have recently been examined in the *Tai Hing Cotton Mill Ltd* v *Liu Chong Hing Bank* case. Recent developments in areas of letters of credit, letters of comfort, cheques and negotiable instruments, insolvency law, and the obligations of receivers are examined in the book. All these developments are considered in the context of their effect on banking law.

In addition to the common law changes, the recommendations of the Jack Committee Report are examined in detail. The response of the government, and the banks and other financial institutions is also examined, in particular with regard to the effect of the Cheques Act 1992.

Finally, I would like to thank all those people who have encouraged and assisted me in the completion of this project. My thanks are due to Patrick Bond from Pitman Publishing and the secretarial staff in the Faculty of Law at the University of Liverpool, especially Miss Ann Doherty for all her hard work and patience. Finally, I would like to thank my husband for his encouragement.

A. Arora
July 1992

Table of cases

A.E. Lindsay & Co. v Cook [1953] 1 Lloyd's Rep 328 *194*
A.L. Underwood Ltd v Bank of Liverpool [1924] 1 KB 775 *81, 178*
Accurist Watches Ltd v King [1922] FSR 80 *250*
AGIP (Africa) Ltd v Jackson & Others [1991] 3 WLR 116 *49, 171, 173*
Allcard v Skinner [1887] 36 Ch D 145 *219*
Alliance Bank v Kearsley [1891] LR 6 CP 433 *44*
Aluminium Industrie Vaasen BV v Romalpa Aluminium Ltd [1976] 2 All ER 552
    247, 248
Amalgamated Investments & Property Co. Ltd v Texas Commerce International
Bank Ltd [1982] 1 Lloyd's Rep 27 *233*
American Express v Hurley [1985] 3 All ER 564 *225, 241*
Anglo Overseas Agencies Ltd v Green [1961] 1 QB 1 *46*
Arab Bank Ltd v Barclays Bank [1952] AC 495 *120*
Arab Bank Ltd v Barclays Bank (Dominion, Colonial and Overseas) Ltd [1952]
    WN 529 *65*
Arab Bank Ltd v Ross [1952] 2 QB 216 *151*
Arrow Transfer Co. Ltd v The Royal Bank of Canada and Bank of Montreal [1972]
    SCR 845 *168*
Ashbury Railway Carriage & Co. v Riche [1875] LR 7 HL 653 *46*
Astro Exito Navegacion SC v Chase Manhattan Bank NA (*The Messiniake Tolmi*)
    [1988] 2 Lloyd's Rep 217 *201*
Attock Cement Co. Ltd v Romanian Bank for Foreign Trade [1989] 1 All ER
    1189 *217*
Auchteroni & Co. v Midland Bank Ltd [1928] 2 KB 294 *154, 175*
Austin v Bunyard [1865] 6 B & S 687 *135*

Baden, Delvaux and Lecuit v Société General pour Favoriser le Developpement du
Commerce et de l'Industrie en France SA [1983] BCLC 325 *48, 49*
Baines v National Provincial Bank Ltd [1927] 96 LJKB 801 *175*
Baker v Australia & New Zealand Bank Ltd [1958] NZLR 907 *79, 80*
Baker v Barclays Bank Ltd [1955] 1 WLR 822 *182*
Balmoral Supermarket Ltd v Bank of New Zealand [1974] 2 NZLR 155 *62*
Banbury v Bank of Montreal [1918] AC 626 *104*
Bank of Baroda v Panessar [1982] 2 BCC 288 *117*

Bank of Baroda v Shah [1988] 3 All ER 24 *220*

Bank of Chettinad Ltd of Colombo v Inland Revenue Commissioners of Colombo [1948] AC 378 *4*

Bank of Credit and Commerce International SA v Aboody [1989] 2 WLR 759 *220*

Bank of Credit and Commerce International SA v Dawson and Wright [1987] FLR 342 *152, 228*

Bank of Cyprus (London) v Gill [1980] 2 Lloyd's Rep 51 *240*

Bank of England v Riley [1922] 2 WLR 840 *8*

Bank of England v Vagliano Brothers [1891] AC 107 *137, 138, 139, 144*

Bank Melli Iran v Barclays Bank DCO Ltd [1951] 1 Lloyd's Rep 367 *200*

Bank of Montreal v Stuart [1911] AC 20 *219*

Bank of Montreal v The Exhibit and Trading Co. Ltd (1906) 11 Com Cas 250 *160*

Bank of Scotland v Wright (QB, 13 July 1990) *233*

Bank of Tokyo v Karoon [1984] 1 AC 45 *90*

Bankers Trust Co. v Shapira [1980] 3 All ER 353 *85*

Bankers Trust Co. v State Bank of India (*The Times*, 25 June 1991) *204*

Banque Belge pour l'Etranger v Hambrouck [1921] 1 KB 321 at p. 334 *170*

Banque Brussels Lambert SA v Australian National Industries (JBL May 1919 p. 282) *236*

Banque de l'Indochine et de Suez v Euroseas Group Finance Co. Ltd [1981] 3 All ER 198 *143*

Banque de L'Indochine et de Suez SA v J.H. Rayner (Mincing Lane) Ltd [1983] 1 All ER 468 *202*

Barber & Nicholls v R & G Associates (London) Ltd [1985] CLY 129 *143*

Barclays Bank Ltd v Aschaffenberger Zellstoffwerke AG [1967] 1 Lloyd's Rep 387 *131*

Barclays Bank Ltd v Astley Industrial Trust Ltd [1970] 2 QB 527 *178, 228*

Barclays Bank Ltd v Beck [1952] 1 All ER 549 *239*

Barclays Bank Ltd v Harding [1963] 1 WLR 102 *94*

Barclays Bank Ltd v Khaira & Another (*The Times*, 19 December 1991) *241*

Barclays Bank Ltd v Okenarhe [1966] 2 Lloyd's Rep 87 *41, 71, 72*

Barclays Bank Ltd v Quincecare Ltd [1988] 1 FTLR 507 *94*

Barclays Bank Ltd v Quistclose Investments Ltd [1970] AC 567 *50, 73*

Barclays Bank Ltd v W.J. Simms Son & Cooke (Southern) Ltd and Another [1980] 1 QB 677 *169*

Barlow v Broadhurst [1820] 4 Moor CP 471 *136*

Barnes v Addy [1874] 9 Ch App 244 *48*

Barnes v Williams & Glyn's Bank Ltd [1981] Com LR 205 *58*

Batra v Ebrahim [1982] QB 208 *208*

Bavins Jnr & Sons v London & South Western Bank [1900] 1 QB 270 *134*

Beavan, Davies, Bank & Co v Beavan [1913] 2 Ch 595 *110*

Bechuanaland Exploration Co. v London Trading Bank [1989] 2 QB 658 *123*

Beeman v Duck [1843] 11 M & W 251 *155*

Bell Houses Ltd v City Wall Properties Ltd [1966] 1 QB 207 *46*

Bhogul v Punjab National Bank [1988] 2 All ER 296 *73*

Bodenham *v* Hoskins [1852] 21 LJ Eq 846 at 869 *47*
Bolivinter Oil SA *v* Chase Manhattan Bank NA [1984] 1 Lloyd's Rep 251 *209*
Bolivinter Oil SA *v* Chase Manhattan Bank and Others [1984] 1 WLR 392 *216*
Bondina Ltd *v* Rollaway Shower Blinds Ltd [1986] 1 All ER 564 *142*
Borden (UK) Ltd *v* Scottish Timber Products Ltd [1979] 2 Lloyd's Rep 168
    248, 251
Bourne, Bourne *v* Bourne [1906] 2 Ch 427 *44*
Box *v* Midland Bank Ltd [1972] 2 Lloyd's Rep 391 *104*
Bradford Old Bank Ltd *v* Sutcliffe [1918] 2 KB 833 *70, 73*
Brandao *v* Barnett [1846] 12 Cl & Fin 787 *124, 226, 227*
Brewer *v* Westminster Bank Ltd [1952] 2 All ER 650 *42*
Brewer *v* Westminster Bank Ltd & Another [1952] 2 TLR 568 *145*
British Airways Board *v* Parish [1979] 2 Lloyd's Rep *143*
British Guiana Bank Ltd *v* Official Receiver [1911] 27 TLR 454 *74, 119*
Brook *v* Hook [1871] 47 LR 6 Ex 89 *145*
Brown *v* Westminster Bank Ltd [1964] 2 LR 187 *99*
Buckingham & Co. *v* London & Midland Bank Ltd [1895] 12 TLR 70 *73*
Burnett *v* Westminster Bank Ltd [1966] 1 QB 742 *102*
Bute (Marquess) *v* Barclays Bank Ltd [1955] 1 QB 202 *183, 184*

Calzaturificio Fiorella Spa *v* Walton and Another [1979] CLY 23 *130, 143*
Caparo Industries plc *v* Dickman [1990] 2 AC 605 *18, 19*
Carpenters' Company *v* British Mutual Banking Co. Ltd [1938] 1 KB 511 *173*
Carreras Rothmans Ltd *v* Freeman Mathews Treasure Ltd [1985] Ch 207 *51*
Catlin *v* Cyprus Finance Corporation (London) Ltd [1983] QB 759 *42*
Cebora SNC *v* SIP (Industrial Products) Ltd [1976] 1 Lloyd's Rep 271 *129*
Central Motors (Birmingham) Ltd *v* A. and S.N. Wadsworth [1983] CAT 82/231 *45*
Chamberlain *v* Young [1893] 2 QB 206 *136*
Chapman *v* Smethurst [1909] 1 KB 927 *142*
Chase Manhattan Bank NA *v* Israel British Bank (London) Ltd [1981] Ch 105 *171*
Chatterton *v* London & County Banking Co. Ltd (*The Times*, 21 January 1891) *101*
Chemco Leasing SpA *v* Rediffusion plc [1987] 1 FTLR 201 *234, 235*
China and South Sea Bank Ltd *v* Tan [1990] 1 Lloyd's Rep 113 *225*
Choice Investments Ltd *v* Jeromnimon (Midland Bank Ltd, garnishee) [1981] 1 All
    ER 225 *236*
Clare & Co *v* Dresdner Bank AG [1915] 2 KB 576 *107*
Claydon *v* Bradley [1978] 1 WLR 521 *135*
Clough Mill Ltd *v* Martin [1985] 1 WLR 11 *249*
Clutton *v* Attenborough [1897] AC 90 *139*
Co-operative Centrale Raiffaisen-Boerleenbank BA *v* Sumitomo Bank Ltd (*The
    Royan*) [1988] 2 Lloyd's Rep 250 *191, 204*
Coghlan & Amalgated Investments [1982] 1 QB 84 *233*
Cohn *v* Boulken [1920] 36 TLR 767 *136*
Cole *v* Milsome [1951] 1 All ER 311 *133, 134*
Commercial Bank of Scotland *v* Rhind [1860] 3 Mac. 643 *96*

Commissioners of Taxation *v* English, Scottish & Australian Bank Ltd [1920] AC 683 *39, 40*

Cooper *v* Meyer [1839] 10 B & C 468 *155*

Cooper *v* National Provincial Bank Ltd [1945] 2 All ER 641 *231*

Cornish *v* Midland Bank plc [1985] 3 All ER 513 *222*

Cory Brothers Co. *v* Mecca Turkish SS (Owners), *The Mecca* [1897] AC 286 *70*

Crears *v* Hunter [1887] 19 QBD 341 *150*

Cripps (Pharmaceuticals) Ltd *v* Wickenden [1973] 1 WLR 944 *117*

Crouch *v* Credit Foncier Co. of England (1873) LR 8 QB 374 *123*

Crumplin *v* London Joint Stock Bank Ltd [1913] 30 TLR 99 *182, 185*

Cuckmere Brick Co. Ltd *v* Mutual Finance Ltd [1971] 2 All ER 633 *118, 224, 225, 240, 241*

Currie *v* Misa [1876] LR 10 Exch 153 *126*

Cutts (a Bankrupt), *ex parte* Bognor Mutual Building Society *v* Trustee of TW Cutts [1956] 1 WLR 728 *114*

D. and C. Rees Builders Ltd *v* Rees [1966] 2 QB 617 *126*

Dakin *v* Bayly [1933] 290 US 143 *62*

Davidson *v* Barclays Bank Ltd [1940] 1 All ER 499 *79*

Davis *v* Bowsher [1795] 5 Term Rep 488 *227*

Davis *v* Kennedy [1868] 3 Ir R Eq 31 *5*

Deeley *v* Lloyds Bank Ltd [1912] AC 756 *67, 68, 243*

Delbrueck & Co *v* Manufacturers Hanover Trust Co. 609 F ed 1047 (2d Cir [1979]) *158*

Depositors Protection Fund *v* Dalia & Another (*The Times*, 9 July 1991) *20*

Devaynes *v* Noble – Clayton's case [1816] 1 Mer 572 *68, 69, 70, 242, 243*

Diamond *v* Graham [1968] 1 WLR 1061 *150*

Dix *v* Grainger [1992] 10 LILR 496 *193*

Douglass *v* Lloyds Bank Ltd [1929] 34 Com Cas 263 *66*

Drew *v* Nunn [1879] 4 QBD 661 *110*

Durham Fancy Goods Ltd *v* Michael Jackson (Fancy Goods) Ltd [1968] 2 All ER 987 *143*

Eaglehill Ltd *v* J. Needham Builders Ltd [1973] AC 992 *161*

EB Savory & Co *v* Lloyds Bank Ltd [1932] 2 KB 122 *174*

EDF Man Ltd *v* Nigerian Sweets and Confectionery Co. Ltd [1977] 2 Lloyd's Rep 50 *127*

Edward Owen Engineering Ltd *v* Barclays Bank International Ltd [1978] 1 All ER 976 *207, 212*

El-Nakib Investments (Jersey) Ltd *v* Longcroft [1990] 2 WLR 1930 *19*

Elliott *v* Bax-Ironside [1925] 2 KB 301 *142*

Ellison *v* Collingridge [1850] 9 CB 570 *135*

English, Scottish and Australian Bank *v* The Bank of South Africa [1922] 13 LILR 21 at 24 *200*

E.Pfeiffer Weinkellerei- Weineinkauf GmbH *v* Arbuthnot Factors Ltd [1987] 3 BCC 608 *249*

Equitable Trust Company of New York v Dawson Partners Ltd [1925] 25 LILR at 93 *191*

Equitable Trust Company of New York v Dawson Partners Ltd [1926] 25 LILR 90 *211, 212*

Equitable Trust Company of New York v Dawson Partners Ltd [1927] 27 LILR 49 *199*

Esal (Commodities) Ltd v Oriental Credit Ltd [1985] 2 Lloyd's Rep 546 *214*

Esdaile v La Nauze [1835] 1 Y & C Ex 394 *145*

Etablissements Chainbaux v Harbormaster Ltd [1955] 1 Lloyd's Rep 303 *193, 194, 198*

Ferson Contractors Ltd v Feris [1982] CLY 14 *130*

Fleming v New Zealand Bank Ltd [1900 AC 577 *105*

Floating Dock Ltd v Hong Kong and Shanghai Banking Corp. [1986] 1 Lloyd's Rep 65 *204*

Foley v Hill [1848] 2 HL Cas 28 *60, 61, 62, 63, 190*

Ford & Carter Ltd v Midland Bank Ltd [1979] 129 New LJ 543 *233*

Forestal Mimosa Ltd v Oriental Credit Ltd [1986] 2 All ER 400 *191*

Foti v Banque Nationale de Paris (17 March 1989) *106*

Garcia v Page & Co. Ltd [1936] 55 LILR 391 *193, 195*

Garnett v M?Kewn [1872] LR 8 Ex 10 *71, 72*

Garrard v James [1925] Ch 616 *232*

Gian Singh & Co Ltd v Bank de l'Indochine [1974] 1 WLR 1234 *207*

Gibbons v Westminster Bank Ltd [1939] 2 KB 882 *79*

Giddens v Angle-African Produce Co. Ltd [1923] 14 LILR 230 *197*

Gillespie Bros & Co. Ltd v Roy Bowles Transport Ltd [1973] QB 400 *225*

Gomba Holdings UK Ltd v Homan [1986] 1 WLR 1301 *116*

Gomba Holdings UK Ltd v Minories Finance Ltd [1989] 1 All ER 261 *118*

Goodwin v Robarts [1875-76] 1 App Cas 476 *123*

Gorgier v Mieville [1824]   3B & C 45 *124*

Gray v Johnston [1868] LR 3 HL 1 at 11 *48*

Great Western Railway Company v London and County Banking Company [1901] AC 414 *38, 39, 40, 162, 163*

Greenhough v Munroe [1931]   53 F 2d 362 *211*

Greenwood v Martins Bank [1932] 1 KB 371 *80, 98, 146*

Griffiths v Dalton [1940] 2 KB 264 *135, 160*

Guaranty Trust Co. v Van den Berghs Ltd [1926] 22 LILR 447 *201*

H. & J.M. Bennett Europe Ltd v Angrexco Co. Ltd (unreported, 6 April 1990) *192*

Hadley (Felix) & Co. v Hadley [1898] 2 Ch 680 *126*

Halesowen Pressworks & Assemblies Ltd v Westminster Bank Ltd [1971] 1 QB 1 *71, 228*

Halifax v Lyle [1849] 3 Exch 446 *155*

Hamilton v Watson [1845] 12 Cl & Fin 109 *230*

Hansan v Willson [1977] 1 Lloyd's Rep 431 *148, 149*

Harlow and Jones v American Express Bank and Creditanstalt-Bankerein (Third Party) [1990] 2 Lloyd's Rep 343 *204*

Hedley Byrne & Co. Ltd v Heller & Partners Ltd [1963] 2 All ER 575 *103, 222*

Henry v Burbidge [1837] 3 Bing NC 501 *156*

Hibernian Bank Ltd v Gysin and Hanson [1939] 1 KB 483 at p. 486-87 *163, 166*

Hick v Raymond & Reid [1893] AC 22 *194*

Hirschorn v Evans [1938] 2 KB 801 *43, 238*

Holland v Manchester and Liverpool District Banking Co [1909] 25 TLR 386 *96*

Holt v Markham [1923] 1 KB 504 *96*

Hong Kong and Shanghai Banking Corporation v Kloeckner & Co. AG [1990] 3 WLR 634 *72*

Hopkinson v Rolt [1861] 9HL Cas 514 *68, 242*

House Property Co. of London and Others v London County and Westminster Bank [1915] 89 LJKB 1846 *164, 166*

Howe Richardson Scale Co. Ltd v Polimex-Cekop & National Westminster Bank Ltd [1978] 1 Lloyd's Rep 161 *214*

Hunter v Hunter and Others [1936] AC 222 *239*

Imperial Bank of India v Abeysinghe [1927] 29-30 Ceylon NLR 257 *169*

Importers Co. Ltd v Westminster Bank Ltd [1927] 2 KB 297 *41*

In re a Company (No.001992 of 1988) [1988] BCLC 9 *116*

In re a Company (No.005009 of 1987), *ex p* Copp [1989] BCLC 13 *245*

In re B. Johnston & Co (Builders) Ltd (1955) Ch 634 *118*

In re Bishop deceased [1965] Ch 450 *43*

In re Bond Worth [1979] 3 All ER 919 *249*

In re Bottomgate Industrial Co-operative Society [1891] 65 Lt 712 *4, 11*

In re Brightlife Ltd [1978] Ch 200 *244*

In re Byfield, *ex p.* Hill Samuel & Co Ltd [1982] 1 All ER 249 *113*

In re Castell & Brown [1898] 1 Ch 315 *243, 244*

In re Charge Card Services Ltd [1988] 3 WlR 764 *128*

In re Consumer and Industrial Press Ltd [1988] BCLC 68 *115*

In re Court of Appeal [1983] 1 ALL ER 1137 *203*

In re Diplock [1948] Ch 465 *171, 172*

In re District Savings Bank, *ex parte* Coe [1861] 3 De GF & J 355 *3*

In re EJ Morel Ltd [1961] 1 All ER 796 *73*

In re EVTR [1987] BCLC 646 *51*

In re FLE Holdings Ltd [1967] 1 WLR 1409 *114*

In re Gray's Inn Construction Co. Ltd [1980] 1 WLR 711 *111, 112*

In re Gross, *ex p.* Kingston [1871] 6 Ch App 632 *46*

In re Hallett's Estate [1880] 13 Ch D 696 *13, 70, 248, 249*

In re Hone (a Bankrupt), *ex parte* Trustee v Kensington Borough Council [1951] Ch 85 *57*

In re Keever [1966] 3 All ER 631 *228*

In re M. Kushler Ltd [1943] 2 All ER 22

In re Multi Guarantee Co. Ltd [1987] BCLC 257 *51*

In re Potters Oils Ltd (No.2) [1986] 1 All ER 890 *117, 241*
In re Produce Marketing Consortium Ltd (No.2) [1989] BCLC 520 *246*
In re Romer & Haslam [1989] 2 QB 286 *125*
In re Russian Commercial and Industrial Bank [1955] Ch 148 *121*
In re Shields Estate [1901] 1 Ir R 172 *4, 11*
In re The Court of Appeal [1983] 1 All ER 1137 *203*
In re Wigzell, *ex p.* Hart [1921] 2 KB 835 *112*
In re Woodroffes (Musical Instruments) Ltd [1986] Ch 366 *244*
In re Yeovil Glove Company Ltd [1965] Ch 148 *68*
Intraco Ltd *v* Notis Shipping Corp. (*The Bhoja Trader*) [1981] 1 Lloyd's Rep 256 *214*

Jackson *v* White & Midland Bank Ltd [1967] 2 Lloyd's Rep 68 *42*
Jade International Steel Stahl and Eisen GmbH *v* Robert Nicholas (Steels) Ltd [1978] 3 WLR 39 *130*
Jefferys *v* Agra and Masterman's Bank [1866] LR 2 Eq 674 *227*
Joachimson *v* Swiss Bank Corporation [1872] LR 8 Ex 10 *108, 109, 175*
Joachimson *v* Swiss Bank Corporation [1921] 3 KB 110 *58, 61, 63, 78, 175, 239*
Jones *v* Gordon [1876-77] 2 App Cas 616 *152, 154*
Jones *v* Maynard [1951] Ch 572 *43*
Joseph Samson Lyons, *ex p.* Barclays Bank Ltd *v* The Trustee [1934] 51 TLR 24 *113*

Karak Rubber Co Ltd *v* Burden (No.2) [1972] 1 All ER 210 *48, 93, 94, 95*
Keane *v* Robarts [1819] 4 Madd 332-357 *48*
Kelly *v* Solari [1841] 9 M & W 54 *169*
Kepitigalla Rubber Estates ltd *v* National Bank of India Ltd [1909] 2 KB 1010 *100, 102*
Kleinworth Benson Ltd *v* Malaysia Mining Corporation Berhad [1988] 1 All ER 714 *235*
Koch *v* Dicks [1932] 49 TLR 24 *160*
Korea Exchange Bank *v* Debenhams (Central Buying) Ltd [1979] 1 Lloyd's Rep 549 *135*
Korea Industry Co. *v* Andoll [1990] 2 Lloyd's Rep 183 *208*
Kreditbank Cassel GmbH *v* Schenkers [1927] 1 KB 826 *145*
Kwei Tek Chao *v* British Traders & Shippers Ltd [1954] 1 All ER 779 *146, 160, 200*
Kydon Compania Naviera SA *v* National Westminster Bank Ltd [1981] 1 Lloyd's Rep 68 *201, 204*

Ladbroke *v* Todd [1914] 30 TLR 433 *40*
Landes *v* Marcus [1909] 25 TLR 478 *142*
Larner *v* L.C.C [1947] 2 KB 114 *96*
Latchford *v* Beirne [1981] 3 All ER 705 *225*
Leach *v* Buchanan [1802] 4 Esp 226 *145*

Leader & Co. *v* Direction der Disconto-Gessellschaft [1914-15] TLR 83 *108*
Lewes Sanitary Steam Laundry Co. Ltd *v* Barclays & Co. Ltd [1906] 11 Cm Cas
   255 *100*
Libyan Arab Foreign Bank *v* Bankers Trust Co. [1987] 2 FTLR 509 *64*
Libyan Arab Foreign Bank *v* Bankers Trust Co. [1988] 1 Lloyd's Rep 259 *88*
Liggett (Liverpool) Ltd *v* Barclays Bank Ltd [1928] 1 KB 48 *81*
Limpgrange *v* Bank of Credit and Commerce International SA [1986] FLR 36 *66*
Lipkin Gorman *v* Karpnale Ltd [1989] 1 WLR 1340 *47*
Lipkin *v* Gorman [1991] 3 WLR 10 *48, 49, 172*
Lipkin *v* Karpnale Ltd & Lloyds Bank plc [1988] 1 WLR 987 *94*
Little *v* Stackford [1828] 1 Mood & M 171 *135*
Lloyds Bank plc *v* Margolis and Others [1954] 1 WLR 644 *239*
Lloyds Bank Ltd *v* Bundy [1975] QB 326 *219, 220*
Lloyds Bank Ltd *v* Dolphin (1920) (*The Times*, 2 December) *161*
Lloyds Bank *v* Savory & Co [1933] AC 201 *179, 181*
Lloyds *v* Citicorp Australia Ltd [1985] 11 NSWLR 286 *106*
London and Foreign Trading Corporation *v* British and North European Bank
   [11921] 9 LILR 11 *201*
London Intercontinental Trust Ltd *v* Barclays Bank Ltd [1980] 1 Lloyd's Rep 241
   99, 102
London Joint Stock Bank Ltd *v* Macmillan and Others [1918] AC 777 *100*
London Joint Stock Bank *v* Simmons [1892] AC 201 *150, 154*
London and River Plate Bank *v* Bank of Liverpool [1896] 1 QB 7 *169*
Lumsden and Co. *v* London Trustee Savings Bank [1971] London Trustee Savings
Bank [1971] 1 Lloyd's Rep 114 *181, 186*

M.S. Fashions Ltd & Others *v* Bank of Credit and Commerce International SA &
Another (*The Times*, 23 June 1992) *234*
McEvoy *v* ANZ Banking Group Ltd [1988] ATR 80 *106*
McEvoy *v* Belfast Banking Co. [1935] AC 24 *43, 44*
MacGregor *v* Rhodes [1856] 6 El & Bl 266 *156*
Mackenzie *v* Royal Bank of Canada [1934] AC 468 *221*
Mackinnon *v* Donaldson, Lufkin and Jenrette Securities Corp. [1986] Ch 482 *85*
McInerny *v* Lloyds Bank Ltd [1973] 2 Lloyd's Rep 389 *103*
Madras Official Assignee *v* Mercantile Bank of India Ltd [1935] AC 53 *229*
Manus Asia Co Inc. *v* Standard Chartered Bank (*see* May 1989, *Journal of
   Business Law,* p. 257) *49*
Mardorf Peach & Co. Ltd *v* Attica Sea Carriers Corporation of Liberia [1976] 2 All
   ER 249 *157, 158*
Marfani *v* Midland Bank Ltd [1968] 1 WLR 956 *179, 180*
Marreco *v* Richardson [1908] 2 KB 584 *126, 158*
Marshall *v* Crutwell [1875] LR 20 EQ 328 *43*
Maxform Spa *v* Mariani and Goodville Ltd [1979] 2 Lloyd's Rep *143*
Metropolitan Police Commissioner *v* Charles [1977] AC 177 *54, 55*
Midland Bank Ltd *v* Seymour [1955] 2 Lloyd's Rep 147 *201*

Midland Bank Ltd *v* Shephard [1988] 3 All ER 17 *220*
Midland Bank *v* Reckitt [1933] AC 1 *140, 179, 184*
Misa *v* Currie [1876] 1 App Cas 554 *227*
MK International Development Co. Ltd *v* Housing Bank (unreported, 21 December 1990) *147*
M'Kenzie *v* British Linen Co [1881] 6 App Cas 82 *80, 146*
Momm *v* Barclays Bank International Ltd [1977] 2 WLR 407 *157, 158*
Morison *v* London County and Westminster Bank Ltd [1914] 3 KB 356 *99, 141, 185*
Morzetti *v* Williams & Others [1830] 1 B & Ad 415 *78*

Nathan *v* Ogden [1905] 94 LR 126 *134*
National Bank of Commerce *v* National Westminster Bank plc [1990] 2 Lloyd's Rep 514 *65*
National Bank of Greece SA *v* Pinios Shipping Co. (No.2) (*The Times*, 1 December 1989) *190*
National Bank of Greece SA *v* Pinios Shipping Co. (No.1) [1989] 1 All ER 213 *105*
National Bank of Greece SA *v* Pinios Shipping Co. [1990] 2 Lloyd's Rep 225 *59*
National Provincial Bank of England *v* Brackenbury (1906) 22 TLR 796 *232, 233*
National Provincial Bank of England *v* Glanusk [1913] 3 KB 335 *231*
National Provincial Bank Ltd *v* Ainsworth [1965] AC 1175 *241*
National Westminster Bank Ltd *v* Barclays Bank International Ltd and Another [1965] 1 QB 654 *168*
National Westminster Bank Ltd *v* Halesowen Presswork & Assemblies Ltd [1972] AC 785 *74, 118, 119*
National Westminster Bank Plc *v* Morgan [1985] AC 686 *218, 219, 220*
Neste Oy *v* Lloyds Bank plc [1983] 2 Lloyd's Rep 658 *52*
North & South Wales Bank Ltd *v* Macbeth [1908] AC 137 *139*
North European Bank Ltd *v* Zalstein [1927] 2 KB 92 *97*
North and South Insurance Corporation Ltd *v* National Provincial Bank Ltd [1936] 1 KB 328 *133*
Nova (Jersey) Knit *v* Karngarn Spinnerei GmbH [1877] 2 All ER 463 *130*
Nu-Stilo Footware Ltd *v* Lloyds Bank Ltd [1956] 77 JIB 239 *182*

Oelbermann *v* National City Bank of New York [1935] 79 F 2d 354 *212*
Offord *v* Davies and Another [1862] 12 CB (NS) 748 *232*
O'Hara *v* Allied Irish Banks Ltd [1985] BBCLC 52 *222*
Oliver *v* Davis [1949] 2 KB 727 *149*
Orbit Mining and Trading Co. Ltd *v* Westminster Bank Ltd [1963] 3 All ER 565 *132, 181*
Osterreichische Landerbank *v* S'Elite Ltd [1980] 2 All ER 651 *114*

Parker *v* Marchant [1843] 1 Ph 356 *61*
Parker *v* Winlow [1857] 7 E & B 942 *142*
Parker-Tweedle *v* Dunbar Bank plc (*The Times*, 29 December 1989) *226*

Parkside Leasing Ltd v Smith (Inspector of Taxes) [1985] 1 WLR 310 *158*

Parr's Bank Ltd v Thomas Ashby & Co. [1898] 14 TLR 563 *156, 157*

Partridge v Bank of England [1846] 9 QB 396 *124*

Paulger v Butland Industries Ltd (unreported, 25 October 1989) (*see* JBL May 1991, p. 281) *236*

Peat v Gresham Trust Ltd [1934] 50 TLR 345 at 347 *113*

Penmount Estates Ltd v National provincial Bank Ltd [1945] 89 Sol Jo 566 *184, 185*

Plasticmoda Spa v Davidson (Manchester) Ltd [1952] 1 Lloyd's Rep 527 *198*

Plunkett v Barclays Bank Ltd [1936] 2 KB 107 *238*

Potton Homes Ltd v Coleman Contractors (Overseas) Ltd [1984] 128 SJ 282 *216*

Price Waterhouse v BCCI (Luxembourg) SA and Others (*The Times*, 30 October 1991) *19*

Prosperity Ltd v Lloyds Bank Ltd [1923] 29 TRL 372 *108*

R.D. Harbottle (Mercantile) Ltd v National Westminster Bank Ltd [1977] 2 All ER 862 at p. 870 *213, 215*

R v Crown Court of Leicester, *ex parte* DPP [1987] 3 All ER 654 *88*

R v Gilmartin [1983] 1 All ER 829 *55*

R v Halai [1983] Crim LR 624 *56*

Ranoustsos v Raymond Hadley Corporation of New York [1917] 2 KB 473 *197*

Raphael and Another v Bank of England [1855] 17 CB 161 *153, 174*

Ravia & Co. v Thurmann-Neilsen [1952] 2 QB 84 *195*

Rayner & Co. v Hambros Bank Ltd [1942] 2 All ER 649 *200*

Redmond Bank v Allied Irish Banks plc [1987] FLR 307 *95*

Rekstin v Severo Sibirsko AO 9 [1933] 1 KB 47 *157*

Richards v Oppenheim [1950] 1 KB 616 *194, 198*

Rimmer v Rimmer [1953] 1 QB 63 *43*

Ringman v Hackett and Another [1980] 124 SJ 201 *45*

Robinson v Midland Bank [1925] 41 TLR 402 *40*

Rogers v Whitely [1898] AC 118 *237*

Rolfe Lubell & Co. v Keith and Another [1979] 1 All ER 860 *141*

Rolin v Stewart [1854] 14 CB 592 *79*

Rowlandson v National Westminster Bank [1978] 3 All ER 370 *48*

Royal Bank of Scotland v Christie [1841] 8 A & Fin 214 *68*

Ruben v Great Fingall Consolidated [1906] AC 439 *144, 145*

S.C.F. Finance Co. Ltd v Masri [1987] 2 WLR 58 *9, 11*

Sales Continuation Ltd v Austin Taylor & Co Ltd [1967] 2 All ER 1092 *210*

Santley v Wilde [1899] 2 Ch 474 *238*

Saunders v Anglia Building Society [1971] AC 1004 *223*

Scarth v National Provincial Bank ltd [1930] 4 LBD 241 *111*

Schering Ltd v Stockholms Enskilda Bank Aktiebolag [1946] AC 19 *120*

Schioler v Westminster Bank Ltd [1970] 2 QB 719 *94*

Selangor United Rubber Estates Ltd v Cradock and Others (No.3) [1968] 2 All ER 1073 *94, 95*

Selangor United Rubber Estates *v* Cradock (No.3) [1968] 1 WLR 1555 *48*

Shamji *v* Johnson Matthey Bankers Ltd [1986] BCLC 278 *117*

Shamsher Jute Mills Ltd *v* Sethia (London) Ltd [1987] 1 Lloyd's Rep 388 *128*

Siebe Gorman & Co. Ltd *v* Barclays Bank Ltd [1979] 2 Lloyd's Rep 142 *244*

Sinclair *v* Brougham [1914] AC 398 *170, 171, 172*

Siporex Trade SA *v* Banque Indosuez [1985] 2 Lloyd's Rep 546 *214*

Skyring *v* Greenwood & Cox [1825] 4 B & C 28 *97*

Slingsby *v* District Bank Ltd [1932] 1 KB 544 *101, 159, 160, 184*

Sohio Supply Co *v* Gatoil (USA) Inc. [1989] 1 Lloyd's Rep 588 *196*

Soproma SpA *v* Marine and Animal By-Products Corporation [1966] 1 Lloyd's
   Rep 367 *127*

Space Investments Ltd *v* Canadian Imperial Bank of Commerce Trust Co.
   (Bahamas) Ltd [1986] 3 All ER 75 *62*

Specialist Plant Services Ltd & Another *v* Braithwaite Ltd [1987] 3 BCC 119 *250*

Stafford and Another *v* Conti Commodity Services Ltd [1981] 1 All ER 691 *106*

Standard Chartered Bank *v* Walker [1982] 1 WLR 1410 *223*

Standard Chartered Bank *v* Walker [1983] 3 All ER 938 *118*

Starke *v* Cheeseman [1699] Carth 509 *156*

State Trading Corporation of India *v* E.D. & F. Man (Sugar) Ltd & Another [1981]
   Com LR 235 *216*

Stoberg-Carlson Corporation *v* Bank Melli Iran [1979] 467 F Supp 530 *216*

Stony Stanton Supplies (Coventry) Ltd *v* Midland Bank Ltd [1966] 2 Lloyd's Rep
   373 *40*

Suffell *v* Bank of England [1882] 9 QBD 555 *160*

Sunderland *v* Barclays Bank Ltd [1938] *88*

Szteyn *v* Henry Schroder Banking Corporation [1941] 31 NYS 2d 631 *207*

Tai Hing Cotton Mill Ltd *v* Lin Chong Hing [1986] QC 80 *77, 98, 101, 102, 105*

Talbot *v* Von Boris [1911] KB 854 *154*

Tatung (UK) Ltd *v* Galex Telesure Ltd [1989] 5 BCC 25 *249, 251*

Taylor *v* Plummer 3M & S 562 *170*

Tenax Steamship Co Ltd *v* The Brimnes (Owners), (*The Brimnes*) [1974] 3 All ER
   88 *157*

Thairwall *v* Great Northern Railway Co. [1910] 2 KB 509 *134*

Thoni GmbH & Co. *v* RTP Equipment Ltd [1979] 2 Lloyd's Rep 282 *130*

Thorton and Others *v* Maynard [1875] LR 10 CP 695 *131*

Tournier *v* National Provincial and Union Bank of England [1924] 1 KB 461 *83,
   84, 88, 89, 90, 91, 95*

Trans Trust SPRL *v* Danubian Trading Co. Ltd [1952] 1 Lloyd's Rep 348 *192*

Transpetrol Ltd *v* Transol Olieprodukten Nederland BV [1989] 1 Lloyd's Rep
   309 *196*

Trustee Savings Bank of Wales and Border Counties *v* Taylor (*Financial Times,* 23
   June 1989) *84, 87*

Tukan Timber *v* Barclays Bank plc [1987] 1 FTLR 154 *208*

Union Bank of Australia Ltd v Murray-Aynsley & Another [1898] AC 639 72
United Bank of Kuwait v Hammound [1988] 1 WLR 1051 45
United Bank Ltd v Banque Nationale de Paris (unreported, 7 June 1991) 205,
    207, 212
United City Merchants (Investments) Ltd v Royal Bank of Canada [1983] 1 AC
    168 205, 207, 212
United Dominion Trust v Kirkwood [1966] 1 All ER 969 1, 2, 3, 5, 11
United Overseas Bank v Jiwani [1976] 1WLR 964 97, 98
United Trading Corporation SA and Murray Clayton v Allied Arab Bank Ltd
    [1985] 2 Lloyd's Rep 554 217
Universal Guarantee Property Ltd v National Bank of Australasia Ltd [1965] 1
    WLR 691 163
Universal Guarantee Property Ltd v National Bank of Australasia Ltd [1965] 2 All
    ER 98 165
Uttamchandami v Central Bank of India [1989] 139 NJL 222 73

Vinden v Hughes [1905] 1 KB 795 139

W.J. Alan & Co v L. Nasr Export and Import Ltd [1972] 2 All ER 127 127
Wealdon Woodlands (Kent) Ltd v National Westminster Bank Ltd [1983] 133 NLJ
    719 102
West Mercia Safetywear Ltd v Dodd [1988] BCLC 250 247
West v Williams [1899] 1 Ch 132 243
Westminster Bank Ltd v Cond [1940] 46 Com Cas 60 70, 232
Westminster Bank v Zang [1966] AC 182 161, 177, 179
Westminster Bank v Hilton [1926] 43 TLR 124 81, 93
Whistler v Forster (1863) 14 CB (NS) 248 135
Whitaker v The Governor & Co. of the Bank of England [1835] 1 CM & R 744 79
Williams & Glyn's Bank v Boland and Another (1981) AC 487 241, 242
Williams & Glyn's Bank Ltd v Brown [1980] 2 All ER 408 241
Williams & Glyn's Bank v Barnes [1981] Com LR 205 189
Williams & Others v Summerfield [1972] 2 QB 512 85
Wilson v Kelland [1910] Ch 306 244
Wilson Smithett & Cope Ltd v Teruzzi [1976] QB 683 208
Windsor Refrigeration Co. Ltd v Branch Nominees Ltd [1961] Ch 375 117
Woods v Martins Bank Ltd [1958] 3 All ER 166 36, 41, 104, 105
W.P. Greenhaugh & Sons v Union Bank of Manchester [1924] 2 KB 153 69, 71, 73

XAG v A Bank [1983] 2 All ER 464 89, 92

Young v Grote [1827] 4 Bing 253 100
Yourell v Hibernian Bank Ltd [1918] AC 372 59

Table of statutes

Administration of Justice Act (1956),
  s. 38 *237*

Bank of England Act (1946) s. 4(1) *36*
Bankers' Books Evidence Act (1879)
  5, 84, 86
  s. 3 *85*
  s. 7 *84, 85*
Banking Act (1979) *6, 7, 9, 10, 15, 20,*
  22, 36
  s. 1(6)(a) *9*
  s. 2 *7*
  s. 3 *17*
  sched. 11 *17*
Banking Act (1987) *1, 5, 6, 17, 18, 22,*
  24, 36, 37, 86, 88, 121
Meaning of Deposit Order (1991) *20*
  s. 1(4) *18*
  s. 3 *8*
  s. 3(1) *6, 7*
  s. 4 *7*
  s. 5 *9*
  s. 5(2)(a) *9*
  s. 5(4) *10*
  s. 6(1) *10, 11*
  s. 21–6 *16*
  s. 39 *19*
  s. 42 *8*
  s. 42(4) *8*
  s. 47 *19*
  s. 67 *15*
  sched. 2 *7*
  sched. 3 *11–14*
Bankruptcy Act (1914) *119*
  s. 45(d) *228*

Bills of Exchange Act (1882) *5, 38, 39,*
  114, 132, 133, 145, 156
  s. 2 *143*
  s. 3(1) *132, 134*
  s. 3(4)(a) *135*
  s. 6(2) *142*
  s. 7(1) *136*
  s. 7(3) *137, 138, 140*
  s. 10 *135*
  s. 11 73 *132, 133*
  s. 20 *160*
  s. 20(1) *136*
  s. 21(1) *143*
  s. 21(2)(b) *161*
  s. 23 *140*
  s. 24 *80, 137, 144, 151*
  s. 25 *140, 141*
  s. 26 *141*
  s. 26(2) *142*
  s. 27 *147*
  s. 27(1)(b) *148, 149*
  s. 27(2) *149*
  s. 27(3) *178, 179, 228*
  s. 29 *174*
  s. 29(1) *151*
  s. 29(1)(b) *178, 179*
  s. 29(2) *155*
  s. 38(2) *154, 155*
  s. 50(2)(c) *169*
  s. 51(2) *155*
  s. 53(2) *187*
  s. 54 *155*
  s. 55(1) *156*
  s. 55(2)(b) and (c) *156*

s. 60 *173, 174, 175, 176*
s. 61(1) *159*
s. 64(1) *146*
s. 64 *159*
s. 76 *162*
s. 80 *164, 167, 175, 176*
s. 81 *162, 163, 164*
s. 82 *173–4, 180, 183*
s. 91(1) *140*
ss. 27 and 38 *150*
ss. 30(2) *154*
ss. 54-5 *140*
ss. 60 and 80 *159*
Bills of Exchange Act (1909) *39*
Bretton Woods Agreements Act
(1945) *208*
Building Societies Act (1986) *7, 75,*
76, 86

Cheques Act (1957) *5, 38, 132, 135*
s. 1 *176*
s. 2. *176, 177, 178*
s. 4 *41, 133, 165, 174, 176, 179,*
182, 185
s. 4(1) *179*
s. 4(1)(a) *133*
s. 4(2)(b) *133*
Cheques Act (1992) *29, 132, 162, 163,*
164, 166, 176
s. 1 *162, 164, 176*
s. 1(1) *175*
s. 1(2) *164*
Companies Act (1948) *119, 121*
  s. 108(4) *142, 143*
Companies Act (1982) *45*
s. 35(1) *46*
Companies Act (1985) *46, 86, 88*
s. 93 *250*
s. 349(4) *142*
s. 395 *251*
  s. 741(1) *247*
Companies Act (1989) *45, 46*
s. 93 *46*
s. 108 *250*
s. 396 *250*

Consumer Credit Act (1974) *31, 88*
s. 51 *31, 33*
s. 84 *31, 33*
s. 145(8) *90*
ss. 83 *31*
Credit Unions Act (1979) *7*

Data Protection Act (1984) *91*
Drug Trafficking Offences Act (1986)
72, 86, 87
s. 24 *86, 87*
s. 27(1) *86*
s. 27(2) *86*
s. 31 *86*

European Communities Act (1972) 45
Evidence (Proceedings in Other
Jurisdictions) Act (1975) *93*

Financial Services Act (1986) *88*
s. 183 *16*
Friendly Societies Act (1974) *7*

Gaming Act (1845) *177*
s. 18 *172*

Income Tax Ordinance of Ceylon (1932)
4, 5
Indian Contract Act (1872) *229*
Insolvency Act (1986) *74, 86, 111, 112,*
113, 114, 115, 116
s. 212 *247*
s. 214 *245, 246*
s. 239 *245*
s. 251 *245*
Insurance Companies Act (1974) *7*

Land Registration Act (1925), s. 70 *241*
Law of Property Act (1925), s. 94 *243*
Law Reform (Contributory Negligence)
Act (1945) *185*
Law Reform (Miscellaneous
Provisions) Act (1934) *59*

Matrimonial Homes Act (1967) *242*

Mental Health Act (1983) *110*
Moneylenders Acts (1900) and
 (1927) *2, 3*
 ss. 4 *5*
 ss. 6 *5*

Police and Criminal Evidence Act
 (1984) *87, 88*
Post Office Savings Act (1861) *38*
Prevention of Terrorism (Temporary
 Provisions) Act (1989) *87*

Sale of Goods Act (1979) s. 19 *248*
Single European Act (1986) *21, 23*
Solicitors Act (1843) *126*
Statute of Limitations (1980) *66,
 67, 239*
 s. 5 *66*
Supply of Goods Act (1982) *93*

Supply of Goods and Services Act
 (1982) *95*

Theft Act (1968) s.15 *56*
Theft Act (1978) *56* s.1 *56, 57*
Theft Act (1987) *56*

UCP
 Art. 8(e) *192, 205*
 Art. 10 *197*
 Art. 10(b)(iii) *191*
 Art. 16(f) *202*

Unfair Contracts Terms Act (1977) *34,
 77, 102, 225*

Uniform Customs and Practice for
 Documentary Credits *see* UCP

1 Parties to the Banker– Customer Relationship

The banker–customer relationship is based on contract and parties to that contract owe certain obligations to each other. This chapter will examine the characteristics of the parties to the banking contract.

WHAT IS A BANK OR BANK INSTITUTION?

The business of banking and finance has grown into a complex and specialised field, governed by stringent rules of law and commercial practice, but any study will clearly reveal that there is no definition of the term bank or banking organisation. It is because of the expansion and diversification into the traditional banking areas of non-banking institutions that the definition has become more complicated. Early statutory attempts to define the term bank or banking institution were remarkably unimaginative and unhelpful.

More recently, the Banking Act 1987 has shied away from the task of defining the term bank or banking institution and instead the Act lays down certain minimum criteria which an institution must satisfy in order to obtain recognition as an 'authorised institution' (a term used by the First EC Banking Directive).

EARLY ATTEMPTS TO DEFINE THE TERM BANK

Although the Banking Act 1987 now lays down requirements which an institution must satisfy in order to obtain authorisation from the Bank of England, it is interesting to examine early attempts to define the term bank, both at common law and by statute.

The common law

Probably the single most important decision of the courts which attempted to define the term bank or banker is the *United Dominion Trust* v *Kirkwood* case ([1966] 1 All ER 969). The case laid down extensive guidelines on the nature of the business a bank had to undertake in order for it be treated as carrying on the business of banking.

It is interesting to note that many of the guidelines established in the *Kirkwood* case are incorporated in the Banking Act 1987. The common law has, therefore, to some extent been incorporated into the central piece of legislation which now regulates the banking sector.

United Dominion Trust v Kirkwood [1966] 1 All ER 968

The defendant was a managing director of a company that financed the purchase of cars through loans from UDT. The loans were secured by the company accepting bills of exchange drawn by UDT and the defendant indorsing them so as to guarantee payment. The company went into liquidation and the bills of exchange were dishonoured by the company's liquidators. UDT brought an action against the defendants, as indorsers, who argued that UDT, as moneylenders, were not registered under the Moneylenders Acts 1900 and 1927, and so were not entitled to recover the money or enforce the security for the loans. UDT claimed that as bankers they were exempted from the provisions of the Moneylenders Acts. The court, therefore, had to determine the status of UDT.

Mocatta J found for the plaintiffs and said:

'words banking and banker may bear different shades of meaning at different periods of history, and their meaning may not be uniform today, in countries of different habits and different degrees of civilisation.'

Mocatta J also held that the plaintiffs must be 'bona fide' bankers for the purpose of exemption from the Moneylenders Acts but the motive for making particular loans was irrelevant, except where the genuineness of its business as a banking institution was in doubt.

The defendant appealed.

The Court of Appeal held in favour of the plaintiffs and said that UDT were carrying on the business of bankers, as commonly understood within the banking community. Lord Denning examined the nature of banking business and said that there are two main characteristics usually found in bankers today (p. 975):

'(i)   They accept money from, and collect cheques for, their customers and place them to their credit;

(ii)   they honour cheques or orders drawn on them by their customers when presented for payment and debit customer accounts accordingly.'

Lord Denning continued that these two characteristics carry with them a third, namely:

'(iii) They keep current accounts, or something of that nature, in their books in which the credits and debits are entered ... No-one and nobody, corporate or otherwise, can be a "banker" who does not (i) take current accounts; (ii) pay cheques drawn on himself; (iii) collect cheques for his customers.'

The guidelines enunciated by the Court of Appeal have been widely accepted.

Lord Denning in the Court of Appeal accepted the view expressed by Paget (*Paget's Law of Banking* 1961, 6th ed., p.8) who said that three essential characteristics were found in bankers today, namely:

(a) They [banks] must accept money from and collect cheques for their customers and place them to their credit;
(b) they must honour cheques presented or orders drawn on them by their customers according to the mandate; and
(c) they must keep current accounts or something of that nature in their books in which the credits and debits as between themselves and their customers are entered.

The minimum services required to be provided by a bank according to Lord Denning in the *Kirkwood* case are almost identical to the guidelines laid down in *Paget's Law of Banking*.

The Court of Appeal further held that banking need not be the only activity undertaken by a company for it to qualify as a bank but it must be a substantial and independent activity, and not merely incidental to some other activity. In fact UDT provided banking facilities only for customers who were dealers in motor vehicles as an adjunct to the hire-purchase business. Lord Denning examined individually the various types of transactions conducted by UDT and if the criterion laid down by the court had been strictly applied UDT would not have come within the guidelines.

The transaction which had the greatest resemblance to the business of a banker and which UDT undertook was the provision of current accounts by it for motor vehicle dealers but even this, said Lord Denning, was a facility used in connection with hire-purchase transactions and incidental loans. The current accounts were not used for general purposes.

The court decided that, although the usual characteristics of a banking business were not complied with by UDT, nevertheless it was a bank for the purposes of exemption under the Moneylenders Acts because it was treated (even if incorrectly) by other banks as an institution carrying on a banking business. The court took into account that UDT was allowed to participate in the London clearing system. The reputation that UDT had, as a bank, within the banking community was given special significance by the Court of Appeal.

Lord Harman (dissenting, p. 983) took the view that UDT were not carrying on a 'bona fide' business of banking so as to allow it exemption from the Moneylenders Acts. He took the words 'bona fide' to mean 'that a real business of banking is being carried on', which he felt was not being carried on. Moreover, he held that an established reputation as a banker within the banking community should not alone be sufficient to grant an institution the status of a bank or banker.

Other cases relating to definition

Prior to the *Kirkwood* case the courts had examined the nature of a bank or banking institution in a number of cases.

In *District Savings Bank Ltd ex parte Coe* ((1861) 3 De GF & J 355) Turner LJ held that a savings bank was not carrying on a banking business, even though it provided some banking services, because its business taken as a whole differed materially from the ordinary course of bankers. The facts of the case were that a company (called 'The District Savings Bank') was registered with the objects of being able to receive deposits, to grant loans on security and to conduct the business of emigration agents. The company did not provide facilities for the drawing of cheques, and deposits could only be withdrawn by giving notice. The court held that the company was not a bank although its business had some resemblance to the business of bankers; it was in other respects very dissimilar to the business of banking.

It is, however, unnecessary that the institution should undertake all activities associated with a banker. In *Re Bottomgate Industrial Co-operative Society* ((1891) 65 LT 712) Smith J held that the statutory prohibition on industrial and provident societies carrying on the 'business of banking' extended to all kinds of business normally undertaken by a bank, and so the prohibition was infringed by a co-operative society accepting deposits of money from the public which could only be withdrawn on a certain agreed period of notice being given. The co-operative society provided no cheque account facilities. The learned judge outlined the nature of business an institution must undertake if it is to be regarded as a bank or banking institution and said (p. 714):

> 'It is not necessary, in our judgment, in order to constitute a banking business prohibited by the statute, that the society should carry on every part of a business carried on by some bankers; it is sufficient to bring the business within the prohibition, if the society carried on what is a principal part of the business of a banker, viz., receiving money on deposit, allowing the same to be drawn against as and when the depositor desires, and paying interest on the amounts standing on deposit.'

In *Re Shields Estate* ([1901] 1 Ir R 172) the court looked at the essence of banking and said:

> 'The business of banking, from the banker's point of view, is to traffic with the money of others, for the purpose of making a profit ... the essence of the trade, business or calling of a banker, is not primarily or essentially to be found in the mode in which he disposes of the money which is deposited with him, but in the mode in which he receives the money of others. If he keeps open shop for the receipt of money from all who choose to deposit it with him, if his business is to trade for profit in money deposited with him for that purpose, he answers the description of "Banker"... If a banker's business was confined to honouring cheques on demand, he could not make any profit at all, those who take money on deposit account are just as much bankers as those who hold it on current account ...'

More recently, in *Bank of Chettinad Ltd of Colombo* v *Inland Revenue Commissioners of Colombo* ([1948] AC 378) the Privy Council said that the test for determining whether a Ceylon branch of a non-resident bank could itself be described as a bank was whether it (p. 379):

> 'carried on as its principal business the accepting of deposits of money on current account or otherwise, subject to withdrawal by cheque, draft or order.'

In the *Bank of Chettinad Ltd of Colombo* case the appeal concerned the amount at which the appellant company was liable to be assessed to income tax under the Income Tax Ordinance of Ceylon of 1932, in respect of income and profits of its Ceylon branch conducted at an office in Colombo. The question was whether in computing the amount of the income and profits, a deduction should be allowed in respect of a sum debited to the Ceylon branch by way of interest on balances due to the head-office. If the Ceylon branch were a bank that interest would be deductible.

The answer depended on the construction given to the rules made under the Income Tax Ordinance of Ceylon which provides that 'Ceylon branch' means the business carried on in Ceylon by any bank. The Privy Council held that the acceptance of deposits was clearly not the principal business of the branch since its main activities were in other areas and the deduction of interest was disallowed. The fact that the head-office accepted deposits was immaterial in deciding whether the branch in question was a bank.

These and other cases (see *Davies* v *Kennedy* ([1868] 3 Ir R Eq 31)) laid down guidelines which were adopted by the Court of Appeal in the *Kirkwood* case to give a comprehensive and modern definition of the term bank or banker at common law.

Statutory definition

The few statutory attempts to define the term bank or banking institution have been totally unsatisfactory. The Banking Act 1987 makes no attempt to provide a definition but merely enumerates the conditions that have to be fulfilled for an institution to be granted recognition as an authorised institution. All early attempts to define the term bank or banker were ambiguous or inadequate. For example, the Bankers' Books Evidence 1879 Act, which allows banks to produce certified copies of bank records in litigation, gives no definition of what constitutes a bank and provides that the exemption from producing originals applies to any:

'Persons or company carrying on the business of banking.'

Similarly, the Bills of Exchange Act 1882 and the Cheques Act 1957 both fail to provide anything amounting to a definition and the 1882 Act provides the term bank includes:

'Any body of persons, whether incorporated or not, who carry on the business of banking.'

By ss. 4 and 6 of the Moneylenders Acts 1900 and 1927, banks were given special exemption from the necessity of having to obtain licences and the stringent regulations relating to advertising by moneylenders. The only definition of a bank or banker in the Act is:

'Any person bona fide carrying on the business of banking.'

These illustrations of the term bank are still relevant for they are given for specialised purposes and are by no means repealed by the Banking Act 1987.

The need for a definition of a bank was avoided by the Department of Trade being given exclusive powers of recognition. This was done by the Department of Trade certifying that the institution had satisfied certain standards of efficiency, propriety and reliability.

THE BANKING ACT 1987

The First Banking Co-ordination Directive was implemented by the Banking Act 1979 (repealed and replaced by the Banking Act 1987). The 1979 Act was the first statute governing the licensing and supervision of banks and other deposit-taking institutions in the UK. The 1979 Act has been superseded by the 1987 Act, which introduced restrictions on the acceptance of deposits to institutions authorised under the Act. More significantly, the Banking Act 1987 considerably reinforced the powers of the Bank of England to advise, supervise and control the banking sector.

Section 1 of the Act imposes on the Bank a general duty to supervise certain authorised institutions. In exercising its supervisory functions the Bank of England is under a duty to keep under review any developments in the banking sector and the operation of its powers and duties. The Act recognises the changing nature of the banking sector and for this reason the Bank is expected to operate and take account of current practices and circumstances. To assist the Bank of England in its supervisory activities the Bank must establish a Board of Banking Supervision consisting of officers of the Bank and independent representatives from outside the banking sector. The independent members of the Board of Banking Supervision will be expected to give such advice as they think fit to the *ex officio* members, either generally or in a particular respect. To assist the Board to carry out its functions the Bank of England is required to submit regular reports to the Board on any matters the Bank considers relevant in connection with its supervisory functions. The independent members of the Board are not limited merely to considering the information the Bank of England has decided to make available to them, but they can require the Bank to supply them with such other information they may reasonably require in the discharge of their duties.

In order to ensure that the Bank of England and the Board of Banking Supervision carry out their duties with independence and confidence, the Act provides that neither the Bank nor any member of its Board of Directors, or any officer or servant or employee of the Bank, or any independent member of the Board of Banking Supervision, will be liable for damages for any act or omission committed or arising in the discharge of their duties, unless done in bad faith (ss. 1(4) and 2(7)). Immunity is only granted so long as the Bank, its servants, or members of the Board of Banking Supervision act in good faith. In neither case will immunity be conferred where the Bank or members of the Board of Banking Supervision have acted outside their powers or in bad faith.

It is not intended to survey the Act as a whole but to examine merely the provisions relating to obtaining authorisation under the Banking Act 1987 and the tendency to move away from the idea of defining the term bank or banker.

Restrictions on the acceptance of deposits

Section 3(1) of the Banking Act prohibits the acceptance of deposits in the UK in the course of carrying on (whether in the UK or elsewhere) a business which is a deposit-taking business unless that person is an institution which is:

(a) authorised by the Bank of England; or
(b) exempt under Schedule 2 to the Act; or
(c) exempt from obtaining authorisation under regulations made by the Treasury.

Section 3 is fundamental to the Act because the system of banking supervision derives from the need of deposit-taking institutions to obtain authorisation from the Bank of England. Although the section places an absolute prohibition on the acceptance of deposits unless the institution is authorised, s. 4 (enacting s. 2 of the 1979 Act with minor variations) goes on to exempt certain persons, institutions and transactions entered into by certain institutions from the necessity of obtaining authorisation. Section 4 exempts from the general prohibition any deposit accepted by the Bank of England. Schedule 2 to the 1987 Act contains a list of those institutions which, for one reason or another, it has been unnecessary or inappropriate to bring within the Bank of England's supervisory ambit. These institutions include the central banks of other EC member states, the National Savings Bank, local authorities, municipal banks and certain other public bodies, building societies, friendly societies where deposits are accepted in the course of carrying out transactions permitted by the rules of the society, insurance companies where deposits are accepted in the course of carrying on an authorised insurance business and the Crown Agents. Institutions listed under Schedule 2 to the Act are exempt not only from the need to apply for authorisation but also from the obligation to contribute to the deposit protection scheme. The central banks of other EC member states are exempt from the requirement to obtain authorisation in accordance with the 1977 EC Banking Directive. The Act does not, however, exclude non-EC central banks. The National Savings Bank is exempt because, as part of the Department of National Savings, it is an integral part of central government and as such is not deemed to require supervision. Similarly, local authorities and other public bodies are excluded, since local authority borrowing is subject to close statutory regulation. Insurance companies authorised under the Insurance Companies Act 1974 are exempt from obtaining authorisation under the Banking Act 1987 because they are closely supervised by the Department of Trade. Friendly societies and credit unions are supervised under the Friendly Societies Act 1974 and Credit Unions Act 1979. Building societies are also excluded from the supervision of the Bank of England because they are regulated under the Building Societies Act 1986.

Section 4(2), however, provides that institutions subject to Schedule 2 may have their exemption curtailed if they accept deposits for purposes other than those relating to their business. Thus, friendly societies under the Friendly Societies Act 1974 are exempt from authorisation under the Banking Act 1987 only to the extent that deposits are accepted in the course of transactions permitted under the rules of the society. Similarly, insurance companies are exempt from the provisions of the Banking Act, but only for the purposes of accepting deposits in the course of carrying on their authorised insurance business.

The section abolishes the distinction between recognised banks and deposit-taking institutions introduced by the Banking Act 1979. Instead, a single supervisory regime and a single set of criteria for authorisation is imposed by the 1987 Act.

B

In what is probably the first case to deal with a breach of s. 3 of the 1987 Act the court held that a defendant is not entitled to claim reliance on the privilege against self-incrimination as a reason for not answering interrogatories or disclosing documents under the Act.

Bank of England v *Riley* [1992] 2 WLR 840

Between 1983 and 1989 the defendant ran two organisations and in the course of business she accepted deposits from members of the public. In 1989, she was arrested and charged with obtaining money by deception and theft. The Bank of England commenced proceedings under the Banking Act 1987 for an injunction restraining the defendant from obtaining deposits contrary to s. 3 (prohibiting the unauthorised acceptance of deposits) of the Act and from dealing with or otherwise disposing of the assets. The defendant claimed to rely on the privilege against self-incrimination in relation to the anticipated prosecution under s. 3 of the Banking Act 1987 and the pending prosecution for obtaining money by deception.

The Court of Appeal held that the defendant was not entitled to claim the privilege against self-incrimination under s. 42 of the Banking Act 1987 which enabled the Bank of England, where it suspected a breach of s. 3 or s. 35 of the 1987 Act, to require the person responsible for the breach to provide the Bank with such information and such documents as the Bank may reasonably require for its investigation. Ralph Gibson LJ examined the powers given to the Bank of England where it suspects a breach of s. 3 or s. 35. These powers are contained in s. 42 of the Act and provide:

'Where the bank has reasonable grounds for suspecting that a person is guilty of contravening section 3 or 35 ... the bank or any duly authorised officer, servant or agent of the bank may by notice in writing require that or any other person – (a) to provide, at such place as may be specified in the notice and either forthwith or at such time as may be specified, such information as the bank may reasonably require for the purpose of investigating the suspected contravention; (b) to produce, at such place as may be specified in the notice and either forthwith or at such time as may be so specified, such documents the production of which may be reasonably required by the bank for the purpose; (c) to attend at such place and time as may be specified in the notice and answer questions relevant for determining whether such a contravention has occurred.'

Subsection 42(4) continues:

'Any person who without reasonable excuse fails to comply with a requirement imposed on him under this section or intentionally obstructs a person in the exercise of the rights conferred ... shall be guilty of an offence ...'

Gibson LJ concluded that the defence of 'reasonable excuse' under s. 42(4) could not justify construing s. 42 as retaining the privilege against self-incrimination. He said that Parliament did not intend that s. 42 should be 'operated subject to the continuation of the privilege against self-incrimination'.

Meaning of deposit

The term deposit is widely defined and s. 5 virtually repeats the wording used in the Banking Act 1979. Almost any form of borrowing from the general public is a deposit for the purposes of the Act. Section 5 defines a deposit as:

'a sum of money paid on terms under which it will be repaid, with or without interest or a premium and either on demand or at a time or in circumstances agreed by or on behalf of the person making the payment and the person receiving it.'

The currency in which payment is received is immaterial.

Section 5(2)(a) provides that where a deposit is paid and is referable to the provision of property or services or the giving of security under a contract of sale, hire or the provision of other property or services, then any such payment is not a deposit under the Act. Subsection (2)(a) re-enacts s. 1(6)(a) of the 1979 Act but the drafting of the subsection is altered and places beyond doubt that a sum of money will be excluded from the definition of 'deposit' only if the contract is for the sale of specific goods or services. The standing committee of the House of Commons took the view that the meaning of 'deposit' was intended to cover credit card budget accounts where credit balances can be built up in the customer's favour, because these are not built up with a view to the provision of specific goods or services. The subsection covers 'returnable deposits' on goods, or services supplied on a sale or return basis.

S.C.F. Finance Co. Ltd v *Masri* [1987] 2 WLR 58

The plaintiffs were licensed dealers carrying on business as brokers in futures. At the request of the first defendant, the plaintiffs agreed to open an account for him with a deposit of 50,000 US dollars. The agreement with the defendant provided that the customer was promptly to 'furnish and maintain such deposits and margins' as and when the plaintiffs would require in order to enable them to enter into various contracts of sale and purchase and to receive commission. They accepted the risk of loss and of primary liability to brokers for which they were indemnified by the defendant. The first defendant suffered heavy losses and went into deficit with the plaintiffs. The deficit was reduced on a number of occasions. In January 1984, the plaintiffs closed his account resulting in a balance outstanding to them of $910,031. The first defendant failed to pay and the plaintiffs brought an action to recover the amount.

Leggatt J held that the plaintiffs' claim was for reimbursement of losses incurred through the first defendant trading and that they did not carry on a deposit-taking business contrary to the Banking Act 1979.

The first defendant appealed.

The Court of Appeal held that money paid to the plaintiffs in connection with dealings in the commodity futures market was not accepted as deposits under the Banking Act, since it related to the provision of services by the plaintiffs. Slade LJ said that on the facts the services which the plaintiffs undertook for the defendant comprised three elements:

(a) entering into various contracts of sale and purchase on the defendant's behalf;
(b) the extending of credit (for which they were entitled to interest);
(c) the acceptance of the risk of loss and of primary liability to the brokers with whom the contracts were made (in respect of which they were entitled to be indemnified).

Moreover, he continued, a person 'holds himself out to accept deposits on a day to day basis' (p. 76):

> 'If (by way of an express or implicit invitation) he holds himself out as being generally willing on any normal working day to accept such deposits from those persons to whom the invitation is addressed who may wish to place moneys with him by way of deposit.'

The plaintiffs were, therefore, entitled to recover the amounts outstanding to them.

The Act then goes on to exclude certain payments from the word deposit and provides that a payment will be referable to the provision of property and services and, therefore, not a deposit, if payment is made payable by way of security or the performance of a contract or services supplied or to be supplied. This covers the sort of 'deposit' required by British Gas or British Telecom before services are provided for new account-holders. Another situation where the 'deposit' is referable to property or services is where the sum is paid as security for the safe return of property, e.g. caution money required by landlords.

Sums paid by one company to another when one is a subsidiary of another, or when both are subsidiaries of a third, are also exempt from the definition of 'deposit'. A technical difficulty that arose in the application of the 1979 Act involved loans made by a partnership where the partners were 'directors, controllers or managers' of the company to which a loan was made. The 1979 Act removed loans by 'directors, controllers and managers' from the definition of the word 'deposit', but left unclear the position of persons who carried on a partnership business together where the business comprised the making of loans. This is now resolved by s. 5(4) of the 1987 Act which provides that if a person making a loan is a partner in a partnership in which all the partners are either 'directors, controllers or managers' of the company to which the loan is made, it is not a 'deposit' for the purposes of the Act.

Meaning of deposit-taking institution

Whilst the Banking Act 1987 restricts the circumstances in which a person may accept a 'deposit', it does not *per se* make unlawful the carrying-out of a deposit-taking business. Section 6(1) provides that an institution is a deposit-taking institution if in 'the course of the business, money received by way of a deposit is lent to others', or 'where any activity of the business is financed ... out of capital or the interest on money received by way of deposit.' It is then that authorisation is required under the Banking Act 1987.

The section recognises the traditional basis of the banking business namely 'receiving money on deposit, allowing the same to be drawn against as and when the depositor desires, and paying interest on amounts standing on deposit.' Section 6 gives effect to the view held at common law that a person who deals with other people's money to make a profit is carrying on the business of banking (i.e. a deposit-taking business) (see *Re Bottomgate Industrial Co-operation Society* (1891) 65 LT 712 and *Re Shields Estate* [1901] 1 Ir R 172). In *Re Shields* the court said the essence of banking is:

'to traffic with the money of others, for the purpose of making a profit.'

Moreover, s. 6 goes on to say that a business will not be a deposit-taking business if the person carrying it on does not hold himself out as accepting deposits on a daily basis although regard may be had to the frequency of those occasions, or if deposits are accepted only on particular occasions (see the *Kirkwood* case and *SCF Finance Ltd* v *Masri*).

The prohibition on the acceptance of deposits applies only to deposits accepted in the course of carrying on a business. The Act offers no definition of these words, although the courts have examined the word 'business' in several cases.

For the purposes of deciding whether a business is a deposit-taking business all the activities which a person carries on by way of business will be treated as a single business. However, the business will not be a deposit-taking business if the deposits are not used in the way described in s. 6(1), i.e. if the money deposited is not used to make loans to others or to finance wholly or to any material extent, any business activity of the recipient. For example, credits on budget accounts with retail stores are technically deposits, but a store taking such deposits does not necessarily carry on a deposit-taking business.

Application for authorisation under the Banking Act 1987

The Bank of England, as the supervisory body, is responsible for handling applications for authorisation as a deposit-taking institution. The Act requires that an application for authorisation must be made in the manner directed by the Bank of England and be accompanied by a statement setting out the nature and scale of the deposit-taking business which the applicant intends to undertake and any future plans for the development of the business. The Bank will not grant an application for authorisation unless certain minimum criteria set out in Schedule 3 to the Act are complied with and the Bank may take into account any matters relating to any person who is, or will be employed by or associated with the applicant for the purposes of the deposit-taking business.

Overseas institutions

Overseas institutions with offices in the UK will require authorisation if they wish to accept deposits in the UK. For UK branches of overseas institutions, authorisation is granted to the institution as a whole. The Bank may have regard to the criterion relating to the fitness of directors, controllers and managers and to the requirements relating to the conduct of the business (i.e. the business is conducted in a prudent manner and with integrity and professional skill). Authorisation will be granted if these requirements are satisfied and the Bank of England is satisfied that the overseas bank is properly supervised in its home state and those authorities inform the Bank of England that they are satisfied about the management and financial soundness of the applicant institution.

Statutory criteria for authorisation

The minimum statutory requirements which must be satisfied before the Bank can grant authorisation are set out in Schedule 3 to the Act. If, following authorisation, it appears to the Bank that the criteria are not being, or have not been, fulfilled with respect to an institution, then the Bank has power to revoke or restrict the scope of authorisation. The following are the minimum requirements set out in Schedule 3:

(a) *Directors to be fit and proper persons.* The Act provides that every person who is, or is to be, a director, controller or manager of an authorised institution must be a 'fit and proper' person to hold the particular position which he holds, or will hold. With regard to a person who is a director, executive controller or manager of an institution the Bank may have regard to a number of considerations, e.g. a person's probity and whether he has sufficient skills, knowledge, soundness of judgment and experience to properly undertake and fulfil his particular duties and responsibilities and the diligence with which the person is likely to fulfil his responsibilities.

   The Bank will have regard to the previous business conduct, or financial conduct and activities of the person concerned. The Bank will also take into account the person's reputation and character, including whether he has a criminal record. Convictions for fraud or other dishonesty are particularly relevant. Any evidence of contravention by him of regulations designed to protect members of the public against financial loss due to dishonesty, incompetence or malpractice in the provision of banking, insurance or other financial services or in the management of such institutions, or against financial loss due to the person concerned being a discharged or undischarged bankrupt is especially relevant.

   Once an institution is authorised, the Bank has continuing regard to the performance of the person in the exercise of his duties. The standards demanded are more onerous for those with primary responsibility for an institution's affairs, although they will vary according to the scale and nature of the business concerned.

(b) *Two persons must direct the business.* The schedule provides that at least two individuals must effectively direct the business of an authorised institution. The Bank would not regard it as sufficient for either person to make some decisions, however significant, relating only to a few specific aspects of the business. The Bank expects that the individuals concerned will be either executive directors or persons granted executive powers by, and reporting immediately to, the board.

(c) *Board of directors.* In the case of a UK incorporated institution, the directors must include such number (if any) of directors without executive responsibility for the management of its business as the Bank considers appropriate, having regard to the circumstances of the institution and the nature and scale of its operations.

(d) *Business to be conducted in a prudent manner.* An authorised institution must conduct its business in a prudent manner. All applicant institutions are required to submit a programme of operations setting out the nature and scale of the intended business, and plans for the future development of the business based clearly on defined and realistic objectives. In deciding whether this programme is likely to be carried out in a prudent manner, the Bank will have regard to certain aspects of the future conduct of the business, e.g. the mix and type of assets to be acquired. An institution will not be regarded as conducting its business in a prudent manner unless:

  (i) it does, or will, maintain adequate liquid assets and liquidity. The Bank will have regard to the extent of such assets and the times when they mature, the institution's actual and contingent liabilities, the times at which such liabilities will, or may, fall due and any other factors which appear relevant. The Bank may, to any extent it considers appropriate, take into account liquid assets of the institution (e.g. short-term Treasury bonds) and any facilities available to it capable of providing liquidity within a reasonable period (e.g. borrowing from other banks);

  (ii) it makes, or will make, adequate provision for the depreciation or diminution in the value of its assets (including provision for bad debts or doubtful debts);

  (iii) it maintains, or will maintain, adequate accounting and other records of its business, including adequate systems of control, records and verification methods.

(e) *Net assets and other financial resources of an amount commensurate with nature and scale of the business.* The institution seeking authorisation must ensure that its investment in the business is on a scale which bears a resemblance to its liabilities, so that there is a reasonable assurance that its liabilities will be met in all circumstances.

(f) *Adequate liquidity.* In order that an institution can repay deposits as they fall due, its assets and liabilities must be organised so that it can accommodate unexpected or irregular withdrawals.

(g) *Adequate provision for depreciation.* It is necessary that bad and doubtful debts should be recognised and adequate provision made. Thus the quality of an institution's asset portfolio should be regularly reviewed by the management committee.

(h) *Adequate accounting and other records and adequate systems of control.* Adequate records and control systems are essential for sound banking. Any returns made to the Bank should be complete, accurate and timely. The Bank must be satisfied that these requirements will be complied with by an applicant before authorisation is granted. After authorisation the institution's conduct in this area will be monitored regularly.

(i) *Integrity and professional skills appropriate to the nature and scale of the institution's activities.* The requirement that the institution's business will be carried on with integrity and appropriate professional skills clearly envisages that it will be under the direction and control of persons who are fit and proper persons. This requirement goes beyond the question of suitability of particular persons; it involves the institution as a whole in showing the highest professional, ethical and business standards.

(j) *Minimum net assets*. The Act requires an authorised institution to have, at the time authorisation is granted, net assets of at least 1 million. In the case of a body corporate this is defined as paid-up capital and reserves. In the case of an overseas institution having a branch in the UK the institution as a whole must meet the minimum level.

The Banking Act obliges the Bank of England to give notice in writing of the grant or refusal of authorisation.

OTHER METHODS OF REGULATION THROUGH THE BANKING ACT

Apart from the requirement that all deposit-taking institutions must seek authorisation and the Bank of England's monopoly to grant authorisation, the Act gives other powers to the Bank of England to supervise the banking sector. It is now intended to discuss the other requirements of the Act by which control is imposed over authorised institutions.

Continuous duty to supervise the banking sector

The Bank of England is under a continuing statutory duty to supervise the banking sector, having regard to current banking practices, developments and innovations. Therefore, once authorised, all institutions are subject to the Bank's continuing duty to supervise the banking industry. Institutions are required to submit regular returns giving details about the business. Supervision is conducted on a consolidated basis, in accordance with the EC Credit Institutions Consolidated Supervision Directive (83/350/EC), taking account of the operations of the banking and other financial companies connected with the authorised institutions. Whilst the Act sets out in general terms the criteria which must be fulfilled with respect to all institutions, they are interpreted and applied to the circumstances of individual institutions. These returns form the basis for discussions with management of institutions incorporated in the UK. Although the Bank of England generally arranges meetings with the management of authorised institutions, in the event of the management becoming aware of any significant changes in the institution's business they should inform the Bank immediately. The Bank also expects to be consulted before an institution amends or departs significantly from the programme of operations submitted in support of its application for authorisation.

The Bank has power to require the provision of information and documents, and reports by accountants on that information. The Bank may require reports on authorised institutions' returns and their accounting and other records and internal controls. The Bank of England may also appoint investigators.

Restrictions on the use of banking names

The Act includes a wide prohibition on the use of banking names. The Act gives the Bank power to regulate the names of authorised institutions and of overseas institutions with representative offices in the UK. An authorised institution incorporated in the UK may use a banking name if it has at least £5 million of paid-up share capital and/or undistributable reserves. However, an authorised institution under the Banking Act 1979, when the 1987 Act came into effect, may retain its current name. Section 67 provides that, with certain exceptions, no person carrying on a business in the UK will use any name which indicates or may reasonably be understood to indicate that it is a bank or banker or carrying on a banking business. The exceptions include the authorised institutions, central banks of member states of the European Community, certain savings banks and certain other institutions. In addition, any authorised institution, which is not otherwise eligible to use a banking name, may, if it is a wholly owned subsidiary of an authorised institution with a banking name, use a name which includes the banking name of its parent for the purposes of indicating a connection between the two companies.

Monetary control requirements

All authorised institutions are required to hold minimum cash ratio deposits and comply with monetary control provisions. The cash ratio deposit scheme requires all reporting institutions with eligible liabilities of 10 million or more to hold non-interest deposits with the Bank equivalent to 0.45 per cent of eligible liabilities.

Additionally, institutions with eligible liabilities of 10 million or more may be called upon from time to time to place special deposits with the Bank for monetary control purposes.

Advertising for deposits

The Treasury is empowered to introduce regulations governing the issue, form and content of deposit advertisements after consultation with the Bank and Building Societies Commission. Any person who issues or causes in the UK an advertisement which is prohibited by the regulations or which does not comply with the requirements is guilty of an offence.

Notification requirements under the Act

The Banking Act enables the Bank of England not only to supervise and regulate the banking sector but it also allows the Bank to veto the involvement of individuals in authorised institutions. Thus, to some extent, the Bank of England has statutory powers to control and supervise not only the management of an institution but persons who may hold controlling interests in an authorised institution. It is intended to examine in outline the various notification requirements under the Act which enable the Bank to supervise shareholder control.

Notification of changes of control

Any person (whether an individual or an institution) who is considering acquiring shares in an authorised institution, or becoming an indirect controller (defined in the Act) of such an institution must have regard to ss. 21–26 of the Act. It is the responsibility of the person who seeks to acquire a shareholding in an authorised institution to comply with the terms of the Act.

The Act establishes a vetting procedure for any person who proposes to become a shareholder controller (defined in the Act) of an authorised institution and for any existing shareholder controller who proposes to increase his shareholding above 50 per cent or above 75 per cent. The procedure also applies to persons who propose to become indirect controllers. Any such person is required to give notice in writing of his intention to the Bank, together with any information and documents it requires.

The Bank of England may object unless it is satisfied that the person is a fit and proper person to hold the particular position and it is satisfied regarding certain other matters. A person who fails to comply with the notification requirement or who becomes a controller despite having been given notice of objection commits a criminal offence. The requirements relating to changes of control are additional, for example, to the Takeover Code etc.

Objection by direction of the Treasury

The Treasury is empowered to direct the Bank to serve a notice of objection on a person who has given notice of intention under s. 21 to become a controller or who has become such a controller without giving the required notice. The Treasury may exercise this power if it appears to it that, in the event of the person becoming, or as a result of a person having become, a controller a notice could be served on the institution by the Treasury under s. 183 of the Financial Services Act 1986. The latter section empowers the Treasury to disqualify or restrict the authorisation of an institution authorised under the Banking Act on the ground that it is connected with a country which does not offer equal treatment to UK persons or institutions in the investment, insurance or banking sectors.

Objection to existing shareholder controller

The Bank of England is empowered to serve a notice of objection on a person who is a shareholder controller of an authorised institution which is incorporated in the UK if it appears to it that a controller is no longer a fit and proper person to be such a controller of the institution. Prior to the Bank serving such a notice of objection the Bank is required to give a preliminary notice stating that it is considering serving a notice and specifying the reasons for objection.

Restrictions on the sale of shares

Where a person becomes or continues to be a shareholder controller having received a notice of objection, the Bank may direct that dealings or rights attached to the shares are restricted, e.g. the Bank may direct that the transfer of shares is void or suspend the right to vote in respect of those shares. The Bank may apply to the court for an order of sale in respect of those shares.

Limitations or withdrawal of authorisation

In certain circumstances the Bank of England may revoke or impose restrictions on an authorised institution. The Bank's powers to revoke or impose restrictions become exercisable if it appears that any one of a number of established circumstances, in s. 11 of the 1979 Act, are applicable. These include a failure to comply with the minimum requirements set out in Schedule 3 to the Act; that the institution has failed to comply with any requirement of the Act; that a person has become controller although he has been served with a notice of objection; that false, misleading or inaccurate information has been provided by the institution; that a resolution has been passed for its winding-up; that a winding-up order has been made; that in respect of an institution whose main or principal place of business is outside the UK the relevant supervisory authority has withdrawn authorisation; or that the interests of depositors or potential depositors have been threatened.

HAS REGULATION UNDER THE BANKING ACT 1987 BEEN SUCCESSFUL?

In order to restore confidence in the banking sector after the collapse of the Johnson Matthey Bank it was felt that more stringent regulations were required to supervise the banking sector. The Banking Act 1987 was enacted in order to restore the loss of confidence and to strengthen control over banks and banking institutions. The Act does not appear to have been entirely successful and on 5 July 1991 the Bank of England (under its regulatory capacity) acted to close down the operations of the Bank of Credit and Commerce International (BCCI). As events unfolded the enormous extent of the fraud involved sent reverberations throughout the banking world. Account-holders (being unsecured creditors) have been denied any access to their credit balances. Several local authorities had deposited very large sums with BCCI – in the case of the Western Isles Council it had a credit balance of £23 million. Until the closure of BCCI, the bank appeared on an officially published list of banks.

There has been much talk of whether the Bank of England should have acted earlier to close BCCI. The Bank of England claims that it was only presented with concrete evidence of fraud in June 1991. In October 1990 the Bank of England received a report from Price Waterhouse (BCCI auditors) indicating fraud and corruption within BCCI. Earlier in the same year a letter from a member of the BCCI staff alleging fraud and corruption was received by the Treasury. A similar letter was sent to the Bank of England in June 1990. BCCI is now in provisional liquidation. For the depositors who continue to suffer hardship and the loss of security the question must be asked what remedies are available?

Can an action be brought against the Bank of England?

The Bank of England is under a continuous duty to supervise deposit-taking institutions. This duty is owed under the Banking Act 1987, which requires the Bank to authorise such institutions and then to continue to monitor them. The question which will prove difficult to provide an answer to is when did the Bank have sufficient notice of fraud to close down BCCI? If it can be established that the Bank of England was negligent in not stepping in earlier, certainly those depositors who opened accounts with BCCI after the Bank of England had, or should have had, notice of the fraud, may be able to allege negligence. However, s. 1(4) of the Banking Act 1987 places a considerable obstacle towards any successful claim. The section provides 'Neither the Bank nor any person who is a member of its Board of Directors or who is or is acting as an officer or servant of the Bank shall be liable in damages for anything done or omitted in the discharge or purported discharge of the functions of the Bank under this Act unless it is shown that the act or omission was in bad faith.' Evidence of such bad faith will require a great deal of further investigation and probably be impossible to establish.

The liability of auditors

The auditors of BCCI (Price Waterhouse) had two specific functions.

To carry out the traditional functions of auditors
A company must each year at the general meeting at which copies of its profit and loss account and balance sheet for a financial year are laid appoint an auditor or auditors to hold office until the conclusion of the next general meeting at which such accounts for its next succeeding financial year are laid. The standard of care and skill auditors must exhibit in carrying out their tasks is that of the ordinary reasonable auditor. In *Re London and General Bank (No. 2)* on the duty to comply with SSAPs Woolf J said 'while they are not conclusive so that a departure from their terms necessarily involves a breach of the duty of care, ... they are very strong evidence as to what is the proper standard which should be adopted and unless there is some justification, a departure from this will be regarded as constituting a breach of duty.'

Although it is established that auditors owe a duty of care to shareholders it is unlikely that such a duty of care is owed to depositors and account-holders of a bank on the liquidation of a bank. In *Caparo Industries PLC* v *Dickman* ([1990] 2 AC 605) the House of Lords held that in deciding whether auditors owe a duty of care to persons who rely on the published accounts in buying shares the proximity of the relationship is vital and this requires more than just foreseeability of reliance. It must be shown that the auditors knew the accounts or any statement made in connection with them would be communicated to the investor either as an individual or as a member of a group. The *Caparo* case has been applied in *El-Nakib Investments (Jersey) Ltd* v *Longcroft* ([1990] 2 WLR 1930) where the court concluded that the defendants did not owe a duty of care to the plaintiffs in respect of transactions involving the purchase of shares in the market in that the prospectus and interim reports had been issued for a particular purpose (a rights issue) and were used by the plaintiffs for another purpose (buying shares in the market).

It is unlikely that the auditors would be held to owe a duty of care to depositors of BCCI and even if the auditors could have qualified previous years' accounts no liability is likely to arise in an action by defrauded depositors.

To report to the Bank of England on certain areas under the Banking Act

Under the Banking Act 1987, auditors are required to submit certain confidential reports to the Bank of England. Reports may be required at various stages by the Bank of England. In considering applications for deposit-taking authority, the Bank may require the applicant to provide a report by an accountant or other professional approved by the Bank on any aspect of the information submitted by the applicant. Once an institution is authorised the Bank of England expects to receive copies of the annual accounts and audited accounts for every authorised institution. However, under s. 39 of the Banking Act 1987, the Bank may by notice in writing require an authorised institution to provide it with a report, by an accountant or other approved person, on any area of business conducted by that institution. Under s. 47 auditors and reporting accountants are released from the restrictions on disclosure to the Bank of information about the institution obtained in the course of their work, provided that the information is relevant to the Bank's supervision of the institution and the information is disclosed in good faith. Although the Act specifically provides that information disclosed to the Bank of England in the course of the supervisory function is protected by privilege, a similar rule has been applied to disclosure of information made in the course of an inquiry into the collapse of BCCI. In *Price Waterhouse* v *BCCI (Luxembourg) SA and Others* (*The Times*, 30 October 1991) Millett J held that it was in the public interest for confidential information to be disclosed to the inquiry into the BCCI affair set up at the request of the Bank of England. The court said:

'If it was in the public interest to require confidential information to be disclosed to the Bank of England to enable it to carry out its supervisory functions, there was at least as great a public interest in the disclosure of such information to an inquiry set up to review the Bank's past performance of its statutory functions, provided that dissemination of such information was no wider in the latter case than would be authorised in the former case.'

It therefore appears that the role of auditors in connection with the supervision of authorised institutions is special and any information which may indicate negligence on the part of the Bank or auditors will be privileged information.

Deposit protection scheme

The Banking Act 1979 established the Deposit Protection Fund from which depositors are entitled to recover a proportion of their credit balances. The Banking Act 1989 continues to operate the deposit protection fund scheme and establishes a Deposit Protection Board to manage the fund. However, before the depositor can recover under this scheme the bank must be wound up. The depositor is then entitled to recover three-quarters of his credit balance with the bank, up to a maximum of £20,000.

Thus a depositor owed £20,000 by an authorised institution which has failed will receive £15,000 from the deposit protection board. A depositor owed £100,000 or £50,000 or any other sum exceeding £20,000 would also only receive £15,000.

In order to maximise the amount of payments from the deposit protection fund, some depositors took the precaution of assigning sums of £20,000 to trusted friends and relatives who would then each be compensated £15,000 out of the deposit protection fund in respect of the £20,000 assigned to them. This loophole was plugged by the Banking Act 1987 (Meaning of Deposit) Order 1991 (made on 30 July 1991). It provided that in future the definition of 'deposit' in the Act excluded a sum to which a person became entitled, otherwise than by operations of law, after presentation of a winding-up petition. In *Depositors Protection Fund* v *Dalia & Another* (*The Times*, 9 July 1991) the question arose whether the assignees of deposits in an insolvent bank were entitled to claim compensation from the deposit protection fund where the assignments were made after the presentation of a winding-up petition but before 31 July 1991, when the Banking Act 1987 (Meaning of Deposit) Order (SI 1991 No. 1776) came into force. Sir Donald Nicholls, VC held that the legal right to money subject to an assignment was transferred to the assignee who was entitled to all the 'legal remedies to recover the money and he could give a good discharge to the bank without the concurrence of the assignor'. In the event of insolvency of the bank, it followed that the assignee was entitled to seek compensation from the deposit protection board. The court concluded than an 'assignment of a deposit, in whole or part, made while a bank was trading normally was not struck down'.

Compensation from the majority shareholder

The majority shareholder in BCCI may to some extent compensate the creditors of BCCI but this is an undesirable way of protecting depositors' interests. Moreover, there is no guarantee that in any future bank failures majority shareholders will be willing (and indeed capable) of compensating depositors.

The only safeguard therefore is a strong and aggressive supervisory body.

New regulation of international banks

As a direct result of the BCCI collapse, leading industrial countries announced on 6 July 1992 that new measures would be adopted to regulate international banks. The main safeguard is that international banks operating on a world-wide basis will be regulated on a world-wide basis with a single bank regulator. The standards announced by the Basle Committee on Banking Supervision were indorsed by the central bank governors from the Group of Ten leading industrial countries, together with Luxembourg and Switzerland. The four main features to the standards are:

(a) any international banking group should be supervised on a 'consolidated basis', taking account of its operations anywhere in the world, by a single home authority;
(b) if a bank wants to set up branches in a jurisdiction outside its home country, it will need the consent of both its home country and the regulating body in the 'host' country where the branch is to be established;
(c) the home country supervisor will have the right to receive information on the international operations of banks under its supervision. This will require co-operation between the home and 'host' country;
(d) if a country is unhappy about the international supervision of a bank whose domicile is elsewhere, it can impose 'restrictive measures' on branches of that bank on its territory. This would, if necessary, include banning the branches from the 'host' country or allowing a branch to operate in the 'host' country with a fence on the assets of the branch in that country.

THE INFLUENCE OF THE EUROPEAN COMMUNITY

The Treaty of Rome of 1957, Article 2, envisages:

'... By establishing a common market and progressively approximating the economic policies of Member States, to promote throughout the community a harmonious development of economic activities, a continuous and balanced expansion, an increase in stability, an accelerated raising of the standard of living and closer relationships between States belonging to it.'

Article 8 of the Treaty calls for the common market to be 'progressively established' during a period of twelve years. The Single European Act 1986 added Article 8(a) to the Treaty of Rome and this provided for the completion of the internal market 'over a period expiring on 31 December 1992'. Article 8(a) defines an internal market as an 'area without internal frontiers in which the free movement of goods, persons, services and capital is ensured in accordance with the Treaty of Rome.'

With the aims of the Treaty of Rome in mind it is intended to examine the extent to which developments in the banking law area have been shaped and influenced by the European Community.

The First Banking Co-ordination Directive

The First Banking Co-ordination Directive had two major aims. In the first instance, it was intended to harmonise the laws of the member states for the licensing of banks by providing common basic licensing criteria. In order to produce a common definition the term 'credit institution' was adopted and defined as 'an undertaking whose business is to receive deposits or repayable funds from the public and to grant credits for its own account'.

This definition and the licensing criteria were implemented in the UK by the Banking Act 1979 (which has now been entirely repealed by the Banking Act 1987). The UK, however, introduced the distinction between a recognised bank and licensed deposit-takers and one of the main failings of the Act was that the powers of the Bank of England over recognised banks proved to be inadequate. Moreover, the regulations required the licensing of deposit-takers only, and not of lenders. The Second Banking Directive of 1989 will require that prohibitions be implemented so that bodies other than 'credit institutions' may not accept deposits.

The second aim of the 1977 Directive was to provide for co-operation among member states' supervisory authorities, including the exchange of information concerning the management and ownership of banks.

The Consolidated Supervision Directive and revision of the 1975 Concordat

In 1983 the G-10 group (a group of 10 industrialised countries within the framework of the IMF) revised the 1975 Concordat which aimed to provide that no bank would escape supervision. It sought to do this by providing that the primary responsibility for monitoring the solvency of a banking group would lie with the 'home' authority of the group. At the same time and in similar terms the EC produced a Directive on the Supervision of Credit Institutions on a Consolidated Basis. The consolidated supervision provisions apply not only to credit institutions but also to financial institutions. 'Financial institutions' are undertakings other than credit institutions whose principal activity is to grant credit facilities, to acquire 'participations' (ownership of at least 25 per cent of the capital of another credit or financial institution) or to make investments.

The purpose of the Directive is to make it mandatory for the supervisory authorities to apply consolidated supervision. The Directive is intended to apply only to groups of banks. Consolidation is designed to ensure that no bank escapes supervision. Supervision will take place at least once a year and will be undertaken by the competent authorities of the home country of the credit institution concerned.

In 1990, draft proposals for amendments to the 1983 Directive were produced and the Second Consolidated Supervision Directive was adopted on 6 April 1992. The new proposals have the following aims:

(a) there should be consolidated supervision where the parent undertaking of a group is not a bank but a financial holding company (a non-bank financial institution whose subsidiaries are mainly credit or financial institutions);
(b) to require a parent of a bank (if neither is a bank nor a financial holding company) and its non-bank subsidiaries to provide information requested by the banking regulators of the group's banks;
(c) to specify the areas covered by the consolidated supervision, e.g. solvency, large-scale exposure;
(d) to specify consolidation methods reflecting the Directive on the annual accounts and consolidated accounts of banks.

The Single European Act 1986

The Single European Act 1986 provides for a single internal market designed to produce a free market in goods, services, persons and capital. By 1992 it is anticipated that there will be:

(a) freedom of capital movements;
(b) a single licence for banking, insurance and investment services;
(c) a 'level playing field' for supervisory and prudential rules.

The Second Banking Co-ordination Directive

The Second Banking Directive was adopted in December 1989. It has three main purposes, namely:

(a) single licence for banks based on the idea that the home country will be responsible for authorisation of branches;
(b) a list of activities to be permitted under the licence;
(c) common supervisory rules.

The single European banking licence under the Second Directive

The single banking licence will enable banks and other credit institutions which are nationals of a member state to expand their activities throughout the Community either through branches in other member states or by offering cross-border services. Only credit institutions established in member states as corporations will be able to extend their business activities in this way and not those which are established as branches or agencies. Moreover, banks recognised in member states may only establish branches in other member states and not subsidiaries.

The freedom to expand depends on the initial recognition and 'establishment' in a member state. The Commission has taken the view that a company is 'established' in a member state when it has a real and continuous link with the economy of that country. The Commission also takes the view that the nationality of the directors and shareholders is irrelevant although some member states disagree with this view.

The single licence will be applicable to all 'credit institutions', which includes banks. Once the institution is 'established' in its home country it can establish a branch in a 'host' country subject only to certain notification requirements. The institution will not be required to obtain local authorisation or licensing or compliance with local capital adequacy rules. Alternatively, cross-border services may be provided, e.g. advertising for deposits from the home state.

An important qualification to the possession of the single banking licence is that a firm or institution will not be granted the single 'passport' without actually undertaking in its home state the business for which the authorisation is given to the institution. In the case of credit institutions this means taking deposits and lending money (the First Banking Directive of 1977 defined a credit institution as 'an undertaking whose business is to receive deposits or other repayable funds from the public and to grant credits for its own account'). A credit institution is, therefore, defined by the functions which it actually undertakes and not merely by the fact that authorisation is granted for those functions. The First Directive (and therefore the Banking Act 1987) actually provides for authorisation to be revoked if an authorised institution does not undertake the business for which it is granted.

The definition of credit institutions covers deposit taking and lending. In the UK, however, only those engaging in the business of deposit taking need to obtain authorisation under the Banking Act 1987.

Obtaining the licence

In order to enjoy the benefits conferred by the single licence an institution must first apply to the competent authority for the credit institution status. The First and Second Directives apply to 'credit institutions' and therefore the licence is not restricted merely to banks but is available to institutions which take deposits or repayable funds from the public and grant credit on their own account. It is, therefore, suggested that this includes building societies although some member states have expressed doubt.

A credit institution must comply with certain criteria in order to obtain the single licence:

(a) maintain adequate minimum funds of five million ECU (approximately £3.5 million);
(b) its business must be directed by at least two persons of good repute;
(c) inform the competent authority of the identity of the owners or controllers of the institutions;
(d) submit a list of the types of business the applicant intends to carry on and details of its structural organisation.

Activities permitted by the single licence

Once a bank has a single licence from its home country it can carry on in any member state a list of permitted activities. The single licence will enable banks to operate not only through branches, but they may supply banking services to one member state from another member state. The activities permitted under the single banking licence are:

(a) acceptance of deposits and repayable funds from the public;
(b) lending, including consumer credit, mortgage credit, factoring and other financing of commercial transactions;
(c) financial leasing;
(d) money transmission services;
(e) issuing and administering means of payment, e.g. credit cards, traveller's cheques, etc;
(f) guarantees and commitments;
(g) trading for own account or for the account of customers in:
　　(i) money market instruments (cheques, bills, etc.);
　　(ii) foreign exchange;

(iii) financial futures and options;
(iv) exchange and interest rate instruments; and
(v) transferable securities.
(h) participation in share issues and the provision of services related to issues;
(i) advice to undertakings on capital structure, industrial strategy and related questions, including questions relating to mergers and the purchase of undertakings;
(j) money broking;
(k) portfolio management and advice;
(l) safekeeping and administration of securities;
(m) credit reference services;
(n) safe custody services.

The wide list of activities permitted under the single licence is not exhaustive and further activities may be added to the list. The rules of the home country in which the single licence is given will govern the regulation of activities undertaken from the list. Member states are not required to harmonise their rules on the permitted activities.

It is possible for a member state unilaterally to extend the list of permitted activities for banks established or which operate within its boundary. Activities not included in the list of permitted activities may be provided freely in a host country without new authorisation if the activities are licensed and properly supervised in the home country, whether or not the institution undertaking them is a credit institution.

Reciprocity

In April 1989, the Commission introduced modifications to the Draft Second Banking Directive in order to simplify the procedures for individual banking applications from non-EC countries and to make it clear that in return for opening its markets the EC expects reciprocal facilities for EC banks. The modifications have the following main elements:

(a) requests for authorisation by non-EC banks will be notified to the Commission;
(b) the Commission will monitor on a continuous basis how EC banks are treated in non-EC countries;
(c) the Commission will negotiate with the other relevant country where equivalent treatment to EC banks is not granted;
(d) where equal treatment is not granted to EC credit institutions the relevant authorities of the member states must limit or suspend their decisions regarding requests pending authorisation or future requests for authorisation from the non-EC country refusing equal treatment.

These rules do not apply to applications made by institutions already authorised in the Community and which wish to establish new subsidiaries.

Annual accounts and consolidated accounts of banks and other financial institutions

The Fourth Company Law Directive of 1978 allowed member states to 'exempt banks and other financial institutions' from the accounting provisions which applied generally to companies. The Bank Accounts Directive of 1986 covers the exemption. It provides that the Fourth Company Law Directive is to be followed except in specific instances where differences in terminology, layout, valuation rules, etc., require departure. The accounts provisions provide for the layout of the balance sheet. Valuation rules are laid down.

Publication of annual accounting documents by branches

The Council Directive of 13 February 1989 (89/117/EC) relates to the provisions of the annual accounting documents published by branches established in a member state by institutions having their head-offices outside that member state. The Directive applies to branches where the parent institution's head-office is outside the state where the branch is maintained, and even if it is outside the EC entirely. Branches with head-offices in a different member state must publish the annual accounts, consolidated accounts, the annual report, the consolidated annual report and the opinions of the person responsible for auditing the annual accounts and consolidated accounts of the relevant institution. Such documents must be drawn up and audited in the manner required by the law of the member state in which the institution has its head-office. Certain provisions of the Seventh Company Law Directive (given effect by the Companies Act 1989) concerning disclosure requirements in respect of branches opened in a member state by certain types of companies will apply to banks.

Branches may not be required to publish annual accounts relating to their own activities.

Large Exposures Directive

The Commission has produced a Recommendation and a draft proposal for a Directive intended to discourage an excessive concentration of exposure to a single client or client group by introducing reporting requirements for large exposures. A 'large exposure' is defined as a commitment in excess of 15 per cent of own funds. A common position was reached in June 1992 and it is proposed that the Directive will be implemented by 1 January 1994.

Capital adequacy ratios

There are two Directives relevant to the question of capital adequacy for institutions engaging in 'banking' activities. One concerns the definition of 'own funds' (Directive on the Own Funds of Credit Institutions adopted in 1989) and the other the 'solvency ratio' (Directive on a Solvency Ratio for Credit Institutions also adopted in 1989). In addition a Capital Adequacy Directive (if adopted) may regulate the position of all firms involved in the investment business, including banks. For credit institutions matters such as capital adequacy, administrative and accounting procedures and internal control mechanisms are under the jurisdiction of home country regulators but host member states co-operate with the home supervisory authority for supervision of the liquidity of branches. Host countries have complete control for measures resulting from the implementation of its monetary policies.

Reorganisation and the winding-up of credit institutions

The Commission has proposed a Directive on the reorganisation and the winding-up of credit institutions and deposit-guarantee schemes (in the UK up to £20,000 of a depositor's funds are already protected). The Directive provides that the home country authorities are principally responsible for the reorganisation and winding-up of banks with financial problems. The Directive is expressed to apply to credit institutions and their branches set up in a member state other than that in which they have their head-office.

The concept of winding-up is linked to the idea of compensation for depositors and this is dealt with by the implementation of guarantee protection schemes.

Draft Directive on Deposit Guarantee Schemes

A preliminary Draft Directive on the co-ordination of the laws and regulations to the setting-up of compensation schemes in member states to protect depositors from loss resulting from failure of an EC authorised credit institution is under discussion. It would bring responsibility for deposit protection into line with responsibility for supervision by requiring the 'home state' which authorises a bank to ensure that its Deposit Protection Scheme covers deposits in all EC branches of that bank. The Draft Directive sets the minimum compensation level at 80 per cent of the deposit up to 15,000 ECU.

The position of overseas banks

By Article 58 of the Treaty of Rome subsidiaries established in a member state by a third country bank are treated as Community undertakings. The time for 'establishment' is the final date for the implementation of the Second Directive, that is 1 January 1993. These subsidiaries will have the benefits of the single licence system. For that reason the Second Directive contains proposals for reciprocity. If an overseas bank already has a subsidiary and is fully 'established' when the single licence provisions come into force, these institutions will be protected from the reciprocity provisions. The overseas bank will enjoy all the benefits of other EC established banks, including the ability to expand in other EC countries through branches. However, changes in the ownership of banks may trigger the reciprocity provisions.

These rules do not apply to branches. If an overseas bank has no 'establishment' rights or merely a branch in the EC when the single licence provisions come into force it will be required to apply for authorisation in a member state. The member state will notify any request for authorisation to the Commission. The overseas applicant is subject to the principle of reciprocity which requires that non-EC banks should not be permitted entry into the Community if EC institutions are not given similar access. The Commission determines the question of reciprocity by satisfying itself that the laws and practices of the country which govern the institution (i.e. law of the place in which it is incorporated and has its principal place of business) provide reciprocal market access to all EC credit institutions. The Commission is concerned to ensure that EC banks have access to the financial markets in foreign states which is 'equivalent' to that given to foreign institutions by the EC. If the reciprocity test is satisfied the applicant must meet all the other normal local requirements for authorisation.

OTHER REFORMS IN BANKING LAW AND PRACTICE

A review of banking services law by an independent review body was announced in January 1987. The terms of reference of the review committee were:

> 'to examine the statute and common law relating to the provision of banking services within the United Kingdom to personal and business customers, including payment and remittance services; but excluding taxation, company law and parts of the law whose relevance is to trading or the provision of services in general, rather than particularly to banking.'

The objectives of the review committee were:

(a) to examine the law and its practical implications from the points of view of banker, customer and the general public interest in the availability, reliability, security and efficient and effective operation of payment, remittance and other banking services;

(b) to have regard to:

    (i) current and prospective developments in banking and payment systems, including developments in electronic data processing and electronic funds transfer technology;

    (ii) areas of particular difficulty in or confusion about existing law and practice and the rights and obligations of banks and their customers respectively;...

(c) to prepare a final report, and if necessary interim reports also;

(d) if appropriate and after consultation to recommend the implementation of codes of good practice ...

(e) if necessary and after consultation to make proposals for legislation.

The Jack Committee report (*Banking Services: Law and Practice*) was published in March 1989. The report recommended some changes to the law on banking services. The Committee made some 83 recommendations in the report, and suggested that 43 of these recommendations be given effect in the form of three new pieces of legislation. The Committee therefore recommended:

(a) a Banking Services Act governing the banker–customer relationship, a statutory Ombudsman scheme and the regulation of electronic funds transfers;

(b) a Cheque and Bank Payment Act to regulate cheque usage and payments, and to include and regulate a new non-transferable instrument known as a bank payment order;

(c) a Negotiable Instruments Act to cover technical changes in the existing law on bills of exchange and screen-based transfers.

The Jack Committee expressed the view that other recommendations should be given effect in the form of a voluntary Code of Practice and Appendix L to the report contains an illustrative non-statutory Code of Banking Practice prepared by the Committee. Appendix J to the report contains a Code of Good Practice, proposed by the Office of Fair Trading. Appendix S contains an outline of supporting legislation for a Statutory Code of Banking Practice.

Since the publication of the Jack Committee report there has been a government response in the form of a White Paper on Banking Services (published in March 1990). The banks, building societies and card issuers have adopted a voluntary Code of Banking Practice (adopted in March 1992), and there has been a Cheques Act 1992 which came into force in June 1992.

In this section of the chapter it is intended to deal with those aspects of the Jack Committee (especially in relation to electronic funds transfers (EFT) and plastic cards), the White Paper and the Code which will not be dealt with in later chapters.

The Jack Committee Report

The Jack Committee expressed the view that there was some need for regulation of EFT transactions for a number of reasons. It felt that banks had in the past used their stronger bargaining position to impose onerous terms and conditions on customers who often had little choice but to accept the services provided for them. Moreover, the EFT systems had been operational for some time and the initial problems had been solved. The banks had also safeguarded themselves with the gradual introduction of EFT systems. The Committee also expressed the view that EFT regulation was necessary because customers were not always fully informed of the terms of the EFT contracts and there was widespread uncertainty about the allocation of duties and liabilities amongst the suppliers of services and consumers. The Committee recommended the adoption of a two-tier approach which restricted statutory intervention to a few key areas and issues common to the main EFT systems, with the adoption of standards of best practice to regulate the more detailed issues unique to the specific EFT systems and technologies.

The Jack Committee refers to EFT transfers as any payment messages transmitted either through magnetic material such as magnetic tapes, disks and cassettes, or through purely electronic media such as a telephone, telex and electronic transmission between computers, or between a terminal and a computer. Both methods are near-instantaneous in speed of transmission.

On the basis of the definition of EFT used by the Jack Committee Report electronic funds transfer includes methods of payment such as CHAPS, SWIFT, ATMs, EFTPOS, truncation, home and office banking.

The issues which are of special concern and which the Jack Committee examined deal with customer rights and liabilities.

Authentication of the customer's instructions

A form of authentication of the customer's instructions is necessary in all payment systems. The paper-based payment systems are based on authentication of the customer's signature and a bank which makes payment on a forged signature cannot debit the customer's account. Moreover, s. 24 of the Bills of Exchange Act 1882 deals with forged or unauthorised payments. The Jack Committee was of the view that with EFT systems technology had not evolved to such an extent as to allow payment instructions to be personalised in the same way as paper-based instructions. Where EFT systems are used to transfer funds, a plastic card and Personal Identification Number (PIN) are often used in order to authenticate the customer's identity, gain access to the computer terminal and as a security measure. The validity of the PIN authorisation has not yet been tested in the courts and the PIN is clearly vulnerable to possible breaches in security. The Jack Committee therefore recommended:

(a) A standard of best practice should translate into the context of customer-activated EFT systems the bank's duty to observe the customer's mandate.

In order to comply with this obligation the Jack Committee recommended that banks should adopt the principle that EFT systems must attain certain minimum standards of security in authorisation procedures so that there is an acceptable degree of protection for the customer. Moreover, banks should accept a continuing commitment to upgrade their systems by the introduction of new technology based on the electronic recognition of a signature or their personal characteristics.

(b) A standard of best practice should require banks to take reasonable care when issuing cards and PINs to their customers. In return customers should understand their obligations to take reasonable care in handling their cards and PIN. The Jack Committee recommended that customers should be required to acknowledge the receipt of their cards. In fact many banks and other card issuers already require customers to acknowledge receipt of their cards or to collect their cards from a specified branch (Barclays Bank), or to bring the card into the store to have it activated (Marks & Spencers plc).

(c) The Committee recognised the problem of privacy in customer-activated EFT systems. In order to maintain security the Committee recommended that a standard of best practice should be established which requires banks to ensure the maximum privacy that is reasonably possible:

(i) to prevent internal interception of electronically transmitted information banks should introduce encryption (where this can be operationally justified); and

(ii) to monitor ATM withdrawals so that any fraudulent misuse of the system can be detected.

(d) Legislation should be introduced to ban the unsolicited mailing of payment cards and PINs by banks to their customers (credit cards are already covered by s. 51 of the Consumer Credit Act 1974).

Liability in case of fraud or technical failure

The existing terms and conditions employed by banks do not always deal with the question of customer grievance in respect of EFT transactions and the customer is often unaware of (a) against whom he has redress, and (b) against whom the dispute may be pursued. The Jack Committee recommended that a standard of best practice should be introduced requiring the bank or other card issuer to deal with its own customer where the dispute relates to an EFT system. The bank may then pursue the claim against any third party involved.

The Jack Committee recommended that where loss arises to a customer due to fraud-provisions similar to those in the Consumer Credit Act 1974 should be enacted to apply to EFT payments. The Consumer Credit Act 1974 (ss. 83 and 84) limits the liability for misuse of credit and debit cards to £50. Moreover, the Act provides that a customer's liability should cease from the moment he notifies the bank of the loss of the card and/or compromise of the PIN, or notifies the bank of an error on his bank statement whether or not it is combined with the discovery of the loss of the card and/or compromise of the PIN.

The customer's liability for loss caused by the customer's negligence, however, is not dealt with by the Consumer Credit Act.

The Committee recognised that loss may be caused to a customer by a system's malfunction either in a customer-activated system or in an internal bank-to-bank terminal. Any rule dealing with the question of allocation of liability should deal with direct and consequential losses but the measure of damages may be reduced if the failure is due to causes beyond the control of the bank or if 'intent or gross negligence on the customer's part has contributed to the fault.' Moreover, where the customer is, or should be, aware of the malfunction, the bank's liability should be limited to the correction of any errors on the customer's account. Again the Jack Committee recommended that any questions of liability, or of action, against the third party should be dealt with by the bank.

Burden of proof

Where there is a customer-activated EFT terminal disputes may arise about the underlying facts, i.e. whether a transaction recorded by the bank or appearing on the bank statement was in fact authorised by the customer or whether it took place at all. The Committee concluded that rules are necessary to ensure that the resolution of EFT disputes 'starts from a fair contractual base, and guide the actual process of resolution.'

Under proposals recommended by the Jack Committee the law would ensure that notwithstanding any agreement to the contrary any loss arising from a disputed EFT transaction is apportioned by reference to the extent to which the acts or omissions of the parties contribute to the loss. The apportionment of any loss should take into account factors such as:

(a) the steps taken by a customer to protect the security of his card and PIN;

(b) the extent to which the system provided by the bank protects the customer against unauthorised transactions on his account;

(c) the relative weight of the evidence by the parties in support of their respective contentions, and whether the transaction was authorised or not.

The Jack Committee recommended that the customer should be notified of this rule.

Revocation of payment

By the very nature of paper-based methods of payment the customer has an opportunity to countermand payment. Where the payment method is instantaneous the customer may be denied his opportunity to countermand the mandate (see p.157). The Jack Committee concluded that banks should formulate their own contractual rules on countermand for each individual EFT system. However, where possible the customer should be given the opportunity to countermand and banks should take steps to notify their customers of the rules of countermand as they apply to different payment systems.

When is payment made?

The Committee noted that payment may be complete between the parties at a different time from payment between banks. It made recommendations relating to the completion of payment between banks and concluded that statutory rules were necessary to define completion of payment under EFT systems and the rules should provide:

(a) payment is to be regarded as complete between two accounts at the point where the payee's bank (or its agent) having actual or ostensible authority accepts payment for the payee's account and provided that payment has become unconditional; and

(b) where the transfer is between two accounts at the same time, payment should be regarded as complete when the bank has taken the decision to treat the instructions for the transfer as irrevocable. These rules should be capable of modification by contractual agreement between the parties.

Plastic cards

The Jack Committee examined the expansion and use of plastic cards with regard to both EFT and paper-based transfer systems. It made a number of recommendations.

Multi-function cards

The Committee saw the development of multi-function cards as both inevitable and desirable. It therefore recommended a standard of banking practice:

(a) to allow the customer the right to choose the functions he wants and to block off unwanted functions; and

(b) that the customer should not be liable for any loss resulting from the use of functions which the customer did not require or want.

Card notification agencies

The Committee accepted that there is often confusion regarding notification of loss of cards. As a matter of banking practice all card-issuers should inform customers:

(a) of whether they will accept notification of loss and/or compromise of PIN;
(b) whether notification may be to an agent and whether that discharges the customer from having to notify the bank.

The White Paper

The Jack Committee report on banking services was followed by a White Paper which announced that a committee under the chairmanship of Sir George Blunden had been set up to oversee the preparation of a Code of Banking Practice, and the scope of the Code. The White Paper also announced that legislation would follow in certain areas. Again it is intended here to deal with those proposals in the White Paper which will not be discussed in later chapters.

Rules on electronic funds transfers

The White Paper made a number of recommendations on EFT systems. It recommended that the Code of Banking Practice deal with:

Authentication of the customer's instructions

The White Paper accepted that EFT systems should meet certain minimum standards of security in the authorisation procedures. It therefore recommended that the Code contain a provision giving an undertaking that banks will continue to maintain existing minimum standards of security in all EFT systems.

Written record of ATM withdrawals

The White Paper accepted that written records of all ATM withdrawals should be made available to the customer. In a disputed EFT transaction which involves more than one party the customer should be informed of his right of redress and to whom he should apply for redress.

The White Paper also states that a number of issues will form the basis of new legislation. In connection with EFT payments legislation will be introduced in connection with:

Unsolicited mailing of payment cards

The government proposes to introduce legislation to ban the mailing of unsolicited credit and other payment cards and other similar credit facilities. Section 51 of the Consumer Credit Act 1974 will be extended to cover all payment cards and s. 84 of the Act will establish the limits of liability to cover such cards so that the customer is only liable for a maximum of £50 for loss resulting from theft of the card.

EFT systems breakdown

The White Paper proposes legislation in the case of customer-activated EFT systems whereby banks will not be able to exclude liability for systems breakdown by contract. The bank will be liable for any foreseeable loss due to a failure of customer-activated EFT equipment despite any contractual provisions to the contrary. At present, any such terms excluding or restricting liability are subject to the Unfair Contracts Terms Act 1977.

Code of Banking Practice

The White Paper was followed by the Code of Banking Practice which was adopted by the banks, building societies and other card issuers when dealing with personal customers. The Code deals with a number of issues regarding EFT systems and plastic cards. The Code provides that any written terms and conditions relating to plastic cards will be expressed in plain language and will provide a fair and balanced view of the customer and card issuer. The Code provides:

Terms and conditions
That any change in the terms and conditions of service will be notified to customers prior to the variation and where there have been several changes over a 12-month period a single consolidating document will be supplied. Any changes in the interest rates will be notified by publication in the branches or stores or in the press or in the statement of account or by all these methods where the change takes effect immediately.

Issue of cards
The Code provides that card issuers will issue cards only when requested in writing, or to replace or renew existing cards. Where the card performs more than one function the customer must be notified and the issuer must comply with any request not to be issued with a PIN. The Code did not adopt the recommendation of the Jack Committee that customers should have the option of blocking off functions on multi-function cards.

Security of cards
The Code requires card issuers to issue cards and PINs to customers separately (this is already done by the majority of card issuers). Card issuers must notify customers of their obligation to safeguard their cards and PINs to prevent fraud. It should be emphasised to customers that they should not disclose their PIN to another person, that they keep the PIN and card secret at all times, and not write the PIN on the card. Moreover, if the PIN is written down reasonable attempts should be made to disguise it.

The Code does not adopt the Jack Committee recommendation that customers should acknowledge both receipt of the card and PIN.

Lost cards

The Code requires customers to notify card issuers 'as soon as reasonably
ble' of the loss or theft of the card, or that the PIN is compromised or the ba..
statement shows a wrong entry.

Card issuers will at regular intervals be notified of telephone numbers where
details of lost cards and PINs can be given. The Code requires a 24-hour service.
Once notified of the loss of the card or compromise of the PIN the card issuer will
be required to 'take action to prevent further use of the card.'

Card issuers will, on request, notify customers whether notification of loss to a
card notification agency will be sufficient.

Liability for loss

The Code provides that card issuers will bear the full loss incurred where the card
never reaches the customer; for all transactions not authorised by the customer after
the card issuer is informed of the loss of the card or compromise of the PIN; and any
loss suffered by the customer due to systems malfunction unless the fault was
obvious or advised by notice.

Once loss or compromise of the card is notified to the card issuer the customer is
only liable for the first £50 of any loss unless the customer is responsible for the
fraud or is grossly negligent.

Records

Card issuers will provide customers with written records of their statements, in addition to the immediate computer receipt.

Handling customer complaints

Each card issuer must have its own internal complaints procedure which must be
notified to customers. Any customer who wishes to complain must be informed of
the procedure. Card issuers are required to belong to the various conciliation
schemes (see p.75 on the Banking Ombudsman scheme).

THE UK BANKING STRUCTURE

The UK banking system has developed gradually over the last three centuries and is
still undergoing change. In this section of the chapter it is intended to examine the
structure of the banking system in the UK and the role the banks have developed for
themselves. It should be remembered that there are no specific facilities or services
which the banks must supply to their customers. The provisions in the Banking Act
requiring banks to provide certain types of services to their customers are fairly basic
(e.g. the supply of current account facilities) and were introduced with a view to
facilitate the recognition of certain types of institutions (i.e. deposit-taking institutions). Apart from that requirement in the Banking Act there are no statutory
provisions which govern the type of services that banks must undertake. It is true to

say that banking business has expanded beyond recognition but that has been more in response to competition from other financial institutions than any statutory or other obligation. In *Woods* v *Martins Bank Ltd* ([1958] 3 All ER 166) (see p.41) Salmon J said (p. 172):

> 'In my judgment, the limits of a banker's business cannot be laid down as a matter of law. The nature of such a business must in each case be a matter of fact and, accordingly, cannot be treated as if it were a matter of pure law.'

The Bank of England

The Bank of England, which stands at the head of the banking system, has been a public corporation since the acquisition of its shares by the Treasury in 1946. Until the Banking Act 1979 (now the Banking Act 1987) the banking sector was supervised informally by the Bank of England. It had powers of recommendation and direction under the Bank of England Act 1946, which were in fact never used.

The Bank of England is administered by a Governor, a Deputy Governor and a board of directors appointed by the government under the 1946 Act. They act in close consultation with the Treasury and other government departments. Under s. 4(1) of the Bank of England Act the Treasury may from time to time give such directions as it thinks fit and the Bank is managed subject to these directions.

Functions of the Bank of England

The functions of the Bank are not exhaustively listed either in statute or in its charter. The Bank attends to the issue and registration of government stock and is responsible for the issue of Treasury bills required to meet the excess in government expenditure over current revenues. It is the only bank which may issue notes in England and Wales. In Scotland, however, the Royal Bank of Scotland may issue notes and in Northern Ireland the banks may issue notes. The total volume of notes in circulation at any given time is determined by direction of the Treasury and since the abandonment of the Gold Standard, only part of the note issue, known as the fiduciary issue, is backed by gold.

The Bank of England's Banking Department maintains accounts for the government, nationalised industries, public and local authorities and some overseas governments. It also holds accounts for the commercial banks and certain overseas banks. The legal relationship between the Bank of England and these banks is that of banker and customer, but the Bank of England does not offer current account facilities.

The Bank of England is used by the government as a means of regulating the economy through the minimum lending rate, and its open market and exchange operations. For this reason it is only on the directions of the Treasury that the Bank of England will alter its minimum lending rate.

One of the most important functions of the Bank of England is to exercise supervisory powers over the activities of the other banks and to give effect to government policies. The supervisory powers of the Bank of England are now contained in the Banking Act 1987.

The retail banks

These banks are also known as the high street banks and provide services to the customer (either individual customers or business customers). These banks are regulated by the Banking Act 1987 and must obtain authorisation under the Act. They provide a varied range of services for their customers, including cheque and deposit accounts, traveller's cheques and finance of international trade, finance and investment facilities, insurance and probate. Due to increased competition banks have entered into a wide range of activities, including mortgage lending for house purchase to individuals.

A major feature of the retail banking system is the branch system which operates in the UK.

The clearing banks

The clearing banks are merely a grouping of the retail banks. They are members of the London clearing system and at the conclusion of the business each day, balances between the banks are settled by means of accounts maintained with the Bank of England. More recently, the banks have introduced electronic means of payment to reduce the time taken to complete payment transactions and effect economies of scale. Banks charge their customers for the services provided although most banks will not impose bank charges in respect of current accounts which have a credit balance or which maintain a minimum credit balance.

In order to assist with the resolution of banking disputes the banks have set up a voluntary Banking Ombudsman scheme.

Merchant banks

Merchant banks (some being subsidiaries of the clearing banks) include accepting and issuing houses and investment bankers. Merchant banks provide the same services as commercial banks but for a restricted range of customers. The main activities undertaken by these banks include financing imports and exports and world trade by the acceptance of bills of exchange. Merchant banks are heavily involved in arranging finance for companies and the issue or sale of shares to the public and other securities of public companies and authorities. Although merchant banks act primarily as intermediaries between parties, they undertake commercial ventures themselves by making loans or by subscribing or underwriting issues of shares or securities.

Most merchant banks specialise in a particular area of business or undertake work mainly originating from the part of the world with which they have historical connections.

The merchant banks which engage in the acceptance of bills of exchange are represented on the Accepting Houses Committee.

Finance houses

Finance houses include subsidiaries of the clearing banks, independent deposit-takers and subsidiaries of foreign financial institutions. Their business is based mainly on instalment credit, e.g. hire-purchase, credit sales, etc.

Discount houses

Discount houses are responsible for making markets in a variety of short-term sterling financial instruments and for providing a means by which the Bank of England can make itself felt in the money markets.

Government savings institutions

The main savings banks in the UK are the Trustee Savings Bank and the National Savings Bank.

The Trustee Savings Bank Act 1976 granted each trustee savings bank the power 'to carry on the business of banking'. Trustee savings banks do grant overdrafts and loans, including personal loans and home improvement loans. They issue cheque cards, provide traveller's cheques and since 1978 they have issued Visa credit cards.

The National Savings Bank was established by the Post Office Savings Act 1861. Business may be conducted through any post office. Interest is paid on accounts held by the customer.

WHO IS A CUSTOMER?

The term 'customer' is easier to define and the law is fairly settled on the point. There is, however, no statutory definition of the term and it is, therefore, necessary to examine the case law. It is necessary to determine who is a customer of a bank because the banker–customer relationship imposes certain obligations on the parties to the contract. The question is also relevant in the context of the Bills of Exchange Act 1882 and the Cheques Act 1957 because many of the statutory defences available to the banks are only available when a bank deals with a customer.

The Jack Committee concluded that the legal definition of the term 'customer' resembles closely the meaning given to it by the general public. For that reason the Committee recommended that the existing law should not be altered.

The view has always been taken that for a person (whether an individual or company) to be treated as a customer there must be a regular or recognisable course of dealing between him and the bank.

Great Western Railway v London & County Bank [1901] AC 414

The manager of a bank had over a number of years cashed cheques over the counter for one Huggins, although he had no account with the bank. In 1898, Huggins obtained a cheque from the appellant company by false pretences. The cheque was drawn in his favour and crossed 'not negotiable'. This cheque was also cashed over the counter. When the fraud was discovered the true owner of these cheques brought an action against the bank for conversion.

At first instance the court held that Huggins was a customer of the bank on the grounds that the bank had for many years collected cheques for him. The bank appealed and the Court of Appeal affirmed the decision. The bank appealed.

The House of Lords held that since Huggins did not maintain an account with the bank, he could not be a customer of the bank, despite the habitual dealings he had with the bank and so the bank could not rely on the protection conferred by the Bills of Exchange Act 1882. Although, Huggins had had dealings with the bank over an extended period of time, he did not become a customer because he did not have an account with the bank. Davey LJ (p. 420):

> '... I think that there must be some sort of account, either a deposit or a current account or some similar relation, to make a man a customer of a banker.'

And later Lindley LJ said (p. 425):

> 'I cannot think that Huggins was in any sense a customer of the bank; no doubt he was known at the bank as a person accustomed to come and get cheques cashed, but he had no account of any sort with the bank. Nothing was put to his debit or credit in any book or paper kept by the bank.'

Commissioners of Taxation v English, Scottish & Australian Bank Ltd [1920] AC 683

An action was brought by an Australian taxpayer who delivered to the offices of the Commissioner of Taxation, in Sydney, a cheque in payment of taxes. All cheques payable to the Commissioner of Taxation were drawn made payable in 'cash'. The cheque was stolen and a person calling himself Thallon opened an account with the respondent bank and paid in the stolen cheque. The cheque was cashed and Thallon then drew a number of cheques against the credit balance on his account.

The Commissioner of Taxation brought an action against the bank for conversion. The bank argued that it was protected by s. 88 of the Bills of Exchange Act 1909 (Commonwealth of Australia) which is similar to s. 88 of the Bills of Exchange Act 1882. The Commissioner argued that the bank had been negligent and additionally Thallon was not a customer of the bank under the Act. The trial judge and, on appeal, the Supreme Court of New South Wales found for the bank. The Commissioner of Taxation appealed.

The Judicial Committee of the Privy Council held that the bank was not guilty of negligence in allowing cheques to be drawn against the misappropriated funds standing to the credit of its customer's account, Thallon. Lord Dunedin said (p. 687):

'... the word "customer" signifies a relationship in which duration is not of the essence. A person whose money has been accepted on the footing that they undertake to honour cheques up to the amount standing to his credit is ... a customer of the bank irrespective of whether his connection is of short or long standing.'

The effect of the House of Lords' decision in the *Great Western Railway* case is that anyone who claims to be a customer of a bank must show that he maintains an account with the bank. It is not enough to enter into a course of dealings, however regular. In the *Commissioner of Taxation* case the court held that a bank will only be protected if it makes payment to a customer. The Privy Council contrasted between a person for whom the bank performs a casual service and a person who has an account of his own with the bank. It is only the latter who is a customer of the bank.

In *Ladbroke* v *Todd* ((1914) 30 TLR 433) the plaintiffs posted a letter to a client, one Jobson, enclosing a cheque drawn to his order and crossed 'A/C payee'. The cheque was stolen and the thief fraudulently indorsed Jobson's name on it. He opened an account with the defendant bank in Jobson's name. The cheque was specially cleared and the thief absconded with the proceeds. The plaintiffs brought an action to recover the proceeds of the cheque. The court held that it was unnecessary that the customer should have drawn on the account or be in a position to be able to draw on the account, in order that he should be a customer. The mere fact the an account has been opened is sufficient.

In *Robinson* v *Midland Bank* ((1925) 41 TLR 402) it was said that a person does not become a customer of a bank unless he opens an account personally or instructs an agent to act for him. If an account is opened in a person's name by someone who impersonates him or who falsely represents himself as having authority to open an account, there is no account with the person in whose name the account is being opened. Similarly, in *Stony Stanton Supplies (Coventry) Ltd* v *Midland Bank Ltd* ([1966] 2 Lloyd's Rep 373) it was held that a banker–customer relationship had not been entered into when it was discovered that the bank's mandate to open the account had been forged. This was despite the fact that the bank had opened an account relying on the mandate and the account had been operated. The facts of the case were that one Fox, an undischarged bankrupt, formed a company which had the name of Stony Stanton Supplies (Coventry) Ltd. The two directors of the company were the proprietors of the company registration firm through which the company was formed. Fox agreed with a Mr Taylor to the purchase of his grocery business and was introduced by Mr Taylor to his bank manager. In due course, Fox produced the necessary form to open an account in the name of Stony Stanton Company. Although the forms were purported to be signed by the two directors of Stony Stanton Ltd they were in fact forgeries. After the account was opened money coming into the grocery business was paid into the account of Stony Stanton Company Ltd and used by Fox for his personal benefit. When the fraud was discovered Fox received a prison sentence and a winding-up petition was obtained against Stony Stanton Ltd. The present action was brought to recover some £9,000, the amount withdrawn by Fox from the Stony Stanton account. The Court of Appeal held that there was no duty of care owed to Stony Stanton in connection with the operation of the bank account since there was no banker–customer relationship. Moreover, the court held that the bank had not been negligent in opening the bank account.

In *Barclays Bank Ltd* v *Okenarhe* ([1966] 2 Lloyd's Rep 87) (see p. 71) it was suggested by Bailhache J that the mere offer to open an account, and its acceptance by the bank, will create a binding contract on the basis of the general law of contract (a view expressed by Chorley, *Gilbert Lectures*, 1955). This is in line with banking practice even though the customer has not paid anything into the account. In many cases banks ask for a credit to be placed to the customer's account on opening the account.

It is possible for one bank to become the customer of another bank, e.g. where one bank uses another to clear cheques. In *Importers Co. Ltd* v *Westminster Bank Ltd* ([1927] 2 KB 297) Atkin LJ said:

> 'The remaining point was that Heilmanns, being a bank, could not be a "customer". In my opinion, on the evidence, they were customers in every sense of the word. They had a drawing account with the respondents. But if they were in a different position, it seems to me that if a non-clearing bank regularly employs a clearing bank to clear its cheques, the non-clearing bank is the "customer" of the clearing bank.'

Although, the banker–customer relationship is only created when an account is opened for the customer it has been held that the bank may be liable to a prospective customer. In *Woods* v *Martins Bank Ltd* ([1959] 1 QB 55) the plaintiff invested money in a company after receiving advice from the manager of the defendant bank. The bank also acted in that capacity for the company in which investment was recommended. The plaintiff lost money as a result of relying on the investment advice given by the manager and sued in negligence. The court held where the plaintiff was a prospective customer, and the bank was aware of the facts as the defendant bank was, it owed a duty of care in giving investment advice. Such a duty is owed not only to customers of the bank but also to a prospective customer where it is understood that the person will open an account.

The Jack Committee examined the question of the degree of inquiries a bank should undertake to verify the identity of a person who applies to open an account. The Committee concluded that the common law had not given consistent guidance on the question and the Committee concluded that it was necessary to re-establish the relevance of these inquiries with special regard to the protection conferred on the bank under s. 4 of the Cheques Act 1957.

CAPACITY TO CONTRACT AND TYPES OF CUSTOMER

It is assumed that the normal rules of contract and capacity to enter into that contract apply to the banker–customer relationship. There are, however, certain categories of customer who may not enjoy full capacity. It is intended to look merely at some of the types of person, whether legal or natural, who may be in a special position.

Joint accounts

Where an account is opened in the name of more than one person, the joint account holders will instruct the bank whether any one, or some of them, or all of them jointly must sign the mandate.

Jackson v *White & Midland Bank Ltd* [1967] 2 Lloyd's Rep 68

The plaintiff entered into negotiations with a view to entering into a partnership with the first defendant. The plaintiff paid £2,000 into a joint account at the branch of the defendant bank and instructed the bank that cheques could only be drawn against the joint signature of himself and the first defendant. The first defendant forged several cheques which were honoured by the bank. The first defendant refused to repay the money misappropriated from the joint account when negotiations with the plaintiff, to join the business, broke down. The plaintiff applied for an injunction ordering the bank to re-credit the account with the amount of the forged cheques and for an order requiring the bank to honour cheques drawn by the plaintiff, alone.

The court held for the plaintiff. Park J said:

'The bank made an agreement with the plaintiff and the first defendant jointly that it would honour any cheques signed by them jointly, and also a separate agreement with the plaintiff and the first defendant severally that it would not honour any cheques not signed by the plaintiff, the plaintiff is entitled to sue for breach of that separate agreement.'

A similar view was expressed in *Catlin* v *Cyprus Finance Corporation (London) Ltd* ([1983] QB 759) where once again the bank honoured a cheque, in breach of its mandate, which did not bear the signature of the joint account-holders. The court said that although the account was a joint account the bank owed a separate duty to conform to the mandate to each of the joint account-holders. Bingham J said that the bank's agreement to honour instructions by both account-holders imposed a negative agreement not to honour instructions not signed by both. He said that a duty on the joint account-holders which could only be enforced jointly would be worthless where the purpose of the account was to safeguard against the misconduct of one of the account-holders.

The nature of the bank's liability to joint account-holders was in doubt as a result of the *Brewer* v *Westminster Bank Ltd* ([1952] 2 All ER 650) case where it was held that an action on a joint account could only be brought by the joint holders and, therefore, an action against the bank failed because one of the joint account-holders having forged the signature of the other account-holder could not maintain an action against the bank. The survivor's legal title to the balance on the joint account following the death of one of the joint account-holders is never in question. The bank is within its rights to pay out any credit balance to the survivor. A dispute may, however, arise as to the equitable title, i.e. whether the survivor is entitled to keep the money or whether he is treated as holding it for other persons who have a beneficial interest in the money.

The presumption is that equitable title follows the legal title. This presumption can be displaced by showing the intention of the parties, i.e. it can be shown by the intention of the parties that a true joint account was not intended (see *Marshall* v *Crutwell* ((1875) LR 20 Eq 328) where it was held that the presumption of survivorship was displaced when it was shown that all the money credited to the joint account was provided by the husband (who was in ill health) and the withdrawals made by the wife were for housekeeping). However, there must be clear evidence of ownership of the money (see *Hirschorn* v *Evans* ([1928] 2 KB 801) where it was held that there was clear evidence of the beneficial ownership of the money and a garnishee order against the husband could not attach to the bank account. In *Jones* v *Maynard* ([1951] Ch 572) a husband and wife had a joint account into which the husband's salary and investment income was credited, although the wife had a little investment income of her own. Any surplus on the bank account was regularly invested in the husband's name. When the husband and wife divorced, the wife claimed that she was beneficially entitled to half the investments. The husband argued that she was only entitled to such investments as were proportionally represented by her own contributions to the account. Vaisey J held in favour of the wife and said:

> 'In my view a husband's earnings or salary, when the spouses have a common purse, and pool their resources, are earnings made on behalf of both ... the money which goes into the pool becomes joint property.'

The reasoning in *Jones* v *Maynard* was approved in *Rimmer* v *Rimmer* ([1953] 1 QB 63). However, in *Re Bishop, deceased* ([1965] Ch 450) the husband and wife had separate accounts into which their respective salaries were paid and from which investments were made in the name of the husband alone or the wife alone. The court held that there was nothing to displace the legal titles indicated in the individual accounts and purchases.

Partnership accounts

A partnership account resembles a joint account in that it will be opened in the name of more than one person. Unlike registered companies a partnership does not enjoy legal status and the account is in effect a joint account in the name of the specified partners. A partner acts as an agent of his co-partners for the purposes of opening the account and not only must he act within the authority conferred on him but once the account is opened, the bank must conform to any mandate given by the partners. A partner has no authority to open a partnership account in his own name. The rules of survivorship, as applied in the case of joint accounts, are merely a presumption in the case of partnership accounts and may be rebutted.

McEvoy v *Belfast Banking Co.* [1935] AC 24

In 1921, JM deposited £10,000 with the respondent bank in a joint account opened in the names of his son and himself. The mandate given to the bank enabled either joint account-holder to sign on the account and, in the event of the death of either partner, any balance would be made over to the survivor. J.M. subsequently made a will leaving the residue on trust for the son until he reached the age of 25. On J.M.'s death the executors received the £10,000 from the bank and re-deposited it in their own names. Between the death of the father and the son's 25th birthday, the executors carried on the deceased father's business with the son taking a more active role. After the son reached his 21st birthday but before his 25th birthday the executors withdrew the balance of the £10,000 and paid it into their own personal account which was overdrawn. On reaching his 25th birthday the son brought an action against the bank for the amount standing to the credit of the deposit account at the time of his father's death and the interest accrued.

The House of Lords held that the executors were entitled to receive the money and apply it in the due course of the administration. Nevertheless, the House of Lords held that steps should have been taken to protect the interests of the infant son. Lord Warrington of Clyffe said that the real question is not whether the appellant would in contract be entitled to repayment of the money but what in the view of a court of equity would be the position between him and the executors.

Alliance Bank v Kearsley (1871) LR 6 CP 433

The defendant and his brother, James, carried on a business as partners under the name of 'George Kearsley & Company'. James opened an account in his own name because he was the only partner resident locally. The account became overdrawn and the bank brought an action against the defendant.

The court held that the bank could not recover the amount of the overdraft because it is not in the ordinary course of business for one partner to open a banking account in his own name on behalf of the partnership and so bind the co-partners as to the state of the account. Montague Smith J said:

> '... I do not think a judge can take it upon himself to assume, without evidence, that it is within the ordinary course of business for one partner to open a banking account in his own name on behalf of the partnership so as to bind the co-partners to the state of that account whatever it may be. That being so, the foundation of the implied authority entirely fails ... an account opened by a man in his own name is prima facie his private account ... '

Re Bourne, Bourne v Bourne [1906] 2 Ch 427

A partnership business was carried on by Grove and Bourne. On the death of Grove, the remaining partner, Bourne, continued the business in the partnership name until his death. At the time of Grove's death, the partnership account was overdrawn by £6,476. Bourne deposited with the bank, as security, title deeds over certain partnership assets in order to secure a further overdraft. At the time of Bourne's death the bank account was overdrawn by £4,463. Bourne's estate being insolvent, the question that arose was whether the bank or Grove's executors had priority to the proceeds of sale of the property charged in favour of the bank.

The court held that the bank had priority to the proceeds of sale. Grove's executors appealed.

The Court of Appeal held for the bank and said that the surviving partner had the power to give a good title to purchasers and mortgagees. Anyone dealing with the surviving partner was entitled to assume that he was acting in good faith and entitled to liquidate the partnership. Romer LJ said:

> 'When a partner dies and the partnership comes to an end, it is not only the right, but the duty, of the surviving partner to realise the assets for the purpose of winding up the partnership affairs, including the payment of the partnership debts. It is true that in a general sense the executors or administrators of the deceased partner may be said to have a lien upon the partnership assets in respect of his interest in the partnership account, but that lien is not one which affects each particular piece of property belonging to the partnership so as to effect that property in the hands of any person dealing with the surviving partner in good faith ...'

A partner in a trading partnership will bind his co-partners if he acts in the ordinary course of the partnership business. If he acts outside the ordinary course of business he will make himself personally liable. A partner therefore has implied authority to open a bank account in the name of the partnership, to extend credit and to draw cheques and other negotiable instruments. A partner will not be deemed to have authority to open a bank account in his own name for partnership purposes. In *Ringham v Hackett and Another* ((1980) 124 SJ 201) a partner who signed a cheque bearing the name of the partnership was held to bind all the partners. In that case the first defendant, without the knowledge of the other partner, drew a cheque for £500 under the printed name of the partnership. He subsequently disappeared and the remaining partner countermanded payment on all outstanding cheques drawn by him. The Court of Appeal held that the remaining partner was liable to make payment on the cheque and where a cheque is drawn by one partner it is unnecessary that the cheque should be signed in such a way as to indicate it is signed in a representative capacity. This case was followed in *Central Motors (Birmingham) Ltd v A. and S.N. Wadsworth* ([1983] CAT 82/231). In *United Bank of Kuwait v Hammound* ([1988] 1 WLR 1051) a solicitor fraudulently gave a security undertaking in the name of the partnership. In an action to enforce the security against the co-partners the Court of Appeal held that a partner is deemed to have ostensible authority to give security in the ordinary course of business and the co-partners were bound.

Registered companies

A call for the reform of the *ultra vires* rule was made as long ago as 1945 when *The Report of the Committee on Company Law Amendment* (Cm. 6659) recommended its repeal. The question was examined again in 1962 and some modifications made to the common law under the Companies Act 1982 (amending s. 9 of the European Communities Act 1972). In 1985 the Prentice Committee was set up 'to examine the legal and commercial implications of abolishing the *ultra vires* rule'. The new rules were enacted in the Companies Act 1989.

A company registered under the Companies Act 1985 is a separate legal entity and may therefore enter into contracts on its own behalf. Any limitations on the capacity of the company to enter into contracts with a third party have been removed. A company can, therefore, not only open an account with a bank but borrow money without the third party falling foul of the *ultra vires* rule. The new s. 35(1) of the Companies Act 1985 (s. 108 of the Companies Act 1989) provides:

'The validity of an act done by a company shall not be called into question on the ground of lack of capacity by reason of anything in the company's memorandum.'

The new s. 35 does not overrule the *Ashbury Railway Carriage & Co.* v *Riche* case ((1875) LR 7 HL 653) but it provides that neither the company nor the third party to a contract or transaction can question its validity on the ground that the act or transaction is outside the objects or powers of the company. The new provisions make it possible for a company to enforce a contract which but for the validating provisions would be *ultra vires* the company. This is a departure from the old rules under which the company could not sue to enforce a contract which was outside the objects of the company (see *Anglo Overseas Agencies Ltd* v *Green* ([1961] 1 QB 1) and *Bell Houses Ltd* v *City Wall Properties Ltd* ([1966] 1 QB 207)). There are, however, some changes to the wording of the new s. 35 which requires the third party to have acted in 'good faith' but the third party is still deemed to have acted in good faith even though he has knowledge that the contract is outside the scope of the objects clause. The company's lack of capacity cannot be relied on by either the third party or the company. The section applies to 'acts' rather than transactions and will therefore extend to powers, e.g. gifts made to a charity will be valid.

Moreover, the new provisions make ineffective against the third party dealing with the company any limitations on the power of the board of directors to enter into transactions through provisions in the memorandum or articles, or any limitations imposed by the passing of board resolutions.

Consequently, the *ultra vires* rule is repealed in its external effect insofar as acts or transactions could be held to be unenforceable on grounds of lack of capacity of the company or the directors.

Trust accounts

Where a bank has actual knowledge of trust money it must not deal with the fund in a manner which is inconsistent with the trust.

Re Gross, ex p. Kingston (1871) 6 Ch App 632

Gross, a treasurer for Suffolk, kept a private account with the National Provincial Bank. He paid into his private account funds received in his capacity as treasurer. He subsequently opened a separate account headed 'police account' into which he transferred certain amounts from his private account. The bank paid interest due on both the accounts into his personal account. Gross became insolvent and disappeared leaving his private account overdrawn and the 'police account' in credit. The bank sought to set off the accounts to produce an overall credit balance. At the time the 'police account' was opened the bank manager knew that Gross was the county treasurer and had knowledge that he had been in the habit of paying county money into his personal account.

The county court at Ipswich made an order that the bank was entitled to a lien on the credit balances to satisfy the net indebtedness. The magistrates representing the county appealed. The Chief Judge in Bankruptcy found against the bank which appealed.

The court held that the bank had no right to set off the accounts but that the county was entitled to amounts standing to the credit of the trust account. Sir George Mellish LJ said:

> 'If an account is in plain terms headed in such a way that a banker cannot fail to know it to be a trust account, the balance standing to the credit of that account will, on the bankruptcy of the person who kept it, belong to the trust. The banker need not open such an account unless he pleases ... ; and if the customer, when his general account is overdrawn, asks that it may be further overdrawn for the purpose of paying money into the trust account, the banker is entitled to refuse such an accommodation.'

A bank may make itself liable to the beneficiaries of a trust under circumstances where it knowingly participates in the breach of trust. The question which the courts have been asked to determine is what type of knowledge will make the bank liable as a constructive trustee?

Lipkin Gorman v *Karpnale Ltd* [1989] 1 WLR 1340

The plaintiffs were a firm of solicitors. Between 1978 and 1980 one Norman Cass, a partner in the firm, used his authority to sign cheques on the firm's client account for his gambling purposes. The fraudulent partner was convicted of theft and sentenced to imprisonment. An action was brought against the first defendants, who operated a gambling casino, for negligence and for money had and received and against the second defendants, Lloyds Bank plc, to hold them liable as constructive trustees for funds misappropriated by Norman Cass.

At first instance Alliott J held that the claim against the casino failed, but the bank was liable as a constructive trustee. There were appeals and cross-appeals resulting from these findings.

The Court of Appeal allowed the appeal by the bank against the finding that it was liable to the plaintiffs as a constructive trustee. May LJ considered first the liability of the bank to pay against cheques drawn by the customer (and citing Kindersley VC in *Bodenham* v *Hoskins* ((1852) 21 LJ Eq 864 at 869) he said (p. 1353):

> '... the banker looks only to the customer, in respect of the account opened in that customer's name, and whatever cheques that customer chooses to draw, the banker is to honour. He is not to inquire for what purpose the customer opened the account; he is not to inquire what the monies are that are paid into that account, and he is not to inquire for what purpose monies are drawn out of that account: that is the plain general rule, as between banker and customer.'

May LJ then continued, citing Cairns LC in *Gray* v *Johnston* ((1868) LR 3 HL 1 at 11), and said:

> '... in order to hold a banker justified in refusing to pay a demand of his customer, the customer being an executor, there must, in the first place, be some misapplication, some breach of trust, intended by the executor, and there must in the second place, as was said by Sir John Leach, in the well known case of *Keane* v *Robarts* (1819) 4 Madd 332–357, be proof that the bankers are privy to the intent to make this misapplication of the trust funds.'

May LJ then considered the liability of the bank as a constructive trustee. He rejected the argument that the bank was aware of the fraud in that the manager had actual knowledge of it, or had wilfully shut his eyes to the obvious, or had wilfully or recklessly failed to make inquiries as an honest and reasonable man would have made. He concluded that nothing less than knowledge, as defined in one of the first three categories set out in *Baden, Delvaux and Lecuit* v *Société Général pour Favoriser le Developpement du Commerce et de l'Industrie en France SA* ([1983] BCLC 325), of an underlying dishonest intent is sufficient to make a stranger liable as a constructive trustee.

The *Lipkin* v *Gorman* case went on appeal to the House of Lords ([1991] 3 WLR 10) but the question of liability as a constructive trustee was not examined.

In *Barnes* v *Addy* ((1874) 9 Ch App 244) it was held that a person who assists in the disposal of trust property in breach of trust will be held liable as constructive trustee if he knowingly:

(a) assists the dishonest trustee; or
(b) receives or deals with a trust fund in breach of trust.

However, in *Selangor United Rubber Estates* v *Cradock (No. 3)* ([1968] 1 WLR 1555) the court applied the rule and said that liability will be imposed on a stranger who assists in the disposal of trust property if either:

(a) he knew of the breach;
(b) or ought to have known of the breach of trust.

The facts of the *Selangor* case were that a bank provided financial assistance in connection with a takeover bid, and because of inexperience its officials failed to realise that a company which was its customer was indirectly financing the acquisition of its own shares. The court held that where a bank knowingly participates in a breach of trust by which the trustee wrongfully disposes of the credit balance of an account the bank is liable to compensate the beneficiary for knowingly participating in the wrongful act.

The view in the *Selangor* case was followed in *Karak Rubber Co.* v *Burden (No. 2)* ([1972] 1 All ER 1210) and in *Rowlandson* v *National Westminster Bank* ([1978] 3 All ER 370). In the latter case it was said that in order to establish liability as a constructive trustee on the part of a third party, who assisted in a breach of trust, it was necessary to show that the third party had assisted with knowledge of a dishonest and fraudulent design. In the *Rowlandson* case the plaintiffs brought an action for a declaration to the effect that a sum of £2,000 deposited with the Curzon Street branch of the defendant was held by the bank as a trustee and it was liable as a constructive trustee in allowing the account-holder, fraudulently, to draw against the amount. The court held that no express trust had been declared, created or accepted by the bank. However, when an account described as a 'trust account' had been opened for the plaintiffs, the bank came under a fiduciary duty to the plaintiffs in respect of the account and was liable if it knowingly assisted in a dishonest and fraudulent design on the part of the trustees.

In more recent cases the courts have examined the type of knowledge which will be sufficient to impose liability as a constructive trustee. In *Baden* v *Société Général* ([1983] BCLC 325) the court said that a person may have the following types of knowledge of a breach of trust, namely:

(a) actual knowledge;
(b) knowledge that he would have obtained but for wilfully shutting his eyes to the obvious;
(c) knowledge which he would have obtained but for wilfully and recklessly failing to make such inquiries as an honest and reasonable man would make;
(d) knowledge of facts which would indicate the facts to an honest and reasonable man;
(e) knowledge of circumstances which would put a reasonable man on inquiry.

In *Lipkin* v *Gorman* May LJ was of the opinion that only the first three types of knowledge will impose liability on a stranger to a trust and hold him liable as a constructive trustee.

In *AGIP (Africa) Ltd* v *Jackson & Others* ([1991] 3 WLR 116) the defendants, a firm of accountants in the Isle of Man, who participated in money laundering operations, were held liable as constructive trustees who had knowingly assisted in the fraud. The Court of Appeal concluded that the common law right to trace the proceeds would be available only if the money paid to the credit of J & Co.'s account 'was the product of or substitute for the original thing.'

The constructive trustee doctrine examined in *Lipkin Gorman* was applied by the Supreme Court of Hong Kong in *Manus Asia Co Inc.* v *Standard Chartered Bank* (unreported: see 1989 May, *Journal of Business Law* p. 257). The case arose out of an action instituted against one Fred Lee by the US Securities and Exchange Commission (SEC) in respect of insider dealing. The parties to the present proceedings were a company controlled by Lee and the bank which held the proceeds of insider dealing on deposit. At trial the facts were no longer in dispute and Lee had admitted that he had issued instructions for the transfer of funds by the bank's New York office to its Hong Kong office. The SEC demanded that the bank's New York office pay the money to it, and eventually the bank was ordered by the Southern District Court of New York to transfer the funds. The bank paid subject to protest and Lee demanded that the amount involved be paid to his solicitors in Hong Kong. On the bank's refusal to comply with his instructions, Lee brought an action against the bank in Hong Kong. One of the defences raised by the bank was that if the bank paid in accordance with Lee's instructions it would be liable as a constructive trustee to the victims of Lee's insider trading activities. Cruden DJ gave judgment for the bank on this ground. He pointed out that the bank obtained express knowledge of the *cestui's* claim whilst the money was still in its hands and relying on Alliott J's judgment in *Lipkin Gorman* the judge said the bank was entitled to refuse to make payment. He was not disturbed that the trust arose because of the effect of a foreign and confiscatory Act. There was no dispute about the 'knowledge' of the bank which the bank admitted to and it is questionable that the case involved a constructive trust.

Money paid into account for specific purpose
Where money is paid into an account for a specific purpose the bank is under an obligation to apply it for that specific purpose.

Barclays Bank Ltd v Quistclose Investments Ltd [1970] AC 567

R Ltd was in serious financial difficulties and, being overdrawn with their bank, the appellants, commenced negotiations with X Ltd, a financier, to obtain a loan of £1,000,000. This loan from X Ltd was agreed on the condition that R Ltd found a sum for £209,719 8s 6d to pay a dividend which R Ltd had declared but which remained unpaid. R Ltd succeeded in obtaining a loan for the payment of the dividend from the respondents on the condition that it would be used for the purpose of paying the dividend. Before the dividend could be paid R Ltd went into voluntary liquidation and X Ltd brought an action claiming that, the purpose for which the money was paid having failed, it was held on a resulting trust for them and that the appellants had notice of the trust and were therefore constructive trustees of the money.

The House of Lords held that, the money having been paid into a bank account for the specific purpose (that purpose being made known to the bank), the bank was fixed with a trust and when the purpose failed the money could not be used as intended. The bank, therefore, had no right of set-off. Lord Wilberforce said that arrangements for the payment of a person's creditors by a third person give rise to (p. 580):

'a relationship of a fiduciary character or trust, in favour, as a primary trust, of the creditors, and secondarily, if the primary trust fails, of the third person ...'

Lord Wilberforce rejected the argument that the lender only has contractual rights in a loan transaction and said:

'There is surely no difficulty in recognising the co-existence in one transaction of legal and equitable rights and remedies: when the money is advanced, the lender acquires an equitable right to see that it is applied for the primary designated purpose.'

The *Quistclose* rule has been applied in a number of cases. In *Re Northern Developments (Holdings) Ltd* (unreported) Northern was the parent company of a group of companies including one, Kelly, which was in financial difficulties. A number of banks agreed to provide funds in an attempt to rescue Kelly and money was credited to a bank account in the name of the parent company for the express purpose of providing funds for Kelly's unsecured creditors. At a time when only approximately half the credit balance had been used, Kelly was put into receivership and the question arose as to who was entitled to the balance of the fund. Sir Robert Megarry VC held that there was a *Quistclose* type of trust attaching to the fund and the purpose of the trust was enforceable by identifiable individuals, namely the banks as lenders, Kelly for whose immediate benefit the fund was established and Kelly's creditors. The judge accepted that the *Quistclose* type of trust gave rise to a relationship of a fiduciary character or trust in favour of the creditors and he drew a parallel with the position of a beneficiary entitled to a share under a will. He said:

> 'What he has is not a beneficial interest in any asset forming part of residue, but a right to compel the executor to administer the assets of the deceased properly. It seems to me that it is that sort of right which the creditors of Kelly had.'

In *Carreras Rothmans Ltd* v *Freeman Mathews Treasure Ltd* ([1985] Ch 207) the court rejected the submission that third party creditors of a company who 'had paid into a special account had no enforceable rights' when the money was specifically to be used to pay off debts of the company.

In *Multi Guarantee Co. Ltd* ([1987] BCLC 257) Multi Guarantee Ltd (MG) was incorporated to market warranties for domestic appliances which provided insurance after the manufacturer's guarantee had expired. Vallance (V) owned a chain of shops and it operated the MG scheme. V collected premiums from its customers and them paid them over to MG. V, being concerned that MG had not obtained proper insurance cover for the scheme, entered into negotiations with MG with a view to protecting its customers' interests. At the time the negotiations were commenced MG agreed to deposit the amount of the premiums into a joint account from which funds could only be withdrawn against the joint signatures of MG's and V's solicitors. MG went into liquidation and V claimed that when the funds were deposited into a joint account MG constituted itself a trustee of the funds. The Court of Appeal held that MG had not intended to divest its beneficial interest in the funds. Indeed it had always contemplated that it would have access to the insurance money, either to arrange further cover for itself or to meet any claims by V's customers. On the question whether a trust had been created the court held that there was no intention to create a trust, and the requirement that there should be certainty of words was not satisfied. The account into which the money had been deposited was a mere holding device.

In contrast, *Re EVTR* ([1987] BCLC 646) is an illustration of where the *Quistclose* rule may be applied successfully to preserve the creditor's assets from the consequences of a debtor's insolvency. In *Re EVTR* money was deposited with a solicitor with the specific instructions that it should be used for the sole purpose of buying new equipment. Some of the money was used for that purpose, but the amounts were refunded when EVTR went into liquidation. The receiver was granted a declaration that the money was part of the general assets of the company. The creditors appealed. The Court of Appeal held that the original advance was for a specific purpose and that purpose having failed a resulting trust arose in favour of the creditor. It therefore followed that amounts repaid on EVTR's insolvency were held on the terms of the original trust.

Where the bank benefits from the transaction

A bank may be a constructive trustee where it benefits from the transaction, e.g. applies the misappropriated funds to reduce an overdraft. In *Neste Oy* v *Lloyds Bank plc* ([1983] 2 Lloyd's Rep 658) a bank having learnt that a company which was its customer had decided to cease trading and that a debenture-holder was about to appoint a receiver, received a payment which it credited to the customer's bank account. The bank wished to set off the amount so credited against the amount owing to the bank under another account held by the customer. The court held that the bank should have made inquiry as to the circumstances of the receivership and that would have revealed that the funds deposited in the customer's account were subject to a trust in favour of the receiver. The bank had, therefore, knowingly received trust funds.

The Jack Committee on Banking Services recommended that the whole area of constructive trusts should be reviewed by a government-appointed committee.

2 The bank account

This chapter will examine the nature of the commonest types of bank accounts available to the customer, the representations made by a customer when drawing cheques against his account, the effect of drawing cheques when the customer has an insufficient credit balance and the nature of the overdraft.

TYPES OF BANK ACCOUNT

Current account

The current account is used by the customer for regular transactions where cash 'on demand' is required by him. The drawing of a cheque is a mandate to the bank to honour the instruction given in the form of the cheque. Cheques payable by the customer can be credited to the customer's account and at the same time amounts owed by the customer may be settled by the drawing of cheques against the customer's account. In some cases customers may ask that amounts owed to them be credited against their account directly through the Giro system. The drawing of cheques is backed by cheque cards which guarantee payment provided the amount of the cheque drawn is within the limit of the cheque card. A customer can also withdraw cash from his account by the use of a cheque card and PIN. Regular bank statements are supplied by the bank giving details of credit and debit entries.

The current account is probably the most common type of account. In recent years banks and building societies have tended not to impose bank charges for the operation of the current account where the account remains in credit or the balance remains above a certain minimum figure. Overdraft facilities may be permitted either by express agreement or through banking practice. In 1968, Mr D.J. Roberts, Chairman of the Committee of London Clearing Bankers, explained to the Governor of the Bank of England why it was difficult for the banks to comply with the request to reduce lending and said:

> 'Bank advances in this country are controlled, in the main, by pre-arranged overdraft limits. This means that customers are given a permitted limit of overdraft up to which they may draw at any time while the agreement is in being. These limits usually run for a year, and it therefore follows that major customers can without notice draw on us in very large sums.'

In cases where an overdraft facility is agreed upon in advance it is probably not open to the banks to demand repayment of the whole or part of the advance prior to the agreed date, unless the bank makes it clear to the customer that it reserves that right. Where the customer is persistently overdrawn in excess of the agreed overdraft then, of course, the bank may have the right to call in the overdraft.

Deposit account

The deposit account or the savings account cannot be overdrawn since the bank will not allow an overdraft facility against such an account. The credit balance will accrue interest (although this may also be available against the current account) and higher rates of interest are available to customers who agree to give lengthy notices, e.g. 90 days' notice.

Loan account

The most usual method of lending money to a customer is by way of overdraft on a current account. However, banks may advance a fixed sum by way of a loan account. Interest is calculated on the amount outstanding on a daily basis.

Personal loan accounts

In 1958 some banks introduced personal loan accounts. The special feature of the account is that the bank receives no security for the loan, and the loan and interest is repayable by equal monthly instalments over a period from six months to five years.

REPRESENTATIONS MADE IN DRAWING A CHEQUE

Until the *Metropolitan Police Commissioner* v *Charles* ([1977] AC 177) case was decided, the view was that a number of representations were made in the drawing of a cheque, namely:

(a) that the drawer has an account on which the cheque is drawn;
(b) that he has authority to draw on the account for the amount;
(c) that the cheque as drawn is a valid order for the amount.

The House of Lords, however, in *Metropolitan Police Commissioner* held that in fact only one representation is made in the drawing of a cheque, namely that the existing state of facts is such that 'in the ordinary course the cheque will be met.'

Metropolitan Police Commissioner v *Charles* [1977] AC 177

The defendant was granted an overdraft facility of £100 by his bank and given a cheque card on which was printed an undertaking to honour cheques for up to £30 in certain circumstances. The defendant used the cheque card to draw several cheques of £30 each which took him over the £100 overdraft limit. The bank manager informed the defendant that he could not draw more than one cheque for £30 a day at the bank. He was also issued with a further cheque book. The defendant used the cheque card to back 25 cheque forms, for £30 each, at a gambling club. The defendant was convicted of obtaining a pecuniary advantage by deception contrary to s. 16 of the Theft Act 1962. The conviction was upheld by the Court of Appeal and he appealed to the House of Lords.

The House of Lords held that the defendant's conviction under s. 16 of the Theft Act 1962 should stand. The Lords looked at the effect of drawing a cheque and Lord Diplock held (p. 182):

> '... It is no doubt true to say that all the payee is concerned with is that the cheque should be honoured by the bank, and that to induce the payee to take the cheque all that the drawer is concerned to do is to assure him that as far as can be reasonably foreseen this is what will happen. But payment by the bank cannot be reasonably foreseen as likely unless the fact be that the cheque is one which the bank on which it is drawn is bound, by an existing contract with the drawer ...'

Lord Diplock then examined the effect of the cheque card and said:

> 'When a cheque is brought into the transaction, it still remains the fact that all the payee is concerned with is that the cheque should be honoured by the back. I do not think that the fact that a cheque card is used necessarily displaces the representation to be implied from the act of drawing the cheque.'

It is, however, likely not to be the main inducement for accepting a cheque and Lord Diplock said:

> 'By exhibiting to the payee a cheque card containing the undertaking by the bank to honour cheques drawn in compliance with the conditions endorsed on the back, and drawing the cheque accordingly, the drawer represents to the payee that he has actual authority from the bank to make a contract with the payee on the bank's behalf that it will honour the cheque on presentment for payment.'

R v *Gilmartin* [1983] 1 All ER 829

The appellant ran a stationery business which he carried on through a company which owed money to a creditor. The company's bank account was overdrawn. The appellant gave the creditor a postdated cheque which he signed on behalf of the company. He also obtained stationery from suppliers by giving them also postdated cheques. On presentation the cheques were dishonoured. The appellant was charged with (a) dishonestly obtaining goods by deception under s. 15 of the Theft Act 1968; and (b) dishonestly obtaining deferment of a debt due to the creditor by deception under s. 16 of the Theft Act. It was alleged that the deception consisted of a false representation that the cheques in question were good and valid orders for the payment of the sums specified in the cheques. The appellant submitted that no such representation could be inferred from the mere act of giving postdated cheques.

The court upheld the appellant's conviction. It reviewed the earlier authorities (see pp. 833–834) and concluded that by drawing a cheque, whether a postdated cheque or not, the drawer implicitly represents that the state of facts existing on the date of delivery of the cheque is such that in the ordinary course of events the cheque will be honoured on presentation.

It is settled law that the drawing of a cheque involves certain representations of fact. The extent of these representations was examined in the *Charles* case. Similar representations are made when a cheque is backed by a cheque card. By using a cheque card the customer cannot be guilty of deception in representing that the cheque will be met, even if the drawer knows that there will be no funds or insufficient funds to meet the cheque. However, the customer does represent that as between himself and the bank he is authorised to use the cheque card. If, therefore, the customer's authority to use the card has been revoked then the use of such a card amounts to deception on the part of the customer.

OBTAINING SERVICES

Where an individual obtains the opening of a bank account under false pretences does that amount to an offence?

Section 1 of the Theft Act 1978 provides that it is an offence to dishonestly obtain services from another by deception. The offence is committed when a person is induced to provide services or confer some other benefit by doing some act, or causing or permitting some act to be done, on the understanding that the benefit has been or will be paid for.

R v Halai [1983] Crim LR 624

The defendant applied for a mortgage at a time when he had a credit balance of £28 in his bank account. He said that he had held his present job for 18 months when in fact he had only been in his present employment for two months. He drew a postdated cheque for £40 to pay for the survey undertaken by the building society and also opened a savings account with another postdated cheque for £500. He was issued with a pass book showing a credit of £500. He then went to another branch of the building society and paid in a cheque to the credit of his account for £250. At the same time he withdrew £100 from the account representing that the £500 paid into the account was a cash payment. All three cheques were dishonoured. The defendant was convicted on various counts under the Theft Act 1978 and s. 15 of the 1968 Act.

On count 1, obtaining the preparation of a surveyor's report and valuation, the court said there was a false representation and it was immaterial that the cheque was post-dated. There was a benefit received because it was an essential step towards obtaining a mortgage.

The other counts were bad because no services were obtained. No benefit is conferred by a bank or building society on a customer when an account is opened and s. 1 of the Theft Act 1987 requires payment for the benefit conferred by the deception. The court said (p. 625):

'Where a customer pays £500 into a bank, by no stretch of the use of the ordinary English can anyone suggest that the bank is conferring a benefit on the customer ...'

The court felt it necessary to distinguish between the opening of an account and the payment of money into that account. A person who deceives a bank into opening an account in his favour induces the bank to confer a benefit on him but the customer does not pay for that facility; he will only pay for the bank's services if he overdraws or does not maintain a minimum balance to the credit of his account. The court, therefore, held that merely obtaining the opening of an account and having money credited to the account is no offence under s. 1 of the 1978 Act because the service is not paid for.

It appears that no offence is committed under s. 1 of the 1978 Act unless the service provided for by the deception is provided on the understanding that it has been or will be paid for. Opening a bank account is not a service which normally has to be paid for and therefore deception in obtaining that service is not an offence under s. 1 of the Act. Deception in the operation of the account may, however, lead to an offence under s. 1 of the Theft Act 1987.

NATURE OF AN OVERDRAFT

A bank is obliged to allow a customer to overdraw if it has agreed to allow the customer an overdraft or if such an agreement can be inferred from a course of dealings on the account. An overdraft is money lent to the customer by the bank usually under an arrangement. An overdraft is normally repayable on demand but this right to repayment should be exercised so as not to unduly prejudice the customer's interests.

Re Hone (a Bankrupt), ex parte Trustee v *Kensington Borough Council* [1951] Ch 85

On 4 November 1949, a cheque was paid into the banking account of a borough council. At the time of drawing the cheque the drawer's account was overdrawn. On the same day the drawer filed a petition in bankruptcy and was adjudicated bankrupt. The cheque was honoured by the bank a few days later and credited to the council's account. An action was brought to determine whether the amount of the cheque was money belonging to the bankrupt at the time of her bankruptcy.

The court held that payment was not made to the council until after the bankruptcy order had been made and that the money was an asset belonging to the drawer and it had been paid without the authority of the trustees in bankruptcy. On the question whether the title in the money vested in the bankrupt or the bank advancing the overdraft Harman J held (p. 89):

'... Her account was overdrawn. Therefore, it is said, this money with which the debt was paid was not her money – never was an asset of the bankrupt. The bank paid it, and it was the bank's money and never the bankrupt's. In my judgment, that is not right, for this reason: that a payment by a bank, under an arrangement by which the customer has an overdraft, is a lending by the bank to the customer of the money. It is the customer who pays the money and not the bank. Otherwise, the bank may be able to sue the payees of the cheque for the money, which they clearly cannot do. They have paid it as agent for the customer just as if she had money there.'

Therefore, the money out of which payment was made to the council belonged to the bankrupt.

REPAYMENT OF AN OVERDRAFT

The question of repayment of an overdraft has been examined in a number of cases, for example in *Joachimson* v *Swiss Bank Corporation* ([1921] 3 KB 110)(see p. 61 for facts) and *Barnes* v *Williams & Glyn's Bank Ltd* ((1981) Com LR 205). In the *Joachimson* case it was held that:

> '... in the absence of an express term as to the date of repayment, an overdraft facility for use by a customer in his business must contain an implied term that the money borrowed under the facility was repayable only on reasonable notice. The length of that notice was to be determined by reference to the commercial use which the bank knew the customer would make of the money.'

Barnes v *Williams & Glyn's Bank* (1981) Com LR 205

The defendant was the founder, chairman and majority shareholder of NDH, a property development company which from 1965 banked principally with the plaintiff bank. In 1972, when the company's overdraft limit was £6.5 million, the bank lent the plaintiff £1 million personally to enable him to buy more shares in the company. It was understood that the loan would be repaid out of funds the company owed to him. The property market collapsed and the bank eventually appointed receivers over the company. The bank brought an action against the defendant to recover the money lent to him personally, who argued that the action raised various claims and counter-claims.

Gibson J held that no defence to the personal action could be founded on the bank's conduct towards the company. But in any event the learned judge reviewed the various issues raised in the action. As regards the overdraft he said that an overdraft is repayable on demand, unless it is expressly or implicitly agreed otherwise. Gibson J said:

> 'There is an obligation upon the bank to honour cheques drawn within the agreed limit of an overdraft facility and presented before any demand for repayment or notice to terminate a facility has been given. That obligation, however, does not by itself require any period of notice beyond the simple demand.'

The decision in the *Barnes* case recognises banking practice in lending to customers. Although in normal cases an overdraft is repayable on demand, Gibson J also recognised that that may not always be commercially viable. He remarked that whilst the customer is free to replace the borrowing or amount of the overdraft without notice if he can find facilities on better terms, the financial state of the business may be such that no other lender will advance loans and in such circumstances the bank may be forced to continue to support a customer.

Although the overdraft facility tends to be more informal than the loan facility the rules established in the *Barnes* case would apply equally. The differences between a loan and overdraft are more a matter of banking practice than law, since in both advances are made to the customer.

INTEREST

The charging of interest is a matter of banking practice. It can be recovered on the basis of the implied contract or on the basis of a course of dealings or mercantile usage. Interest may be given under s. 3 of the Law Reform (Miscellaneous Provisions) Act 1934, although the Act does not authorise charging compound interest. In *Yuorell* v *Hibernian Bank Ltd* ([1918] AC 372) Lord Atkinson considered it 'a usual and perfectly legitimate mode of dealing between banker and customer'. In *National Bank of Greece SA* v *Pinios Shipping Co.* ([1990] 2 Lloyd's Rep 225) contractors who had built and delivered a ship demanded payment under a guarantee opened in their favour by the bank at the instruction of the purchasers. The bank, in turn, exercised its right of reimbursement against the purchasers and a third party who had executed a counter guarantee in the bank's favour. Although the bank's right to reimbursement was not in issue, the two defendants contested the bank's right to charge compound interest on the amount outstanding, arguing that the bank was entitled to plain interest on the amount outstanding. The House of Lords held that the usage under which banks are entitled to charge compound interest prevails generally as 'between bankers and customers who borrow from them and do not pay interest as it accrues.' Lord Goff of Chieveley further said:

> '... if it be equitable that a banker should be entitled to capitalise interest at, for example, yearly or half yearly rests because his customer has failed to pay interest at the due date, there appears to be no basis in justice or logic for terminating that right simply because the bank has demanded payment of the sum outstanding in the customer's account.'

A point which is uncertain is whether the same method of calculation could be used in situations in which the original debt did not involve periodic repayments leading to the compounding of interest. In *Minories Finance Ltd* v *Daryanani* (unreported, 13 April 1989) the repayment of certain loans, granted by a bank in London to a Nigerian company, was blocked by an embargo imposed by the Nigerian government. The bank served a demand in London on the guarantors. On the question of compound interest the Court of Appeal held that as the facility letter did not include an express provision entitling the bank to charge compound interest, the question of the bank's right to charge compound interest was a triable issue and leave to defend was granted.

The Court of Appeal relied on the *National Bank of Greece* case and Neill LJ held that whilst a bank's right to charge compound interest could not be doubted in the case of overdrafts, in which the customer's account might move from a credit to a debit balance, it was less certain whether it applied equally in the case of term loans which did not involve a revolving arrangement and in which the parties anticipated a gradual reduction of the debit balance.

It should be remembered that in the *Daryanani* case the issue arose only in respect of interest charged prior to the date on which the bank made its demand.

THE DEBTOR–CREDITOR RELATIONSHIP

The banker–customer relationship is based on contract law (see Chapter 4) but in the operation of the current account the relationship is that of debtor and creditor. This was established in *Foley* v *Hill* ((1848) 2 HL Cas 28) with the consequence that the bank is treated as the absolute owner of any amounts deposited with the bank and in the insolvency of the bank the depositor is treated merely as an unsecured creditor (the position of BCCI customers has been examined in Chapter 1). Moreover, the bank can invest or otherwise in the course of its business deal with the amounts deposited by customers without the need to obtain authorisation from each individual customer. The bank is only required to return an amount equivalent to the credit balance shown on the customer's account and not the money deposited by the customer in species.

Foley v *Hill* (1848) 2 HL Cas 28

In 1829, the plaintiff opened an account with the defendant banker and made an initial credit payment of £6,117 10s. It was agreed that interest at 3 per cent per annum would be payable on the account. There were two withdrawals made from the account for £1,700 and £2,000.

In 1838, the plaintiff sought to recover the credit balance on his account by bringing, in Chancery, an action on account. The account, being a simple account, was held not a matter for a court of equity. The plaintiff thereupon claimed that the relationship of a banker and customer was by analogy that of an agent and his principal, and he was therefore entitled to an account. Further, the relationship being of a fiduciary nature, the Statute of Limitations did not apply.

The House of Lords held the relationship was that of debtor and creditor, and therefore was not one suitable for an account in equity. Lord Cottenham LC said (pp. 1005–1006):

'Money, when paid into a bank, ceases altogether to be the money of the principal; it is then the money of the banker, who is bound to return an equivalent by paying a similar sum to that deposited with him when he is asked for it. The money paid into the banker is money known by the principal to be placed there for the purpose of being under the control of the banker; it is then the banker's money; he is known to deal with it as his own; he makes what profit of it he can, which profit he retains to himself, paying back only the principal according to the custom of bankers in some places, or the principal and a small rate of interest, according to the custom of bankers in other places. The money placed in the custody of a banker is, to all intents and purposes, the money of the banker, to do with it as he pleases; he is guilty of no breach of trust in employing it; he is not answerable to the principal if he puts it into jeopardy, if he engages in a hazardous speculation; he is not bound to keep it, or deal with it, as the property of his principal, but he is of course answerable for the amount, because he has contracted, having received that money, to repay to the principal, when demanded, a sum equivalent to that paid into his hands ... the banker is not an agent, or factor, but he is a debtor.'

The principle in *Foley* v *Hill* has been approved in later cases.

Joachimson v Swiss Bank Corporation ([1921] 3˙KB 110)

The plaintiff firm was a partnership between two Germans and a naturalised Englishman. The partnership business was conducted in Manchester. On 1 August 1914, one of the Germans died and the partnership was dissolved. The partnership account had a credit balance of £2,321. On the outbreak of war, a few days later, the other German became an enemy alien.

On 5 June 1919, the naturalised partner commenced an action in the name of the partnership to recover the sum standing to the credit of the account, the cause of the action allegedly having arisen on 1 August 1914.

The firm had not made any demand for the repayment of the credit balance and the bank pleaded that the action could not be maintained.

The Court of Appeal held that where money is standing to the credit of the customer's account at a bank, a previous demand is necessary before an action can be maintained against the bank for the balance. Bankes LJ said (p. 119):

'Having regard to the peculiarity of that relation there must be, I consider, quite a number of implied super-added obligations beyond the one specifically mentioned in *Foley* v *Hill* and *Potts* v *Clegg*. Unless this were so, the banker, like any ordinary debtor, must seek out his creditor and repay him his loan immediately it becomes due – that is to say, directly after the customer has paid the money into his account – and the customer, like any ordinary creditor, can demand repayment of the loan by his debtor at any time and place ... It seems to me impossible to imagine the relation between banker and customer as it exists today, without the stipulation that, if the customer seeks to withdraw his loan, he must make application to the banker for it.'

The *Foley* v *Hill* case did not establish a new principle of law but it did remove doubts that had existed until the House of Lords' judgment.

In *Foley* v *Hill* the court approved *Parker* v *Marchant* ((1843) 1 Ph 356) where the testator divided his property into three classes, namely: (a) ready money, securities and money in certain funds; (b) real estate; and (c) jewels, plate, wine, carriages, etc. The question before the court was whether the first category included the credit balance on a current account. The court having held that the credit balance on the bank account passed under the first category as ready money, said that where the parties enter into the banker–customer relationship it follows from that relationship being that of debtor and creditor that the money ceases to be that of the account-holder. It is then the money of the bank which is obliged to return merely an equivalent sum on demand. The money paid to the credit of the customer's account is at the absolute and unfettered disposition of bank and not available merely for restricted purposes. The bank is then free to deal with the money as its own, to make and retain any resulting profit subject to its obligation to pay the interest (if agreed). The bank is not guilty of a trust in employing the money in any manner it chooses, including investing the funds in risky investments.

The customer has no proprietary interest in the bank's funds on the ground the bank holds the customer's money mixed with that of all other customers. The law makes no distinction between the different sources from which a banker receives money which is credited to the customer's account and once the money has been credited to the account the new balance is treated as one single debt. The application of the debtor–creditor relationship to the operation of the bank account accords entirely with the practical operation of the business of banking. The normal rules of the debtor–creditor relationship have been modified, however, so that the creditor is under an obligation to seek out the debtor (the bank) and make a demand for repayment.

The Jack Committee on banking services concluded that the rule in *Foley* v *Hill* was not in need of reform.

American law recognises the fundamental rule that in the case of an ordinary or general deposit of money with a bank, the money so deposited becomes the property of the bank. In *Dakin* v *Bayly* ((1933) 290 US 143) the US Supreme Court held that the unrestricted indorsement and deposit of cheques to the credit of a bank account creates the relationship of debtor and creditor so that in receiving the amount of the cheques from the paying bank the bank acts, not as agent for the account-holder, but as owner of the money received.

The question which must be asked is at what stage does title in the money pass to the bank? In *Balmoral Supermarket Ltd* v *Bank of New Zealand* ([1974] 2 NZLR 155) the plaintiff's employee entered the defendant bank's premises with the intention of depositing some cash and cheques in the plaintiff's account. The cash was emptied out of a bag onto the counter and whilst the bank assistant was counting the money bank robbers entered the bank and stole the money. The plaintiff brought an action against the bank claiming the cash stolen by the robbers and alleging that property stolen had passed to the bank. The claim failed. The Supreme Court of New Zealand held that, until the money (to be deposited) had been checked and the bank had signified its acceptance, the money had not been deposited with the bank and title remained with the customer.

More recently, the court examined the *Foley* v *Hill* Case and it was held that money placed in a trust account with a bank may still become the property of the bank.

Space Investments Ltd v *Canadian Imperial Bank of Commerce Trust Co. (Bahamas) Ltd* [1986] 3 All ER 75

The Mercantile Bank and Trust Co. Ltd (MBT) was appointed trustee of certain settlements which empowered it, *inter alia*, to open bank accounts and to deposit any part of the trust funds. The trustees, MBT, deposited certain funds with MBT as bankers. MBT became insolvent and an action was brought to recover the funds under the trust.

Both the Supreme Court and the Court of Appeal in the Bahamas ruled that money so deposited was subject to the trust and in the event of MBT becoming insolvent the beneficiaries of the trust were entitled to payment in priority to the bank's other customers and other unsecured creditors. Space Investments Ltd, representing the unsecured creditors, appealed to the Privy Council.

The Privy Council held that the appeal would succeed. MBT, as trustees, were expressly authorised to deposit trust funds into bank accounts and a breach of trust was not involved when MBT, as trustees, placed the funds on deposit with MBT as bankers.

Lord Templeman giving judgment said the money (p. 78):

'became the property of MBT in law and equity and MBT were entitled to use that money for the purposes of MBT and in any manner they pleased ... On the insolvency of that independent bank the trustee MBT could only rank as unsecured creditor for the amount of the deposit account.'

Following *Foley* v *Hill* Lord Templeman said (p. 76):

'A customer who deposits money with a bank authorises the bank to use that money for the benefit of the bank in any manner the bank pleases. The customer does not acquire any interest in or charge over any asset of the bank or over all the assets of the bank. The deposit account is an acknowledgment and record by the bank of the amount from time to time deposited and withdrawn and of the interest earned. The customer acquires a chose in action, namely the right to payment by the bank of the whole or any part of the aggregate amount of principal and interest which has been credited or ought to be credited to the amount. If the bank becomes insolvent the customer can only prove in the liquidation of the bank as unsecured creditor for the amount which was, or ought to have been, credited to the account at the date when the bank went into liquidation.'

In order to protect the beneficiary of a trust, any trust funds deposited in a bank account must clearly be deposited in a trust account so that the trust money does not cease to be impressed with the trust.

Although it has long been established that the banker–customer relationship in respect of the operation of a bank account is that of debtor–creditor, in other respects the normal agency relationship will apply, e.g. with regard to the honour of the customer's mandate by making payment on a cheque, or the acceptance of documents under a letter of credit.

CUSTOMER'S RIGHT TO RECOVER CREDIT BALANCES

The effect of the decisions in *Foley* v *Hill* and *Joachimson* v *Swiss Bank Corporation* is that the customer must make a demand for the repayment of any balance standing to the credit of his account. The demand must be made at the branch where the account is maintained and it must be made during normal working hours. The debt is then repayable immediately to the customer. Additionally, if the customer has a deposit account other conditions may have to be satisfied by the customer, e.g. the production of a deposit receipt may be essential or an agreed period of notice may be required.

The customer's right to demand his money in cash was looked at in a recent case.

Libyan Arab Foreign Bank v *Bankers Trust Company* [1987] 2 FTLR 509

In January 1986 the plaintiffs (the Libyan bank) had a call account with the defendants' (Bankers Trust) London branch in US dollars. Interest was payable on this account and on 8 January the balance was $131,506,389.93.

The Libyan bank also had a demand account with Bankers Trust New York denominated in US dollars. No interest was payable on this account and on 8 January the balance was $251,129,084.53.

Relations between the United States and Libya had deteriorated to such an extent that on 8 January at 4.10 p.m. New York time the US President issued an executive order blocking all property and interest of the government of Libya, its agencies '... in the United States or hereafter come within the United States, or are or come within the possession or control of US persons including overseas branches of US persons.'

It was therefore illegal after 8 January, 4.10 p.m. New York time for Bankers Trust to make any payment or transfer of funds to or to the order of the Libyan bank in New York either by way of a debit to the Libyan bank's account or by way of credit or a loan. Similarly, it was illegal by New York law or any other state law for Bankers Trust to make payment or transfer funds in London or anywhere else. Nothing in English domestic law prohibited such a transaction.

The Libyan bank claimed the balance of the $131,506,389.93 standing to the credit of the London account at the close of business and a further $165,200,000 which ought to have been transferred from the New York account on 7 or 8 January to the London account.

The Libyan bank also claimed that certain instructions given to Bankers Trust New York for compliance before 4.10 p.m. on 8 January had not been executed and that Bankers Trust were in breach of the duty of confidentiality in disclosing information about the account to the Federal Reserve Bank of New York.

Bankers Trust contended that they could not and were not obliged to transfer the sums in question without using the payment machinery (clearing through Chips) in New York and performance of the contract became illegal in New York after the presidential order.

Staughton J held that the contract between the banker and customer was governed by the law of the place where the account was kept, and there was no reason to hold that rule did not apply. The London account was governed by English law which would apply unless an infringement of US law on US territory was involved; that indeed was the case in respect of the demand account maintained in New York where clearing took place in New York.

The London account, however, could be operated without infringing US law and the court refused to imply a term that required any transfer of funds from that account to be effected through the United States' clearing system.

There were various methods of clearing which would have infringed the US law but a demand for a cash payment of US dollars in London would not necessarily involve a breach of US law. Moreover, if payment could not be made in dollars then by the contract entered into between the parties payment in sterling would suffice.

Usually the customer's demand for repayment of his credit balance, or part of it, is made by means of a cheque, but an oral demand by the customer at the branch where the account is maintained will suffice. In *Arab Bank Ltd* v *Barclays Bank (Dominion, Colonial and Overseas) Ltd* ([1952] WN 529) Parker J said:

> '... it was contended that under English law ... a written demand is necessary. There is no express authority on the point, and the question was specifically left open by Atkin LJ ... in *Joachimson* v *Swiss Bank Corporation*, where after defining the relation of banker and customer on current account he added: "Whether he must demand it in writing it is not necessary to determine." ... The necessity for a demand at all only results from implying a term, and there seems little necessity in going further and implying that such demand must be in writing.'

By legal action

In English law a customer who has a credit balance in his account can recover the balance, or any part of it, by making a demand for repayment to the bank. The bank has no protection against claims for payment of credit balances which have been dormant for many years and the customer has six years from the time of the demand in which to bring an action to recover the balance.

National Bank of Commerce v *National Westminster Bank plc* [1990] 2 Lloyd's Rep 514

The National Bank of Commerce (NBC) was a Tanzanian bank which maintained a current account as a correspondent bank with National Westminster Bank (NW). It authorised NW to debit its account on receipt of mail transfer orders (MTOs) signed by two authorised NBC officers. On a number of occasions, between 1978 and 1980, NW debited the account with amounts totalling approximately £268,227 in respect of MTOs purported to have been signed by the two authorised officers. NBC alleged that the debit orders were not validly signed and each debit was made under an ineffective mandate. NBC demanded the return of the amounts it alleged were wrongly debited from its account.

In 1988, it brought an action:

(a) for wrongfully failing, and in breach of the agreement governing the account, to repay the sums demanded which were due and owing; and

(b) that NW was liable in damages for breach of contract.

The defences raised included the contention that the cause of action accrued on the date on which each debit was made and, accordingly, the claim was statute barred. Section 5 of the Limitation Act 1980 provides that an action based on simple contract cannot be brought after the expiration of six years from the date on which the cause of action accrued.

Webster J held that an action founded on simple contract for repayment of sums which have been wrongfully debited is not simply a claim to correct the balance on the account, but it is a claim in debt arising out of the banker–customer relationship. It is, therefore, a pre-condition that a demand be made for repayment and an action arises when the demand is made and the six-year limitation period runs from that date, and not from the date of the debit. Referring to *Limpgrange* v *Bank of Credit and Commerce International SA* ([1986] FLR 36), the facts of which were basically the same except that no question was raised regarding the limitation of action, Webster J adopted the reasoning of Staughton J who said:

> 'If debits were made without authority they should be disregarded, and the [customer] can claim as the money owed to [him] by [the bank] the credit balance remaining when those debits are left out of account, or, if there would still be an overdraft, the [customer] would be liable to [the bank] only for such amount as the account was overdrawn after deletion of the disputed debits.'

As a bank's obligation to make payment only arises once a demand has been made (and can be enforced for six years after) the bank has no protection against claims for repayment of credit balances which have been dormant for many years. There is, however, a common law presumption that if a debt has not been claimed for a long time, i.e. 60 years, it is presumed to have been repaid. In *Douglass* v *Lloyds Bank Ltd* ((1929) 34 Com Cas 263) a daughter, going through the papers of her deceased mother, found a deposit receipt dated 12 May 1866, issued at the Birmingham office of the defendant bank to a Mr Fenwicke, her father, who had died in 1893. No mention was made of the receipt in her father's will, or personal papers. An action was brought by the surviving executor of Mr Fenwicke. The bank admitted that it could find no records of the Birmingham office before 1873, but contended that there was a presumption that the money had been repaid, and that in any event the plaintiff was debarred by his delay in bringing the action. The court decided in favour of the bank and accepted that the presumption of repayment applied.

The case is an exceptional one. The bank was allowed to produce its oldest surviving deposit ledgers, which showed that no account in the name in question existed. This was accepted as supporting the bank's claim that the deposit had been repaid. Roche J said (p. 272):

> 'On the facts I recognise to the full the strength of the fact that the plaintiff produces this deposit receipt, but I cannot ignore what experience tells me, and the evidence in this case shows, that people lose or mislay their deposit receipts at the time when they want to get their money back, and that money is paid over, if they are respectable persons and willing to give the necessary indemnity or receipt, without the production of the deposit receipt ...'

It must be noted that the bank did not plead the Statute of Limitations and it is unlikely that, in similar circumstances, a bank would hide behind the Statute, for to do so would be to admit the debt. In any event the limitation period does not begin to run until a demand for repayment has been made (see *Joachimson* case).

By self-help remedies

A bank is not obliged to allow its customer to overdraw on a current account unless either there is an express agreement or such an agreement can be implied from conduct, e.g. where the bank honours cheques without a previously agreed overdraft with the customer.

The question that now arises is whether a bank has any rights to recover a debit balance from a customer who is overdrawn without resorting to an action in the courts.

APPROPRIATION

Where the customer has more than one account, then unless it is otherwise agreed, the customer has the right to appropriate the funds to whichever account he chooses.

Deeley v *Lloyds Bank Ltd* [1912] AC 756

The defendant bank had advanced money against a second mortgage. A subsequent mortgage was executed in favour of the borrower's sister, Mrs Deeley. The bank continued to operate the account after notice of the third mortgage was given to it, despite a rule that the account should be ruled off and further transactions be conducted through a separate account. The account continued to operate and amounts were paid into it which were more than the amount of the bank's mortgage. Within another two weeks the amounts credited to the account exceeded the whole of the indebtedness, both secured and unsecured. The customer subsequently became bankrupt and the bank entered into possession of the mortgaged property which was eventually sold for an amount sufficient to pay off the first and second mortgages only. Mrs Deeley claimed an account as against a mortgagee in possession. Judgment was given in favour of the bank.

The Court of Appeal dismissed the appeal but the House of Lords allowed the further appeal and held that payments to the credit of the account after notice of the third mortgage wiped out the total advance made by the bank at the time of the notice. However, subsequent withdrawals made after the notice was given were subject to Mrs Deeley's mortgage which had priority.

Lord Shaw of Dunfermline, approving Eve J's words (p. 783) said:

'... where a creditor having a right to appropriate moneys paid to him generally, and not specifically appropriated by the person paying them, carries them into a particular account kept in his books, he *prima facie* appropriates them to the account, and the effect of that is that the payments are *de facto* appropriated according to the priority in order of the entries on the one side and on the other of that account.'

Lord Dunfermline continued:

> 'I understand that to mean this: According to the law of England, the person paying the money has the primary right to say to what account it shall be appropriated; the creditor, if the debtor makes no appropriation, has the right to appropriate; and if neither of them exercises the right, then one can look on the matter as a matter of account and see how the creditor has dealt with the payment, in order to ascertain how he did in fact appropriate it. And if there is nothing more than this, that there is a current account kept by the creditor, and he carries the money to that particular account, then the Court concludes that the appropriation has been made ...'

The *Deeley* case depended on the combined application of the rule in *Clayton*'s case and *Hopkinson* v *Rolt*. The latter case established the rule that in the absence of any specific appropriation by either party, the payments are appropriated according to the priority in order of the entries on the one side and on the other of the account. Until the account is communicated to the customer the bank continues to have the option of applying the several payments as it thinks fit, but after communication, the bank cannot alter the mode of appropriation laid down in the *Clayton*'s case. The former case established that a mortgage by a customer to a bank to secure his current account does not entitle the bank to priority over a subsequent mortgage in respect of moneys becoming due to the bank after the bank has received notice of the subsequent mortgage.

In *Deeley*'s case the court found that the bank had received notice of the mortgage in favour of Mrs Deeley on the date of execution and the bank continued the account as unbroken. Consequently, the total balance on the date the notice was given was wiped out and its mortgage discharged. Mrs Deeley's mortgage therefore had priority.

In *Royal Bank of Scotland* v *Christie* ((1841) 8 A & Fin 214) a partner in a trading firm mortgaged his own land to secure advances made to the firm by its bank. At the date of the partner's death the firm had overdrawn on its account but on the death of the partner the account was continued unbroken. The surviving partners paid into the account amounts which exceeded the debit balance at the deceased partner's death, and then withdrew an even larger balance. The court held that the rule in *Clayton*'s case required payments into the account by the surviving partners to be credited first against the earlier debit items in the account; the account being overdrawn, the payments into the account after the death of the partner went to pay off the mortgage.

In *Re Yeovil Glove Company Ltd* ([1965] Ch 148) a company created a mortgage over the whole of its assets by way of a floating charge to secure its existing and future indebtedness to the bank. The company went into liquidation within 12 months of the creation of the charge with the result that the charge was void except as security for 'cash paid to the company at the time of, or subsequently to the creation of, and in consideration for, the charge.' The Court of Appeal held that the floating charge was valid security for advances made by the bank after it was created, but not for earlier advances. However, because the company had paid amounts into its current account since the creation of the charge, those amounts went towards satisfying its existing indebtedness under *Clayton*'s case and the advances made since the creation of the floating charge were still owing and secured by the charge.

The customer can appropriate within a particular account. In *WP Greenhalgh & Sons* v *Union Bank of Manchester* ([1924] 2 KB 153) the court held that there had been an equitable assignment of the proceeds of three bills paid into the customer's account when the payee was notified by the customer that the proceeds of the bills would be used to pay amounts due to him and the bank had knowledge of the ultimate destination of the proceeds.

The *WP Greenhalgh* case is unusual because the customer had actually notified the third party that the proceeds of the bills would be used to pay him and the bank was aware of the ultimate destination of the funds.

THE DEFAULT RULE CASE

If neither the customer nor the bank specifically appropriates a payment and it is credited to the account, the presumption is that the rule in *Clayton*'s case will apply so that in the case of a current account items credited to that account are deemed to satisfy earlier debits before later ones, so that debit and credit items are set off against each other chronologically.

Devaynes v *Noble – Clayton's* case (1816) 1 Mer 572

Clayton had an account with a banking partnership. One of the bank's partners died, and at that time the bank owed Clayton a certain sum, for which the deceased partner's estate was jointly liable with the other partners. The bank, however, continued to operate the account, so that the credit balance on Clayton's account of £1,713 at the time of the death of the partner was reduced to £453 with no further payments being made into the account. The partnership subsequently became bankrupt at a time when the total withdrawals on the account amounted to considerably more than the £1,713. Clayton, however, claimed that the sum of £453 was due to him from the dead partner's estate, on the ground that subsequent withdrawals from the account were to be set against later credits.

Sir William Grant MR examined the general area of appropriation of payments and distinguished those situations from one where the question of appropriation relates to a bank account. He said (p. 609):

> 'But this is a case of a banking account, where all sums paid in form one blended fund, the parts of which have no longer any distinct existence. Neither banker nor customer ever thinks of saying, this is to be placed to the account of the £500 paid in on Monday, and this other to the account of the £500 paid in on Tuesday. There is a fund of £1,000 to draw upon, and that is enough. In such a case, there is no room for any other appropriation than that which the receipts and payments take place, and are carried into the account. Presumably, it is the sum first paid in, that is first drawn out. It is the first item on the debit side of the account, that is discharged, or reduced, by the first item on the credit side. The appropriation is made by the very act of the two items against each other. Upon that principle, all accounts current are settled, and particularly cash accounts.'

On the principle of appropriation as explained in the judgment the action by Devaynes against the deceased partner's estate failed.

The rule in *Clayton*'s case does not apply in a number of instances, namely:

(a) Where a trustee pays trust money into his personal account, thus mixing trust funds with his own funds. In *Re Hallett's Estate* ((1880) 13 Ch D 696) a solicitor misappropriated client funds and paid the money into his own account. He then withdrew amounts from his account which were in excess of his personal savings. The court held that the presumption that a trustee is deemed to withdraw his personal funds first applied, thus leaving trust funds wrongly paid into the account intact.

(b) The rule does not apply to separate bank accounts even if with the same branch. In *Bradford Old Bank Ltd* v *Sutcliffe* ([1918] 2 KB 833) a customer had a loan account and a current account and it was held that payments to the credit of the current account must be appropriated to that account. Accordingly, a guarantor for the loan account could not claim that such payments should be used to reduce the loan account. Scrutton LJ said (p. 847):

> 'The sums paid into the current account are appropriated by the customer to that account, and cannot be used by the bank in discharge of the loan account without the consent of the customer. No customer could otherwise have any security in drawing a cheque on his current account if he had a loan account greater than his credit balance on current account.'

(c) The rule does not apply where the parties have merely entered into a series of transactions without opening a current account. In *Cory Brothers Co.* v *Mecca Turkish SS (Owners), The Mecca* ([1897] AC 286) it was said that the rule in *Clayton*'s case does not apply where there is no current account between the parties, nor where it is clear from the circumstances that the creditor intended to reserve the right.

(d) The rule does not apply where the account has been stopped, i.e. where payments in and out do not take place.

(e) Finally, the rule does not apply where the bank agrees not to apply the first-in, first-out rule. Thus, in *Westminster Bank Ltd* v *Cond* ((1940) 46 Com Cas 60) the guarantor argued that because the bank had continued the account unbroken after making a demand on him, the loan had been paid off by subsequent payments into the account. The court rejected this argument on the grounds that the guarantee form contained an express clause to prevent the operation of the rule.

CONSOLIDATION OF ACCOUNTS (BANKER'S SET-OFF)

Where the customer has two or more accounts with the same bank it has a right to combine or consolidate any debit balances against any credit balances the customer maintains on another account with the same bank. Consequently the bank may produce an overall balance for which it is accountable to the customer. This right of set off is only available to a bank when the customer has more than one account with the bank and some of these accounts are overdrawn. A set-off involves the setting-up of cross-claims against the amounts due to the customer.

Garnett v M'Kewan (1872) LR 8 Ex 10

The customer having a credit balance at one branch of the defendant bank drew a cheque for the full amount of the credit balance. At the same time the customer was indebted to the bank on another account held with a different branch of the same bank which reduced his overall credit balance to a few shillings. The bank without notice to the customer dishonoured the cheque on presentation. An action was brought against the bank for wrongful dishonour.

The court held that the dishonour of the cheque was justified although the bank had not given any notice of its intention to combine the accounts. The customer is not entitled to expect his cheques to be honoured at one branch of a bank where he has an account in credit, if at the same time the credit balance is counterbalanced by a debit against him at another branch of the same bank and there is no duty on the part of the bank to keep the accounts separate.

This rule was challenged in *W.P. Greenhalgh & Sons v Union Bank of Manchester* ([1924] 2 KB 153) where Swift J said that:

'If a banker agrees with his customer to open two or more accounts, he has not, in my opinion, without the assent of the customer, any right to move either assets or liabilities from the one account to the other; the very basis of his agreement with his customer is that the two accounts shall be kept separate ...'

The *Greenhalgh* case ignored the decision of the court in *Garnett v M'Kewan* where it was settled that the bank has, in the absence of an express or implied agreement to the contrary, the right to combine the accounts of a customer and it can exercise that right without notice to the customer (again unless the contract provides otherwise). In *Halesowen Pressworks & Assemblies Ltd v Westminster Bank Ltd* ([1971] 1 QB 1) the bank was held entitled to combine a current account with a loan account when the banker and customer relationship was terminated because of the customer's insolvency. The court said that requiring the bank to give notice could serve no purpose under the circumstances.

Although the *Halesowen* case was decided on its special facts, i.e. the insolvency of the customer which enabled the bank to combine a current account which was in credit with a loan account which was in debit, the case reaffirmed the rule laid down in the *M'Kewan* case that the bank can combine two accounts to produce an overall balance for the customer where the debit and credit items are immediately payable on demand.

The rule has been affirmed recently in *Barclays Bank Ltd v Okenarhe* ([1966] 2 Lloyd's Rep 87) where the defendant, having stolen C's building society pass book, went to the plaintiff bank's Sloane Square branch and representing himself to be C instructed the bank that he wished to withdraw £1,590 from the building society and open a deposit account. The defendant then withdrew the amount from the bank against the building society's uncleared cheque credited to his bank account. The defendant then paid approximately £1,785 into current and deposit accounts he opened with the Battersea branch of the plaintiff's bank. When the building society dishonoured the cheque, the bank sought a declaration to combine the accounts held by the defendant with its Sloane Square and Battersea branches. The court held that the bank had intended to deal with the person physically present at the Sloane Square branch, although it was thought he was C and there was, therefore, an agreement to open a deposit account. As regards the right to combine accounts Mocatta J examined the authorities and held:

> '... It is plain that the general principle is that the bank is entitled to combine the two accounts. There is clear authority for this in the case of *Garnett* v *M'Kewan* (1872) LR 8 Ex 10 ...'

In *Re K* (unreported, 29 June 1989) an amount of money given as a gift to the bank's customer by persons who were subsequently convicted of offences under the Drug Trafficking Act 1986 was paid to the credit of a fixed deposit account as security for the customer's overdraft. The bank obtained from the customer a letter of set-off which was stated to be given in addition to the bank's right to combine at common law. The bank was unaware of the origins of the amount. The court held that the bank was entitled to combine the customer's accounts. It was said that although the Drug Trafficking Act 1986 had a draconian effect as between persons guilty under the Act, it did not affect the bank's right. The bank was treated as if it were an innocent purchaser of the money in question and on that basis banks' right to combine remained unaffected by the 1986 Act.

In *Hong Kong and Shanghai Banking Corporation* v *Kloeckner & Co. AG* ([1990] 3 WLR 634) the question that arose was whether an issuing bank could set off against the amount demanded by the beneficiary under a standby credit an amount due to the bank from the beneficiary. The question arose because the issuing bank, which happened to have dealings with the beneficiary, had granted at his request certain facilities in respect of the transactions which became the subject of the dispute. Hirst J rejected the argument that the doctrine of the autonomy of the letter of credit of necessity led to the conclusion that a set-off could not be permitted. The nature of the letter of credit prevented the grant of an injunction to stop payment and disputes relating to the underlying contract could not be raised but a set-off did not abrogate the independence of the letter of credit. Hirst J said :

> '... it would seem to me anomalous that such a set-off should be unavailable in letter of credit cases, but available against bills of exchange which ... are closely analogous in that a bill of exchange is also virtually equivalent to cash.'

Exceptions to the rule

Mocatta J in the *Okenarhe* case recognised the following exceptions to the rule:

(a) There is no right to combine in relation to accounts maintained with a bank by one person but in two different capacities, e.g. where the customer maintains an account in his personal capacity and also holds a trust account. In *Union Bank of Australia Ltd* v *Murray-Aynsley & Another* ([1898] AC 693), however, the Privy

Council held that where there are several accounts in the name of the same customer with a bank, but the customer does not make it clear to the bank and the bank does not know which of those accounts is a trust account, the bank is entitled to combine all the accounts.

(b) The right to combine does not arise if there is an express or implied agreement not to combine the accounts. For example, in the *Bradford Old Bank Ltd* v *Sutcliffe* ([1918] 2 KB 833) the right to set off was not permissible where the bank had agreed with the customer that the two accounts would be kept separate. In that case the bank had opened a current account and Scrutton LJ said that amounts paid into that account cannot be used by the bank in discharge of the loan account without the customer's consent. Similarly, in *Buckingham* v *London & Midland Bank Ltd* ((1895) 12 TLR 70) it was held that the bank had no right to combine a loan account (secured) with a current account. Again, In *Re E.J. Morel Ltd* [1961] 1 All ER 796 the court recognised the right of the bank to combine, but this time only to a limited extent as the bank was not allowed to combine all three accounts. In the *Morel* case a company maintained a No. 2 account and a wages account, and the arrangement was that the credit balance on the No.2 account would always be sufficient to cover the wages account. It was held that the No. 2 account and the wages account were in substance one as between the bank and the company.

(c) If money is deposited with the bank for a special purpose the bank cannot combine. In the *W.P. Greenhalgh* case the bank had knowledge of the ultimate destination of the proceeds of certain bills deposited by the customer to the credit of his account and for that reason the court held the bank had no right to combine accounts. In *Barclays Bank Ltd* v *Quistclose Investments Co.* ([1970] AC 567) it was held that money paid into a bank account was paid in with the knowledge of the bank for a specific purpose, i.e. payment of wages, and that purpose having failed due to the liquidation of the customer the bank could not claim a set-off against other indebtedness of the customer.

(d) Combination is not possible for contingent liabilities. In *Jeffreys* v *Agra & Mastermans Bank* ((1886) LR 2 Eq 674) a customer being indebted to the bank handed to it certain bank receipts from another bank representing deposits lodged with that other bank. The court held that the bank could only set off such sums as were due and payable immediately and it could not retain the balance as security for amounts the customer might owe the bank in future.

(e) Set-off is not available where there is any doubt as to the identity of the account-holder. In *Bhogul* v *Punjab National Bank* [1988] 2 All ER 296 it was held that the right of set-off against funds held in several different accounts depends on the several different accounts belonging to the same person. Similarly, in *Uttamchandami* v *Central Bank of India* ((1989) 139 NJL 222) the defendant bank sought to set off accounts held in different names on the ground that in each case the accounts were 'nominee' accounts and that in each case the customer was in reality a Mr Vaswani. The Court of Appeal, affirming the decision of Hobhouse J held that the bank had no right to combine the accounts. Lloyd LJ said:

'... Set-off has never been allowed save where the accounts are of the same customer, held in the same name, and in the same right. Even then, the right of set-off may be excluded by agreement express or implied. What is unusual about the present case is that the bank is seeking to set off accounts held in different names ...'

Statutory right of set-off

The customer's bankruptcy

Section 323(1) and (2) of the Insolvency Act 1986 provides that where before the commencement of the bankruptcy there have been mutual credits, mutual debts or other mutual dealings between the bankrupt and any creditor of the bankrupt proving for a bankruptcy debt, an account must be taken of what is due from each party to the other in respect of mutual dealings and the sums due from one party must be set off against the sums due from the other. However, s. 323(3) of the Act provides that sums due from the bankrupt to another party must not be included in the account taken under this provision if the other party had notice at the time they became due that a bankruptcy petition relating to the bankrupt was pending.

The customer's liquidation

In the winding-up of companies, the rules as to set-off in bankruptcy apply (Insolvency Rules 1986, R 4.90). In *British Guiana Bank* v *Official Receiver* ((1911) 104 LT 754) a company which was indebted to a bank on a current account opened another current account under a written agreement which provided that the bank would not, without the knowledge and consent of the company, appropriate any of the funds which at any time might be standing to the credit of the new account in reduction of the debt due to the bank. A few years later the company was wound up. There was a substantial sum owing under the original account and a considerable credit balance in favour of the company in the second account. The Judicial Committee of the Privy Council held that the bank had a right to set-off the one sum against the other. In *National Westminster Bank Ltd* v *Halesowen Presswork and Assemblies Ltd* ([1972] AC 785) the House of Lords held that the statutory set-off provisions in bankruptcy and winding-up cannot be excluded by agreement. If the bank, however, has notice that the credit balance held in the company's account is trust money then the statutory rights are not available.

THE BANKING AND BUILDING SOCIETIES' OMBUDSMEN

So far the chapter has examined the self-help remedies available to a bank if money is owed by a customer. Nevertheless, disputes will arise within the banker–customer relationship which are not necessarily resolved by discussion either at branch or head-office level. Apart from expensive litigation the customer may use the services of the Banking or Building Societies' Ombudsman.

The existing schemes

The UK is unique in having a specialised Ombudsman in the field of financial services. The Banking Ombudsman is sponsored by the banking sector through a voluntary scheme which was adopted in January 1986, in response to an initiative by the National Consumer Council. The Building Societies Ombudsman scheme has been in operation since July 1986 and was established under the Building Societies Act 1986. The function of both Ombudsmen is the resolution of disputes between their members and their private customers by an informal process of arbitration provided free of charge.

The Banking Ombudsman

The Banking Ombudsman scheme is modelled on the Insurance Ombudsman scheme. The object of the scheme is to receive unresolved complaints about the provision of banking services and to 'facilitate the satisfaction, settlement or withdrawal of such complaints'. The scheme is constituted as an unlimited company set-up under the Companies Acts and headed by a Board of Directors, appointed by the banks from among their own full time executives. The Board has three main tasks:

(a) to levy and channel funds from the industry and to approve the budget for the scheme;
(b) to appoint, and where appropriate re-appoint, Council members with a final say in the appointment of the Ombudsman himself;
(c) to approve the Ombudsman's terms of reference, and any amendments to them.

Under the Board is the Council of the Banking Ombudsman, consisting of seven members with the following duties:

(a) to appoint the Ombudsman and monitor his terms of reference, both these being subject to the approval of the Board;
(b) to give him continuing assistance and guidance;
(c) to receive his annual report;
(d) to approve a financial budget for recommendation to the Board.

Under the Council is the Ombudsman himself. A dispute may be referred to the Ombudsman by an individual customer or group of such customers (but not a company) after the internal banking complaints procedure has been exhausted and provided the complaint falls within the terms of reference of the Ombudsman. Certain types of complaint are specifically excluded, e.g. complaints more than six months old, a bank's commercial decision about lending, a bank's general policy, e.g. rates of interest, and claims above £100,000. The Ombudsman may seek to promote a settlement between the applicant and the bank, failing which he may recommend a settlement or withdrawal of the complaint. If his recommendation is, within one month, accepted by the applicant but not the bank, he may make an award against the bank, not exceeding £100,000. The award will be binding, if accepted by the applicant within one month, on the applicant and the bank.

The Building Societies' Ombudsman

This scheme was established under the Building Societies Act 1986 and requires every building society to be a member of one or more recognised adjudication schemes. The Act gives the Building Societies Commission the function of granting recognition of schemes and of withdrawing recognition it has granted. The Act also lays down the matters to be provided for in the schemes and the requirements for recognised schemes as regards matters of complaint, grounds of complaint, functions of adjudicator, etc. The single scheme which has in fact been produced under the Act resembles the Banking Ombudsman scheme in its structure, including the balance of representatives on the Council. A major difference under the Building Societies scheme, however, is that fixing the terms of reference is within the ambit of the independent Building Societies Commission.

Recommendations of the Jack Committee

The Jack Committee on Banking Services expressed concern about the fairness of the Banking Ombudsman scheme and therefore concluded that a statutory scheme, similar to the Building Societies scheme, should be adopted. The scheme should ensure comprehensive coverage of authorised banks above a certain minimum size by one of the recognised adjudication schemes. An impartial and independent body with some knowledge of banking matters should be given the functions performed by the Building Societies Commission in granting recognition to schemes and monitoring them. The Jack Committee recommended that the Bank of England be given the role of the Building Societies Commission and the responsibility for approving a statutory scheme or schemes. Any Act giving effect to the Jack Committee proposals for a statutory Banking Ombudsman scheme would have to deal with the requirements for recognised schemes, e.g. grounds for complaints, functions of the adjudicator, etc.

The Jack Committee was also of the view that the Banking Ombudsman scheme should be extended to small businesses.

4 The banking contract

The contract entered into by a bank on opening an account for its customer is one the terms of which are implied by the law. The mandate signed by the customer is a general request to provide banking facilities but the legal obligations imposed on the parties have largely been developed by the common law. A consultee to the Jack Committee on Banking Services said:

> 'We are doubtful if many people have any clear idea of what duties are owed to them by their bankers, or of what remedies are available to them in the event of any of these duties not being performed. By the same token the general public would be unaware of the obligations which they themselves owe to their banker ...'

The Jack Committee rejected the idea of a standard term contract even for business customers. The Committee felt that the absence of a requirement for a written contract when a customer applies for an account to be opened allows flexibility and room to manoeuvre. However, regulation was said to be desirable where banks choose to set out terms and conditions in an express contract; and where banks seek to vary contractual terms a reasonable length of notice should be given to the customer.

In some instances banks do impose express terms, for example when a bank issues a cheque card or credit card or opens a letter of credit facility. Where such terms are imposed they are subject to the Unfair Contracts Act 1977, and it is for the bank to establish that the term it seeks to rely on is 'reasonable'. Moreover, in *Tai Hing Cotton Mill Ltd* v *Lin Chong Hing Bank* ([1986] AC 80) the Privy Council held that where banks wish:

> 'to impose upon their customers an express obligation to examine their monthly statements and to make those statements, in the absence of query, unchallengeable by the customer after expiry of a time limit, the burden of the objection and the sanction imposed must be brought home to the customer.'

The Privy Council then went on to say that the test is so rigourous because:

> 'the bankers would have their terms of business so construed as to exclude the rights which the customer would enjoy if they were not excluded by express agreement.'

DUTIES OWED BY THE BANK TO ITS CUSTOMER

In *Joachimson* v *Swiss Bank Corporation* ([1921] 3 KB 110) the plaintiff firm was a partnership between two Germans and a naturalised Englishman, carrying on business in Manchester. One of the German partners died on 1 August 1914 and the partnership was dissolved. On the outbreak of war the other German became an enemy alien. On 1 August the partnership account with the defendant bank was £2,321 in credit. In 1919, the naturalised partner brought an action in the name of the firm to recover the credit balance on the account, the cause of action having arisen on or before 1 August 1914. The firm had not made a demand for the credit balance and the bank pleaded that no cause of action accrued. The Court of Appeal held that where money was standing to the credit of a customer on a current account, a previous demand was necessary before an action could be maintained against the bank. The Court of Appeal gave judgment for the bank. Atkin LJ said:

> 'I think that there is only one contract made between the bank and its customer. The terms of that contract involve obligations on both sides and require careful statement ... The bank undertakes to receive money and to collect bills for its customer's account. The proceeds so received are not to be held in trust for the customer, but the bank borrows the proceeds and undertakes to repay them. The promise to repay is to repay at the branch of the bank where the account is kept, and during banking hours. It includes a promise to repay any part of the amount due against the written order of the customer, addressed to the bank at the branch, and as such written orders may be outstanding in the ordinary course of business for two or three days, it is a term of the contract that the bank will not cease to do business with the customer except upon reasonable notice ...'

The paying bank is under a duty to conform to the customer's mandate and this includes an obligation to honour cheques drawn by its customer if the cheque is regular and unambiguous in form and if the customer has a sufficient credit balance or if the cheque is within any agreed overdraft limit. The obligation to make payment is counterbalanced by an obligation to refrain from making payment when there is an effective countermand.

Duty to make payment

Morzetti v *Williams & Others* (1830) 1 B & Ad 415

The plaintiff was a trader in London and maintained a current account with the defendants, who carried on a banking business. It was an accepted custom within the banking community that a customer could draw cheques or issue drafts against any credit balances standing to his account. The customer had a credit balance of £1,091 19s 6d and issued a cheque for £871 7s 6d to be paid against his account. When the cheque was presented for payment the defendant bank wrongfully refused to honour it. The plaintiff brought an action for the wrongful dishonour.

The court held that the plaintiff could maintain an action against the defendant bank although he had suffered no actual loss. In the course of the judgment it was said that a banker is bound by law to pay a cheque drawn by a customer, within a reasonable time, after the banker has received sufficient funds belonging to that customer. The customer may maintain an action for breach of contract or in tort against the bank's refusal to make payment in such circumstances. Lord Tenterden said:

> 'It is a discredit to a person, and therefore injurious in fact, to have a draft refused payment for so small a sum, for it shows that the banker had very little confidence in the customer.'

The duty to honour cheques and other similar instruments exists so long as the documents are presented in the normal course of the banking business and during normal banking hours (see *Whitaker* v *The Governor & Co. of the Bank of England* (1835) 1 C M & R 744).

Wrongful dishonour

Gibbons v Westminster Bank Ltd [1939] 2 KB 882

The plaintiff, Mrs Margaret Gibbons, was a customer of the defendant bank. On 19 July 1938, she issued a cheque in favour of her landlords, Ainslie & Co. Ltd, in payment of rent. The cheque was presented for payment on 22 July 1938, and was dishonoured by the defendant bank on the ground that the plaintiff's account did not have a sufficient credit balance. The plaintiff in fact had paid to the credit of her account in due time sufficient funds to meet the cheque but due to an error of the defendant's employee the amount was credited to the wrong account. On the dishonour of the cheque the plaintiff interviewed the manager of the branch where the account was maintained and was paid the sum of one guinea.

The plaintiff brought an action against the defendant bank for wrongful dishonour but pleaded no special damage. The defendants admitted that they had been in breach of contract but pleaded that they gave the plaintiff the sum of one guinea in full discharge of her cause of action.

The court held that the customer is entitled to sue for breach of contract. However, the court only awarded nominal damages. It took the view that a person who is not a trader is not entitled to recover substantial damages unless particular damage is both alleged and proved (see *Rolin* v *Stewart* (1854) 14 CB 592). In *Baker* v *Australia & New Zealand Bank Ltd* ([1958] NZLR 907) it was held that a lady who was a substantial shareholder and a working director of a company was not a trader and therefore not entitled to recover substantial damages for breach of contract when the defendant bank wrongfully dishonoured cheques drawn by the plaintiff.

Where a private customer cannot recover general damages for loss of reputation by bringing an action for breach of contract, general damages may be recoverable by bringing an action in defamation if the reason given for the dishonour appears to convey a defamatory meaning. In *Davidson* v *Barclays Bank Ltd* ([1940] 1 All ER 499) the court held that the bank could not raise the defence of qualified privilege when it by mistake dishonoured a cheque drawn by the customer and marked it 'not sufficient' (see also *Baker* v *Australia & New Zealand Bank Ltd* [1958] NZLR 907 where the court held that a cheque wrongfully dishonoured and marked with the words 'present again' was reasonably capable of a defamatory meaning because it conveyed the impression that the plaintiff had insufficient funds to the credit of his account on the original presentation of the cheque).

Payment outside the mandate
The bank must not make payment outside the limits of the customer's mandate. There are a number of instances where the bank will be treated as acting outside the mandate.

Where the bank makes payment on a forged instrument
The bank can only debit the customer's account where it has either express authority (where a cheque is drawn by the customer) or ostensible authority (where the rules of estoppel can be applied against the customer as in *Greenwood* v *Martins Bank Ltd* [1933] AC 51). Where the drawer's signature is forged or there is some other material falsification of the instrument then s. 24 of the Bills of Exchange Act 1882 renders the instrument void and the bank cannot debit the customer's account.

M'Kenzie v *British Linen Co.* (1881) 6 App Cas 82

The names of A and B appeared on a bill of exchange, as drawers and indorsers to the BL Co. The BL Co.'s bank discounted it for C, who signed it as acceptor. The bill was dishonoured on maturity and notice of the dishonour was sent to A and B and received late on the same day, a Saturday. On the following Monday, C brought to the BL Co. a blank bill with A and B's signatures on it, as drawers and indorsers. It was agreed to accept the bill as a renewal of the previously dishonoured bill but for a smaller amount, the difference being paid in cash by C. Three days before payment became due on this bill, notice of the due payment was sent, through agents, to A and B, but the bill was dishonoured again on presentation.

A fortnight later notice was given that the signatures of A and B were forged. The agents brought an action against A for payment of the bill alleging that he had either authorised the use of his name or had subsequently adopted the bill and therefore was estopped from denying his liability on the bill.

The House of Lords held, reversing the Court of Appeal, that on the facts A had neither authorised nor consented to the use of his name on the bill of exchange and that estoppel could not arise against him. Lord Watson (p. 109) said:

> 'It would be a most unreasonable thing to permit a man who knew the bank were relying upon his forged signature to a bill to lie by and not to divulge the fact until he saw that the position of the bank was altered for the worse. But it appears to me that it would be equally contrary to justice to hold him responsible for the bill because he did not tell the bank of the forgery at once, if he did actually give the information, and if when he did so the bank was in no worse position than it was at the time when it was first within his power to give the information.'

Where the bank pays a cheque drawn by an agent in excess of his authority

The bank fails to conform to the customer's mandate if it pays a cheque which is signed in excess of the authority conferred on the agent and the bank could have had that authority verified. Where the payment is made outside the mandate the bank acts without the authority of its customer and cannot therefore debit the customer's account.

Liggett (Liverpool) Ltd v *Barclays Bank Ltd* [1928] 1 KB 48

One of the directors of a company which maintained a bank account with the defendant bank expressed concern regarding the management of the business and insisted on signing all cheques drawn on the company's account. Subsequently, the bank was notified by the second director of the appointment of a third director, who happened to be his wife. The bank paid cheques which had been improperly drawn by these two directors. It was later discovered that the amounts of these cheques had been paid into the personal account of one of the fraudulent directors. The company brought an action against the bank for money had and received.

The defendant bank had acted negligently and contrary to the express instructions of the customer. Where a bank is put on inquiry with regard to the appointment of a new director it is guilty of negligence in not investigating the circumstances. The bank is not entitled to assume that the appointment of an additional director is valid and proper notice of the appointment has been given.

The *Liggett* case follows *A.L. Underwood Ltd* v *Bank of Liverpool* ([1924] 1 KB 775) where the sole director of a company paid into his personal account cheques drawn in favour of the company and misappropriated the proceeds. In an action against the bank by a debenture-holder for conversion of the cheques it was held that the act of paying cheques drawn on the company into his personal account was so unusual that the bank should have made inquiry and that failing to do so rendered the bank liable in negligence.

Where the bank pays a cheque which has been effectively and properly countermanded

Westminster Bank Ltd v *Hilton* (1926) 43 TLR 124

The plaintiff maintained an account with the defendant bank, and drew a cheque for £8 1s 6d, payable to one Poate. The cheque was drawn in July 1924, and was postdated 2 August. On 1 August, the plaintiff instructed the bank to stop payment on the cheque but gave the bank the wrong cheque number although the correct amount of the cheque and correct information about the payee was given. On 6 August, when the cheque countermanded was presented for payment, the bank made payment. The plaintiff brought an action for negligence against the bank which failed. The plaintiff thereupon appealed. The Court of Appeal found in favour of the plaintiff and the bank appealed.

The House of Lords held that the bank was not guilty of negligence. The House held that in making payment from the customer's account the bank acts as the customer's agent, so that where the customer gives instructions which are open to ambiguity and capable of interpretation in one of several ways, the bank is not liable if it adopts a reasonable interpretation not intended by the customer. Lord Shaw of Dunfermline said:

> 'When a banker is in possession of sufficient funds to meet such a cheque from a customer, the duty of the bank is to honour that cheque by payment, and failure in this duty may involve the bank in serious liability to its customer. This duty is ended, and on the contrary when the cheque is stopped another duty arises – namely, to refuse payment. In a case of that character it rests upon the customer to prove that the order to stop reached the bank in time and was unequivocally referable to a cheque in existence, and signed and issued by the customer before the notice to stop ...'

On the question of countermand of a postdated cheque Lord Shaw said:

> '... it is, in my view, necessary for the customer to prove and explain the postdating, but further to prove that this fact was brought clearly home to the mind of the banker so as to bring the postdated cheque within the order of stoppage ...'

The customer's instructions must be clear and unambiguous so where the customer countermands a cheque and gives the wrong cheque number by mistake, the bank can pay the cheque intended to be countermanded and debit the customer's account.

In *Lapperton* v *McGeever* (unreported, 7 February 1990) on Friday 25 November 1988, the defendant agreed to grant the plaintiff an interest-free loan for £10,000 and gave him a cheque for the amount. The following day the defendant changed his mind and telephoned the bank to stop payment. In fact the plaintiff had already presented the cheque for payment over the counter and asked that the proceeds be credited to his account which was maintained at the same branch. The credit entry appeared in the plaintiff's account on Monday 28 but the bank reversed the entry on the following day, treating it as having been made under a mistake of fact. The defendant sought leave to defend an action on the grounds that the cheque had not been dishonoured as the plaintiff's account had, originally, been credited. Moreover, the defendant argued that the cheque was unenforceable as no consideration had been given for it. Alliot J gave judgment for the plaintiff under Order 14 of the Rules of the Supreme Court. The Court of Appeal granted the defendant leave to defend. On the question of countermand of the cheque Lloyd LJ however, indicated that he thought the cheque was 'clearly dishonoured since the relevant entries were made without the authority of the plaintiff.' It has been suggested that the better explanation is that at the end of the cycle since the plaintiff's account did not show a credit entry representing the cheque he could not be treated as having received payment.

The Jack Committee accepted that it is not always possible to give the customer an opportunity to countermand his mandate but where possible that opportunity should be made available to the customer and the rules of countermand explained. The White Paper accepted that the Code of Banking Practice should give customers a simple explanation of the clearing cycle and establish rules for countermand of cheques. The White Paper also recognises that the right to countermand is severely reduced in electronic funds transfer systems.

The Code of Banking Practice (para. 10.1) provides that banks and building societies will provide customers with details of how their accounts operate including information about how and when a customer may stop or countermand a cheque or other instrument.

Duty of confidentiality

The bank owes a duty of confidentiality in respect of the customer's affairs. Where a breach is threatened by the bank the customer can obtain an injunction to prevent it from disclosing the information. If disclosure has already been made by the bank the only remedy available to the customer is to sue for damages for breach of contract.

Tournier v *National Provincial and Union Bank of England* [1924] 1 KB 461

The plaintiff was a customer of the defendant bank. In April 1922, the customer's account was overdrawn and he signed a document agreeing to pay off the amount by weekly instalments. On the document, the plaintiff wrote the name and address of a firm, Kenyon & Co, with whom he was about to enter into employment. The customer failed to maintain the weekly instalments and the bank manager telephoned the plaintiff's employers in order to ascertain his private address. In the course of the conversation that followed the bank manager disclosed to Kenyon & C. that the customer was overdrawn on his bank account and that promises to repay the overdraft had not been kept. The manager also informed them that in his opinion the overdraft was due to the customer incurring heavy gambling debts.

As a result of this conversation Kenyon & C. dismissed the plaintiff from his employment. The plaintiff brought an action against the bank for slander and for breach of implied contract resulting from the wrongful disclosure of the plaintiff's banking affairs. Judgment was entered for the bank and the plaintiff appealed.

The Court of Appeal allowed the appeal and ordered a new trial. The court held that there is an implied term of the contract between a banker and his customer that the banker will not divulge to a third party, without the express or implied consent of the customer, either the state of the customer's account or any transactions entered into with the bank. The disclosure constituted a breach of the bank's duty to the customer not to disclose information in respect of the customer acquired in the course of the banker–customer relationship.

Bankes LJ outlined the circumstances in which disclosure would be permitted (p. 473):

(a) 'where disclosure is under compulsion of law;
(b) where there is a duty to the public to disclose;
(c) where the interests of the bank require disclosure;
(d) where the disclosure is made by the express or implied consent of the customer.'

This duty of confidentiality Bankes LJ said (p. 473):

'... does not cease the moment a customer closes his account. Information gained during the currency of the account remains confidential unless released under circumstances bringing the case within one of the classes of qualification I have already referred to. Again the confidence is not confined to the actual state of the customer's account. It extends to information derived from the account itself.'

Similarly, Atkin LJ said the duty of confidentiality (p. 485):

'... goes beyond the state of the account, that is, whether there is a debit or a credit balance, and the amount of the balance. It must extend at least to all the transactions that go through the account, and to securities, if any, given in respect of the account; and in respect of such matters it must, I think, extend beyond the period when the account is closed, or ceases to be an active account. It seems to me to be inconceivable that either party would contemplate that once the customer had closed his account the bank was to be at liberty to divulge as it pleased the particular transactions which it had conducted for the customer while he was such. I further think that the obligation extends to information obtained from other sources than the customer's actual account ...'

The duty not to disclose information about the customer's affairs is not an absolute duty (see *Barclays Bank plc* v *Taylor; Trustee Savings Bank of Wales and Border Counties* v *Taylor* (*Financial Times*, 23 June 1989)) and the *Tournier* case itself recognises a number of situations where disclosure may be justified. It is, however, for the bank to show that where disclosure has been made it falls within one of the exceptions which are considered in detail below.

Disclosure by compulsion of law

Disclosure under this exception may take the form of (a) compulsion by order of a court; or (b) compulsion by statute.

Compulsion by order of the court

An order of the court will usually take the form of a subpoena which when served on an officer of the bank will order him to attend court and bring with him certain books, documents and letters relating to the customer's affairs. The term documents includes films and tapes for this purpose and would apply to computer tapes. An order of the court compelling disclosure may derive its validity from a number of statutes allowing disclosure. Under the Bankers' Books Evidence Act 1879, the courts have made orders compelling disclosure in a number of cases.

The Bankers' Books Evidence Act 1879, s. 7, provides that 'on an application of any party to a legal proceeding a court or judge may order that such party be at liberty to inspect and take copies of any entries in a banker's books for any purpose of such proceedings.' The Act defines any 'legal proceedings' to mean 'civil or criminal proceedings or inquiry in which evidence is or may be given, and includes an arbitration.' The term bankers' books is defined to include 'ledgers, day books, cash books, account books, and all other books used in the ordinary business of the bank'.

The purpose of the section was to relieve banks and their officials from having to appear in court in person to give evidence. Section 3 of the Act provides that 'a copy of any entry in a banker's book shall in all legal proceedings be received as prima facie evidence of such entry, and of the matters, transactions and accounts therein recorded.'

This provision was applied to criminal proceedings in *Williams & Others v Summerfield* ([1972] 2 QB 512) where an order was made to enable a police inspector to inspect and take copies of certain bank accounts. Lord Widgery LJ said that in applying s. 7 of the Act:

> '... in criminal proceedings, justices should warn themselves of the importance of the step which they are taking in making an order under s. 7; should always recognise the care with which the jurisdiction should be exercised; should take into account among other things whether there is other evidence in the possession of the prosecution to support the charge ...'

In particular the judge warned that justices should not allow 'fishing expeditions' and that they should limit the period of disclosure of the bank account to a period 'which is strictly relevant to the charge before them.'

In respect of civil proceedings the rule has been laid down that the statutory power to order inspection should not be inconsistent with the general power to order discovery. An order for disclosure will be made if it is relevant to the proceedings and not privileged from production. In *Bankers Trust Co. v Shapira* ([1980] 3 All ER 353) the Court of Appeal held that the order for discovery may be made at the earliest stages of an action to give effect to a defrauded plaintiff's equitable right to trace and recover property of which he claimed to have been fraudulently deprived. The evidence of fraud against the customer must be very strong for such an order to be made.

With regard to foreign banks carrying on business in the UK the courts are reluctant to make orders which have effect outside the jurisdiction. In *Mackinnon v Donaldson, Lufkin and Jenrette Securities Corp.* ([1986] Ch 482) the plaintiff obtained an ex parte order under s. 7 of the Bankers' Books Evidence Act against an American bank which was not a party to the litigation. The plaintiff was alleging fraud against a company and certain individual defendants. The order required the bank to produce books and papers held at the head-office of the bank in New York and which related to the account of one of the defendants, a Bahamian company. In addition the plaintiff obtained a subpoena against an officer of the London branch of the bank. The bank moved to have the ex parte order and the subpoena discharged on the grounds that they exceeded the jurisdiction of the court and infringed the sovereignty of the United States. Hoffman J discharged both the subpoena and the *ex parte* order. He held that as a matter of principle the court should not, except in exceptional circumstances, impose on a foreigner, especially a foreign bank bound by a duty of confidence under its national law, a duty to disclose information and to produce documents outside the jurisdiction concerning business transacted outside the jurisdiction. The duty of confidentiality is regulated by the law of the country where the account is maintained. Hoffman J continued:

'If every country where a bank happened to carry on business asserted a right to require the bank to produce documents relating to accounts kept in any other such country, banks would be in the unhappy position of being forced to submit to whichever sovereign was able to apply the greatest pressure.'

Compulsion by statute

The Jack Committee Report listed 19 statutory provisions in England which permit disclosure of confidential information relating to the customer's affairs without the consent of the customer. The report contains a list of some of the statutes under which disclosure may be made in Appendix Q. A bank may be compelled to disclose information under the Bankers' Books Evidence Act 1879, the Companies Act 1985, the Insolvency Act 1986, the Drug Trafficking Offences Act 1986, the Banking Act 1987, the Building Societies Act 1986, etc.

Drug Trafficking Offences Act 1986

Under the Drug Trafficking Offences Act 1986, there are three sections which are of importance to banks.

(a) Section 27(1) of the Act provides that for the purpose of an investigation into drug trafficking, the police and customs may apply to a circuit judge for an order in relation to 'particular material or material of a particular description.' The judge may order (under s. 27(2)) that a person who appears in possession of the material to which the application relates shall produce it to a constable for him to take away or give the constable access to it within such a period as the order may specify. Once the order is served to the named person he must comply with it and s. 27(9)(b) provides that the order will have effect despite any obligation of secrecy or other restriction on the disclosure of information whether imposed by statute or otherwise. Where the relationship is one of banker–customer the bank would be obliged to comply with such an order notwithstanding its duty of confidentiality. If an order under s. 27 is not complied with, the constable may apply to the circuit judge for a warrant authorising him to enter and search the premises.

(b) Under s. 31 of the Act a new offence is created of 'prejudicing an investigation' into drug trafficking. The section is intended to deter anyone who may 'tip off' a suspect, e.g. a bank adviser or a bank warning a customer that his affairs are being investigated. Where an order has been made under s. 27 and a person knowing or suspecting that an investigation is taking place makes any disclosure likely to prejudice the investigation, they will be guilty of an offence.

(c) Section 24 is aimed at those involved in laundering the proceeds of drug trafficking. It is an offence for a person (e.g. a bank), knowing or suspecting that a customer carries on or has carried on trafficking in drugs or has benefited from this, to enter into or otherwise be concerned with arrangements for:

  (i) retaining or controlling the proceeds of drugs;
  (ii) placing funds so obtained at the customer's disposal;
  (iii) using funds to acquire property by way of investment.

It is not necessary actually to know that the investor is a drug trafficker and mere suspicion is enough. No offence is committed if the belief or suspicion is disclosed to the police as soon as possible and such disclosure will not be 'treated as a breach of any restriction upon the disclosure of information imposed by contract' (s. 24(3)).

This is the first piece of legislation which requires a bank to disclose information to the police on its own initiative. It is only concerned with the proceeds of drug trafficking and requires the bank to disclose information on suspicion that the account is used for harbouring or diverting the proceeds of drug trafficking.

Prevention of Terrorism (Temporary Provisions) Act 1989
The Act requires banks to disclose, on suspicion, confidential information concerning the location of funds which might be used for or derived from possible terrorist offences. There are two offences of special significance to banks:

(a) s. 9 makes it an offence to solicit, receive or accept contributions of money or property, intending that it shall be used for, or in furtherance of or in connection with acts of terrorism or having reasonable cause to suspect that it may be so applied or used;

(b) s. 11 makes it an offence to enter into or otherwise be concerned in an arrangement to control or retain terrorists' funds.

Section 12 provides that an offence is not committed under ss. 9 and 11 if the person who entered into such a transaction or arrangement acted with the consent of the police or disclosed promptly and on his own initiative to the police a suspicion about the money or property concerned.

Police and Criminal Evidence Act 1984
Section 9 of the Act provides that a constable may obtain access to special procedure material for the purposes of a criminal investigation by making an application under Schedule 1 to the Act. 'Special procedure material' is defined as 'material other than items subject to legal privilege and excluded material, in the possession of a person acquired or created in the course of any trade, business, profession or other occupation and which is held subject to an express or implied undertaking to hold it in confidence.' This clearly includes a bank. The police are entitled to apply for an order if, at any stage, they believe it will assist their investigation of a serious arrestable offence. In *Barclays Bank plc* v *Taylor; Trustees Savings Bank of Wales and Border Counties* v *Taylor* (*Financial Times*, 23 June 1989) the Court of Appeal held that where an order is obtained under s. 9 of the 1984 Act and the bank is compelled to comply with that disclosure, it is not a breach of its duty of confidence. The court held that once an order is obtained against a bank to disclose information the bank (a) is obliged to comply with the order and is not in breach of its duty of confidentiality in failing to oppose the order; (b) it is under no obligation to oppose or probe the evidence given in support of the application; (c) it is not obliged to give the account-holders notice that applications have been made with regard to their accounts; (d) and the police obligation to specify the material and subject matter to the application can be complied with by an oral request to bank officials.

In *R* v *Crown Court of Leicester, ex parte DPP* ([1987] 3 All ER 654) the court had earlier held that the police were not obliged to inform persons subject to a s. 9 order that they were being investigated or an order was sought under the section. This has been extended in the *Barclays Bank* case to banks so that a bank is not obliged to notify its customer that it has received instructions to make disclosure under s. 9 of the Act.

Banking Act 1987

Section 84 of the Act provides for disclosure of information by a bank to various persons, including the Secretary of State or one of his inspectors, the Director General of Fair Trading or one of the self-regulating organisations (under the Financial Services Act 1986), if the Bank of England considers that disclosure would enable or assist that person to discharge the functions specified (including functions under the Financial Services Act 1986, the Consumer Credit Act 1974 and Part 13 of the Companies Act 1985).

Where there is a duty to the public to disclose

Bankes LJ in the *Tournier* case said that there are many grounds where disclosure may be justified on grounds of public duty or public interest although he did not give any illustrations where this exception might be used. Scrutton LJ said that a bank may disclose the customer's account and affairs '... to prevent frauds or crimes'. Atkin LJ said that the disclosure may be made 'to the extent to which it is reasonably necessary ... to protect the bank, or persons interested, or the public, against fraud or crime.'

Since the *Tournier* case the exception has largely been superseded by statutory exceptions dealing specifically with circumstances intended to be covered by this exception. However, in *Libyan Arab Foreign Bank* v *Bankers Trust Co.* ([1988] 1 Lloyd's Rep 259) the case concerned the United States Presidential Order of 8 January 1986 freezing Libyan assets under the control of overseas branches of US banks. The case arose because Bankers Trust in New York had discussions with the Federal Reserve Board on 8 January about Libyan Arab foreign bank accounts. One of the claims made by the plaintiffs involved the scope of the duty of confidentiality and the bank relied on three of the four *Tournier* exceptions, including duty to the public to disclose. Staughton J rejected the first two grounds for justifying disclosure but said:

> 'But presuming (as I must) the New York law on this point is the same as English law, it seems to me that the Federal Reserve Board, as the central banking system in the United States, may have a public duty to perform in obtaining information from banks.'

Where the interests of the bank require disclosure

This exception is illustrated by Bankes LJ in the *Tournier* case as involving a situation where the bank is involved in litigation against the bank, e.g. where it seeks to recover the amount of an overdraft. In *Sunderland* v *Barclays Bank Ltd* ((1938) *The*

Times, 25 November) the bank dishonoured the plaintiff's cheque because there were insufficient funds in her account. The real reason in fact was because she had to the knowledge of the bank been betting. The plaintiff complained to the husband and on his advice the plaintiff telephoned the bank. In the course of the plaintiff's complaints the husband interrupted the telephone conversation and continued to complain on behalf of the plaintiff. The bank then informed the husband that most of the cheques passing through the plaintiff's account were drawn in favour of bookmakers and the bank did not therefore consider the account suitable for an overdraft. Du Parcq LJ took the view that in the circumstances the interests of the bank required disclosure and because the husband took over the complaint the bank had to give him a reason for its policy. The judge also said that the plaintiff had given implied consent to disclose information regarding her account by allowing her husband to interfere in her banking affairs.

In *XAG* v *A Bank* ([1983] 2 All ER 464) and *FDC & Co. Ltd* v *The Chase Manhattan Bank NA* (unreported) it was held that disclosure by the respective banks of certain customers would not be justified on the ground that orders under subpoena granted in the USA had been made. The customers were therefore granted interlocutory injunctions to restrain banks from making disclosure on the ground that the nature of 'interest' justifying disclosure in the *Tournier* case was of a different character from that in the present cases.

Where the disclosure is with the express or implied consent of the customer

Under the *Tournier* case the customer may give express or implied consent to the bank to make disclosure. It is advisable for a bank to seek the express consent in writing and if a customer fails to respond to a request for consent the bank should not assume that consent is given. The courts are likely to demand that consent is freely given by the exercise of an independent and uncoerced judgment.

Recommendations for reform of the duty of confidentiality

The Jack Committee (Cm. 622, published February 1989) on banking services examined the rules on banker–customer confidentiality and recommended considerable changes to the law.

The Committee recommended that the rule in the *Tournier* case should be consolidated in statute and that the opportunity should be taken to update the law. The other main recommendations related to the exceptions to the *Tournier* case, namely:

(a) The exceptions relating to disclosure under compulsion of law should be consolidated in the legislation so that disclosure under the statutory provisions would be under a single statute.

(b) The exception allowing disclosure on grounds of public policy should no longer be recognised. The Committee took the view that this exception had lost much of its effect due to the statutory exceptions to the *Tournier* case and that it was difficult to imagine circumstances in which the general exception might apply.

(c) Where disclosure is required in the interest of the bank it should be limited to the following situations:

(i) in the event of legal action to which the bank is a party;

(ii) disclosure between banking companies within the same group provided the disclosure is for defined purposes and not merely for marketing banking services generally. Disclosure of confidential information should be limited to what is necessary for the purposes of protecting the bank and its banking subsidiaries against loss in relation to the provision of normal banking services. This view is not in keeping with the *Bank of Tokyo* v *Karoon* ([1984] 1 AC 45) where it was held that each corporate entity within the banking group must be viewed as a separate entity for the purposes of the duty of confidentiality;

(iii) disclosure may be permitted in connection with the sale of the bank or a substantial part of its undertaking.

(d) Disclosure should only be permitted with the express consent of the customer.

Disclosure to credit reference agencies

The Jack Report dealt with the question of disclosure to credit reference agencies at considerable length. Such agencies are governed by the Consumer Credit Act 1974 and s. 145(8) provides that a credit reference agent is:

'a person carrying on a business comprising the furnishing of persons with information relevant to the financial standing of individuals, being information collected by the agency for that purpose.'

Until recently banks have been able to use information available to such agencies but not to contribute information to such agencies. In May 1988, an agreement was reached by the banks and credit reference agencies under which (for a one-year trial period) the banks would make available information about customers in default. There is, however, a difference of policy between banks in referrals to credit reference agencies, and in a lecture given to the Chartered Institute of Bankers (29 November 1988) the Governor of the Bank of England said:

'I hope that, even if it had to await a change in the law, the banks and all other lenders will consider very carefully whether they cannot provide more data, subject of course to proper safeguards about its confidentiality. That, it seems to me, will be an essential step towards ensuring that the consumer credit industry operates in the interests of the lenders, of the borrowers, and thus the community as a whole.'

The extent of disclosure was also of concern to the Jack Committee, i.e. whether disclosure should be restricted to customers in default (black information) or whether it should be extended to information generally (white information) about customers not in default. It is difficult to envisage the disclosure of white information about a customer being justified under the *Tournier* exceptions. The President of the Chartered Institute of Bankers in an article in *Banking World* of November 1988 said:

'... the further step of providing "white information" on all customer borrowing was more problematical ... Market research had shown that a high proportion of customers might refuse permission for such disclosure if asked to consent to it voluntarily.'

The Government White Paper on Banking Services

The White Paper on Banking Services accepted many of the recommendations of the Jack Committee on the *Tournier* case but the White Paper specifically rejected the idea of consolidating the *Tournier* rule. The proposal that the second exception to the rule (disclosure in the interests of the public) should no longer be recognised is also rejected. The White Paper recommends that in case of default the bank should be able to disclose information about the customer to credit reference agencies and information should be available within the banking group so that disclosure may be made for marketing purposes. However, information about a customer who is in credit should only be passed to credit reference agencies with the consent of the customer. Finally, the White Paper recommends that the scope of the duty of confidentiality should be fully explained to customers.

The draft Code of Banking Practice

The draft Code adopted the recommendation of the White Paper and incorporated the *Tournier* rule and the exceptions to it. The draft Code accepted that banks owe a strict duty of confidentiality but took the view that disclosure where the customer is in default could be justified to credit reference agencies as in the interests of the bank. The draft Code then added two further exceptions:

(a) disclosure may be permitted within the banking group in order to protect the bank, or its subsidiaries in order to prevent loss or fraud to the group;

(b) disclosure may be permitted within the group so that banking, financial and investment information can be provided to a customer appropriate to his needs.

The draft Code provides that banks will exercise restraint when marketing their services to customers who are minors and when marketing loans and overdrafts.

The Code of Banking Practice

The Code of Banking Practice came into force on 16 March 1992. It adopts the *Tournier* rule as originally established. The Code does not adopt the two additional exceptions established in the White Paper and accepted in the draft Code (i.e. disclosure may be permitted to a credit reference agency where the customer is in default and in order to prevent loss to the group). The Code does provide that disclosure for marketing purposes cannot be justified as being in the interests of the bank. The Code requires the banks to explain the effect of the Data Protection Act 1984 and the customer's right to access files kept on computer tape.

The Data Protection Act 1984

The Data Protection Act was passed to give effect to the 'Convention for the Protection of Individuals with Regard to Automatic Processing of Personal Data.' The Act gives an individual to whom information processed by computer (personal data) relates the right to have access to that data, challenge the data and claim compensation for damage and any associated distress arising from loss, inaccuracy or unauthorised destruction or disclosure of that data. The obligation on data users to follow proper procedure in relation to their use of the data is laid down in the eight Data Protection Principles. Principle 1 states 'the information to be contained in personal data should be obtained and personal data processed, fairly and lawfully.'

Subpoenas from other jurisdictions

Foreign courts can serve a subpoena on local offices of international banks in order to obtain information relating to the overseas branches. The bank may, if it refuses to comply with the subpoena, find itself in contempt of court, or by obeying it, find it has infringed the secrecy laws of the country in which the information is maintained. In *XAG* v *A Bank* ([1983] 2 All ER 464) the plaintiffs (X), a multinational company incorporated under Swiss law and based in Switzerland, and Y, an American subsidiary of X incorporated in Switzerland but with a major branch in New York, were concerned with oil marketing. Both had accounts with the London branch of an American bank. A Grand Jury subpoena was served on the bank to produce all documents relating to the accounts maintained by the plaintiffs at the London branch. The bank declared its intention to comply with the subpoena and the plaintiffs obtained an injunction in the High Court to restrain the bank from producing the documents on grounds of breach of confidentiality. An order was then obtained in New York requiring the bank to comply with the subpoena. The plaintiffs brought proceedings in the High Court to continue the injunction until trial.

The court held that the accounts of the company were opened and maintained in London and English law governed the banker–customer relationship. In determining whether the injunction should be continued the court had to determine the balance of convenience with regard to:

(a) the fact that the order of the New York court would take effect in London in breach of both a private interest (the contract between the bank and customer) and the public interest in maintaining the duty of secrecy;

(b) the fact that the New York court would not treat the bank as in contempt for complying with the injunction issued by the English court which had jurisdiction over the branch where the account was maintained;

(c) the fact that to allow the order of the New York court to be enforced would involve giving a measure of assistance which would involve the UK court in tolerating a breach of the duty of confidentiality which it would in normal circumstances enforce.

Letters of request

Letters of request or letters rogatory involve a request for information made by a foreign court which is seeking information to the court in the place where the records are maintained, or in order to obtain information without infringing the sovereignty of the foreign state. Letters of request are regulated by the Hague Convention on the

Taking of Evidence in Civil or Commercial Matters 1970. This led to the passing of the Evidence (Proceedings in Other Jurisdictions) Act 1975 and enables an English court to make an order for the obtaining of evidence in civil proceedings in other courts or tribunals upon a request from that court or tribunal.

Duty to exercise reasonable skill and care

The existence of an implied contractual duty of care owed by the bank to the customer has been examined in the context of the performance of the mandate, the giving of advice and the taking and execution of security.

In *Westminster Bank Ltd* v *Hilton* ([1926] 43 TLR 124) Atkin LJ and Bankes LJ pronounced:

'I think it is the duty of the bank, arising out of the contract, to exercise reasonable care and skill in dealing with the communications which the customer sends to [him] in relation to his banking business.'

With regard to the banker–customer relationship the learned judges said:

'... in essence it is a contractual relationship which involves, I think, the duty of the bank to take reasonable care in the carrying-out for its customer of its customer's business.'

Banks are also under a statutory duty of care under s. 13 of the Supply of Goods Act 1982. The section provides:

'In a contract for the supply of a service where the supplier is acting in the course of a business, there is an implied term that the supplier will carry out the service with reasonable care and skill.'

Although the 1982 Act does not apply in Scotland the common law has similar effect. The duty of care imposed on banks has been examined in a number of recent cases.

Karak Rubber Co Ltd v *Burden* (No. 2) [1972] 1 All ER 210

The defendants, *Barclays Bank Ltd*, were party to the payment, by means of a bankers draft, of £98,954 in circumstances in which it was alleged that the members of the bank staff involved in the transaction should have realised that the payment was for the purpose of, or related to, the purchase of a company of its own shares. This being illegal under the companies legislation an action was brought against the bank for replacement of the amount or damages for negligence.

The bank was liable for breach of contract. Brightman J said that in exercising the duty of care the question which must be answered is:

'whether the banker is to exercise reasonable care and skill in transacting the customer's banking business, including the making of such enquiries as may, in given circumstances, be appropriate and practical if the banker has, or a reasonable banker would have, grounds for believing that the authorised signatories are misusing their authority for the purpose of defrauding their principal or otherwise defeating his true intentions.'

In *Selangor United Rubber Estates Ltd* v *Cradock and Others* (*No. 3*) ([1968] 2 All ER 1073) a bank provided financial assistance in connection with a takeover bid and because of the inexperience of its officers it failed to realise that a company which was its customer was indirectly financing the purchase of its own shares. The court held that an agent who assists in bringing about the disposal of trust property in breach of trust will be personally liable if he either knew or ought to have known about the breach of trust. Ungoed-Thomas J (*obiter*) approved the extent of the duty of care applied in *Hilton* v *Westminster Bank Ltd* and said:

'... a bank has a duty under its contract with its customer to exercise "reasonable care and skill" in carrying out its part with regard to operations within its contract with its customer. The standard of that reasonable care and skill is an objective standard applicable to bankers. Whether it has been attained in any particular case has to be decided in the light of all the relevant facts, which can vary infinitely.'

Attempts to limit the effect of Selangor United Rubber Estates Ltd *v* Cradock and Others *and* Karak Rubber Co. Ltd *v* Burden

In *Lipkin Gorman* v *Karpnale Ltd* & *Lloyds Bank plc* ([1988] 1 WLR 987) the Court of Appeal criticised the *Selangor* and *Karak* cases as imposing too high a duty of care on the paying bank. May LJ qualified the duty of care imposed on the paying bank and said:

'The relationship between the parties is contractual. The principal obligation is upon the bank to honour its customers' cheques in accordance with its mandate or instructions. There is nothing in such a contract, express or implied, which could require a banker to consider the commercial wisdom or otherwise of the particular transaction. Nor is there normally any express term in the contract requiring the banker to exercise any degree of care in deciding whether to honour a customer's cheque which his instructions require him to pay. In my opinion any implied term requiring the banker to exercise any degree of care must be limited.'

In *Barclays Bank plc* v *Quincecare Ltd* ([1988] 1 FTLR 507) Steyn J noted that the observations on the duty of care in *Lipkin Gorman* were made in the context of a banker transferring money from the customer's current account. He recognised that a balance has to be struck between the bank conforming to its customer's mandate and at the same time ensuring that the bank remains within the ambit of the duty of care. It is therefore a sensible comprise to say that the bank must 'refrain from executing an order if and for so long as the bank was "put on inquiry" in the sense that he had reasonable grounds (although not proof) for believing that the order was an attempt to misappropriate the funds of the company. And the likely external standard of the perception of an ordinary prudent banker was the governing one. That was not too high a standard.'

Unsuccessful attempts to impose a duty of care
In two recent cases the courts have held that the bank is not liable for a breach of the contractual duty of care. In *Schioler* v *Westminster Bank Ltd* ([1970] 2 QB 719) the court held the bank was not in breach of its duty to exercise reasonable care when the

plaintiff had to pay UK income tax on dividend payments received by the bank for her from a Malaysian company. The court held that to place the defendant under an obligation to consult the plaintiff or her accountants because of possible tax repercussions would place an impossible burden on banks.

More recently in *Redmond Bank v Allied Irish Banks plc* ([1987] FLR 307) it was held that a bank is not under a duty of care to advise or warn a customer of the inherent risks of dealing with cheques which are crossed 'not negotiable'. The plaintiff deposited a number of cheques in his account which were crossed 'Not negotiable – account payee only', and which were apparently indorsed generally on the back by the named payee. In fact the cheques had been placed in circulation through fraud, to which the plaintiff was not a party, and the defendant bank eventually settled an action for wrongful conversion which had been brought against it by the drawer of the cheques. In turn, the defendant debited the plaintiff's account with the face value of the cheques which he had deposited in his account. The plaintiff brought an action against the defendant bank to recover, by way of damages for negligence, sums debited from his account. The court held there is no duty on the bank to advise or warn a customer of the risks of dealing with cheques crossed 'not negotiable'.

Saville J (pp. 309–310) took the view that unlike a bank's duty to exercise reasonable care and skill in interpreting, ascertaining and acting on a customer's instructions, which was clearly established (see *Selangor United Rubber Estates Ltd v Cradock and Others (No. 3)* and *Karak Rubber Co. Ltd v Burden (No. 2)*), it was not necessary to impose a duty on the bank to warn customers of the risks of 'that which they wanted to do in order to give contractual efficacy to the contractual relationship between bank and customer.'

With the exception of the *Tournier* case the Jack Committee on Banking Services felt that the duties owed by the bank to its customers were sufficiently well established so as not to require statutory intervention. It also took the view that the common law allowed the desired flexibility for the development of the rules.

It must be remembered that banks owe a general duty of care and that it is imposed on the paying bank. The Jack Committee questioned whether the duty of care imposed on the paying bank was sufficient to meet the needs of modern day society. It came to the conclusion that the existing statutory and common law were adequate. Although the position in Scotland is somewhat different, where the Supply of Goods and Services Act 1982 does not apply, the common law has a similar effect in imposing a duty of care.

DUTY TO ACCOUNT

The bank is under a duty to render accounts to its customers either periodically (e.g. every three months), or on demand. Failure to render an account will entitle the customer to demand repayment of any balance on his account and then (if necessary) to sue for debt.

The real point of interest with regard to the bank's duty to render an account is whether the customer can rely on any credit balance of his account as shown in bank statements supplied by the bank. A situation of this sort arises where the bank under a mistake credits the customer's account with larger credit balances than those actually due to the customer, or the bank – due to an error – fails to debit the customer's account with a payment made from the account.

Holland v *Manchester and Liverpool District Banking Co* (1909) 25 TLR 386

The plaintiff had an account with the defendant bank. On 21 September 1907, the passbook showed a credit entry of approximately £70 17s 9d. The plaintiff, relying on the credit balance, issued a cheque for approximately £67 11s, in payment of a trade debt. On presentation, the cheque was dishonoured by the bank on the grounds that the actual credit balance on the account was only £60 5s 9d; a credit for £10 12s having been entered twice due to a mistake. Although the bank apologised for its mistake when the fact of the dishonour became known to other suppliers the plaintiff was refused credit. The plaintiff brought an action for damages.

The jury assessed the damages to £100, subject to the decision of the court on whether or not the plaintiff was entitled to draw the cheque in such circumstances. On that point the court held that although the effect of an entry in a passbook did not appear to have been clearly resolved in the courts, and although in this case the bank was entitled to have the passbook rectified, the customer was entitled to rely on the bank's statement of the customer's account, as appearing in the passbook, until the erroneous entry was corrected. The passbook being merely *prima facie* evidence of the credit balance standing in favour of the customer's account, the statement can be relied on by the customer until the mistaken entry is corrected.

The bank does not have an absolute right to have an error of this nature corrected, although in the *Holland* case that was actually permitted. The court clearly followed *Commercial Bank of Scotland* v *Rhind* ((1860) 3 Mac. 643) where it was held that a credit entry in a passbook is clearly *prima facie* evidence against the bank which the bank is entitled to have corrected, regardless of the customer's genuine actions by relying on it.

The question which has to be asked is whether the bank will be prevented from having the passbook corrected if the only detriment suffered by the customer is that he has spent the money the bank seeks to recover. In *Larner* v *L.C.C.* ([1947] 2 KB 114) Lord Denning said:

'Speaking generally, the fact that the recipient has spent the money beyond recall is no defence unless there was some fault – as, for instance, breach of duty – on the part of the paymaster and none on the part of the recipient.'

However, in *Holt* v *Markham* ([1923] 1 KB 504) where estoppel was one of the grounds for the decision against the bank the court held:

'The plaintiffs represented to the defendant that he was entitled to a certain sum of money and paid it, and after a lapse of time sufficient to enable any mistake to be rectified he acted upon that representation and spent the money. That is a case to which the ordinary rule of estoppel applies.'

In *Skyring* v *Greenwood & Cox* ((1825) 4 B & C 281) the plaintiff was the administratrix of Major Skyring and the defendants were paymasters of the Royal Artillery. Over a considerable period of time, and in error, the defendants had credited the customer's account with sums in excess of his salary. When the error was discovered the defendants sought to recover the excess of the payments. The customer died in December 1822, and the defendants rendered an account to the plaintiff, by debiting the excess of the credit balances. The plaintiff challenged the right to debit the account with the amount of the mistaken payments. The court held:

'It is of great importance to any man ... that they should not be led to suppose their annual income is greater than it really is. Every prudent man accommodates his mode of living to what he supposes to be his income; it therefore works a great prejudice to any man, if after having had credit given to him in account for certain sums, and having been allowed to draw on his agent on the faith that those sums belonged to him, he may be called upon to pay them back.'

The belief of the customer as to the accuracy of the statement is essential, so that if he is aware of the bank's error, the bank will not be estopped from rectifying the error. In *British and North European Bank Ltd* v *Zalstein* ([1927] 2 KB 92) the bank had credited the customer's account with £2,000 to conceal his excessive borrowing from the bank's auditors. The account was later debited with the same amount, neither entry being known to the customer until he received a statement. When the customer was sued for the amount of the overdraft, he claimed that the credit formed a payment to him which the bank was not entitled to debit. The court rejected the customer's claim and held that the credit and debit entries were merely book entries and to claim a book entry as a payment some other circumstance had to be present (e.g. some express authority to pay or some other communication of the making of the entry and some conduct in pursuance of it).

Thus, the bank is only estopped from disputing the accuracy of the statements of account where the customer honestly believes the statement to be correct and acts on it. In *United Overseas Bank* v *Jiwani* ([1976] 1 WLR 964) the defendant, a resident in Uganda, had an account with the plaintiffs, a Swiss bank in Geneva. In October 1972, his credit balance in the account was $10,000 and the bank received a telex from a bank in Zurich instructing that $11,000 had been paid to the customer's credit and his account should be credited appropriately. Subsequently, the Geneva bank received written confirmation of the telex transmission which it erroneously treated as a further credit payment to the defendant's account. The defendant, who was in the process of buying a hotel issued two cheques for the full amount of the credit balance, including the mistaken entry for the second $11,000. When the plaintiffs discovered the mistake they sought to recover the amount of the overdraft of $11,000.

The court held that the bank could recover the amount. Mackenna J held that if a bank is to be estopped from recovering amounts wrongfully credited to the account of a customer the following three conditions must be satisfied:

(a) that the bank was under a duty to give the customer accurate information about the state of his account, and that in breach of that duty it gave him inaccurate information, or that there was some other misrepresention made about the state of the account for which the bank was responsible;

(b) the customer must show that the inaccurate information misled him about the credit balance on his account, and this caused him to believe that the plaintiffs were his debtors for a larger sum than was actually the case; and

(c) the customer must show that because of his mistaken belief he changed his position in a way which makes it inequitable to require him to repay the money wrongly credited to him.

The court went on to say that the customer who seeks to raise estoppel against the bank must show that he relied on the statement of account and also that he would not have acted in the manner he did unless he honestly believed his credit balance to be as represented by the bank. In the *Jawani* case the bank was not estopped from debiting the customer's account because he could not show that he entered into the transaction in reliance on the statement of account. The facts were such that the customer would have entered into the negotiations in any event and his entering into the transaction was not effected by the mistake credit balance, which a reasonable man would have realised to be a mistake made by the bank.

DUTIES OWED BY THE CUSTOMER TO THE BANK

The customer owes certain duties to the bank with which it has entered into a contractual relationship. In addition to an obligation to repay on demand any sums overdrawn on the current account and the duty to pay reasonable charges for the services of the bank, if no charge has been agreed, the customer owes a number of 'self-regarding' duties, i.e. failure to conform to these duties will prevent the customer from enforcing his rights against the bank. Evidence submitted to the Jack Committee indicated that there was a considerable body of opinion that felt that the *Tai Hing* case demonstrated the extent of the inequity in the duties owed by the customer to the bank. However, the Committee rejected the proposal that legislation should be introduced which had the effect of imposing a statutory duty on customers to examine their bank statements. Instead the Committee recommended that legislation should be enacted whereby in an action for debt or damages arising from an unauthorised payment, the bank may raise the defence of contributory negligence. It would be for the courts to interpret the general provision in a variety of situations. Mere failure to check a bank statement should not in itself amount to contributory negligence.

The self-regarding duties owed by the customer to his bank are considered below.

Duty to notify the bank of known forgeries

Greenwood v *Martins Bank Ltd* [1933] AC 51

A husband and wife had a joint account with the defendant bank. Subsequently, that account was closed and an account was opened in the sole name of the husband, the wife having no authority to draw cheques on the account. The wife had repeatedly forged her husband's signature on the joint account and she continued to forge his name on the account opened by her husband in his own name. During the currency of the sole account the husband became aware of the forgeries. The husband did not notify the bank of the forgeries for eight months. When he did notify the bank his wife committed suicide. The husband brought an action against the bank to recover the sums paid against the forged cheques.

The court held that the plaintiff owed a duty to the defendants to disclose the forgeries when he became aware of them so as to enable the defendants to take steps to recover the amounts wrongfully paid on the forged cheques. The plaintiff was estopped from recovering the amount of the forged cheques because of his failure to notify the bank on discovery of the forgeries. Lord Tomlin (p. 58) said:

> 'The appellant's silence, therefore, was deliberate and intended to produce the effect which it in fact produced – namely, the leaving of the respondents in ignorance of the true facts so that no action might be taken by them against the appellant's wife. The deliberate abstention from speaking in those circumstances seems to me to amount to a representation to the respondents that the forged cheques were in fact in order, and assuming that detriment to the respondents followed there were, it seems to me, present all the elements essential to estoppel. Further, I do not think that it is any answer to say that if the respondents had not been negligent initially the detriment would not have occurred.'

The customer's duty to notify the bank of forgeries in respect of his account only applies to known forgeries. Failure to notify the bank will mean that the customer cannot later sue the bank for recovery of the amounts debited from his account. Moreover, the customer cannot make the bank liable in contributory negligence for a failure to detect the forgeries.

In *Morison* v *London County and Westminster Bank Ltd* ([1914] 3 KB 356) the bank's customer had for a considerable time known of the forged cheques being presented against her account. The bank on several occasions made enquires concerning the genuineness of the cheques and the customer on each occasion represented the cheques to be validly drawn by her. It was held that the bank was entitled to debit her account with the amount of the cheques when her son challenged the debits. A customer of a bank who discovers forgeries against his account owes a duty to notify the bank for two reasons:

(a) to safeguard against further forged cheques or other instruments being paid; and
(b) to enable the bank to take steps towards recovering the amounts wrongfully paid against the forged cheques or other instruments.

Similarly, in *Brown* v *Westminster Bank Ltd* ([1964] 2 LR 187) it was held that the customer was estopped from setting up forgeries of her cheques against the bank when she had actually represented to the bank on several occasions that the cheques were genuine. In *London Intercontinental Trust Ltd* v *Barclays Bank Ltd* ([1980] 1 Lloyd's Rep 241) (see p. 102) the court again held that the knowledge of the company that cheques were being improperly drawn on its bank account prevented it from later bringing an action against the bank to recover the amounts of two cheques.

In *Lewes Sanitary Steam Laundry Co. Ltd* v *Barclays & Co. Ltd* ((1906) 11 Cm Cas 255) the secretary of a company forged a number of cheques on the company's account. When the forgeries were discovered the company brought an action against the bank to recover the amount of the forged cheques. It was alleged that the company had been negligent in the appointment of its secretary and in the security of its books, including cheque forms. The action failed and the court held that the estoppel must be immediate or in connection with the transaction in order to succeed. In *Kepitigalla Rubber Estates Ltd* v *National Bank of India Ltd* ([1909] 2 KB 1010) the secretary of a company over a period of some months forged cheques and received payment on those cheques. In an action against the bank to recover the amounts of the forged cheques it was said that the company was not under a duty to organise its business affairs in such a way so that forgery could not take place.

To draw cheques in such a way so as not to facilitate fraud

London Joint Stock Bank Ltd v *Macmillan and Others* [1918] AC 777

A clerk, employed by the defendants, was entrusted with the duty of filling in cheques for the signature of one of the partners. The clerk presented a cheque for £2 to one of the partners and obtained his signature on it. The clerk subsequently altered the amount of the cheque by inserting the figures '1' before and '0' after the figure £2. He also inserted the words 'one hundred and twenty pounds' on the cheque. The bank debited the partnership account with the amount of the altered cheque and the firm brought an action against the bank contending that the bank could only debit their account with the sum of £2.

The House of Lords held that the bank could debit the full amount of the altered cheque. The House held that there is a duty on the customer, in drawing cheques, to take reasonable precautions against forgery and that the fraudulent alteration was the direct result of a breach of that duty. Lord Finlay LC said:

'... it is beyond dispute that the customer is bound to exercise reasonable care in drawing the cheque to prevent a banker being misled. If he draws the cheque in a manner which facilitates fraud, he is guilty of a breach of duty as between himself and the banker, and he will be responsible to the banker for any loss sustained by the banker as a natural and direct consequence of this breach of duty ... If the cheque is drawn in such a way as to facilitate or almost to invite an increase in the amount by forgery if the cheque should get into the hands of a dishonest person, forgery is not a remote but a very natural consequence of negligence ...'

The House of Lords applied the principle laid down in *Young* v *Grote* ((1827) 4 Bing 253) where it was said that a customer who draws an incomplete cheque leaving its completion to an agent cannot object to the bank debiting him with the full amount fraudulently entered on the cheque even if this is done by way of alteration. The decision also imposed a wider duty of care to ensure that when the customer signs the cheque he does not leave spaces facilitating fraud.

Refusal to extend the customer's duties

The courts have refused to extend the application of the duty to draw cheques in such a way so as not to facilitate fraud and in *Slingsby* v *District Bank Ltd* ([1932] 1 KB 544) the bank was held not entitled to debit the customer's account when the customer had left certain blank spaces on the cheque form which enabled a fraudulent solicitor to insert the words 'per Cumberbirch and Potts' after the name of the payee and before the words 'or order' printed on the cheque form. The court said that the form of the alteration was such that it could not reasonably be anticipated that the cheque would be altered in the way it was.

More recently, in *Tai Hing Ltd* v *Lui Hing Bank* ([1986] 1 AC 80) the Privy Council refused to extend the scope of the duties owed by the customer to include a duty to take reasonable care to operate his bank account.

In that case it was argued that a Hong Kong company could not bring an action against three banks with which it maintained current accounts and from which approximately HK$6,000,000 had been debited by the banks against cheques which were subsequently discovered to be forgeries. When the frauds were discovered and the customer brought an action to recover the amounts paid against the forged cheques, the banks argued that the company had been negligent in failing to supervise the activities of their clerks and in not checking their monthly bank statements. The Hong Kong Court of Appeal accepted the argument of the banks. In rejecting the claim of the company the court said:

> 'After a great deal of hesitation, I find myself finally led to the conclusion that, in the world in which we live today, it is a necessary condition of the relation of the banker and customer that the customer should take reasonable care to see that in the operation of the account the bank is not injured.'

On appeal the Privy Council emphasised that the duties owed by the customer to the bank (in the absence of express agreement) were (a) a duty to notify the bank of forgeries; and (b) a duty to draw a cheque in such a way so as not to facilitate fraud. The express terms of the banking contracts were not sufficiently clear and unambiguous to impose on the company a contractual obligation to examine its bank statements and to accept them as accurately stating the amount of the debits. Lord Scarman said:

> 'The argument for the banks is, when analysed, no more than that the obligation of care placed on banks in the management of a customer's account which the courts have recognised have become so burdensome that they should be met by a reciprocal increase of responsibility on the customer ... They [banks] can increase the severity of their terms of business, and they can use their influence, as they have in the past, to seek to persuade the legislature that they should be granted by statute further protection. But it does not follow that because they may need protection as their business expands the necessary incidents of their relationship with their customer must also change. The business of banking is the business not of the customer but of the bank.'

The rule confirmed in the *Tai Hing* case is one of long standing. In *Chatterton* v *London & County Banking Co. Ltd* (*The Times*, 21 January 1891) Lord Esher MR said that customers were not bound to examine their passbooks. The rule has been applied in several cases since. In the *Tai Hing* case the Privy Council approved the judgment of Bray J in *Kepitigalla Rubber Estate Ltd* v *National Bank of India Ltd* ([1909] 2 KB 1010) where the judge said 'while it is the duty of a customer in issuing his mandates (i.e. his cheques) to the bank to take reasonable care not to mislead the bank, there is no duty on the part of the customer to take precautions in the general course of carrying on his business to prevent forgeries on the part of his servants.'

In *London Intercontinental Trust Ltd* v *Barclays Bank Ltd* ([1980] 1 Lloyd's Rep 241) the company mandate required cheques to be signed by two directors. In fact cheques were only signed by one director and paid by the bank. The plaintiff company sought to recover the amounts of two cheques drawn by only one director. The action failed on the grounds that the company had approved and later ratified the transaction in respect of which the cheques were drawn. The court said that although the company owed no duty to the bank to examine its passbooks, the fact that it had so examined them and failed to notify the bank of the breach of mandate was a representation that the cheques were properly drawn. In *Wealdon Woodlands (Kent) Ltd* v *National Westminster Bank Ltd* ((1983) 133 NLJ 719) McNeill J said that in the absence of legislative intervention no duty would be imposed on the customer to check his bank statements. Failure to verify such statements would not be breach of duty to the bank.

In *Burnett* v *Westminster Bank Ltd* ([1966] 1 QB 742) the court held that a customer does not owe a duty to abstain from altering the printed parts of the cheque forms issued to him. In that case a customer held two accounts with two branches of the same bank and because he had no cheque forms from one of the branches where he maintained an account, he substituted the name and address of the branch from which he had received cheque forms with the name and address of the other branch. It was held that the cheque could be validly countermanded by notifying the substituted branch although the cheque never reached that branch – it having been sent to the branch whose details appeared in magnetic ink at the bottom of the cheque and that branch not having received the countermand paid it on presentation.

The unwillingness of the courts to extend the scope of duties owed by the customer to his bank has resulted in the banks imposing express duties on their customers. In the *Tai Hing* case the banks' attempt to impose on the customer an obligation to verify bank statements and to notify them of any errors within a certain time was unsuccessful. The Privy Council held:

> 'If banks wish to impose upon their customers an express obligation to examine their monthly statements and to make those statements, in the absence of query, unchallengeable by the customer after expiry of a time limit, the burden of the objection and of the sanction imposed must be brought home to the customer. In their Lordships' view the provisions which they have set out above do not meet this undoubtedly rigourous test.'

It should also be remembered that if clauses limiting or excluding liability have been incorporated into the contract their validity will be subject to the Unfair Contract Terms Act 1977.

DUTY OF THE BANK IN TORT

A bank owes a duty, in tort, to the customer to exercise proper skill and care in carrying out any business it agrees to transact. A bank also owes a duty of care to such persons with whom it has a a 'special relationship'.

Hedley Byrne & Co. Ltd v *Heller and Partners Ltd* [1963] 2 All ER 575

The plaintiffs, advertising agents, enquired through their bank, the National Provincial Bank in Bishopsgate, as to the credit of their clients, Easipower Ltd, who banked with the defendant merchant bank. Satisfactory replies were given to two such enquiries, and the plaintiffs, relying on these, placed orders for advertising space in connection with which they lost £17,000 on the liquidation of Easipower Ltd. The defendants had given credit references about Easipower Ltd only after disclaiming liability for negligent advice. McNair J held that the bank had been negligent, but quite apart from the disclaimer, he was bound by precedent to hold that a bank was not liable from loss resulting from mere statements of this kind even if the bank had been negligent. His judgment was affirmed by the Court of Appeal.

The House of Lords held that if a person such as a banker on receiving a request for information or advice in circumstances that show that his skill or expertise is being relied on, gives information or advice without a disclaimer of liability, he will owe a duty of care even if he is not under a contractual or fiduciary duty to the person enquiring. If such a person is liable in negligence an action in damages may be brought. Lord Devlin said (pp. 528–529):

> '... the categories of special relationships, which may give rise to a duty to take care in word as well as in deed, are not limited to contractual relationships, but include also relationships which, in the words of Lord Shaw in *Nocton* v *Lord Ashburton*, are 'equivalent to contract,' that is where there is an assumption of responsibility in circumstances in which, but for the absence of consideration, there would be a contract.'

However, in *Hedley Byrne & Co. Ltd* the bank's disclaimer was held to be sufficient and no liability arose.

The extent of the duty to exercise care, in tort, will depend on the extent of banking services offered by the bank in the course of its business.

McInerny v *Lloyds Bank Ltd* [1973] 2 Lloyd's Rep 389

A bank manager made certain statements in a telex message to his customer. At the customer's request the bank manager repeated the telex message to the plaintiff, with whom the customer was doing business. The plaintiff brought an action in negligence based in part on those statements.

The court held that the action in negligence did not succeed. An action in negligence will lie where either the statement is addressed to the plaintiff directly or through some

E

other person, or formulated for the benefit of anyone in the position of the plaintiff to whom it might be communicated, but the court must be cautious in drawing the same conclusion in a case where the statement has been addressed to a particular person concerning his affairs, even if it is likely to be shown to a third party.

It is a question of fact to be decided in each individual case whether a particular undertaking is within the scope of the bank's business. Although a bank must provide certain minimum services there is no limit on the extent of services it might undertake voluntarily or at the request of the customer. The standard of care expected from them will be that reasonably expected from officials of that standing and competence. In *Woods* v *Martins Bank Ltd* ([1959] 1 QB 55) the manager of the defendant bank agreed to act as financial adviser to the plaintiff. The plaintiff, relying on advice given by the bank manager, invested a substantial amount of money in a company which also maintained a business connection with the defendant bank. To the knowledge of the bank the company had a substantial overdraft on which the bank's head-office was pressing for payment. The investments were made at a time when the company was in fact in financial difficulties and the plaintiff eventually lost a considerable amount of money. The court held that there was a fiduciary duty between the parties which imposed on the bank a duty to exercise reasonable care. On the facts, the court held there were no reasonable grounds on which the bank could have advised the plaintiff that the company was in a strong financial position and that investment in the company was a wise undertaking.

In *Box* v *Midland Bank Ltd* ([1972] 2 Lloyd's Rep 391) the plaintiff was anxious to obtain additional finance in order to enable a company he controlled to carry out a contract. The manager of the Wells branch of the defendant bank informed him that he would like to make the advance but it required the approval of his regional head-office. The manager also advised the plaintiff that if an ECGD policy was obtained, the approval from head-office would be a mere formality. The manager failed to advise between an ECGD policy which was available and an ECGD Bankers' Guarantee (Bills and Notes) policy which was not available. The application for the loan was submitted and the manager forwarded the ECGD quotation for the comprehensive policy. The head-office refused to approve the loan. The plaintiff subsequently applied for the Bankers' Guarantee policy but this was refused. The plaintiff became bankrupt and brought an action against the bank claiming damages around £250,000 for negligence on the grounds that the manager made careless statements about the availability of finance. The court held that a duty of care was owed to the customer arising under the law of negligence. The manager was not obliged to predict the outcome of the plaintiff's application to head-office, but having chosen to do so, he was under a duty to take reasonable care since he knew that the prediction would be relied upon.

In the *Woods* case the court looked at the bank's advertising leaflets and booklets and concluded that giving investment advice was within the scope of the bank's business. The bank had relied on *Banbury* v *Bank of Montreal* ([1918] AC 626) where the House of Lords had held that giving such advice was outside the scope of banking business.

The *Woods* case was decided in 1959. There can be no doubt that in the 1990s the giving of financial advice would be within the scope of the bank's business and a duty of care would be owed to the customer. However, until *Box* v *Midland Bank Ltd* it was unsettled whether a bank is under a duty of care to fulfil any non-contractual assurance given by a bank to its customers when there is a likelihood that such assurances will be relied upon by the customer, e.g. where a bank provides that it will provide overdraft facilities in the future (without a contract bring entered into immediately) and the customer alters his position by entering into commitments he would not otherwise have undertaken. In such a situation the bank may, however, find itself estopped from denying the effects of its representation (see *Fleming* v *New Zealand Bank Ltd* [1900] AC 577 where it was held that a bank was estopped from withdrawing an existing overdraft facility without giving notice to the customer). There is no reason why the bank may not find itself estopped from denying its undertaking to provide an overdraft or other facility in the future.

The *Tai Hing* case provides the leading modern statement on the imposition of a duty of care in tort where the parties are in a contractual relationship. Lord Scarman said:

'Their Lordships do not believe that there is anything to the advantage of the law's development in searching for a liability in tort where the parties are in a contractual relationship. This is particularly so in a commercial relationship. Though it is possible as a matter of legal semantics to conduct an analysis of the rights and duties inherent in some contractual relationships including that of banker and customer either as a matter of contract law when the question will be what, if any, terms are to be implied or as a matter of tort law when the task will be to identify a duty arising from the proximity and character of the relationship between the parties, their Lordships believe it to be correct in principle and necessary for the avoidance of confusion in the law to adhere to the contractual analysis; on principle because it is a relationship in which the parties have, subject to a few exceptions, the right to determine their obligations to each other, and for the avoidance of confusion because different consequences do follow according to whether liability arises from contract or tort ...'

Although this principle has been applied (see *National Bank of Greece SA* v *Pinios Shipping Co. (No. 1)* [1989] 1 All ER 213) there are a number of cases where the principle will not preclude the imposition of a duty of care in tort between parties who stand in a contractual relationship. The exceptions include entering into a general contractual relationship such as that of banker and customer.

BANKERS' LIABILITY FOR ADVICE IN RESPECT OF CURRENCY TRANSACTIONS

The expansion of banking services in recent years has given rise to some new problems. One of the questions which have arisen is whether the bank's duty of care extends to a situation where it provides facilities in order to enable a customer to speculate in risky transactions, e.g. in commodities or currency futures. In such cases the bank grants a line of credit or an overdraft facility which is used for speculation. Where the customer sustains a loss the question which has arisen is whether the bank can have any liability imposed on it, e.g. for failing to warn the customer of the risk. In the UK the courts have tended to restrict the liability of a bank where it can be shown that the customer relied on its advice *(Woods* v *Martins Bank* [1959] 2 QB 55) or where the customer placed his affairs entirely in the hands of the bank. In *Stafford and Another* v *Conti Commodity Services Ltd* ([1981] 1 All ER 691) the plaintiff, an investor on the London commodities futures market, after discussions with the defendants (brokers dealing on the market) gave them a substantial sum to invest. Although the defendants gave the plaintiff advice and brought to his attention different points of view the plaintiff made his own decisions and often rejected advice given by the defendants. The commodities market was unpredictable and the plaintiff sustained a loss of over £19,000. He brought an action against the defendants alleging negligence. Mocatta J held that the brokers were not liable in negligence when giving advice in a market which was unpredictable and in circumstances where the plaintiff had often failed to accept the advice given. This attitude is in contrast with recent Australian cases where the courts have treated a duty of care in tort as concurrent with any contractual obligations. In *Lloyds* v *Citicorp Australia Ltd* ((1986) 11 NSWLR ·286) the bank granted its customer a loan that could be drawn in a number of currencies. The customer, who had substantial experience in land development and business generally used the facility without covering himself by a hedging arrangement. The customer brought an action against the bank for losses sustained due to adverse currency fluctuations on the grounds that the bank failed to advise him generally on the management of the loan and the bank's failure to suggest a hedge. The court dismissed the action and Rogers J said:

> 'The duty [imposed on the bank] called for exercise of skill and diligence which a reasonably competent and careful foreign exchange adviser would exercise; by reason of the nature of the market to which I have already referred, I would take leave to doubt that the content of that duty would be very high. That skill and diligence is of some assistance, I do not doubt. However, the assistance to be derived from it in a market as volatile as the one for the Australian dollar has been is fairly minimal.'

A similar view was taken in *McEvoy* v *ANZ Banking Group Ltd* ([1988] ATR 80) where a businessman of some experience took out a foreign currency loan and eventually sustained heavy losses. The bank knew that the customer had terminated the services of his manager and that he was at times relying on the advice of the bank for specific transactions. It was, however, established that he did obtain advice from other financial institutions and he knew that the bank had a policy not to advise on the type of transactions undertaken by him. The court held that the bank did not owe a tortious duty of care. However, the duty of care cannot be ruled out entirely. In *Foti* v *Banque Nationale de Paris* (unreported; Sup Ct of Sth Aust, 17 March 1989 (see November 1989, JBL, p.499)) the customers, two Italian immigrants who had established successful businesses, obtained a loan from the bank denominated in Swiss francs to finance the purchase of a shopping centre. The purpose of borrowing in foreign currency was to minimise interest. They were given no advice by the bank and were not aware of adverse currency fluctuations. They sustained considerable losses from which they could not be protected by a hedging contract. The court held the bank liable to compensate the customers. Legoe J took into consideration the disparity of the business experience between the parties. Expert evidence indicated that a reasonable banker would have advised a customer (inexperienced) to take out a hedge. The court also accepted that the bank had emphasised its business experience and the fact that the customers had been given the impression that the bank would keep an eye on the foreign currency implications of the transaction.

5 Termination of the banker– customer relationship

The banker–customer relationship is terminated either by one of the parties taking appropriate steps for that purpose or by the occurrence of certain events. The result of the termination is that the bank's mandate to act for the customer is terminated.

TERMINATION BY THE CUSTOMER

A customer may terminate his contract with the bank by demanding repayment of the balance of his current or deposit account. If the customer has more than one account with the bank, the banker–customer relationship will terminate only when all the accounts are closed by the customer. A demand for the repayment of a current account will normally take effect immediately but if the demand is made at a branch other than the branch where the customer maintains his account than the balance should be made available within a reasonable time.

Clare & Company v Dresdner Bank AG [1915] 2 KB 576

The plaintiff had an account at the Berlin branch of the defendant bank which had its head-office in Germany. The bank also had a branch in London. The plaintiff wrote to the London branch after the First World War had started between the UK and Germany demanding repayment of the balance standing to the credit of her account. On refusal the plaintiff sued the bank for repayment of the credit balance without having made a request to the bank in Berlin to pay or to remit the balance to London.

The court held that there had been no breach of contract on the bank's failure to repay the balance on her current account. The plaintiff was not entitled to demand repayment from the London branch and that there had been no breach of contract by the defendant. Rowlatt J said (p. 578):

> '... locality is an essential part of the debt owing by a banker to his customer, and that his obligation to pay is limited to the place where the account is kept. As a rule, no doubt, a debtor has to seek out his creditor and pay him; but in the case of a bank with several branches that cannot be the true relation of the parties ...'

A demand for repayment of the credit balance must be made at the branch where the account is kept if the customer wants repayment of his credit balance immediately.

In *Leader & Co.* v *Direction der Disconto-Gessellschaft* ((1914–15) 31 TLR 83) it was held that the plaintiffs who had an account with the Berlin branch of a German bank and who requested the branch in Berlin on 1 August 1914 to remit the balance to its London branch with the undertaking to pay the necessary commission were entitled to bring an action when the bank refused to act in accordance with the customer's instructions.

It is advisable that the bank obtain in writing the customer's intention to close the account. In *Wilson* v *Midland Bank Ltd* (cited in Milnes Holden: *The Law and Practice of Banking: Vol. 1 Banker & Customer,* 5th ed.,1991 Pitman, p. 117) the plaintiff's cheque for £50 2s 5d was wrongfully dishonoured by the Midland Bank which gave the reason for the dishonour as being 'No account'. The bank alleged that the plaintiff in a conversation with the manager had informed him that he was closing his account. The plaintiff had no recollection of any such conversation with the bank manager. Some time after the alleged conversation, the plaintiff paid into the credit of his account £403 19s 10d at a branch of Lloyds Bank for the credit of his account with the Midland Bank. Due to the mistaken conversation the Midland Bank credited the amount to the joint account of another customer by the name of Wilson. When the plaintiff's cheque for £50 2s 5d was presented it was dishonoured. Sachs J awarded the plaintiff nominal damages for breach of contract and £210 for libel.

A customer who wishes to close a deposit account must give the agreed notice before an action can be maintained against the bank. If the deposit is, however, made for a fixed period then it becomes automatically payable at the end of that period.

TERMINATION BY THE BANK

A bank may terminate its contractual relationship with its customer by giving him notice to that effect and tendering repayment of the credit balance. In *Joachimson* v *Swiss Bank Corporation* ((1872) LR 8 Ex 10) Atkin LJ said that the basis of the banker–customer relationship is that the bank cannot cease to do business with the customer unless it gives reasonable notice of its intention to close his account.

Prosperity Ltd v *Lloyds Bank Ltd* (1923) 39 TRL 372

The plaintiff company was formed to establish a mutual insurance scheme. The scheme was explained to the manager of a branch of the defendant bank which agreed to open an account for the company and to receive applications from subscribers, and to allot the funds received according to the rules of the company. The bank received payments until there was a substantial credit balance on the account but because of the publicity the scheme attracted the head-office of the bank decided it was undesirable to be associated with the scheme. The plaintiff company was, therefore, given one month's notification of the bank's intention to terminate the relationship.

The company brought an action for a declaration that the bank was not entitled to close the account without giving reasonable notice and for an injunction restraining the bank from closing the account.

The court held that the plaintiff company was entitled to reasonable notice of the bank's intention to close the account and that the one month's notice was not sufficient. Moreover, an injunction was not an appropriate remedy.

The court approved *Joachimson* v *Swiss Bank Corporation* ((1872) LR 8 Ex 10) where it was said:

> '... it is a term of the contract that the bank will not cease to do business with the customer except upon reasonable notice, but this, of course, is subject to any express or special agreement between the parties to the contract.'

In the *Prosperity* case the court took the view that (p. 373):

> '... the question of reasonableness must depend on the special facts and circumstances of the case. An account might be a small account drawn upon only by cheques cashed by the customer for his own purposes. In that case a comparatively short notice might be all that was needed ... A customer might also deal with his account by sending cheques, to the knowledge of the bank, to different parts of the continent. In that case ... the existence of such outstanding cheques might place upon the bank a larger burden as to notice ... having regard to the knowledge and approval in the first place of Lloyds Bank of this scheme, and having regard to their knowledge as to the far extent to which the pamphlets and forms were being sent throughout the world, one month was not adequate notice, because it did not give the plaintiffs a sufficient opportunity of dealing with the position created by the decision of Lloyds Bank to end the account.'

It should be noted that the bank is obliged to give reasonable notice in order to terminate the banker–customer relationship. In *Buckingham & Co.* v *London and Midland Bank Ltd* ((1895) 12 TLR 70) the customer had both a loan account and a current account, and at a time when he had a credit balance in his current account of £160 the bank informed him that his account was closed and that the bank would not pay any more cheques or honour any more acceptances. The following day the bank dishonoured two cheques and two bills of the customer. The jury found that the customer was entitled to draw on his current account without reference to his loan account and that he was entitled to reasonable notice before the bank could close the current account.

Where the customer decides to terminate the relationship and the account is an ordinary current account the customer need not give notice.

If the bank decides to close an account the only remedy a customer has is to sue for damages for the inconvenience and any loss of business he suffers as a result of the bank giving insufficient notice. Due to the personal nature of the banker–customer relationship the customer cannot obtain an order of specific performance or an injunction to compel the bank to keep the account.

Where a bank seeks to close a deposit account, notice of closure is not required unless it is expressly agreed that notice is required and so a bank may close a deposit account at any time. If the bank adds interest for the length of a normal notice of withdrawal which its customer would have to give if he initiated the closure, the bank has satisfied its obligations.

TERMINATION BY OPERATION OF LAW

Death of the customer or mental illness

The death of the customer terminates the contract between him and the bank because of the personal nature of the relationship. A bank's duty to pay cheques on the deceased's account is terminated when the bank receives notice of the customer's death and not by the fact of the death if that is unknown to the bank. The credit balance on the death of the customer vests in his personal representatives although they are not entitled to operate the account by drawing cheques on it.

If a customer suffers from a mental disorder to such an extent that he cannot manage his own affairs properly, the banker–customer relationship is terminated. Where the customer becomes of unsound mind the problem faced by the bank is whether or not it is under a duty to continue to honour cheques drawn by the customer. It would seem that the duty to make payment against the customer's account is terminated when the bank receives reliable information of the customer's incapacity. There is no statutory proviso to this effect although the Mental Heath Act 1983 deals with persons of unsound mind.

Where the bank has agreed to act as an agent for a customer, that relationship will terminate when the principal is no longer capable of acting for himself. In *Drew* v *Nunn* ((1879) 4 QBD 661) Brett LJ said 'where such a change occurs as to the principal that he can no longer act for himself, the agent whom he has appointed can no longer act for him.'

Re Beavan, Davies, Bank & Co. v *Beavan* [1913] 2 Ch 595

The plaintiff bank had operated a current account for J.G. Beavan. For two years before his death the customer was of unsound mind but the bank, with the approval of the other members of the customer's family, agreed to continue his account. The authority to draw cheques on the account was given to the eldest son signing cheques 'for J.G. Beavan, S.S. Beavan'. The account was operated for the maintenance of the customer's household in the accustomed manner and on the death of the customer the account was overdrawn.

The bank brought an action against the customer's executors to recover the amount overdrawn including bank charges for interest and commission.

The bank was held entitled to recover from the estate all amounts paid out for necessaries but the interest on the overdraft and commission were held to be irrecoverable. The court took the view that any person who maintains a person of unsound mind is entitled to recoup from his estate any necessary expenditure having regard to the position in life of the person of unsound mind. Anyone who makes an advance to another person who is maintaining a person of unsound mind acquires no right in law by virtue of the advance but in equity the creditor stands in the shoes of those who have been paid for necessaries out of the amount of the advance. The bank could therefore rely on its right of subrogation to recover that part of the advance used to pay for necessaries.

In practice the bank is likely to suspend the customer's account until the appointment of an administrator and any immediate business is likely to be done through a new account. In *Scarth* v *National Provincial Bank Ltd* ((1930) 4 LDB 241) a customer had a credit balance with the defendant bank and in 1919 he was certified a lunatic. The bank on notification refused to allow further transactions on the account or to honour cheques drawn by the customer's wife who had authority to draw cheques 'per pro'. The wife opened a separate account in her own name and the bank transferred the credit balance from the joint account to the credit of her account, in return for the wife entering into an indemnity. The husband later recovered and brought an action against the bank for the balance on his account and transferred to his wife. The defence raised by the bank and accepted by the court was that since the wife had, before the credit balance from her husband's account been transferred to her account, used a larger sum to pay the husband's debts the bank was discharged under its right of subrogation.

It would appear from the *Scarth* case that the banker–customer relationship is terminated on notice of mental incapacity being given to the bank. It is unlikely that the bank would be liable to repay a customer amounts paid from his account when the bank did not have notice of the customer's mental incapacity.

Insolvency, winding-up and bankruptcy

The Insolvency Act 1986 has consolidated the law on company insolvency and winding-up and the law on the insolvency and bankruptcy of individuals.

The bankruptcy of a customer

The law by which an individual may be made bankrupt is now similar to the law by which a company may be put into compulsory liquidation.

Section 278 of the Insolvency Act 1986 provides that bankruptcy begins when the bankruptcy order is made. In the period between the presentation of the petition and the date when the bankrupt's property vests in the trustee the validity of any dispositions made by a bank are void unless either made with the consent of the court or ratified by the court (s. 284(1) of the Insolvency Act 1986).

Re Gray's Inn Construction Co. Ltd [1980] 1 WLR 711

The company maintained an account with the National Westminster Bank. At the time a winding-up petition was presented, on 3 August 1972, the company was overdrawn. The overdraft was secured against a personal guarantee of the managing director. The petition was advertised on 10 August and the head-office of the bank became aware of it on 17 August. A compulsory winding-up order was made on 9 October, the account having been continued unbroken until then. Between 3 August and 9 October, approximately £25,313 had been credited to the account and approximately £24,129 debited from the account.

The liquidator claimed either the amount of the credits paid into the account or alternatively the total amount of the debits (as dispositions of the company's property under s. 227) under the now s. 127 of the Insolvency Act 1986. However, in the course of the proceedings it was agreed that the loss should be restricted to that suffered as a result of the continued trading, approximately £5,000.

The Court of Appeal held that no payment should be validated which resulted in a pre-liquidation creditor being paid in full at the expense of other creditors who would receive a dividend only. The court held:

> 'If a bank decides to continue to afford facilities to a corporate customer against whom a winding-up petition has been presented, having an account in debit at the date of the presentation of the petition, the bank can itself freeze that account and insist on all subsequent dealings being dealt with on a separate account. It can require personal assurances from the directors of the company that no payments out of the new account will be made in discharge of pre-liquidation debts, and that all payments out of the new account shall be in respect of liabilities incurred in the ordinary course of business subsequent to the presentation of the petition.'

Even when the bank has obtained a validation order allowing the business and the account to continue it will be subject to the condition that the continued trading is at a profit and for the benefit of creditors generally.

Although *Re Gray's Inn Construction* examined the effect of the now s. 127 of the Insolvency Act 1986 the same rule now applies to a bankruptcy petition and the bank should refuse to allow a bankrupt to use his account without a validation order from the court. Section 284(4) also requires that the bank seeking the validation order should have acted in good faith, for value and without notice that the bankruptcy petition has been presented. The question of whether or not the bank had notice that the petition had been presented will depend not on constructive notice, but on actual notice.

Re Wigzell, ex p. Hart [1921] 2 KB 835

Wigzell was a customer of a branch of Barclays Bank. A receiving order was made against him on 8 October 1919, but on his application the County Court granted a stay of advertisement of the order and of all proceedings pending an appeal. On 10 November, the appeal was dismissed.

Between the date of the order and the dismissal of the appeal the debtor paid into his account approximately £165 2s 3d, and he withdrew approximately £199 19s 7d. The bank had no knowledge of the bankruptcy proceedings.

The trustee in bankruptcy claimed that he was entitled to £162 2s 3d, and the bank was entitled to deduct any of the debtor's withdrawals. The County Court and the Divisional Court held that the claim was justified. The bank appealed.

The Court of Appeal dismissed the appeal and held that the bank was liable to the trustee for the amount credited to the account without any set-off for the amount debited from the account. The court, however, recognised that the bank could enforce those rights which the bankrupt's creditors could enforce.

Section 284(5) of the Insolvency Act 1986 now provides that where a payment is made from an account at the order of the customer after the commencement of his bankruptcy the debit is provable unless (a) the bank had earlier notice of the bankruptcy, or (b) it is not reasonably practicable to recover the amount involved from the payee.

The bank will not be able to rely on s. 284(5) after the bankruptcy order has been advertised. In *Re Byfield, ex p. Hill Samuel & Co. Ltd* ([1982] 1 All ER 249) the customer's bankruptcy was gazetted on 4 April 1979. On 5 April the bankrupt instructed the bank to transfer £19,500 to her mother's account at another bank. The mother used £12,000 of that amount to pay off some of the bankrupt's creditors. When the trustee claimed the £12,000 from the bank, the bank paid the trustee and then sought to prove for £12,000 as the creditors paid by the mother would otherwise have been claimed in the bankruptcy. The court held that the bank was not entitled under what is now s. 384(5)(b).

Proof of debt

Preference in bankruptcy and winding-up

Re Joseph Samson Lyons, ex p. Barclays Bank Ltd v *The Trustee* (1934) 51 TLR 24

The bankrupt had an account with Barclays Bank with an agreed overdraft limit of £2,000. The overdraft was secured by the guarantee of the bankrupt's father. In early 1932 the bankrupt realised he was bankrupt and in August 1932 he ceased payments to his general creditors. He maintained payments into his account with the result that when a bankruptcy petition was presented the overdraft had been reduced to £1,300. He was adjudicated bankrupt in December 1932 and the trustee sought a declaration that the payments into the account from August constituted a fraudulent preference of the bank and/or the guarantor.

The Court of Appeal overruled the court at first instance and held that the facts did not justify an inference that there was fraudulent preference. Lord Harnworth MR said that the bankrupt continued to use his account and to treat it as an ordinary business account from which cheques were paid and amounts withdrawn. He said that the court at first instance overlooked the essential nature of a fraudulent preference as explained in *Peat* v *Gresham Trust Ltd* ((1934) 50 TLR 345 at 347):

'The onus is on those who claim to avoid the transaction to establish what the debtor really intended, and that the real intention was to prefer. The onus is only discharged when the Court, upon a review of all the circumstances, is satisfied that the dominant intent to prefer was present. That may be a matter of direct evidence or of inference, but where there is not direct evidence and there is room for more than one explanation, it is enough to say, there being no direct evidence, that the intention to prefer must be inferred.'

The Insolvency Act 1986 removes the word 'fraudulent' from the offence under s. 239. The liquidator does not have to show an intention to deceive but merely an intention to prefer and the liquidator has power to take summary proceedings against a wide range of people connected with a company prior to its winding-up.

In order to set aside a transaction on grounds of 'preference' it must be shown that:

(a) there was the desire to prefer;
(b) that debts could not be paid off as they fell due at the time of the preference;
(c) the preference must have been made either within six months of the onset of insolvency or within two years before that date in the case of a person connected with the company.

One of the most common forms of preference occurs where directors have guaranteed the company's overdraft and/or secured it with a charge on their own property. If, in order to release the guarantor of his liability under the security, the directors cause the company to discharge the overdraft, that is a preference of the bank, even though the payment was made to benefit the directors and the offence may be established. In *Re M. Kushler Ltd* ([1943] 2 All ER 22) the guarantor and co-director of a private limited company had been professionally notified that the company was insolvent. Between the date of the advice and the date of a resolution for voluntary winding-up (which was passed two weeks later) the company's overdraft was paid off although certain trade creditors remained unpaid and an important trade creditor had been demanding payment for three months. The court held that there was an inference to prefer creditors.

Where the effect of a preference is to release or reduce the burden on a guarantor or other surety, the Insolvency Act 1986, s. 241(1)(e), provides the court may impose such new or revived obligations as it thinks fit on persons who have been preferred. In such cases the intention of the preference is to reduce the liability of the guarantor or surety and there is rarely an intention to benefit the bank. In *Re F.L.E. Holdings Ltd* ([1967] 1 WLR 1409) and in *Re William Hall (Contractors) Ltd* it was held that the creation of legal mortgages in favour of the bank amounted to the completion of an existing understanding with the bank and maintaining good faith and there was no intention of a fraudulent preference in favour of the bank.

In *Re F.L.E. Holdings* Pennycuick J cited Jenkins LJ in *Re Cutts (A Bankrupt), ex parte Bognor Mutual Building Society* v *Trustee of TW Cutts* ([1956] 1 WLR 728) with regard to the question of the voluntary nature of the preference where it was said:

'... in as much as preference implies selection and selection implies freedom of choice, a payment must in order to constitute a preference be voluntarily made, and that a payment made under pressure, e.g. in the shape of proceedings actual or threatened by the creditor concerned, or fear of such proceedings, is not for this purpose a voluntary proceeding.'

The nature of a fraudulent preference was discussed in *Osterreichische Landerbank* v *S'Elite Ltd* ([1980] 2 ALL ER 651) where the court held that the term fraudulent preference could not be equated with the common law meaning of fraud used under the Bills of Exchange Act 1882. The court said that a fraudulent preference can be made by an insolvent debtor with the honest motive of discharging a valid obligation, and the fraud referred to is simply the unfairness suffered by the other creditors who cannot be paid in full. Consequently, the fraud referred to in the expression 'fraudulent preference' is fraud of an equitable nature and is wider than the common law fraud which may affect the title of a holder in due course to a negotiable instrument.

It should be stressed that the word fraud is now omitted from the offence of preferring one creditor against another.

The liquidation or winding-up of a company

Administration orders

An administration order is an order directing that during the period for which the order is in force, the affairs, business and property of a company will be managed by a licensed insolvency practitioner appointed by the court. The administrator is appointed by the court to manage the company in the interests of everyone involved. The purpose of an administration order is to provide a breathing space, free from the pressures of the creditors' claims, in which to take stock of the situation and to decide whether the business can be profitably rescued. For an administration order to be made the company must be unable, or likely to be unable, to pay its debts. The company must not be in liquidation or administrative receivership unless the debenture-holder has consented to the appointment of an administrator or the debenture is liable to be avoided. Moreover, the court must be satisfied that the administration order 'is likely to achieve' one or more of the following:

(a) the survival of the company, and the whole or any part of its undertaking, as a going concern;
(b) the approval of a voluntary arrangement under the Insolvency Act;
(c) the sanctioning of a scheme under s. 425 of the Companies Act;
(d) a more advantageous realisation of the company's assets than would be effected on a winding-up.

Re Consumer and Industrial Press Ltd [1988] BCLC 68

The company published a magazine which had been established in 1949. By April 1987, after incurring heavy losses, the company was insolvent and it was obvious that the company was or was likely to become unable to pay its debts. In July 1987, the Inland Revenue sought an order for compulsory winding-up of the company and in October the company sought an administration order and dismissal of the winding-up petition. The company claimed that administrators could continue publication of the magazine and so be likely to obtain a higher price on its sale than the liquidator.

Gibson J said that s. 8(1) of the Insolvency Act 1986 had to be satisfied for an administration order to be made, namely that (a) the company is or is likely to become unable to pay its debts and (b) the court is satisfied that the making of an order would be likely to achieve one or more of the purposes specified in s. 8(3). That did not mean that it was merely possible that such purpose would be achieved; the evidence had to go further than that to enable the court to hold that the purpose in question would more probably than not be achieved.

The court accepted that there would be a more advantageous realisation of the company's assets by the administrators than in a winding-up of the company and therefore the statutory preconditions for the discretion were satisfied.

As regards the interest of the creditors Gibson J said:

'I do not think I should ignore the benefit that would accrue to secured creditors ... although I accept that their interests weigh lighter in the scales than the other creditors'. But the administration order, in addition to benefiting the secured creditors, will give at least the possibility of achieving more benefit for the preferential creditors and other unsecured creditors than would a liquidation.'

The administration order is an innovation of the Insolvency Act 1986. It is intended to facilitate a rescue operation of a sick company. Essentially the administrator replaces the directors in the management of the business. After an administration petition has been presented the company cannot be put into liquidation. No steps may be taken to enforce any security over the company's property and no legal proceedings may be brought or commenced against the company without the consent of the court. In *Re A Company (No. 001992 of 1988)* ([1988] BCLC 9), however, it was held that it was appropriate to allow a creditor to present a winding-up petition but to restrain advertisement of the petition until after the hearing of administration petition.

The appointment of an administrator does not affect any existing contracts of the company.

Administrative receivers and receivers

An administrative receiver is a receiver or manager of the whole or substantially the whole of the company's property. A receiver includes a receiver of part only of the company's property or only of the income arising from the property or any part of it. Both the administrative receiver and receiver are appointed by or on behalf of the holders of any debenture of the company's property, e.g. a bank, or by the court. A receiver who is not validly appointed may be liable as a trespasser.

Duties of a receiver

In a series of cases since the Insolvency Act 1986 the courts have examined the extent of duties owed by a receiver.

Gomba Holdings UK Ltd v *Homan* [1986] 1 WLR 1301

The plaintiffs had granted fixed and floating charges to Johnson Matthey Bankers Ltd. The bank appointed receivers under the charges who realised various assets to the value of approximately £11,000. The sole and controlling director of the plaintiffs claimed to have entered into an arrangement with an undisclosed third party which would provide funds to pay off the outstanding debts. The plaintiffs therefore claimed that they were entitled to information about the receivership and details of disposals made or proposed to be made. The plaintiffs also sought an order that five days' notice should be given of any commitment to dispose of further assets.

Hoffman J held that a claim by the plaintiffs that they could shortly redeem the charges did not give them a right to limit the receiver's unrestricted right to sell at any time. As regards the request for information the judge reviewed the duties owed by a receiver and manager who, although nominally an agent of the company, has a primary duty to realise the assets in the interests of the debenture-holders. Moreover, the judge said that the receiver and manager should have the power to carry on the day-to-day management of the company's property without interference from the board and the right to realise the assets of the company.

In *Shamji* v *Johnson Matthey Bankers Ltd* ([1986] BCLC 278) the court again rejected the plaintiffs' claim that receivers should not be appointed on the grounds that negotiations for a sale were near completion.

In *Re Potters Oils Ltd (No. 2)* ([1986] 1 WLR 201) the company had borrowed from Lloyds Bowmaker Ltd to finance the purchase of plant from France. When a winding-up order was made against the company, Lloyds Bowmaker notified the liquidator of their charge and were notified that the court would have to determine the validity of their debenture. Lloyds Bowmaker then appointed a receiver and eventually the plant was sold back to the French company. The proceeds from the sale of plant were sufficient to satisfy the bank's claim but the liquidator challenged the claim from the receiver for his remuneration arguing that the appointment was unnecessary. Hoffman J rejected the claim and held that provided the chargee acts in good faith he is entitled to be guided by his own interests in deciding whether or not to appoint a receiver.

Although a receiver appointed out of court is usually an agent of the company the law does not impose on him the traditional fiduciary duties expected from an agent.

In a number of other cases the courts have looked at the formalities of the appointment of a receiver which must be observed. In *Windsor Refrigerator Co. Ltd* v *Branch Nominees Ltd* ([1961] Ch 375) a debenture stated that the power to appoint a receiver had to be exercised in writing. A demand for payment having been made, the document appointing the receiver was executed but not dated until later, after there had been a failure to make payment. The appointment of the receiver was challenged on the grounds that the document appointing the receiver was invalidly executed. The Court of Appeal held that the document appointing the receiver was valid because the document could be properly made out before it was intended to take effect. In *Cripps (Pharmaceuticals) Ltd* v *Wickenden* ([1973] 1 WLR 944) Goff J held that the appointment of a receiver was valid even if made a mere hour after the demand for repayment was presented to an authorised representative of the company. The company must be given a reasonable time to get the money from a convenient place, e.g. a bank, but it is not entitled to time to embark on a venture to raise the required amount. Similarly, in *Bank of Baroda* v *Panessar* ((1982) 2 BCC 288) it was held that the appointment of a receiver will be valid only if the company is given adequate time to carry out the mechanics of finding the money. The company must be given the time to collect the money from the bank but it is not entitled to time to raise a loan before a receiver is appointed.

Gomba Holdings UK Ltd v *Minories Finance Ltd* [1989] 1 All ER 261

Two partners in a firm of accountants were appointed by the debenture-holder to be receivers and managers of companies which included the plaintiff company. Following the discharge of the receiverships the plaintiff companies obtained an order requiring the receivers to deliver all documents relating to the plaintiff company's affairs. In pursuance of that order the receivers delivered certain documents but refused to deliver other documents, e.g. documents created by the receivers to advise and inform the debenture-holders on the conduct of the receivership and draft accounts. The receivers claimed that although the documents related to the plaintiff company's business they did not belong to the plaintiff company.

The receiver had a duty to advise and inform the debenture-holder regarding the conduct of the receivership and, consequently, documents created for that purpose could not be the property of the company although they related to the company's affairs. The fact that the documents were created by the receiver, technically an agent of the company, was not sufficient to confer ownership of the documents on the company.

In *Re B. Johnson & Co. (Builders) Ltd* ([1955] Ch 634) Lord Evershed MR examined the extent of duties owed by a receiver to the debenture-holder and said:

> '... it is quite plain that a person appointed as receiver and manager is concerned, not for the benefit of the company but for the benefit of the mortgagee bank, to realise the security; that is the whole purpose of his appointment; and the powers which are conferred upon him ... are really ancillary to the main purpose of the appointment, which is the realisation by the mortgagee of the security ... by the sale of the assets.'

Until recently, it was unsettled whether in exercising his powers the receiver owed a duty of care to the company in tort. In *Cuckmere Brick Co. Ltd* v *Mutual Finance Ltd* ([1971] 2 All ER 633) the Court of Appeal held that a mortgagee when exercising his power of sale owed a duty to the mortgagor to take reasonable care to obtain the proper price and that included a duty to advertise the property. Again, in *Standard Chartered Bank* v *Walker* ([1983] 3 All ER 938) the Court of Appeal held that a receiver appointed to realise assets under a debenture owed a duty both to the borrower and to a guarantor of the debt to take reasonable care to obtain the best price possible that circumstances permitted, and in choosing a time for the sale (see p. 223).

Winding-up
A winding-up order will terminate the banker–customer relationship.

National Westminster Bank Ltd v *Halesowen Presswork & Assemblies Ltd* [1972] AC 785

The company maintained its No. 1 account with the appellant bank which by 1968 was overdrawn by approximately £1,338 and dormant. The company had another account with Lloyds Bank which was in credit and through which the company conducted its daily banking transactions. After pressure the account with Lloyds Bank was transferred to the appellant bank on April 4. This account was designated No. 2 account and continued in credit whilst the overdrawn No. 1 account was frozen. It was agreed with the bank that the two accounts would not be combined within the following four months unless there was a material change in the circumstances.

On 20 May, the company called a meeting of its creditors and on 12 June, a resolution for voluntary liquidation was passed. The bank sought to set off the credit balance on the No. 2 account against the debit on the other account. The liquidator argued that it had been agreed to keep the accounts separate and that by agreement the bank had contracted out of s. 31 of the Bankruptcy Act 1914, as applied to companies by s. 317 of the Companies Act 1948.

The House of Lords held that the agreement not to combine the accounts had only been intended to be operative during the existence of the banker–customer relationship and that relationship having terminated with the winding-up resolution having been passed the bank could combine the accounts. A requirement imposing notice of the intention to combine accounts would have served no purpose since the banker–customer relationship had been terminated. Viscount Dilhorne approved *British Guiana Bank Ltd* v *Official Receiver* ((1911) 27 TLR 454) – where the bank had agreed with its customer that a second current account (referred to as No. 2 account) would be opened by the bank and the credit balance on that account would not be combined with any debit balance on another account – where Lord Macnaughten said (p. 454):

> 'the whole question turned upon the meaning of the agreement ... In their Lordships' opinion it was an ordinary business agreement intended to be operative as long as the accounts were alive, but no longer. There was nothing in it to exclude the operation of the right of set off.'

In the *National Westminster* case the parties had not contracted out of s. 31 of the Bankruptcy Act 1914. Indeed the House took the view that it was not possible to contract out of s. 31. Viscount Dilhorne cited Buckley LJ [1971] 1 QB 1 at p. 49:

> '... The agreement was intended to have a temporary effect only, at the end of which the parties contemplated that both accounts would become part of their general relationship as bank and customer. In my judgment, notwithstanding the fact that the agreement had the temporary effect of precluding the bank from appropriating any credit on the No. 2 account towards discharging the debt on the No. 1 account, the dealings giving rise to the obligations were "mutual dealings" within the meaning of section 31 and the credits were "mutual credits".

The case confirmed that the bank has, in the absence of express or implied agreement to the contrary, a common law right to combine accounts of a customer. The right can be exercised without notice to the customer. Further, any ancillary agreement affecting the banker–customer relationship is also terminated with the termination of the banker–customer relationship.

Section 31 of the Bankruptcy Act 1914 provided for the setting-off of claims between the bankrupt and the creditor where there had been 'mutual credits, mutual debits or other mutual dealings'. Section 323 of the Companies Act 1948 extended this and other bankruptcy rules to the winding-up of insolvent companies. Similar provisions still apply to bankrupts and insolvent companies or companies being wound up. Therefore, the rule in the *Halesowen Pressworks* case is still valid law.

OUTBREAK OF WAR

The outbreak of hostilities between the country where a bank is established or where the branch at which the customer maintains his account and the country of which he is a resident does not terminate the banker–customer relationship.

Arab Bank Ltd v Barclays Bank [1952] AC 495

The appellant bank which had its registered office in Jerusalem opened a current account with the Jerusalem branch of the respondent bank which had its registered office in England. In 1948 war broke out between the newly constituted state of Israel and the Arab States. Consequently, performance of the contract became impossible. In 1950 the appellant bank sued the respondent bank for repayment of the amount standing to its credit as money had and received on the ground that the contract had been frustrated by war.

The right to be repaid the credit balance survived the outbreak of the war. That right remained in existence subject to the right to suspend payment. The court approved the judgment in *Schering Ltd v Stockholms Enskilda Bank Aktiebolag* ([1946] AC 19) in which Jenkins LJ said:

> '... a debt contracted before the outbreak of war, but made payable by instalments on dates occurring after such outbreak is not abrogated, but merely suspended as regards enforcement ... I fail to see why it should be held that a debt contracted before the outbreak of war should be cancelled merely because it is payable on demand ...'

Lord Reid in *Arab Bank* expressed the rule as follows:

> 'With certain exceptions the outbreak of war prevents the further performance of contracts between persons in this country and persons in enemy territory. It is not merely that an enemy cannot sue during the war, and that trading and intercourse with the enemy during the war are illegal. Many kinds of contractual rights are totally abrogated by the outbreak of the war and do not revive on its termination. On the other hand, there are other kinds of contractual rights which are not abrogated; they cannot be enforced during the war, but war merely suspends the right to enforce them and they can be enforced after the war.'

The effect of the outbreak of war is merely to suspend the rights of the customer but legislation enacted in the country where the bank is established or where the customer's account is maintained may effectively expropriate (as was in fact the case in the *Arab Bank* case) or freeze the credit balances (as was the case in the war with Libya).

LIQUIDATION OF THE BANK

Re Russian Commercial and Industrial Bank [1955] Ch 148

A bank incorporated in Russia which also carried on business at an English branch was dissolved under Russian law in December 1917. The English branch continued to carry on banking business in the normal way. In 1922 a petition for compulsory winding-up was presented and an order made. A customer who had an account with the English branch sought to prove for a sum in sterling converted at the rate of exchange at the date of the dissolution of the bank in Russia. The liquidator contended that the proper date for conversion was that of the winding-up in England.

The court held that the correct date on which the debt became due was the dissolution of the bank in Russia but for the purposes of the distribution of assets amongst the creditors under the Companies Act, the dissolution of the bank in Russia was to be ignored, so that the relationship between banker–customer was deemed to continue until the commencement of winding-up in England. It was on that date that the debt became due.

Where a bank fails to pay its customer's cheques or to repay the credit balances standing on the customer's account, whether the bank has gone into liquidation or not, the banker–customer relationship is terminated.

The consequence of the bank being in liquidation is that the customer is no longer able to draw on his credit balance and he has an immediate right to repayment of the credit balance. In practice the customer is unlikely to recover his credit balance in full. Until the bank actually goes into liquidation its customers are not likely to have the protection of the deposit protection scheme and the deposit protection fund (established under the Banking Act 1987) applied in their favour (see p. 17 for comment on the position of BCCI depositors).

6 Negotiable instruments

WHAT IS A NEGOTIABLE INSTRUMENT?

A negotiable instrument is a document evidencing an obligation on the part of one person (A) to pay money to another person (B). The obligation is discharged by directing an institution (e.g. a bank, building society or post office) with whom A has a credit balance to make payment when the instrument is presented. However, the essence of a negotiable instrument is that B may not wish to receive payment and may negotiate the instrument to C. If C receives the instrument in good faith and for a valuable consideration he will take free from defects of title and acquire a good title even against the true owner of the instrument.

The legal relationship between the person first bound to make payment (A) and the first person entitled to receive payment (B) is based on the general rules of privity of contract. However, there are many exceptions to the privity of contract rules and the doctrine of negotiability is one such exception.

Conditions to be satisfied if an instrument is to be negotiable and sources of negotiability

It has been said that three essential requirements must be satisfied if an instrument is to be recognised as negotiable (Jacobs in *Bills of Exchange, Cheques, Promissory Notes and Negotiable Instruments Generally,* 4th ed., Sweet & Maxwell, 1943), namely:

(a) that the terms of the instrument must not be incompatible with or such as to negative the idea of negotiability and that there should be no indication that the instrument is only transferable subject to defects of title unknown to the transferee and no indication that it is not transferable by delivery or indorsement and delivery;

(b) that the obligation or rights evidenced by the instrument must be of a nature consonant with the commercial function of a negotiable instrument, namely an obligation to pay;

(c) that the instrument must belong to a class which is treated by the mercantile community as negotiable.

Milnes Holden states (in *The Law and Practice of Banking: Vol. 1 Banker and Customer, op. cit.*) the characteristics of negotiable instruments are:

(a) The instrument and the rights which it embodies are capable of being transferred by delivery, either with or without indorsement according to whether the instrument is in favour of order or bearer; an instrument thus transferred is said to be negotiated.
(b) The person to whom the instrument is negotiated can sue on it in his own name.
(c) The person to whom a current and apparently regular negotiable instrument has been negotiated, who takes it in good faith and for value, obtains a good title to it, even though his transferor had a defective title or no title at all.

An instrument will be negotiable if so recognised by mercantile usage.

Goodwin v Robarts [1875–76] 1 App Cas 476

The plaintiff purchased £5,000 of Russian and Hungarian scrip forming part of loans raised by the Russian and Austro-Hungarian governments respectively. The scrip could be exchanged for bonds when they were issued by the relevant governments. The plaintiff deposited these certificates with his broker, Clayton, who fraudulently lodged them with his banker as security for a loan. The plaintiff sought to recover the scrip from the banker who argued that title had passed to him as scrip was by custom a negotiable instrument.

The House of Lords upheld the Court of Exchequer Chamber and said that scrip was a recognised negotiable instrument capable of passing legal title by delivery to a third party. It is interesting to note the judgment of the Court of Exchequer Chamber where Lord Cockburn CJ said ((1875) LR 10 Ex 337):

> 'It is true the law merchant is sometimes spoken of as a fixed body of law, forming part of the common law, and as it were coeval with it. But as a matter of legal history, this view is altogether incorrect. The law merchant, thus spoken of with reference to bills of exchange and other negotiable securities, though forming part of the general body of the *lex mercatoria*, is of comparatively recent origin. It is neither more nor less than the usages of merchants and traders in the different departments of trade, ratified by the decisions of Courts of Law, which, upon such usages being proved before them, have adopted them as settled law with a view to the interests of trade, and public convenience ... Why is it said that a new usage which has sprung up under altered circumstances, is to be less admissible than the usages of past times? ...'

In *Goodwin* v *Robarts* the courts concluded that a usage once shown to be universal is entitled to judicial recognition even though it did not form part of the law merchant as previously recognised and adopted by the courts.

The courts have examined a number of instruments which have been held to be negotiable under the common law. The *Goodwin* v *Robarts* case was followed by *Bechuanaland Exploration Co.* v *London Trading Bank* ([1989] 2 QB 658) where the court held that debentures purported to be payable to bearer were negotiable instruments. Kennedy J held that the decision in *Crouch* v *Credit Foncier Co. of England* ((1873) LR 8 QB 374) could not be reconciled with *Goodwin* v *Robarts* and the earlier decision must therefore be treated as overruled. In *Crouch* v *Credit Foncier Co. of England* the view taken was that the class of recognised negotiable instruments was closed with the result that the court refused to recognise bearer bonds or debentures as negotiable.

Exchequer and Treasury bills issued by the government to raise short-term loans have been recognised by the courts as negotiable instruments. A blank exchequer bill is payable to '[space for payee's name]' or order, and any person who takes the exchequer or Treasury bill for value and in good faith while the space for the payee's name remains blank will acquire a good title free from the defects in the title of the transferor (see *Brandao* v *Barnett* (1846) 3 CB 519).

Similarly, in *Partridge* v *Bank of England* ((1846) 9 QB 396) dividend warrants payable to order or bearer or simply to a named payee were recognised as negotiable instruments. In that case a dividend warrant was made payable to one Mr Partridge only. A person named Wakefield received the dividend warrant from the bank under a power of attorney given by Partridge and immediately wrote on the face of it an acknowledgment of his having received the full sum which he then misappropriated. Evidence was given that according to a long-standing mercantile custom the banks would pay the money to anyone who presented the warrant and the court held that the bank obtained a good discharge since it acted in good faith.

The courts have recognised a number of other instruments as negotiable under mercantile custom, for example bank notes, banker's drafts, share warrants, dividend warrants and bearer bonds.

Additionally, there are a number of instruments which have received statutory recognition as possessing the quality of negotiability, namely, cheques and bills of exchange, promissory notes and Bank of England notes. These instruments are negotiable if they are in such a state that the true owner, if he so desires, can pass the property in them by delivery or by indorsement and delivery.

There are a number of other instruments whose status as negotiable instruments has not yet been tested before the courts. It is probable that they would be recognised as negotiable. These include instruments such as unit trust certificates to bearer, depository receipts and certificates of deposit issued by banks and other depositories in respect of investment certificates (shares and bonds) deposited with them, and certificates of deposit of currency entitling the bearer to repayment on a fixed future date.

Finally, it needs to be mentioned that in *Gorgier* v *Mieville* ((1824) 3 B & C 45) the courts looked at the question of the negotiability of a foreign instrument (a bond issued by the King of Prussia which was wrongfully pledged with the defendants) and held the instrument to be negotiable by the usage of the English market. The court took the view that the King of Prussia had discharged his liability on the bill by paying the bearer since under the usage of the English market it was a negotiable instrument and it is English market usage which is recognised by the court. The fact that an instrument is recognised as negotiable abroad will not automatically make it negotiable in the UK and it must be shown to be negotiable by commercial usage in this country.

The Jack Committee said that it is 'difficult to be precise about the conditions which must be satisfied in order to achieve negotiability.' It recognised that the concept of negotiability was developed by the law merchant and in negotiable instruments the common law courts have referred to the customs and practices of the merchants. The 'stand-alone' principle which must be satisfied if an instrument is to be recognised as negotiable requires that the instrument should be self-contained, and not include any extraneous references which are necessary to interpret and give effect to the instrument. The Jack Committee said that the 'stand-alone' principle 'was one of the main difficulties we met in attempting to formulate a new test of more general application for negotiability. Many instruments currently regarded as negotiable would by virtue of the collateral references they contain fail the test in the absence of any provision to the contrary.' The Committee recommended a new Bills of Exchange Act suggesting that the Act contain the following formula for determining whether an instrument is negotiable:

(a) if it is a bill of exchange or promissory note defined in the new Act; or
(b) if it complies or substantially complies with the requirements (see below) and shows on the face of it a clear intention of the drawer/maker that it should be negotiable; or
(c) if, although it does not satisfy the requirements of paragraph (b), it closely resembles in form and effect other instruments which are negotiable; or
(d) if it is recognised by the custom and practice of the market as negotiable; or
(e) if in the circumstances it would accord with established market custom and practice for it to be treated as negotiable.

The requirements referred to in paragraph (b) above are that the instrument must be:

(a) in writing
(b) signed by the drawer or maker and
(c) unconditionally promises or directs payment or performance
(d) of a right or obligation which is certain or ordinarily determinable
(e) to a specified payee, or to bearer
(f) on demand or at a fixed or determinable future time
(g) the right or obligation in question to be assignable (transferable) in its nature, and the instrument itself to permit transfer (even if certain persons, or classes of persons, are expressly excluded from potential transferees).

The Jack Committee said that the term 'negotiable' in relation to an instrument means that: (a) the obligation or right represented by the instrument is transferable without notice to the party primarily liable; and (b) is transferable to a holder in due course (a bona fide purchaser who has no notice of any defects in the title of the transferor) vesting in the purchaser a title 'free of equities'.

Does payment by a negotiable instrument amount to an absolute discharge of the debt?

It is a question of fact whether or not a negotiable instrument, drawn in payment of a debt, amounts to an absolute discharge of a debt.

Re Romer & Haslam [1989] 2 QB 286

A number of postdated bills of exchange were issued in favour of solicitors for work carried out by the solicitors, generally and more specifically in connection with an arbitration, for the defendants. An application for taxation of costs was allowed on grounds that the bills of costs contained overcharges.

The court held that the bills of exchange issued by the clients and their acceptance 'in settlement' by the solicitors amounted to payment under s. 41 of the Solicitors Act 1843, and operated to take away the client's right of taxation in the absence of special circumstances.

On the question of payment on a bill of exchange the court said:

> 'It is perfectly well-known law, which is acted upon in every form of mercantile business, that the giving of a negotiable security by a debtor to his creditor operates as a conditional payment only, and not as a satisfaction of a debt, unless the parties agree so to treat it. Such a conditional payment is liable to be defeated on non-payment of the negotiable instrument at maturity ...'

In *Hadley (Felix) & Co.* v *Hadley* ([1898] 2 Ch 680) the court held that a cheque or bill of exchange given in respect of a pre-existing debt operates as a conditional payment only. On that condition being satisfied by actual payment, the debt is discharged and payment relates back to the time when the cheque or bill was given. In *Marreco* v *Richardson* ([1908] 2 KB 584) Farwell LJ said '... the giving of a cheque for a debt is conditional on the cheque being met, that is, subject to a condition subsequent, and if the cheque is met it is an actual payment *ab initio* and not a conditional one.' Similarly, in *Currie* v *Misa* ((1876) LR 10 Exch 153) it was said that the title of a creditor to a bill given on account of a pre-existing debt, and payable at a future day, does not rest upon the implied agreement to suspend his remedies. The true reason is that the negotiable instrument given is a conditional payment of the debt, the condition being that the debt revives if the security is not realised.

In *D. and C. Rees Builders Ltd* v *Rees* ([1966] 2 QB 617) the court looked at the question of whether payment of a smaller sum by cheque was sufficient to discharge a larger debt. Lord Denning held (pp. 839–840):

> '... It is a daily occurrence that a merchant or tradesman, who is owed a sum of money, is asked to take less. The debtor says he is in difficulties. He offers a lesser sum in settlement, cash down. He says he cannot pay more. The creditor is considerate. He accepts the proffered sum and forgives him the rest of the debt. The question arises: is the settlement binding on the creditor? The answer is that, in point of law, the creditor is not bound by the settlement. He can next day sue the debtor for the balance, and get judgment ... Now suppose that the debtor, instead of paying the lesser sum in cash, pays it by cheque. He makes out a cheque for the amount. The creditor accepts the cheque and cashes it. Is the position any different? I think not. No sensible distinction can be taken between payment of a lesser sum by cash and payment of it by cheque. The cheque, when given, is conditional payment. When honoured, it is actual payment. It is then just the same as cash. If a creditor is not bound when he receives a payment by cash, he should not be bound when he receives payment by cheque.'

PAYMENT BY LETTER OF CREDIT

In letters of credit transactions the question has similarly been asked whether the opening of a letter of credit releases the buyer from liability for payment under the contract of sale once the credit is issued. This is especially important where the bank becomes insolvent before it accepts or negotiates the seller's bill of exchange or before it pays bills it has accepted. If the letter of credit were treated as absolute payment of the price owed to the seller, the buyer would be under no further liability to the seller once the credit was issued and the seller would have to accept a dividend in the bank's liquidation. This would not be the situation where funds paid to the issuing bank were appropriated by the buyer for the purpose of honouring bills presented under the letter of credit. The English courts have dealt with the question of the buyer's liability in a number of cases. In *W.J. Alan & Co.* v *L. Nasr Export and Import Ltd* ([1972] 2 All ER 127) Lord Denning said that a letter of credit when issued and accepted by the seller operates merely as conditional payment. It does not operate to discharge the liability of the buyer but the seller cannot look to the buyer personally for payment until the issuing bank has refused payment. Lord Denning went on to say that if the letter of credit is honoured by the bank when the documents are presented to it, the debt is discharged and the buyer then absolved from liability. In the *Alan & Co. Ltd* v *L. Nasr* case it was further said:

> 'that a letter of credit is not to be regarded as absolute payment, unless the seller stipulates, expressly or impliedly, that it should be so. He may do it impliedly if he requires the credit to be issued by a particular bank in such circumstances that it is to be inferred that the seller looks to the particular banker to the exclusion of the buyer.'

Similarly, in *EDF Man Ltd* v *Nigerian Sweets and Confectionery Co. Ltd* ([1977] 2 Lloyd's Rep 50) the buyers under three separate contracts agreed to buy 1,100 tons of sugar from the sellers. It was agreed that payment was to be made in cash against documents presented in London. In March 1973, the contracts were varied by oral agreement so the payment was to be made by means of 90-day drafts drawn on the buyer's bank under an irrevocable letter of credit. In April, three letters of credit were opened by the defendant's bank. The sellers performed the underlying contract and tendered the appropriate shipping documents with their drafts for acceptance. The bank failed to accept the drafts and eventually payment was refused. The sellers brought an action against the buyers for the purchase price under the three contracts. The court held that the liability of the buyers was a primary liability which was superseded by the issue of a letter of credit by the bank but which was re-activated if the issuing bank defaulted on the payment. Ackner J said:

> 'The fact that the sellers have agreed to the identity of the issuing bank is but one of the factors to be taken into account when considering whether there are circumstances from which it can properly be inferred that the sellers look at the particular bank to the exclusion of the buyer. It is in no way conclusive.'

In *Soproma SPA* v *Marine and Animal By-Products Corporation* ([1966] 1 Lloyd's Rep 367) McNair J said:

'Under this form of contract, payment by letter of credit, as it seems to me the buyer performs his obligations as to payment if he provides for the sellers a reliable and solvent paymaster from whom he can obtain payment – if necessary by suit – although it may well be that if the banker fails to pay by reason of his insolvency the buyer would be liable ...'

More recently, in *Shamsher Jute Mills Ltd* v *Sethia (London) Ltd* ([1987] 1 Lloyd's Rep 388) Bingham J dealt with the question of conditional payment under a letter of credit. He explained the position as follows:

(1) If the buyer establishes a credit which conforms or is to be treated as conforming with the sale contract, he has performed his part of the bargain so far.
(2) If the credit is honoured according to its terms, the buyer is discharged even though the credit terms differ from the contract terms.
(3) If the credit is not honoured according to its terms because the bank fails to pay, the buyer is not discharged because the condition has not been fulfilled.
(4) If the seller fails to obtain payment because he does not and cannot present the documents which the terms of the credit, supplementing the terms of the contract, require the buyer is discharged.
(5) In the ordinary case, therefore, the due establishment of the letter of credit fulfils the buyer's payment obligation unless the bank which opens the credit fails for any reason to make payment in accordance with the credit terms against the documents duly presented.

PAYMENT BY CHARGE CARD

In *Re Charge Card Services Ltd* ([1988] 3 WLR 764) the Court of Appeal held that there is no general principle in law that whenever a method of payment is adopted involving risk of non-payment by a third party, a presumption arises that acceptance of payment by that method is conditional on the third party actually making payment. In that case Charge Card Services Ltd ran a scheme, the Fuel Card Scheme, for the purchase of petrol and other fuels from approved garages with the use of charge cards issued by the company. In 1985, Charge Card Services went into voluntary liquidation and at that time it owed substantial amounts to garages which had supplied fuel in return for vouchers signed by the cardholders. Substantial amounts were also owed to the company from cardholders who had bought fuel before the company's liquidation. Under a factoring agreement the company had assigned the amounts owed to it to Commercial Credit who was in dispute with the garages and who claimed that they only accepted payment by means of the charge card as conditional discharge of the payer's obligation. Since the company had failed to pay them they were entitled to recover the amounts from the cardholders. The court examined the nature of the credit or charge card transaction as follows and said that it had the following distinguishing characteristics:

(a) There was an underlying contractual scheme which pre-dated the individual contracts of sale whereby the suppliers agreed to accept the card in payment of the price of the goods bought. The purchasers were entitled to commit the company to pay. The underlying scheme was established by two separate contracts. The first contract arose between the credit company and the seller who agreed to sell in return for payment by card. At the same time the company agreed to pay the supplier the price of the goods, less commission. The second contract was between the company and the card-holder, the holder being provided with the card to pay for goods in return for agreeing to pay the full amount against a statement from the company.

(b) A bilateral contract was then made between the buyer and seller for the sale of goods, the supplier accepting the card in payment on the assumption that the legal consequences would be regulated by the underlying scheme.

(c) As the scheme operated to over-the-counter transactions, the card did not carry the holder's address and the only way of tracing him was through the company.

The Court of Appeal examined the nature of the scheme and said that the correct solution to the scheme was that the retailer's acceptance of the card was an acceptance of that payment in substitution for cash, i.e. as an absolute unconditional payment. Browne-Wilkinson VC said (p.772):

'To my mind, all these factors point to the conclusion that, quite apart from any special features of the fuel card scheme, the transaction was one in which the garage was accepting payment by card in substitution for payment in cash, i.e., as an unconditional discharge of the price. The garage was accepting the company's obligation to pay instead of cash from a purchaser of whose address he was totally unaware. One way of looking at the matter is to say that there was a quasi-novation of the purchaser's liability. By the underlying scheme, the company had bound the garage to accept the card and had authorised the cardholder to pledge the company's credit. By the signature of the voucher all parties became bound ...'

PAYMENT EQUIVALENT TO CASH

Cebora SNC v *SIP (Industrial Products) Ltd* [1976] 1 Lloyd's Rep 271

The plaintiffs entered into an agreement with the defendants, an English company, granting them exclusive rights to sell the plaintiffs' products in the UK The parties terminated the agreement after a dispute and set up their own distributing company in England. The defendants gave instructions that five outstanding bills of exchange for a total of £56,000 should be dishonoured. The plaintiffs claimed summary judgment on the bills but the defendants counterclaimed for delivery of defective goods and loss of profit. The District Registrar entered judgment for the plaintiffs on the bills. The defendants appealed, applying for a stay pending trial of the counterclaim. May J refused the stay and the defendants appealed.

The Court of Appeal dismissed the appeal. Sir Eric Sachs said:

'Any erosion of the certainties of the application by our Courts of the law merchant relating to bills of exchange is likely to work to the detriment of this country, which depends on international trade to a degree that needs no emphasis. For some generations one of those certainties has been that the bona fide holder for value of a bill of exchange is entitled, save in truly exceptional circumstances, on its maturity to have it treated as cash, so that in an action upon it the Court will refuse to regard either as a defence or as grounds for a stay of execution any set off, legal or equitable, or any counterclaim, whether arising on the particular transaction upon which the bill of exchange came into existence, or, *a fortiori*, arising in any other way. This rule of practice is thus, in effect, pay up on the bill of exchange first and pursue claims later ...'

The Court of Appeal emphasised the importance of the bills of exchange's equivalence in the international business community. It applies equally to domestic transactions. The rule was applied to a dishonoured cheque in *Calzaturificio Fiorella SpA* v *Walton and Another* ((1979) CLY 23) and to promissory notes in *Ferson Contractors Ltd* v *Ferris* ((1982) CLY 14) where the Court of Appeal rejected the argument that the instruments to which the rule had been applied were mainly bills of exchange and because of their importance the rule should be restricted to such instruments.

In *Thoni GmbH & Co.* v *RTP Equipment Ltd* ([1979] 2 Lloyd's Rep 282) the defendants appealed against summary judgment on a bill for one million Austrian schillings alleging that they owed only half of that amount. The Court of Appeal refused a stay of execution on the ground that there was an arguable case for the disputed amount. Even apart from any defences on the bill of exchange the court has a discretion to stay execution but in *Cebora* it was emphasised that the discretion should be exercised in 'truly exceptional cases'. In *Jade International Steel Stahl and Eisen GmbH* v *Robert Nicholas (Steels) Ltd* ([1978] 3 WLR 39) the defendants dishonoured a bill drawn in favour of the plaintiffs, alleging delivery of faulty goods. Donaldson J gave judgment to the plaintiffs and refused the defendants leave to defend. They argued that he had discretion to vary the rule between immediate parties to the bill. The learned judge held that they were no longer immediate parties to the bill. The plaintiffs had lost the capacity of drawers when they discounted the bill and were now holders in due course, having received the bill back from the bank.

In *Nova (Jersey) Knit* v *Karngarn Spinnerei GmbH* ((1877) 2 All ER 463) there was a dispute between the English plaintiffs and the German defendants. The defendants resisted payment on the dishonoured bills of exchange on the grounds that arbitration in Germany was pending. The Court of Appeal granted a stay but on appeal the House of Lords reversed their decision. Lord Wilberforce said:

'I fear that the Court of Appeal's decision, if it had been allowed to stand, would have made a very substantial inroad upon the commercial principle on which the bills of exchange have always rested.'

Lord Wilberforce continued (p. 470):

'When one person buys goods from another it is often, one would think generally, important for the seller to be sure of his price: he may (as indeed have the appellants here) have bought the goods from someone else whom he has to pay. He may demand payment in cash; but if the buyer cannot provide this at once, he may agree to take bills of exchange payable at future dates ... Unless they are to be treated as unconditionally payable instruments ... which the seller can negotiate for cash, the seller might just as well give credit. And it is for this reason that English law (and German law appears to be no different) does not allow cross-claims, or defences, except such limited defences as those based on fraud, invalidity, or failure of consideration, to be made.'

However, in *Barclays Bank Ltd* v *Aschaffenberger Zellstoffwerke AG* ([1967] 1 Lloyd's Rep 387) Lord Denning approving *Thorton and Others* v *Maynard* ((1875) LR 10 CP 695) said that where the holder of a bill holds 'it in part as trustee for someone else, then when the holder sues upon the bill, the defendant can raise any defences against the trustee or set off which he would have available against the person who was really behind the transaction ...'

7 Bills of exchange

The Bills of Exchange Act 1882 applies to both cheques and bills of exchange and (apart from when Part 3 of the Act provides otherwise) the provisions of the Act relating to bills of exchange payable on demand apply equally to cheques. There are, however, special provisions, for example ss. 60 and 80 of the Bills of Exchange Act 1882, s. 4 of the Cheques Act 1957 and the Cheques Act 1992, which apply exclusively to cheques.

The Jack Committee recommended that instead of the present Bills of Exchange Act 1882 dealing with negotiable instruments there should be two separate Acts dealing with such instruments, namely:

(a) a new Bills of Exchange Act dealing with its recommendations on negotiability and bills of exchange; and

(b) a separate Act dealing with cheques and the bank payment mandate.

DEFINITION AND CONDITIONS FOR INCURRING LIABILITY

The Bills of Exchange Act 1882 defines both a bill of exchange and a cheque. It is possible to produce a general definition by examining two sections in the Act. Section 73 of the Act provides that:

'A cheque is a bill of exchange drawn on a banker payable on demand'

and s. 3(1) provides:

'A bill of exchange is an unconditional order in writing, addressed by one person to another, signed by the person giving it, requiring the person to whom it is addressed to pay on demand or at a fixed or determinable future time a certain sum in money to or to the order of a specified person or bearer.'

The significance of s. 3(1) is emphasised by the following subsection which provides that:

'An instrument which does not comply with these conditions, or which orders any act to be done in addition to the payment, is not a bill of exchange.'

Orbit Mining and Trading Co. Ltd v *Westminster Bank Ltd* [1963] 3 All ER 565

The plaintiff company had two directors who were authorised, jointly, to draw cheques on the company's account.

One of the directors, Epstein, had some years before joining the company opened a private account with the defendant bank which was unaware of the fact that Epstein had become a director of the plaintiff company.

The co-director on going abroad left several crossed cheque forms signed in blank with Epstein who fraudulently completed them with his own signature (which was illegible) and made the cheques payable 'cash or order' for the credit of his private account.

When the fraud was discovered the company brought an action against the bank for conversion of the cheques.

The court held that the instruments were not cheques and further the bank had lost the protection of s. 4 of the Cheques Act 1957 and s. 17 of the Revenue Act 1883 (now repealed). Moreover, the court held that the instrument was not a cheque within the meaning of s. 73 and s. 82 of the Bills of Exchange Act 1882 (s. 82 is now repealed and replaced by s. 4(2)(b) of the Cheques Act 1957). The bank appealed against the finding of negligence.

The Court of Appeal held that the bank had discharged the burden of proving that it had collected the instrument without negligence and was so protected from liability by s. 4(1)(a) of the Cheques Act 1957. The circumstances were not such that the bank ought to have known that the illegible drawer's signature was that of Epstein, the customer for whom it was collecting the cheque, nor that he was employed by the plaintiffs.

The Court of Appeal, however, upheld MacKenna J, at first instance, and said that the instrument drawn pay 'cash or order' is not a cheque within s. 73 of the Cheques Act 1957. Harman LJ said (p. 577):

'In order to be a cheque within s. 73, the document must be a bill of exchange. This is defined by s. 3(1) of the Act of 1882, under which there must be a sum payable 'to the order of a specified person or bearer'. Clearly 'cash' is not a specified person, and I do not think that unless made expressly in favour of the bearer it is enough to argue that 'cash or order' in the end as a matter of construction means 'bearer' and I agree with the judge below that the mandate to pay bearer must be expressed and not implied. As to s. 4(2)(b), this is clearly a document intended to enable a person to obtain payment of the sum mentioned in the document. 'Person' here means any person, and does not require a named person; therefore, 'cash' is good enough. The question is whether the document was 'issued by a customer of a banker'.

The Court of Appeal expressly rejected the idea that a 'pay cash or order' instrument could be treated as a bearer instrument within s. 7(3) of the Bills of Exchange Act 1882 (see p. 134). In so doing the court approved the judgment in *Cole v Milsome* ([1951] 1 All ER 311) where it was held that an innocent plaintiff who received an instrument drawn 'pay cash or order' from a fraudulent third party was not entitled to recover from the defendant, as drawer, the amount of the instrument. The court rejected the view taken in *North and South Insurance Corporation Ltd v National Provincial Bank Ltd* ([1936] 1 KB 328) that an instrument drawn in such a form was payable to bearer. In that case an instrument drawn 'pay cash or order' was paid by the defendant bank a few days after a winding-up petition (unknown to the bank) had been presented against the drawer company. The liquidator claimed that the bank had wrongfully made payment. The court held that an instrument in the form of a cheque but drawn 'pay cash or order' was not a cheque and the words 'or order' were to be disregarded with the result the instrument was by implication a bearer bill.

In *Cole* v *Milsome* the view taken was that a pay cash document was no more than that and if the amount of the instrument is paid to the person intended to receive it the drawer cannot claim it back from the bank and the person who holds the pay cash instrument is not treated as a nominee of the drawer.

The following guidelines were laid down in the October 1951 issue of the *Journal of the Institute of Bankers* on the payment of 'pay cash or order' or 'pay wages or order' instruments, if they otherwise appear to be in order:

(a) if uncrossed, the instrument may safely be paid over the counter only to the drawer or his known agent and whether indorsed or not (the indorsement of the drawer does not make the instrument transferable);

(b) if crossed and bearing no sign of having been transferred, it may be paid through the clearing or over the counter to another bank without question, whether indorsed by the drawer or not;

(c) it should not be collected, if uncrossed, except for a responsible customer.

Other cases on s. 3(1)

There have been several other cases where the courts have had to examine s. 3(1) of the Bills of Exchange Act 1882. Under the section a bill of exchange or a cheque must be an 'unconditional order' with the result that an instrument which requires as a condition of payment a receipt to be signed by the payee does not fall within s. 3(1). In *Bavins Jnr & Sims* v *London & South Western Bank* ([1900] 1 QB 270) the plaintiff received an instrument in the form of a cheque which required a receipt at the foot of the instrument to be signed and dated. The instrument was stolen from the plaintiff at a time when the part constituting the receipt was unsigned. The instrument was subsequently paid into an account at the defendant bank for collection bearing a forged indorsement and the receipt having been signed. In an action by the plaintiff against the collecting bank it was held that the instrument was not a cheque within the definition of the Bills of Exchange Act because it was not an unconditional order.

Where, however, the instruction to sign a receipt in order to acknowledge payment is addressed to the payee personally and not the bank, the instrument will satisfy s. 3(1) of the 1882 Act. In both *Nathan* v *Ogden* ((1905) 94 LR 126) and *Thairlwall* v *Great Northern Railway Co.* ([1910] 2 KB 509) the courts held that instructions at the foot of the instruments did not make them conditional. In the latter case a dividend warrant contained a note that it was not to be honoured after three months from the date of issue. The instrument was a cheque and the note was merely an indication of what was considered a reasonable time within which to make payment. In any case the direction was addressed to the payee and not the bank. The use of receipt forms has diminished considerably since the Cheques Act 1957, provided that the paid cheque is prima facie evidence of payment although it must now be remembered that banks have done away with the practice of returning paid cheques to the drawer.

In *Little* v *Slackford* ((1828) 1 Mood & M 171) an instrument in the form 'You will oblige your humble servant ...' was held to be a mere request and not a demand to make payment. The instrument must be a mandate so as to oblige the bank to make payment (see *Ellison* v *Collingridge* (1850) 9 CB 570).

The instrument must be payable on demand or at a fixed or determinable time in the future. Section 10 of the Bills of Exchange Act 1882 provides that a bill of exchange is payable on demand when it is expressed to be so payable, or is payable at sight, or on presentation or when no time for payment is expressed. In *Korea Exchange Bank* v *Debenhams (Central Buying) Ltd* ([1979] 1 Lloyd's Rep 549) a bill had been drawn as follows:

'At 90 days D/A of this first Bill of Exchange ... Pay to ... or order.'

The word 'sight', which was part of the printed form, had been deleted by over-typing. The defendants claimed that the bill was defective in form and the question before the court was whether the instrument, as expressed, was payable at a fixed or determinable future time. The court held that there could be sight of the bill without acceptance and to achieve certainty the bill must contain provisions as to the date of maturity in the event of non-acceptance, as well as acceptance. The instrument did not fall within s. 11 of the 1882 Act which provides that a bill is payable at a determinable future time when it is payable at a fixed period after sight or date, or at a fixed period after the occurrence of a specified contingency, though the time of the happening of the contingency may be uncertain. More recently in *Claydon* v *Bradley* ([1987] 1 WLR 521) an instrument drawn in the form 'Received from (the plaintiffs) the sum of £10,000 as a loan to be paid back in full by July 1, 1983' and signed by the defendant was not a negotiable instrument. The Court of Appeal held that the instrument created an uncertainty or contingency as to the time of payment and therefore the instrument was a mere receipt acknowledging a debt.

Postdated cheques

A bank is bound to pay a postdated cheque presented for payment on or after the date of payment. In both *Whistler* v *Forster* ((1863) 14 CB (NS) 248) and *Austin* v *Bunyard* ((1865) 6 B & S 687) it was held that the holders of postdated cheques could recover the amounts for which the cheques were drawn and that the instruments were to be taken to have been drawn according to the date appearing on the face of the instruments.

A somewhat different situation arises under s. 3(4)(a) of the 1882 Act which provides that prima facie the instrument need not be dated. In that case the instrument would presumably be payable on demand or on presentation. In practice banks will refuse to pay undated cheques without the drawer's consent and this refusal of the bank to make payment was upheld in *Griffiths* v *Dalton* ([1940] 2 KB 264) where the defendant gave the plaintiff an undated cheque and the plaintiff purported to fill in the date some 18 months later. The cheque was dishonoured on presentation for payment and the court held that the delay in completing the cheque under the authority given by s. 20(1) of the 1882 Act was unreasonable and the bank justified in refusing to make payment.

A cheque may be drawn or negotiated for any sum of money but it must be for a certain sum which is normally expressed in both words and figures. A cheque drawn 'Pay A after deducting what he owes me' was not held to be a cheque since it was not possible to ascertain the amount payable to the payee without looking beyond the instrument (*Barlow* v *Broadhurst* (1820) 4 Moore CP 471). However, a cheque for French francs was held to be for a certain sum of money although it was required to be paid according to the rate of exchange when the cheque was presented *(Cohn* v *Boulken* (1920) 36 TLR 767).

Finally, the cheque must be payable to a specified person or his order or to bearer. Section 7(1) provides:

> 'Where a bill is not payable to bearer, the payee must be named or otherwise indicated therein with reasonable certainty.'

In *Chamberlain* v *Young* ([1893] 2 QB 206) the court held that an instrument made payable to '... order', the blank never having been filled in, must be construed as meaning that it was payable to 'my order,' i.e. to the order of the drawer.

The Jack Committee made a number of recommendations relating to the requirement that the sum payable under a negotiable instrument should be a 'sum certain' in money. The Committee recommended that the sum payable should no longer have to be certain on the date of issue provided it is 'certain or ordinarily determinable' in accordance with the rules established under the proposed new Act. In order to avoid doubt, and to ensure that the ECU is covered, some further clarification was suggested. The new Act should make provisions so that 'a certain or ordinarily determinable sum' includes instruments expressed in 'a monetary unit of account established by an inter-governmental institution'. Further, the Jack Committee recommended that in order to assist in determining amounts payable on instruments expressed to be otherwise than in sterling, the new Act should provide that:

(a) instruments are ordinarily payable in the currency in which they are expressed;
(b) the amount may be expressed in one currency with provision for payment in another;
(c) if an instrument is expressed in a unit of account which is capable of being freely transferred from one person to another, it is so payable. If it is, however, expressed in a unit of account which is not transferable, and no currency of payment is specified, payment should be made in the currency of the place of payment;
(d) where a currency conversion is necessary to determine the amount payable, the rate of exchange or the method of determining the rate of exchange may be stated on the instrument or, failing that, it should be determined by reference to the paying bank's sight draft rate or some other published rate on the day of payment.

Where interest is payable the rate may be either fixed or variable. If interest is payable at a rate which varies, the reference rate against which the interest payable is calculated must be determined in relation to one or more published or public rates.

Any notations of the type described by the Jack Committee would not render the instrument conditional.

Cheque drawn to a fictitious or non-existent payee

Under s. 7(3) of the 1882 Act where the payee of a bill is a fictitious or non-existent person the bill may be treated as a bearer bill. A genuine indorsement of a bill payable to bearer or to a fictitious payee is impossible because such a person does not exist and unless such an instrument were treated as payable to bearer it would be impossible to receive payment on it. The effect of s. 7(3) is that the mere fact a bill is payable to a fictitious or non-existent person does not affect the rights of a person who subsequently receives or pays it in good faith.

The impact of s. 7(3) has been examined in a number of cases.

Bank of England v Vagliano Brothers (1891) AC 107

The plaintiffs were a firm of merchants in London who banked with the Bank of England and were in the habit of accepting bills drawn payable at the Bank. Among the firm's foreign correspondents was one Vucina, who in the course of business regularly drew bills on Vagliano Brothers in favour of Petridi & Co., a firm in Constantinople. A clerk of Vagliano Brothers forged a series of bills purported to be drawn by Vucina on Vagliano Brothers, in favour of Petridi & Co. In order to obtain Vagliano Brothers' acceptance of the forged bills the clerk also forged corresponding letters of advice purporting to come from Vucina. When Vagliano Brothers had accepted the forged bills they were misappropriated by the clerk and indorsed by him with a forgery of Petridi & Co.'s signature. On maturity the clerk presented the bills at the Bank of England and the Bank, having been advised of the acceptance of the bills by Vagliano Brothers, paid them over the counter to the clerk and then debited the account of Vagliano Brothers. When the fraud was discovered Vagliano Brothers brought an action to determine whether the Bank was entitled to debit their account with the amounts of the misappropriated bills.

It was admitted that as Vagliano Brothers had accepted the bills and advised the Bank of the acceptance they could not dispute the signature of the apparent drawer, Vucina, but they argued that the forged payee's indorsement resulted in payment being made to a person who could not give a good discharge. Accordingly under s. 24 of the Act the Bank was not entitled to debit Vagliano Brothers' account.

On behalf of the Bank it was argued that:

(a) Vagliano Brothers were precluded by their own negligence from setting up the forgery of Petridi's indorsement; and
(b) that the Bank was protected by s. 7(3).

On the question of negligence, Lord Halsbury LC and Lord Selborne were of the opinion that as Vagliano Brothers had accepted the bills and had advised the Bank of their acceptances they could not contend that the payments made by the Bank were unauthorised. There was a difference of opinion between the members of the House on the question of estoppel by negligence, but merely in connection with the inference of fact to be drawn from the evidence in the case and not as to the rule of law. The rule applied was that in order to create an estoppel by negligence, the negligence relied on must have been the direct and proximate cause of the false signature being taken as genuine. It was problematical whether negligence by Vagliano Brothers was the proximate cause of the deception of the Bank.

On the construction of s. 7(3), the House of Lords held that the payees named in the bill (Petridi & Co.) were fictitious or non-existent within the meaning of s. 7(3) and that the bills were payable to bearer so that payment over the counter to the person who presented the bills was sufficient to discharge them. The House of Lords examined the scope of s. 7(3) which provides:

'Where the payee is a fictitious or non-existent person the bill may be treated as payable to bearer.'

Lord Herschell on the meaning of the word 'fictitious' said (p. 152):

'Do the words, "where the payee is a fictitious person," apply only where the payee named never had a real existence? I take it to be clear that by the word "payee" must be understood the payee named on the face of the bill; for of course by the hypothesis there is no intention that payment should be made to any such person. Where, then, the payee named is so named by way of pretence only, without the intention that he shall be the person to receive payment, is it doing violence to language to say that the payee is a fictitious person? I think not. I do not think that the word 'fictitious' is exclusively used to qualify that which has no real existence. When we speak of a fictitious entry in a book of accounts, we do not mean that the entry has no real existence, but only that it purports to be that which it is not – that it is an entry made for the purpose of pretending that the transaction took place which is represented by it.'

And Lord Macnaghten (on p. 161) said:

'Then it was said that the proper meaning of "fictitious" is "imaginary." I do not think so. I think the proper meaning of the word is "feigned" or "counterfeit." It seems to me that the "C. Petridi & Co.' named as payees on these pretended bills were, strictly speaking, fictitious persons. When the bills came before Vagliano for acceptance they were fictitious from beginning to end. The drawer was fictitious; the payee was fictitious; the person indicated as agent for presentation was fictitious. One and all they were feigned or counterfeit persons put forward as real persons, each in a several and distinct capacity; whereas in truth, they were make-believe for the persons whose names appeared on the instrument. They were not, I think, the less fictitious because there were in existence real persons for whom these names were intended to pass muster.'

The House of Lords in the *Vagliano* case was not united on the meaning of fictitious or non-existent payee. Lords Bramwell and Field were of the opinion that the payees were not fictitious, there being a real firm of the name Petridi & Co. in existence, their name being inserted as payee because Vagliano Brothers were accustomed to accepting bills drawn by Vucina in their favour. In determining whether the payee is fictitious Lord Bramwell said it is not a question of intention but a question of fact and the bills were payable to an existing person. If there were no real payee, the name inserted was a mere *nominis umbra* and the payee then, and only then, a fictitious payee.

The *Bank of England* v *Vagliano* case left a number of questions unanswered, for example whether the real or fictitious character of the payee depends on the intention of the person who actually drew the bill; whether the intention of other parties should be taken into account in determining the character of the payee; and whether the character of the payee as a real or fictitious person should be linked to the presence or absence of a real transaction in connection with which the bill was issued.

In *Clutton* v *Attenborough* ([1897] AC 90) a clerk in the accounts department of the appellants by fraudulently representing to them that certain work had been done on their account by a person named B induced them to draw cheques payable to the order of B. The cheques, signed by the appellants, were handed by them to their accounts department for transmission to the payee, B. The clerk obtained possession of the cheques and indorsed the payee's signature on them and negotiated the bills to the respondents, who gave value and took them in good faith. The cheques were paid to the respondents by the appellants' bankers. When the appellants discovered the fraud they brought an action against the respondents to recover the amounts of the cheques as money had and received under a mistake of fact. The House of Lords held that although the cheques were drawn in favour of a person named, B, and there might be a person of that name in existence, the payee of the cheques was nevertheless fictitious because the name, B, had been provided by the person wishing to commit the fraud and they had no knowledge of anyone by that name. The appellants could not have intended the payee to be a real, identifiable person.

The *Clutton* case is distinguishable from *Vinden* v *Hughes* ([1905] 1 KB 795) where a cashier filled in a number of cheque forms with the names of his employer's customers, as payees, and obtained the signature of his employer as drawer. The cashier then forged the signature of the payee by way of indorsement and discounted the cheques to the defendant who obtained payment from the drawer's bankers.

In an action to recover the amounts of the cheques from the defendant the court held that the payee was not a fictitious or non-existing payee because at the time the cheques were drawn the drawer intended certain identifiable persons to receive the amounts of the cheques. Warrington J said (p. 800):

> '... that what one has to look at (and the only thing one has to look at for the purpose of construing the Act) is the state of things at the time the cheque was drawn.'

The importance of the rule that a bill payable to a fictitious or non-existent payee or one which may be payable to bearer arises because it enables any forged indorsement purporting to be that of the payee to be disregarded.

However, the decision in *North & South Wales Bank Ltd* v *Macbeth* ([1908] AC 137) deprives the *Vagliano* case of most of its practical value since it will rarely happen that the drawer of the instrument will sign it without intending it to be payable to an identifiable payee. In that case one White fraudulently induced Macbeth to draw a cheque for £11,250 in favour of 'Kerr or order'. Kerr was an existing person known to Macbeth, and Macbeth, although misled by White as to the intended use of the cheque, fully intended that Kerr should receive the amount of the cheque. White obtained the cheque and forged Kerr's indorsement on it. He then paid the cheque into his account with the appellant bank. Macbeth, on discovering the fraud, brought an action against the bank to recover the money on the ground that the collecting bank was guilty of conversion.

The bank alleged that the payee was a fictitious payee within s. 7(3) of the Act and that the cheque was, therefore, payable to bearer.

The House of Lords held that s. 7(3) did not apply because the drawer of the cheque, Macbeth, intended that a real person known to Macbeth should receive the amount of the cheque and so it could not be said the payee of the cheque was fictitious or non-existent.

The problems raised by s. 7(3) can often be avoided by treating the instrument as a bill by estoppel under ss. 54 and 55 of the Act. Under those sections neither the drawer nor the acceptor can deny to a holder in due course the existence of the payee and his capacity to indorse the bill.

PARTIES TO THE INSTRUMENT AND CONDITIONS FOR INCURRING LIABILITY

The parties to a negotiable instrument are:

(a) the drawer – who brings the instrument into existence;
(b) the drawee – is the person to whom the payment mandate is addressed and who is primarily liable to make payment (e.g. a bank). The drawee may also be the acceptor of a bill of exchange. A cheque does not have to be accepted so there cannot be an acceptor of a cheque;
(c) the payee – who is to receive payment on the instrument or who may indorse it to a third party. The indorser will be secondarily liable to make payment to the indorsee;
(d) indorsee – the person to whom the instrument has been negotiated. An indorsee, if a holder in due course, will take free from defects of title even against the true owner of the instrument.

The Bills of Exchange Act 1882, s. 23, provides that no one is liable on the bill as drawer, indorser or acceptor unless he has signed it. An agent may sign on behalf of the drawer, indorser or acceptor and s. 91(1) allows an agent merely to write the principal's name on the instrument without any indication of agency.

If an agent signs in his own name and adds words that indicate that he signs in a representative capacity, that is notice that the agent has limited authority to sign the instrument and the principal will only be bound if the agent acts within that capacity. The effect of s. 25 has been discussed in a number of cases. In *Midland Bank* v *Reckitt* ([1933] AC 1 at page 16) Lord Atkin made the following comment on s. 25 of the 1882 Act:

'The effect of the statute is to give notice of the limited authority on the face of the document, and this operates as and when the document is negotiated or delivered. The legal consequence of such notice may be to prevent the holder who obtains payment from supporting his right to have received payment ... The rights in respect of a bill after payment are no doubt matters of special consideration; but whether before or after payment the fact that the bill contains on the face of it notice of limited authority to place on it the particular signature continues to be a fact affecting *pro tanto* the rights of the parties both before and after payment.'

Lord Atkin rejected the view taken in *Morison* v *London County and Westminster Bank Ltd* ([1914] 3 KB 356) and said:

'that the operation of this section [25] was limited to the time before the instrument was honoured, but that after a bill so signed in excess of authority has been honoured, s. 25 did not confer a right to recover the proceeds. If the words used meant to mark off a definite period within which alone the section affects legal rights, I see no ground for such a distinction.'

Although the learned judges might have disagreed on the cut-off point of s. 25 they were in no doubt as to the effect of the section and Lord Reading in the *Morison* case stated its effect as follows (p. 367):

'... not withstanding the authority given by the principal to the agent to sign negotiable instruments per procuration so as to bind the principal, the principal is not liable upon the instrument, even to a holder in due course, if the agent in so signing the cheque exceeded the actual limits of his authority.'

Section 26 applies to signatures in a representative capacity. Section 26 provides:

'Where a person signs a bill as drawer, indorser or acceptor, and adds words to his signature, indicating that he signs for or on behalf of a principal, or in a representative character, he is not personally liable thereon; but the mere addition to his signature of words describing him as an agent or as filling a representative character, does not exclude him from personal liability.'

Rolfe Lubell & Co. v Keith and Another [1979] 1 All ER 860

The plaintiffs agreed to supply goods to a company on the understanding that the bills of exchange drawn in payment were personally indorsed by two of the officers of the company. The bills were accepted by the defendants, the managing director and secretary of the company, who also signed the backs of the bills with a rubber-stamp composed of the words 'For and on the behalf of' the company, and the designations 'Director' and 'Secretary'. The bills were eventually dishonoured and the company put into receivership. The plaintiffs sued the defendants claiming that they were personally liable on the bills. The action against the secretary was eventually discontinued but the court looked at the effect of s. 26(1) of the 1882 Act in respect of the personal liability of the managing director.

Kilner-Brown J held for the plaintiffs and in the course of the judgment said (p. 863):

'The two defendants signed for and on behalf of the company and made the company liable on the bill as acceptor. By signing in similar form on the back of the bill they produced what counsel for the plaintiffs described as a mercantile nonsense. An indorsement on the back of a bill amounts to a warrant that the bill will be honoured and imposes in certain circumstances a transfer of liability to the indorser. The only way in which validity can be given to this indorsement is by construing it to bind someone other than the acceptor. As soon therefore as it becomes obvious that the indorsement as worded is meaningless and of no value there is a patent ambiguity which allows evidence to be admitted to give effect to the intentions of the parties.'

On the facts the judge found that the defendant realised that by signing the back of the bills he was accepting personal liability. In giving effect to s. 26(2) of the Act, which provides:

'In determining whether a signature on a bill is that of the principal or that of the agent by whose hand it is written, the construction most favourable to the validity of the instrument shall be adopted.'

the judge rejected the contention that:

'no evidence can be admitted to give a different meaning to words which have an accepted meaning and which seeks to prove a different relationship between the parties than that which is unambiguously expressed.'

An agent who signs a negotiable instrument on behalf of his principal must clearly use words which indicate that he signs as an agent in order to be released from being made personally liable on the instrument. It may not be enough to place the words 'agent' or 'director' after the signature since the words merely refer to the office held or occupied by the signatory and not necessarily that he signs in that capacity (see *Parker* v *Winlow* (1857) 7 E & B 942 and *Landes* v *Marcus* (1909) 25 TLR 478). However, in *Chapman* v *Smethurst* ([1909] 1 KB 927) the placing of the word 'director' after the signature was held to make the instrument a promissory note issued by the company.

Another case where the effect of s. 26(2) was examined is *Elliott* v *Bax-Ironside* ([1925] 2 KB 301) where two directors of the company indorsed the back of a bill of exchange 'in order to guarantee the liability of the company'. The court held that under s. 6(2) the directors would be treated as having indorsed the bill in their personal capacity, as that was the only method of giving the additional guarantee required of them.

In *Bondina Ltd* v *Rollaway Shower Blinds Ltd* ([1986] 1 All ER 564) it was held that a cheque signed by a director of a company without any indication of the capacity in which he signed the instrument was a cheque drawn by the company because in placing his signature on it, the director adopted all the wording on it including the name of the company.

It is impossible to be dogmatic about the words which suffice to negative personal liability since the court is entitled to look at the document as a whole in order to discover the capacity of the signatory.

Where the drawer of the instrument is a company it may be possible to establish the personal liability of the signatory under s. 349(4) of the Companies Act 1985 (formerly s. 108(4) of the Companies Act 1948) which provides that:

'... if an officer of a company or a person on its behalf signs or authorises to be signed on behalf of the company any bill of exchange, promissory note, indorsement, cheque or order for money or goods in which the company's name is not mentioned as required by subsection (1), he is liable to a fine; and he is further personally liable to the holder of the bill of exchange, promissory note, cheque or order for money or goods for the amount of it (unless it is duly paid by the company).'

The word holder has been construed to mean the person to whom the order is addressed and who is to benefit by it. It should be noted that personal liability attaches not only to the person who signs the irregular document, but also to the person who authorises its signature. But a person who gives such an authority is personally liable only if he expressly authorises the signature by another of a document if he knows it will be irregular.

In *Durham Fancy Goods Ltd* v *Michael Jackson (Fancy Goods) Ltd* ([1968] 2 All ER 987) the plaintiffs had drawn a bill on the defendants which wrongly named them as 'M Jackson (Fancy Goods) Ltd' and prepared a form of acceptance in the same way. The director and company signed the acceptance without noticing the misdescription. The bill was dishonoured. It was held that the director was personally liable on the bill but that the company was estopped from enforcing his liability since it was responsible for the error. In *Maxform SpA* v *Mariani and Goodville Ltd* ([1979] 2 Lloyd's Rep) a company director of Goodville Ltd was held personally liable on the bills drawn in its registered business name, Italdesign, without mention on the bills of Goodville Ltd. The court said that the word 'name' in s. 108 of the 1948 Act, could only mean the company's registered corporate name. In *British Airways Board* v *Parish* ([1979] 2 Lloyd's Rep) and *Calzaturificio Fiorella SpA* v *Walton and Another* ([1979] CLY 23) directors of two companies were held personally liable when the word 'Ltd' had been omitted from the company names. In *Banque de l'Indochine et de Suez* v *Euroseas Group Finance Co. Ltd* ([1981] 3 All ER 198) it was held that s. 108 of the 1948 Act would not render the company director personally liable because the abbreviation 'Co.' for 'Company' was well established and understood.

In *Barber & Nicholls* v *R & G Associates (London) Ltd* ([1985] CLY 129) it was held that s. 108 would not apply to impose personal liability on several dishonoured cheques because the bank had omitted the word 'London' from the company's printed name on the cheque forms. The omission was not that of the director but of the bank and s. 108 did not apply.

It should now be remembered that the company cannot plead lack of capacity in order to escape its payment obligations on a contract.

Delivery of the instrument

Although a signature is necessary on a negotiable instrument, it is not itself sufficient to render a person liable. Delivery is also necessary and s. 21(1) of the 1882 Act provides:

> 'Every contract on a bill, whether it be the drawer's, the acceptor's or an indorser's, is incomplete and revocable, until delivery of the instrument ...'

The Act (s. 2) defines delivery as:

> 'Delivery means transfer of possession, actual or constructive, from one person to another.'

Thus, the drawer will not be liable to the payee of the instrument until it has been handed over to the payee and the acceptor will not be liable to the payee until he has signed the instrument and handed it back to the payee (or by an exception under s.

21 signed the acceptance and given notice that he has done so) and an indorser will not be liable until he has signed and handed over the instrument to the indorsee.

Constructive possession occurs where one person holds the instrument on behalf of another. Thus, where the drawer signs the instrument and hands it over to an agent of the payee that will be sufficient delivery.

FORGED SIGNATURES AND FORGERY OF THE INSTRUMENT

Section 24 of the Bills of Exchange Act 1882 provides:

'A person is guilty of forgery if he makes a false instrument with the intention that he or another shall use it to induce somebody to accept it as genuine, and by reason of so accepting to do or not to do some act to his own or any other person's prejudice.'

Consequently, forgery is a defence to a person sued on a bill, cheque or promissory note even as against a bona fide holder for value or a holder in due course. The section deals with forged or unauthorised signatures and lays down the principle that a forged signature is a nullity if the forgery is that of the drawer, acceptor or indorser.

Where the drawer's signature is forged

In *Bank of England* v *Vagliano Brothers* ([1891] AC 107) Lord Halsbury said:

'I have designedly avoided calling these instruments [i.e. instruments on which the drawer's signature was forged] bills of exchange, they were nothing of the kind.'

Ruben v *Great Fingall Consolidated* [1906] AC 439

The secretary of a company without proper authority prepared a share certificate showing himself as the holder of shares in the company and affixed the company seal to it. He further forged the signatures of the directors so that the certificate purported to comply with the company's articles of association. An action was brought against the company for damages for refusing to register the appellants as owners of the shares.

In the absence of any evidence that the company represented its secretary as having authority to do anything other than purely the mere ministerial act of delivering share certificates the company was not estopped from disputing the validity of the share certificate.

Lord Macnaghten said (p. 444):

'This paper [i.e. the share certificate] is false and fraudulent from beginning to end. The representation of the company's seal which appears upon it, is counterfeit, and no better than a forgery. The signatures of the two directors which purport to authenticate the sealing are forgeries pure and simple. Every statement in the document is a lie.'

And later he continued:

'The fact that this fraudulent certificate was concocted in the company's office and was uttered and sent forth by its author from the place of its origin cannot give it an efficacy which it does not intrinsically possess.'

The rule that a forged document is a nullity and of no effect has been applied in a number of cases. In *Kreditbank Cassel GmbH* v *Schenkers* ([1927] 1 KB 826) the memorandum of the defendant company authorised the company to sign, draw, accept and indorse bills of exchange. Under the articles of association of the company the directors of the company were empowered 'to determine who shall be entitled to sign, draw, accept and indorse on the company's behalf ...' The defendants, whose business was that of forwarding agents, had a branch in Manchester under the management of one S. Clarke, who without authority from the defendants, and acting fraudulently, drew seven bills of exchange on behalf of the company. The bills were accepted by Clarke & Walker Ltd, a company in which S. Clarke was interested, and indorsed on behalf of the defendants 'SC Manchester Manager'. The bills were dishonoured by the acceptors and the plaintiffs, who were holders in due course, sued the defendants as drawers of the bills.

The court held that the bills of exchange were forgeries and the defendants not liable. Applying the decision in *Ruben* v *Great Fingall Consolidated* ([1906] AC 439) the Court of Appeal per Bankes LJ said 'I cannot see upon what principle your Lordships can hold that the defendants are liable in this action.'

Again in *Brewer* v *Westminster Bank Ltd & Another* ([1952] 2 TLR 568) the plaintiff was the beneficiary of her father's estate. On the suggestion of the second defendant, a managing clerk for a firm of solicitors which handled her father's legal affairs, she arranged for a joint account to be opened at the Abingdon branch of the defendant bank. A mandate allowing either the plaintiff or the second defendant to draw on the account was given to the bank on its standard form for joint accounts. Following the practice adopted by the bank where one of the joint account-holders was a solicitor, acting as an executor, the bank forwarded periodical statements to the managing clerk. The bank gave the plaintiff no indication of the state of her account. The managing clerk forged the signature of the plaintiff on a number of cheques and over a period of years withdrew approximately £3,000 from the account and used the sum for his own purposes. The forgeries were so skilful that the bank could not be held to have acted negligently. The plaintiff brought an action for a declaration that the bank was not entitled to debit the joint account with the amount of the forged cheques.

McNair J at first instance held a bank paying cheques on which the drawer's signature has been forged does not obtain a discharge, for it pays without a mandate although because of procedural difficulties the defrauded executor could not recover.

Before the Bills of Exchange Act 1882 was enacted the absence of protection of the bona fide holder of a forged instrument was based on the fiction that the forged indorsement was absent (see *Esdaile* v *La Nauze* (1835) 1 Y & C Ex 394).

A forgery can never be ratified (*Brook* v *Hook* (1871) 47 LR 6 Ex 89) but it may acquire some negotiability by a genuine indorsement or by a representation that the acceptance or indorsement is genuine. In *Leach* v *Buchanan* ((1802) 4 Esp 226) the signature of a party to a negotiable instrument was forged. The holder had doubts as to the validity of the signature and asked the signatory whether it was genuine. He received a positive reply and then negotiated the bill to a transferee who assumed that the signature was genuine. The court held that the transferee could recover on the bill and the representor had given credit to the bill and induced others to take it.

Even mere non-disclosure of the forgery may result in an estoppel where there is a duty of disclosure and prevent the representor from denying his representation. In *Greenwood* v *Martins Bank* ([1932] 1 KB 371) the customer's wife forged his name on a number of cheques which were debited against the customer's account. The customer discovered the forgeries but failed to notify the bank until after the suicide of his wife, when he brought an action to recover the amounts of the forged cheques. The House of Lords held that the customer could not be heard to say that his signature was forged and claim to have his account re-credited with the amount of the forged cheques. He owed a duty of care to disclose forgeries when they became known to him (cf. *M'Kenzie* v *British Linen Co.* (1881) 6 App Cas 82 where it was said that even if the disclosure had been made with the utmost diligence estoppel could not be raised).

Forgery of some material part of the bill

A forgery may not necessarily invalidate the bill completely and if the forgery is not apparent a subsequent holder in due course may be able to enforce the bill under s. 64(1) of the 1882 Act. In *Kwei Tek Chao* v *British Traders and Shippers* ([1954] 2 QB 459) Devlin J said (p. 476):

'... if the forgery corrupts the whole of the instrument or its heart, then the instrument is destroyed, but if it corrupts merely a limb, the instrument remains alive, though no doubt defective ...'

The Jack Committee explored the issue of forged signatures on a bill of exchange. Its proposal that the person whose signature has been forged on a negotiable instrument should be able to ratify it found no support and the Committee therefore decided not to pursue the issue any further. However, in relation to the forged signature of other parties, e.g where the forgery consists of forging the signature of the indorser, drawer or acceptor the Committee recommended that a protective rule should be established so that:

(a) in relation to a forged drawer's or acceptor's signature the existing law should be retained so that:

    (i) the bank should be able to recover from the person wrongly paid, unless it is estopped;

    (ii) the bank should not normally be entitled to an indemnity from its customer.

There should, however, be new provisions:

    (i) entitling the bank to be indemnified if the customer has been negligent;

    (ii) but, if the bank was also negligent, the loss should be apportioned between the parties; and

(iii) if the customer has indemnified the bank (whether in whole or in part), then he should be able to recover from the payee, unless he is estopped.

(b) in relation to forged or unauthorised indorsements, the existing law should remain unaltered so that:

(i) the true owner should be able to claim compensation from the bank which has paid the wrong person, and when he has been so compensated the bill is discharged;

(ii) the paying bank's right to recover from the person wrongly paid (unless the bank is estopped) would remain.

There should, however, be new provisions so that:

(i) the paying bank should be entitled to be indemnified from its customer, the drawer or the acceptor;

(ii) but should not be able to rely on the indemnity if it was negligent;

(iii) unless the customer was also negligent, in which case the losses should be apportioned;

(iv) and if the customer has indemnified the bank or is required to contribute to the loss, he should be able to recover from the payee.

The Jack Committee, however, suggested that these rules should be open to variation by contractual agreement.

CONSIDERATION ON A BILL OF EXCHANGE

Section 27 of the 1882 Act provides:

Valuable consideration for a bill may be constituted by:

(a) any consideration sufficient to support a simple contract;
(b) an antecedent debt or liability. Such a debt or liability is deemed valuable consideration whether the bill is payable on demand or at a future time.

MK International Development Co. Ltd v Housing Bank (unreported) 21 December 1990

The case arose from the transactions of a relative of King Hussein of Jordan, one N, who required some office space and some financial accommodation during a short period spent in London in 1983 and 1984. K made the necessary arrangements through two companies controlled by him. MK provided the necessary space against an undertaking given by N to reimburse an amount of £1,000 towards expenses and Y Ltd granted N a substantial loan. When N defaulted, K wrote directly to King Hussein, using MK's letterhead, asking that pressure be put on N to repay his debts. K eventually received a letter from the Chief of the Royal Court, enclosing a cheque for £50,965, drawn by the Housing Bank in Amman on the Arab Bank in London and made payable to MK or bearer. However, before MK had the time to present the cheque for payment, N contacted the King's staff and denied the debt. The cheque was countermanded and payment refused. The question that arose was whether leave to serve a writ on the Housing Bank outside the jurisdiction would be granted. Initially, Master Grant gave MK leave to serve a writ but that order was set aside by Master Tench. Leave to serve the writ was restored by Sir Peter Pain and the decision was affirmed by the Court of Appeal. The Court of Appeal held that leave to serve a summons outside the jurisdiction should be granted because the contract was made in England and governed by English law. However, the court felt that there was an arguable case on the issue of valid consideration given for the cheque.

The issue of consideration arose because the cheque was payable to MK whilst the amount it covered (except the £1,000 in relation to offices expenses) was payable to Y Ltd or K.

MK sought to overcome the problem of consideration by arguing:

(a) that N's debt furnished past consideration which under s. 27(1)(b) was adequate to support an undertaking given in a negotiable instrument; and

(b) that there was sufficient consideration to support a simple contract within s. 27(1)(a) because by relying on the cheque, K and MK forbore from enforcing their respective claims against K and MK.

Mustill LJ, after a review of the authorities, held that N's antecedent liabilities did not furnish a valid consideration for the cheque drawn by the Housing Bank in favour of MK. N was a stranger to the cheque and his past debts, due to Y or to K, were not a valid consideration for the cheque in favour of MK. Mustill LJ adopted the words of Robert Goff J in *Hanson* v *Wilson* 'antecedent debt or liability referred to in s. 27(1)(b) must be antecedent debt or liability of the promissor or drawer of the bill of exchange and not of a stranger to the bill.'

Mustill LJ said:

'the line between the two ways of putting the case seems vanishingly thin, for if the antecedent debt is to furnish any useful consideration this must be because it is regarded as nullified by the substitution of the new obligation; and the distinction between a contract which causes the old debt to cease to exist and one which requires the creditor not to enforce it appears of little practical significance ...'

Mustill LJ then dealt with the forbearance issue. Although he agreed that normally such forbearance would constitute good consideration, the judge pointed out that only a small amount, from the total cheque, was owed to MK. He said the real question was whether the partial absence of consideration provided a good defence to MK's action on the cheque. Mustill LJ said that it was established that 'an ascertained cross-claim under the contract which formed the consideration for the bill [was] a good defence *pro tanto* as against an immediate party.' The learned judge continued: 'There seems no logical reason why, if subsequent failure of consideration is a defence as between immediate parties the same should not be so where, as to part, the consideration was never there in the first place.' Mustill LJ concluded that MK could have a good cause of action on the bill, although limited to the amount of the debt owed to it.

Another attempt to establish the existence of a valid consideration was based on the effect of s. 27(2) which provides that 'where value has at any time been given for a bill, the holder is deemed to be a holder for value ... ' It was asserted that as the King had given value for the cheque, MK was deemed to be a holder for value. Mustill LJ indicated that the authorities suggested that s.27(2) applied only where the instrument had been negotiated and not in favour of the original payee. He was also of the view that the consideration under s. 27(2) would have to move from a promissee of the bill and not from a stranger, such as the King.

The final attempt to establish consideration was based on the fact that the cheque was payable to 'MK or bearer'. Mustill LJ observed that if the cheque was accordingly payable to bearer then the King could be considered its first holder. The consideration furnished by him would then inure in favour of any subsequent holder, such as MK.

It should be remembered that the judgments in the *MK International* case were delivered in a preliminary hearing and that the points raised might be discussed and examined in more detail in a full hearing.

Hansan v *Willson* [1977] 1 Lloyd's Rep 431

The plaintiff, a finance broker acting on behalf of an unnamed government, wished to sell a large quantity of gold coins. He was introduced to Smith who, acting on behalf of another government, wished to purchase some 400 tons of gold coins. A contract for the sale of the coins was entered into which was subsequently defaulted on and which left Smith liable to pay £50,000 to the plaintiff. In order to circumvent provisions in the companies legislation prohibiting loans to directors, Smith persuaded the defendant to draw two cheques (one for £50,000 in favour of the plaintiff and a second cheque for £5,000 in favour of P Ltd) in return for Smith's wife issuing a cheque on P Ltd for £55,000 in favour of the defendant. Smith then paid the defendant's cheque, for £50,000, to the plaintiff but the cheque was dishonoured because the defendant, having discovered that the cheques drawn by Smith's wife were worthless, had countermanded payment of the cheque drawn by him.

Goff J held that consideration had wholly failed and although under s. 27(1)(b) valuable consideration might be constituted by an 'antecedent debt or liability', such a debt or liability must be the liability of the promissor or the drawer of the bill and not that of a stranger. Consequently, there could be no liability on the defendant's part under s. 27 because the plaintiff was a stranger. Moreover, the defendants signature had been obtained by fraud.

In *Hansan* v *Willson* Goff J applied the earlier case of *Oliver* v *Davis* ([1949] 2 KB 727). In that case the plaintiff lent £350 to Davis, who gave him a postdated cheque for £400. Davis could not meet the cheque and persuaded a Miss Woodcock to send the plaintiff a cheque for £400. Prior to the cheque being presented for payment, she became aware of certain facts and countermanded payment of her cheque. The plaintiff brought an action against Miss Woodcock who contended that there had been no consideration for the cheque. The plaintiff succeeded in the High Court and Miss Woodcock appealed. The Court of Appeal allowed the appeal and held that the antecedent debt of a third party was not good consideration and the defendant was entitled to stop payment of her cheque. Sir Raymond Evershed MR said (p. 735):

'I think for myself that the proper construction of the words in (b) "An antecedent debt or liability" is that they refer to an antecedent debt or liability of the promissor or drawer of the bill and are intended to get over what would otherwise have been prima facie the result that at common law the giving of a cheque for an amount for which you are already indebted imports no consideration, since the obligation is past and has already been incurred.'

And relying on *Crears* v *Hunter* ((1887) 19 QBD 341) Sir Raymond Evershed MR continued:

'This at any rate is plain – that if the antecedent debt or liability of a third party is to be relied upon as supplying "valuable consideration for a bill", there must at least be some relationship between the receipt of the bill and the antecedent debt or liability. And for practical purposes it is difficult to see how there can be any distinction between a case in which there is a sufficient relationship for this purpose between the bill and the antecedent debt or liability and a case in which, as a result of that relationship, there is in the ordinary sense a consideration passing from the payee to the drawer of the bill. Otherwise the creditor might recover both from the third party and on the cheque from the drawer.'

In *Diamond* v *Graham* ([1968] 1 WLR 1061), however, the plaintiff gave a cheque for £1,650 to a third party on the condition that he gave a cheque to the plaintiff or £1,665. Both the cheques were dishonoured and in an action for the dishonour of the larger cheque the defendant argued that no consideration had passed from the plaintiff to him. The court of appeal held that the plaintiff's cheque to the third party was sufficient consideration. Danckwerts LJ went on to say that consideration was also provided by the third party's cheque to the defendant.

THE HOLDER IN DUE COURSE

The Bills of Exchange Act 1882 (ss. 27 and 38) establishes a hierarchy of holders ranging from the mere holder followed by the holder for value and concluding with the holder in due course. The mere holder will not have given value for the bill, nor be able to take advantage of value having been given at an earlier stage. The holder for value will either himself have given value or be able to rely on the fact that value has been given earlier. He cannot be defeated by want of consideration from suing on the bill but he may be defeated by defences based on defects of title, e.g. an earlier transfer of the bill was obtained by fraud. The holder in due course enjoys all the benefits of negotiability. The position of the holder in due course and the protection conferred to a holder in due course was emphasised in *London Joint Stock Bank* v *Simmons* ([1892] AC 201) where Lord Herschell observed (p. 215):

'The general rule that is, where a person has obtained the property of another from one who is dealing with it without the authority of the true owner, no title is acquired as against that owner, even though full value has been given and the property be taken in the belief that an unquestionable title thereto is being obtained.'

Having stated the general rule Lord Herschell continued:

> 'There is an exception to the general rule, however, in the case of negotiable instruments. Any person in possession of these may convey a good title to them, even when he is acting in fraud of the true owner and although such an owner does nothing tending to mislead the person taking them.'

The conditions to be satisfied in order to be a holder in due course of a bill of exchange are set out in s. 29(1), which provides:

> 'A holder in due course is a holder who has taken a bill, complete and regular on the face of it, under the following conditions, namely:
>
> (a) that he became the holder of it before it was overdue, and without notice that it had been previously dishonoured, if such was the fact;
> (b) that he took the bill in good faith and for value, and that at the time the bill was negotiated to him he had no notice of any defect in the title of the person who negotiated it.

BILL MUST BE REGULAR ON THE FACE OF IT

Arab Bank Ltd v *Ross* [1952] 2 QB 216

In part payment for certain shares the defendant gave two promissory notes for £10,000 each, made payable in favour of 'Fathi and Faysal Nabulsy Company'. The plaintiff bank discounted the bills which were indorsed in its favour by the payee indorsing the back of the bills 'Fathi and Faysal Nabulsy'. The defendant alleged that he had been induced to draw the bills by the fraud of the payee and the plaintiff bank was not entitled to payment. The plaintiff bank claimed that it had given value for the promissory notes and as holder in good faith it was entitled to payment. McNair J, at first instance, held that the plaintiffs were entitled to payment as holders in good faith.

The defendants then claimed that the promissory notes were not complete and regular on their face because the indorsements were irregular as the word 'Company' had been omitted. The judge held that the indorsements were known and recognised as signatures of the payees and they left no doubt that the payee intended property to pass. In his opinion the notes were regular and complete. The defendant appealed.

The Court of Appeal held that the indorsements were sufficient to pass title to the bank, but the bank did not become a holder in due course because the indorsements were irregular, in that they did not set out the name of the indorser in full. The need for regularity was expressed by Lord Denning (at p. 226):

> 'Regularity is a different thing from validity ... On the one hand an indorsement which is quite invalid may be regular on the face of it. Thus the indorsement may be forged or unauthorised and, therefore, invalid under s. 24 of the Act, but nevertheless there may be nothing about it to give rise to any suspicion. The bill is then quite regular on the face of it. Conversely, an indorsement which is irregular may nevertheless be valid. Thus, by a misnomer, a payee may be described on the bill by the wrong name, nevertheless, if it is quite plain that the drawer intended him as payee, then an indorsement on the back by the payee in his own true name is valid and sufficient to pass the property ... Regularity is also different from liability ...'

Lord Denning continued (p. 227):

> 'A bill of exchange is like currency. It should be above suspicion. But if it is asked: When does an indorsement give rise to doubt? I would say that is a practical question which is, as a rule, better answered by a banker than a lawyer. Bankers have to consider the regularity of indorsements every week ...'

GOOD FAITH REQUIREMENT

Jones v *Gordon* (1876–77) 2 App Cas 616

A London agent of a firm drew bills on the firm for £1,727. The firm accepted the bills. At the time both the drawer and acceptor of the bills were insolvent and contemplating bankruptcy and the transaction was entered into in order to defraud the creditors of the acceptor. The drawer offered the bills to the plaintiff who had knowledge that the acceptor was in financial difficulties but that he might be able to pay part of the face value, and who purchased them for £200. Before the purchase the plaintiff also knew someone from whom he could acquire further information but he made no inquires. The acceptor subsequently became bankrupt and the plaintiff brought an action to recover the full amount of the bills.

The court held that the plaintiff had sufficient knowledge of the affairs of the acceptor to realise that he was, or might be, a party to a fraud and he could not therefore prove for the full amount of the bills. Lord Blackburn examined the meaning of good faith and stated (p. 629):

> 'But if the facts and circumstances are such that a jury, or whoever has to try the question, came to the conclusion that he was not honestly blundering and careless, but that he must have had a suspicion that there was something wrong, and that he refrained from asking questions, not because he was an honest blunderer or a stupid man, but because he thought in his own secret mind – I suspect there is something wrong, and if I ask questions and make further inquiry, it will no longer be my suspecting it, but my knowing it, and then I shall not be able to recover – I think that is dishonesty.'

Bank of Credit and Commerce International SA v *Dawson and Wright* ([1987] FLR 342)

A tradesman, one Smith, made an improper arrangement with a branch manager of the plaintiff bank by which Smith obtained a running credit balance of approximately £500,000. The manager mis-stated the transactions on the bank's computer in such a way that the bank was deceived. The defendants, who were in the same trade as Smith, had prior dealings with him but had ceased trading with him when he had failed to pay a substantial debt to them. Eventually, when the debt was paid off they recommenced trading with Smith on the understanding that none of the cheques would be met until the goods purchased by them were delivered. The first defendant then gave him two cheques before delivery of certain goods. The defendants never received the goods. Soon after Smith wrote out a cheque, in the presence of the first defendant and the branch manager, the sum being the amount owed by him to one of the defendant's companies; the manager guaranteed that the cheque would be cleared through his branch of the plaintiff bank and on that basis the first defendant gave a further cheque which he said would be cleared only when all the goods had been received.

Subsequently, Smith's cheque was dishonoured, the goods were not delivered and the defendants received no value for their cheques. They brought proceedings to recover the debt owed to them but received nothing due to Smith's bankruptcy. The plaintiff bank pursued Smith and obtained judgment for nearly £500,000 and secured the right to enforce specific performance of a bill of sale over Smith's stock. Having exhausted proceedings against Smith, the plaintiff asked the defendants for payment of the value of the three cheques since the plaintiff was the holder in due course of the cheques. The defendants denied liability and the plaintiff commenced proceedings.

Drake J held that the plaintiff was not a holder in due course of the cheques either by taking them for collection or by having a lien on them. He rejected the argument that for these purposes 'the bank' means only the directors of the bank and the bank is not tainted or in any way bound by the fraud of its employee, the bank manager. The learned judge said:

'It cannot be said that only the directors of the bank could take the bills; they were in fact taken, as in the normal course of business they would, by the manager Singh. It is my judgment, the bank did not take these bills in good faith. Accordingly it is not entitled to claim that it is deemed to be a holder in due course so as to have a lien on the bills.'

Raphael and Another v *Bank of England* (1855) 17 CB 161

In 1852 bank notes issued by the defendants were stolen in Liverpool, and payment of the notes stopped. The loss was advertised. Raphael was the English correspondent of St Paul, a moneychanger in Paris, whose firm regularly changed English notes. In June 1854, one of the stolen notes was presented to St Paul for changing, and after seeing the passport of the person presenting the note, and getting his name and address in writing, he changed the money into French francs. St Paul did not look at the file of notices of lost and stolen notes although it was shown that he had received notice of the theft of the notes in 1853. The plaintiff sued the defendants for the amount of the notes and interest.

The defendants alleged that the plaintiffs were not bona fide holders for value of the note because they had received notice that it was stolen. Judgment was entered for the plaintiffs and the defendants appealed.

The appeal was dismissed. Cresswell J said:

'A person who takes a negotiable instrument bona fide for value has undoubtedly a good title, and is not affected by want of title of the party from whom he takes it. His having the means of knowing that the security had been lost or stolen, and neglecting to avail himself thereof, may amount to negligence ... He could not have taken it bona fide, if at the time he took it he had notice of knowledge that the note was a stolen note.'

Two important points arise out of Lord Blackburn's judgment in *Jones* v *Gordon* namely:

(a) if a man suspects something is wrong with a negotiable instrument, that is enough to prevent him from taking in good faith. The suspicion need not be accurate provided it is near the truth; and

(b) if a man admits he was careless in not discovering a defect in the title to the bill, he is entitled to be treated as having acted in good faith, but when a man says he was careless the court may conclude that he was not in fact merely careless but that he did suspect something to be wrong and wilfully closed his eyes to it. In that case he has not acted in good faith.

The possible significance of constructive as opposed to actual notice was looked at in *Jones* v *Gordon* where the court said what is relevant is not whether the person who took the instrument ought reasonably to have suspected a defect of title to it, but whether he must in fact have suspected it in the light of the reasonable knowledge he actually possessed.

In *London Joint Stock Bank* v *Simmons* ([1892] AC 201) the House of Lords held that there were no circumstances in which the bank might have become suspicious when a broker pledged negotiable securities belonging to other persons in return for a personal advance and Lord Herschell said (p. 223):

'I apprehend that when a person whose honesty there is no reason to doubt offers nego-tiable security to a banker, or any other security, the only consideration likely to engage his attention is whether the security is sufficient to justify the advance required. And I do not think that the law lays upon him [the banker] the obligation of making enquiry into the title of the person whom he finds in possession of them; of course, if there is anything to arouse suspicion to lead to a doubt whether the person purporting to transfer them is justified in entering into the contemplated transaction, the case would be different; the existence of such suspicion or doubt would be inconsistent with good faith ... It is of the very essence of a negotiable instrument that you may treat the person in possession of it as having authority to deal with it, be he agent or otherwise, unless you know to the contrary.'

This dictum of Lord Herschell was quoted with approval in *Auchteroni & Co.* v *Midland Bank Ltd* ([1928] 2 KB 294). The distinction between the holder for value and the holder in due course was of significant importance in the *Arab Bank* case where the Court of Appeal held that the bank could be a holder for value but not a holder in due course. The reason for the distinction is that ss. 30(2) and 38(2) give protection to a holder in due course only from defects in title.

Section 30(2) provides:

'Every holder of a bill is prima facie deemed to be a holder in due course; but if in an action on a bill it is admitted or proved that the acceptance, issue or subsequent negotiation of the bill is affected by fraud, duress, or force and fear, or illegality, the burden of proof is shifted, unless and until the holder proves that subsequent to the alleged fraud or illegality, value has in good faith been given for the bill.'

In *Talbot* v *Von Boris* ([1911] KB 854) it was held that s. 30(2) does not apply to a holder who is the person to whom it was originally delivered and in whose posses-sion it remains.

Section 38(2) provides:

'Where he is a holder in due course, he holds the bill free from any defect of title of prior parties, as well as from mere personal defences available to prior parties among themselves, and may enforce payment against all parties liable on the bill.'

The list of defects enumerated in s. 29(2) from which a holder in due course takes free is not exhaustive. The personal defences referred to in s. 38(2) refer to such defences as set-off and counterclaim.

ESTOPPEL AND BILLS OF EXCHANGE

The purpose of the rules governing estoppel in respect of bills of exchange is to complete the protection given to a holder in due course if he seeks to recover the amount of the instrument from a person who became a party to it before him. The estoppels operate by each successive party to a bill being assumed to have passed it to the next party in normal circumstances. There is a rebuttable assumption that each party will be precluded from denying the regularity and validity of the bill, and the validity and effectiveness of all signatures on it prior to his own and the capacity of the next person to take it and negotiate it further.

Section 54 of the Bills of Exchange Act 1882 provides that the acceptor undertakes to pay the bill in 'according to the tenor of his acceptance' and under s. 54(2) the acceptor cannot deny the genuineness of the drawer's signature.

Beeman v *Duck* (1843) 11 M & W 251

The plaintiff brought an action on a bill of exchange, drawn by B & W (a really existing firm) payable to their order, and indorsed by them. The bill was negotiated by the acceptor with that indorsement on it. In fact the drawing of the instrument and its indorsement were forgeries.

The court held that where the name of a real person is forged as that of the drawer and payee, a drawee who accepts the bill in ignorance of the forgery is estopped from denying the validity of the drawer's signature, but not the forged indorsement of the payee although in the same handwriting.

The case actually goes further than the wording of s. 51(2), which precludes an acceptor from denying the capacity of the drawer to indorse, but not the genuineness or validity of his indorsement. Counsel for the defence sought unsuccessfully to distinguish *Cooper* v *Meyer* ((1839) 10 B & C 468) from *Beeman* v *Duck* on the grounds that the drawers in the former case were fictitious whereas in the latter case he really existed. Again, in *Halifax* v *Lyle* ((1849) 3 Exch 446) it was said that the acceptor of a bill, payable to the order of another, cannot deny the capacity of the person who draws it or the person who indorses it as payee. In that case an action was brought on a bill of exchange drawn by AB & Co. and payable to their order twelve months after the date of issue. It was accepted by the defendant and indorsed by AB & Co. to the plaintiffs and it was argued that the company was a body corporate without the authority to indorse, issue or negotiate a bill.

The Bills of Exchange Act 1882 (s. 55(1)) also deals with the liability of the drawer and provides that the drawer of a bill by drawing it undertakes that on due presentation the bill will be accepted and paid and in case of dishonour he will compensate the holder or any previous indorser. In *Henry* v *Burbidge* ((1837) 3 Bing NC 501) the defendant drew a bill of exchange on James Pearson requiring him to pay the amount of the bill to the order of the defendant. The defendant indorsed the bill on the plaintiffs and on the maturity of the instrument James Pearson failed to pay it. In an action to recover the amount of the bill the court held that an acceptance constitutes, in effect, a promise to pay but if the acceptor fails to make payment, there arises an obligation against the drawer, by implication of law, a promise to pay the bill (see also *Starke* v *Cheeseman* (1699) Carth 509).

By s. 55 (2)(b) and (c) the indorser is precluded from denying to a holder in due course the genuineness and regularity of the drawer's signature and all previous indorsements and is precluded from denying to his immediate or subsequent indorsee that the bill was at the time of the indorsement a valid and subsisting bill. In *MacGregor* v *Rhodes* ((1856) 6 El & Bl 266) the declaration charged that one Pinkney drew a bill of exchange payable to his own order and indorsed it to the defendants, who indorsed it to the plaintiff. The bill was duly presented for payment and dishonoured. The defendants admitted that they indorsed the bill to the plaintiff but sought to deny that Pinkney had indorsed to them. The court held that the fact of the indorsement to the plaintiff's would be conclusive evidence of the validity of Pinkney's indorsement to the defendants and estopped them from showing that Pinkney's indorsement was a forgery. The court further held that when a person indorses a bill he undertakes that, if the drawee or acceptor fails to make payment, he (as the indorser) will make payment and he cannot deny the payee's mandate.

PAYMENT AND DISCHARGE OF A NEGOTIABLE INSTRUMENT

The Bills of Exchange Act 1882 specifies a number of methods by which a bill may be discharged. The most common method by which a bill may be discharged is by actual payment and the question which must be asked is: when is payment made?

Parr's Bank Ltd v *Thomas Ashby & Co.* (1898) 14 TLR 563

A cheque was presented through the clearing house by the plaintiff bank to the defendant bank. The clearing house rules then in force required the drawee bank to return an unpaid cheque on the same day. The defendant bank to whom a cheque had been presented for payment, instead, returned the cheque the following day but the plaintiff bank acting on the assumption that the cheque had been paid honoured a bill accepted by its customer. The plaintiff bank argued that there had in fact been payment by the defendant bank.

The court held that the plaintiff bank was entitled to recover the sum paid on the bill from the defendant bank on the ground that its delay in returning the dishonoured cheque amounted to a representation that the cheque had been paid and the plaintiff bank had acted on that representation by paying on the bill of exchange.

The *Parr's Bank* case arose out of a situation where the paying and collecting bank were two separate banks. Where there is only one bank acting for both the payer and payee the payment will not be effected through the clearing system and therefore different rules will apply. In *Rekstin* v *Severo Sibirsko AO* ([1933] 1 KB 47) it was held that payment between accounts at the same bank was not effected until the payer's account was debited and the payee's account credited with the amount of the payment. It was also suggested in the case that payment had actually to be notified to the payee although this was rejected in *Momm* v *Barclays Bank International Ltd*.

Other methods of payment

The question when payment is complete depends on the method of payment employed and is of considerable importance. Different rules apply when some method other than a cheque or bill of exchange is used as a means of payment. In *Tenax Steamship Co. Ltd* v *The Brimnes (Owners)* (*The Brimnes*) ([1974] 3 All ER 88) the payment in dispute was a transfer from one account to another account of Morgan Guaranty Trust in New York, the transfer having been initiated by telex from London. The Court of Appeal held that the payment was made not when the telex was received but after the message had been processed and the decision to effect a transfer of the funds made. In *Mardorf Peach & Co. Ltd* v *Attica Sea Carriers Corporation of Liberia* ([1976] 2 All ER 249) charterers failed to pay the hire price on the day it fell due and on the following day the shipowners warned them that they were considering withdrawing the ship. The charterers instructed their bank to make an immediate payment and the charterer's bank, on issuing 'the payment order,' credited the owner's bank with the amount. On receipt of the payment order the owners' bank made an entry on its inter-bank account debiting the charterer's bank. The owners' bank then began to process the payment order, in order to collect payment from the Bank of England where the charterers' bank had an account. It took approximately 24 hours for the owner's account to be credited and when they were informed that payment had been received the shipowners gave instructions to their bank to refuse acceptance of the payment order. The owners' bank complied with these instructions and simultaneously the owners gave notice to the charterers withdrawing the ship. The Court of Appeal held that as the banks regarded the method of payment as equivalent to cash, the payment for the hire of the ship took place when the payment order was handed to the owners' bank and accepted by them without objection. The subsequent processing of the order was merely an internal banking process which did not affect the legal position of the shipowner and charterer.

The *Mardorf Peach* case was followed in *Momm* v *Barclays Bank International Ltd* ([1977] 2 WLR 407) where B, an employee of the defendants' bank, on receiving instructions from the H bank, authorised a transfer of £120,000 to the plaintiffs' account and set its computer process in motion to credit the plaintiffs' account and debit the H bank correspondingly. The credit balance on the customers' account would not, however, be known until the following day when all the day's debit and credit entries on the computer had been taken into account. On the same day, shortly after payment had been authorised, the H bank announced that it was going into liquidation. On the following day the defendants reversed the entries in the account of the H bank and the plaintiffs claimed payment of the £120,000 as money due to them by the defendants' bank. The defendants contended that the decision to effect the transfer to the credit of the plaintiffs' account was conditional and not finalised until the plaintiffs' account had been credited with the amount on the day following that on which the instruction had been given, or alternatively, that since neither the H bank nor the plaintiffs had been informed that the defendants had complied with the H bank's instructions the transfer had not been completed at the time it was cancelled. The court followed *Mardorf Peach* and held that payment was complete when the defendants' bank decided to accept the H bank's instructions to credit the plaintiffs and the computer process was set in motion because the defendants would not have accepted a countermand of the instructions from the H bank.

In *Delbrueck & Co.* v *Manufacturers Hanover Trust Co.* (609 F 2d 1047 (2d Cir. 1979)) the American courts reviewed the technology used in a Chips transfer (the American system allowing electronic transfer of funds) and held that payment was irrevocable when made. A transfer executed through an autonomous network invariably reached the recipient bank almost instantaneously once it was released throughout the computer terminals of the transferor. Moreover, the system of payment was based on the fact that funds would be available to the payee once the payment message was received by the collecting bank.

The Code of Banking Practice requires banks to explain to their customers the payment process and when payment is made.

The alternative question which has often arisen is: when is payment made as between the drawer and payee? There is a distinction between the drawing and delivery of a cheque to the payee and the actual payment of the cheque. So in *Marreco* v *Richardson* ([1908] 2 KB 584) Farwell LJ said '... the giving of a cheque for a debt is conditional on the cheque being met, that is, subject to a condition subsequent, and if the cheque is met it is an actual payment *ab initio* and not a conditional one.'

In *Parkside Leasing Ltd* v *Smith (Inspector of Taxes)* ([1985] 1 WLR 310) a cheque received on 9 April and paid into the bank on 11 April was taxable in the period beginning on 10 April and not in the period ending 9 April. It was said by Scott J (p. 314):

'Money credited to a person's bank account in accordance with his instructions must, in common sense and in law, be regarded as money thereby received by that person. But the receipt of a cheque seems to me to stand on a rather different footing. The receipt of a cheque does not of itself place the sum for which the cheque is made out or the proceeds of the cheque to the payee's disposal. It is not certain that the cheque will be honoured. It may be cancelled by the drawer before it is presented ... If the proceeds of the cheque are not received by the payee of the cheque I do not see how it can be said that the sum therein comprised was at the payee's disposal ... There is a critical difference between the receipt of the cheque and receipt of the proceeds of the cheque ...'

ALTERATION OF A BILL OF EXCHANGE

Section 61(1) of the 1882 Act states that a bill may be discharged by alteration 'except against a party who has himself made, authorised or assented to the alteration and subsequent indorser'.

Slingsby & Others v District Bank Ltd [1932] 1 KB 544

The plaintiffs were executors of an estate, and maintained an executor's trust account with the defendants. They used Cumberbirch and Potts, a firm of solicitors to assist them in work connected with the estate. The plaintiffs agreed with one JC, a partner in the firm of solicitors, to invest money through a firm of stockbrokers. JC regularly drew cheques on the executor's account for signature by the plaintiffs (as drawer) and on this occasion he drew a cheque for £5,000, in the form 'Pay John Prust & Co. ... or order', with a space between the words 'Co.' and the words 'or order'. The executors signed the cheque, and JC then added in the blank space the words 'per Cumberbirch and Potts'. He then indorsed the cheque 'Cumberbirch and Potts' and paid the cheque to the credit of an account with the Westminster Bank in the name of Palatine Industrial Finance Co. Ltd, in which he had an interest. The cheque was paid on presentation.

When the fraud was discovered the plaintiffs brought an action against Westminster Bank, the collecting bank, which was unsuccessful. They did not appeal but brought an action against the defendant bank. The judge held in favour of the plaintiffs and the bank appealed.

The Court of Appeal held that the cheque had been 'materially altered' within the meaning of s. 64 of the Bills of Exchange Act 1882, and was therefore avoided as between the plaintiffs and the defendants. The defendants could not therefore rely on the protection conferred by ss. 60 and 80 of the Act. Scrutton LJ held (p. 559):

'This cheque, having been signed by the executors in a form which give Cumberbirch no rights, was fraudulently altered by Cumberbirch before it was issued and, it was not disputed, altered in a material particular by the addition of the 'per Cumberbirch & Potts'. The cheque was thereby avoided under s. 64 of the Bills of Exchange Act. A holder in due course might not be affected by an alteration not apparent, such as this alteration ... and the cheque when presented to the District Bank, was invalid, avoided, a worthless bit of paper, which the District Bank was under no duty to pay.'

It is not always easy to recognise a material alteration on a bill of exchange. In *Suffell* v *Bank of England* ((1882) 9 QBD 555) Brett LJ said 'Any alteration of any instrument seems to be material which would alter the business effect of the instrument ...' In *Koch* v *Dicks* ((1932) 49 LTR 24) where the alteration related to the place of drawing of the instrument (from London to a German town) it was not material because it did not affect the rights in the bill. In *Kwei Tek Chao* v *British Traders and Shippers Ltd* ([1954] 2 QB 459) the material alteration of a bill of lading was examined and the court held that the forgery, although a material alteration, did not render the bill of lading a nullity as it did not go to the essence of the document – the primary purpose of the bill of lading still being achieved.

An alteration of a crossing on a cheque is a material alteration of the instrument and must therefore comply with the provisions of the legislation.

The significance of the *Slingsby* decision is that the courts will hold an instrument which has been materially altered as 'avoided, a worthless piece of paper'. If the alteration of the instrument is not apparent, the holder in due course 'may enforce payment of it according to its original tenure.' In *Bank of Montreal* v *The Exhibit and Trading Co. (Limited)* ((1906) 11 Com Cas 250) a promissory note was drawn in Liverpool and posted to Canada under which the defendants promised to pay to the order of 'The Goderich Organ Co.' a certain sum of money. The Goderich Organ Co. having been converted into a limited company called The Goderich Organ Company Ltd, an officer of that company, without the consent or knowledge of the defendants, as makers of the note, inserted the word 'Limited' on the face of the note which was then indorsed to the plaintiffs who took it as holders in due course. The plaintiffs took the note without knowledge of the alteration and on dishonour the plaintiffs sued to recover the value of the promissory note. The court held that the insertion of the word 'Limited' on the face of the note was, even if a material alteration, not an apparent alteration and the note was payable according to its original tenure – that is, payable as if the word 'Limited' had not been inserted.

A situation where alteration of a negotiable instrument is permitted is under s. 20 of the Act where a holder may complete an incomplete instrument within a reasonable time (but in *Griffiths* v *Dalton* ([1940] 2 KB 264) the insertion of the date on a cheque after 18 months was held to be unreasonable delay).

DISHONOUR OF A NEGOTIABLE INSTRUMENT

Where a negotiable instrument has been dishonoured the 1882 Act requires that notice of the dishonour should be given. There are intricate rules relating to the protesting of bills of exchange etc. but these do not apply to cheques. The question which is of importance relates to the timing of the notice of dishonour.

Eaglehill Ltd v *J Needham Builders Ltd* [1973] AC 992

The defendants were drawers of a bill of exchange for £7,660 on a furniture company, and payable on 31 December 1970. The plaintiff company discounted the bill and on 28 December the furniture company went into liquidation. Both the plaintiff company and the defendants had knowledge of this and knew that the bill would not be paid. A notice of dishonour, dated 1 January, was prepared and by mistake posted on December 30 and arrived at the defendants on 31 December. On the same day the bill arrived at the bank, by post, and was dishonoured. The defendants argued that the notice of dishonour was ineffective as it was given before the dishonour. At first instance it was held that the notice was effective but the Court of Appeal reversed this. On appeal to the House of Lords.

The House of Lords allowed the appeal and held:

(a) that a notice of dishonour was not avoided by the mere fact that it was posted before the bill became due for payment. It constituted a good notice of dishonour unless it was received before the bill itself was dishonoured;

(b) that a notice of dishonour was given at the time when the drawers received it, which was when it was opened in the ordinary course of business and in the circumstances the bill was presumed to have been dishonoured before the notice of dishonour was given.

Viscount Dilhorne said (p. 1005):

'In my opinion, if the notice was received as soon as or after the bill was dishonoured the statement in it that the bill had been dishonoured was true and the notice a good notice.'

The effect of a failure to give notice of the dishonour of a bill of exchange is that the drawer and indorser will be discharged from liability on the bill. However, mere return of the dishonoured bill to the drawer or indorser is sufficient notice of the dishonour. In *Westminster Bank Ltd* v *Zang* ([1966] AC 182) the view was taken that a collecting bank who claimed to be a holder in due course of a cheque which had been paid in by a customer to his account, lost its right of action against the drawer of the cheque by returning the cheque to its customer intending thereby to give notice of the dishonour. The argument that the release of the instrument was conditional under s. 21(2)(b) was not explored in the *Zang* case (see also *Lloyds Bank Ltd* v *Dolphin* ((1920) *The Times*, 2 December; *Legal Decisions Affecting Bankers*, **111**, 230).

8 Cheques

The scope of this chapter is to examine merely the rules and cases relating to cheques. The authorities on the definition of cheques and other rules common with bills of exchange have already been discussed in Chapter 7.

The cheque is the most common method of making non-cash payments, although the rate of increase in the volume of cheques in circulation is beginning to decline. However, despite this decline the cheque continues to be of crucial importance to the UK banking system. The Jack Committee, therefore, made a number of important recommendations relating to cheques. Where possible the recommendations are made with a view to making the cheque a safer instrument. The Jack Committee proposed a new and separate Cheques Act should be enacted to deal with the law relating to cheques, bank payment orders and analogous instruments.

CROSSINGS ON CHEQUES

A crossing is an instruction to the paying bank relating to the institution to whom payment must be made. The forms of crossings are set out in s. 76 of the Bills of Exchange Act 1882 and s. 1 of the Cheques Act 1992. A general crossing consists of two transverse lines across the face of the cheque and requires that the cheque should be presented for payment by a bank (payment may be made on the cheque through any bank), whilst the special crossing consists of two transverse lines between which the name of a specified bank is written and that bank alone should receive payment.

In addition to the types of crossings recognised in s. 76 the law recognises the 'account payee' crossing and the 'not negotiable' crossing. The 'not negotiable' crossing is provided for by s. 81 of the 1882 Act and although the 'account payee' crossing was not expressly authorised under the 1882 Act, the common law gave effect to it. Although the Jack Committee recommended that the 'account payee' crossing should no longer be recognised, the Cheques Act 1992 has given statutory effect to it.

Great Western Railway Company v *London and County Banking Company* [1901] AC 414

Huggins, a rate collector at Newbury, by falsely pretending to the appellants that rates were due from them obtained a cheque drawn by them on the London Joint Stock Bank, payable to one Huggins or order. The cheque was crossed '& Co.' and marked 'not negotiable'. Huggins indorsed the cheque and presented the cheque for payment at the respondent bank. At his request the bank paid part of the amount of the cheque into the current account of one of the bank's customers, and the balance was paid to Huggins in cash which he misappropriated. The respondent bank crossed the cheque in favour of themselves and sent it to their head-office for collection through the clearing system. When the fraud was discovered the appellants sued the respondent bank. Bingham J held that the defendants received payment in good faith and without negligence. He also held that Huggins was a customer of the bank. The decision was affirmed by the Court of Appeal.

On appeal the House of Lords allowed the appeal and said that Huggins was not a customer of the bank. In relation to the crossing Lord Halsbury LC said (p. 418):

'I think it is very important that every one should know that people who take a cheque which is upon its face "not negotiable" and treat it as a negotiable security must recognise the fact that if they do so they take the risk of the person from whom they negotiate it having no title to it.'

The effect of the crossing was also examined by the Court of Appeal in the *Great Western Railway* case and although the decision of the Court of Appeal was reversed its explanation of s. 81 and the 'not negotiable' crossing is generally accepted as correct. Vaughan Williams LJ said ((1900) 2 QB 464 at p. 474):

'The section does not say that the person to whom the payee of the cheque gives a crossed cheque marked "not negotiable" shall not become a transferee of the cheque, but merely that he shall not take a better title than that which the person from whom he took it had. The transferability of the cheque is not affected by the words 'not negotiable' but only its negotiability.'

The purpose of crossings is to minimise the risk of loss if the cheque is lost or stolen, particularly if the post is used to deliver the cheque to the payee or indorsee. As the paying bank has to ensure that payment is made to the credit of an account, anyone misappropriating the cheque may be more easily traced than if the cheque were merely cashed over the counter. In *Universal Guarantee Property Ltd* v *National Bank of Australasia Ltd* ([1965] 1 WLR 691) (a case dealing with the impact of the 'account payee' crossing prior to the 1992 Act) the court explained (p. 697) the effect of the 'not negotiable' crossing and said that such a crossing does not prevent a cheque from being negotiated but means 'that the holder of the cheque cannot have and is not capable of giving a better title to the cheque than the holder from whom he obtained it.'

In *Hibernian Bank Ltd* v *Gysin and Hanson* ([1939] 1 KB 483 at p. 486–487) council for the respondents explained the effect of the 'not negotiable' as follows:

'Those words indicated an intention ... that the bill should not be transferable. When the transfer of a bill is prohibited, the bill is not negotiable, and that cannot be done more effectually than by writing across the bill the words 'Not negotiable'. It must be inferred that those words, when written across a bill of exchange, have the same meaning as they have under s. 81 when written across a cheque ...'

The words 'not negotiable' have no effect unless combined with the general or special crossing and a cheque bearing these words without a crossing is not a crossed cheque and has no effect in hindering the negotiability of the instrument.

The words do not have to appear within the crossing provided they appear on the face of the cheque. In evidence submitted to the Jack Committee it was clear that there was confusion about the effect of the various types of crossings. The Committee recommended that a minimum number of crossings should be effective in law and each should be readily understood and its effect clear. The existing form of crossings should remain (with the exception of the 'account payee' or 'account payee only' crossings and special crossings).

Not negotiable crossing

The Committee examined the words 'not negotiable' and concluded that although the 'not negotiable' crossing is often used, the words are rarely properly understood and the 'not negotiable' crossing is often erroneously treated as synonymous with 'not transferable'. It recommended that all crossed cheques, in addition to being payable to a bank, should be 'not negotiable' without the need for express words. The cheque would remain transferable but only subject to equities and consequently a holder to whom it had been negotiated would not be given the protection at present conferred on a holder in due course.

'Account payee' crossing

The words 'account payee' or 'account payee only' are frequently used in cheques although they are not expressly authorised by the Bills of Exchange Act 1882.

The Cheques Act 1992 amends s. 81 of the Bills of Exchange Act 1882, and provides:

'Where a cheque is crossed and bears across its face the words 'account payee' or 'a/c payee', either with or without the word 'only', the cheque shall not be transferable, but shall only be valid as between the parties thereto.'

The Cheques Act 1992, s. 1, gives legal effect to the 'account payee' crossing so that such cheques will only be collected for the named payee. The Act denies such cheques negotiability and transferability. However, the statutory protection for both the paying and the collecting banks will be preserved if they have acted without negligence. Consequently, if the cheque is collected for someone other than the named payee but who has an account in the same name as the payee (e.g the cheque is collected for the wrong John Smith) neither the paying nor the collecting bank will be liable unless there is negligence. Section 1(2) of the Cheques Act 1992 amends s. 80 of the Bills of Exchange Act 1882, and provides that a bank will not be negligent simply because of its failure to concern itself with any purported indorsement on the cheque. It is submitted that an instrument crossed 'account payee' is no longer a negotiable instrument; the Bills of Exchange Act 1882 requiring that such instruments be capable of negotiation.

The common law gave recognition to the account payee crossing and the position was examined in *House Property Co. of London and Others* v *London County and Westminster Bank* ([1915] 89 LJKB 1846). In that case the plaintiff company were dealers in real property, the other plaintiffs being trustees of a trust account known as 'Bingley Trust', to which the plaintiff company in the course of its business had mortgaged property. Norman, a solicitor to the trustees, fraudulently wrote a letter calling in the mortgage on the grounds of depreciation. After negotiation, the plaintiff company arranged to repay £800 of the mortgage money and sent a cheque to the solicitor. The cheque was drawn to the trustees 'or bearer' and crossed 'Account payee'. The solicitor misappropriated the cheque and payment was made to the credit of his personal account. An action was brought on the ground that the collecting bank had been negligent in receiving a cheque so crossed for someone other than the named payee. The bank argued that the cheque was a bearer cheque, and the bank, having collected the cheque for the payee as bearer, was not liable in conversion. It was held that the bank was not negligent. Rowlatt J held (p. 1847):

> 'They [Counsel for the defendants] say: This cheque is payable to Hanson and others or bearer, and is a cheque to bearer, and Norman was the bearer, and in passing it to his account we only passed it to the account of the payee, because the payee was the bearer, and the bearer was Norman. I am bound to say that this is a somewhat shallow argument, because on the meaning of this document I cannot in the least doubt that 'a/c payee' does not mean the account of the man who in the process of negotiation is the owner of the cheque at the time it is collected.'

The common law accepted that the words 'account payee' were merely a memorandum of instruction to the collecting bank that the proceeds of the cheque were not to be collected for any account other than that of the named payee without full inquiry (see *Paget's Law of Banking*, 10th edition, p. 377). Consequently, if the collecting bank received payment to the credit of anyone other than the customer without making sure that the payee consented, the bank was liable in negligence and would lose its protection of s. 4 of the Cheques Act 1957. But if the bank had made reasonable inquiries it was protected by s. 4 of the 1957 Act.

A more recent variation to the 'account payee' crossing was the insertion of the word 'only' after the words 'account payee'. In *Universal Guarantee Property Ltd v National Bank of Australasia* ([1965] 2 All ER 98) an employee of the appellant company, one M, defrauded his employers of approximately £59,000. The frauds were perpetrated by M obtaining cheques, properly signed on behalf of the company by himself and another authorised signatory, which were in respect of non-existent transactions and were payable to a fictitious named payee 'or order'. The cheques were drawn 'not negotiable account payee only' and M, having obtained the cheques, then wrote the name of the payee on the back and also wrote on the back of the cheques 'indorsement guaranteed', impressed a rubber stamp which read 'per pro' the company and signed his name underneath. The cheques were then paid by M into the company's account in substitution for equivalent sums of cash which should have been paid into the account but which M misappropriated. An action was brought by the company against the bank for breach of contractual duty. The Privy Council held that the bank was not in breach of its contractual duties to its customer, the company, because in the circumstances the bank was not put on inquiry which would have led it to be suspicious in dealing with the cheques drawn. In dealing with the effect of crossings Lord Upjohn said (p. 102):

'The words 'not negotiable' do not prevent the cheque from being negotiated but mean that the holder of the cheque cannot have, and is not capable of giving, a better title to the cheque than that of the holder from whom he obtained it ...'

In respect of the 'account payee' crossing Lord Upjohn continued:

'The addition of the words 'a/c payee' or 'a/c payee only' refers to the payee named in the cheque and not the holder at the time of presentation (*House Property Co. of London* v *London County & Westminster Bank*), but they do not prevent, at law, the further negotiability of the cheque. The words merely operate as a warning to the collecting bank that if it pays the proceeds of the cheque to some other account it is put on inquiry and it may be in a difficulty in relying on any defence ... in action against it for conversion of the cheque.'

The words 'account payee only' were treated merely as a variation on the words 'account payee' and imposed the same restriction on the collecting bank.

The Jack Committee recommended that the 'account payee' or 'account payee only' crossing should no longer be recognised. The government White Paper accepted that legislation was necessary to simplify the law relating to crossings. This has, to an extent, been achieved by changes introduced by the Cheques Act 1992, which clarify an area of banking law and practice which was generally misunderstood. The changes are to be welcomed.

RESTRICTION OF THE PAYMENT INSTRUCTION

The Jack Committee accepted that at common law the only effective way of restricting the transferability of a cheque was by drawing it in favour of 'Pay X only', with the deletion of the words 'or order' on the cheque form. The Committee examined the question of whether the duty of ensuring that the named payee received payment should fall on the collecting or paying bank. The Committee concluded that in such an instance the onus should fall on the collecting bank. In *Hibernian Bank* v *Gysin and Hanson* ([1939] 1 KB 483) the court held that the use of the word 'only', together with the 'not negotiable' crossing, prohibits the transfer of the bill altogether, and so the plaintiffs could not recover on the bill since they were not the named payee. The court said that the use of the word 'only' on its own would have been just as effective in restricting the transferability of the cheque.

In order to improve the level of security and confer greater protection on the customer the Jack Committee recommended that a new non-transferable order be introduced by legislation. The Committee recommended that the new instrument should be called a 'bank payment order' and that it should have the following features:

(a) Unlike a cheque the proceeds should only be available to the person specified in the new bank payment order (thus preventing negotiation or transfer).

(b) But like a cheque:

    (i) it would be addressed by the account holder or his agent;

    (ii) to the bank who holds his account;

(iii) requiring the bank to pay on demand;

(iv) a specified sum;

(v) only through the collecting bank (or by internal transfer if both the payer and payee have accounts with the same bank).

Attributes of the bank payment order

The bank payment order would retain many of the attributes of a cheque and a number of legal rules governing the use of cheques would apply in their entirety to the new instrument. Thus, for example:

(a) the payee of a bank payment order would be able to sue on it in his own name;

(b) a forged or unauthorised drawer's signature would be wholly inoperative and the drawee bank would be unable to debit its customer's account;

(c) a bank payment order would be discharged by payment in due course, or if the payee renounced his rights against the drawer, or if the payment order was intentionally cancelled by the payee, or if it was fraudulently altered or materially altered by anyone but the drawer. It would not be discharged if it was marked as cancelled or paid under a mistake of fact;

(d) the paid order, or a photocopy or other reproduction by electronic means, would be regarded as evidence of the receipt by the payee of the sum specified thereon;

(e) the presentment of a bank payment order would not operate as an assignment of funds in the hands of the drawee bank;

(f) rules governing the presentment for it would still be required and should specify that presentment is made if a demand for payment is made by a bank, and that such demand for payment may be by exhibiting the payment order to the drawee bank or by any other means whereby the identity of the payment order is reasonably certain and in a form intelligible to, or decipherable by, the drawee bank. Since, however, these instruments could be presented only by a bank to the drawee bank, it should not be necessary to be more specific as to the place of presentment;

(g) provided it had acted in good faith and without negligence, the paying bank should have protection on the same lines as that currently given by s. 80 of the Bills of Exchange Act 1882, so that it would be protected if it paid to the bank presenting the order for payment but not otherwise; and

(h) the collecting bank should be protected against claims by the true payee on the same basis as cheques.

In other areas the law relating to cheques would not apply to bank payment orders, e.g. the rules relating to indorsements or crossings would have no effect. Finally, it was recommended the words 'Bank Payment Order' should be printed on blank forms and the word 'only' preprinted against the space for the payee's name instead of the words 'or order'. Appendix M to the Jack Committee report contains an illustrative 'Bank Payment Order'.

The bank payment order is along the lines of a similar instrument introduced in Australia.

RECOVERY OF AMOUNTS INCORRECTLY PAID

Where due to an error the bank makes payment under a mistake of fact (e.g. payment is made on a cheque that has been countermanded or payment is made on a cheque where the drawer's signature is forged or the same mandate is erroneously acted upon twice and the payee's account is credited twice) the paying bank may seek to recover the amount paid from the person to whom payment is made.

National Westminster Bank Ltd v *Barclays Bank International Ltd and Another* [1965] 1 QB 654

A blank cheque had been stolen in Nigeria from a customer of the plaintiffs, National Westminster Bank in London, without the customer's knowledge. The second defendant, one Ismail, was a Nigerian businessman anxious to move substantial funds out of Nigeria, contrary to the strict exchange control regulations in force. He agreed to purchase, at a premium, a cheque for £8,000 drawn on the National Westminster Bank, at a branch in London, but before paying for it he sent it to his own bank in London, Barclays Bank International, for special collection. The cheque was duly presented for payment and honoured and Ismail paid for it in Nigeria. It was subsequently established that the cheque form had been stolen and its completion involved a forgery of the signature of the customer to whom it had been issued by the National Westminster Bank. The plaintiffs, National Westminster Bank, brought an action for recovery of the money and the second defendant, Ismail, resisted the claim arguing that the plaintiffs had acted negligently and since he had acted to his detriment (by making payment for the cheque in Nigeria) they were estopped from claiming repayment.

Kerr J held that the plaintiffs were entitled to recover the amount of the payment under the forged cheque and that he could not regard payment of the cheque as a representation that it was genuine. In paying a cheque the bank does not make a representation to the recipient as to the genuineness of its customer's signature. Kerr J, in the course of the judgment, said (p. 647):

'... Mr Ismail can only succeed in raising an estoppel against the plaintiffs if the mere fact of a banker honouring a cheque on which his customer's signature has been undetectably forged carries with it an implied representation that he believes the signature to be genuine ... Furthermore, I think that the law should be slow to impose upon an innocent party who has not acted negligently an estoppel merely by reason of having dealt with a forged document on the assumption that it was genuine.'

Kerr J rejected a number of other propositions on which it had been alleged that the bank had been negligent. The learned judge also held that because a cheque is presented for special collection it does not mean, and it should not be assumed, that the cheque is a forgery.

The court also considered two conflicting commonwealth authorities. In *Arrow Transfer Co. Ltd* v *The Royal Bank of Canada and Bank of Montreal* ([1972] SCR

845) cheque forms were extracted from the plaintiff company's cheque book by an employee who forged the signatures of the authorised signing officers and made cheques payable either to cash or a firm of which he was the proprietor. The plaintiff company brought an action for conversion and for money had and received against the paying and collecting banks. The Court of Appeal of British Columbia gave judgment for the banks. The judgments were confined mainly to the conversion issue and the action did not lie because there could be no conversion of an instrument on which the drawer's signature was a forgery. In *Imperial Bank of India* v *Abeysinghe* ((1927) 29–30 Ceylon NLR 257) the defendant received a cheque payable to himself in part payment of an amount payable under a fictitious transaction which he had been instructed to handle on behalf of a supposed vendor of certain property. The cheque was a complete forgery and the defendant received and paid it over to his principal. The bank brought an action to recover the money paid to the defendant. Fisher CJ, rejected the view that the paying bank is under a duty to the recipient of the amount of a cheque to know its customer's signature and even if there were such a duty it does not extend to the signature of a third party, e.g. the payee of a cheque. Fisher CJ distinguished *London and River Plate Bank* v *Bank of Liverpool* ([1896] 1 QB 7).

Kerr J accepted the rule established in *Kelly* v *Solari* ((1841)) 9 M & W 54) that the mere fact that the defendant has acted to his detriment by spending or paying the money away, in reliance upon having received the payment, is not a sufficient bar to the plaintiff's right to recover.

In *Barclays Bank Ltd* v *W.J. Simms Son & Cooke (Southern) Ltd and Another* ([1980] 1 QB 677) a housing association drew a cheque for £24,000 on its account with the plaintiff bank, in favour of a building society. The following day a receiver was appointed to call in the building society's assets. Consequently, the association countermanded payment of the cheque and confirmed the stop in writing. The bank's computer was programmed accordingly but the next day payment on the cheque was made, contrary to the stop instruction. The bank claimed repayment from the receiver, who refused and it brought an action against the company and the receiver. Goff J held that the plaintiff bank was entitled to recover the full amount of the cheque and that money paid under a mistake of fact was prima facie recoverable. However, the claim may fail if (p. 695):

'(a) the payer intends that the payee shall have the money at all events; or (b) the payment is made for good consideration, in particular if the money is paid to discharge, and does discharge, a debt owed to the payee (or a principal on whose behalf he is authorised to receive the payment) by the payer or by a third party by whom he is authorised to discharge the debt; or (c) the payee has changed his position in good faith or is deemed in law to have done so.'

It was also argued by the defendants, following *Cocks* v *Masterman,* that the bank's failure to give immediate notice of the mistake invalidated its claim for repayment. The judge, however, said that it was a prerequisite for that defence that the defendants should be under a duty to give notice of the dishonour, whereas s. 50(2)(c) of the Bills of Exchange Act 1882 states that notice is dispensed with where the drawer has countermanded payment.

Bank's right to trace the proceeds

A bank which seeks to recover money paid under a mistake may not only recover from the collecting bank or the person whose account was credited but it may also recover from anyone who holds the money by derivation from the recipient provided it can still be identified. At common law, therefore, funds sought to be recovered must still be identifiable. In *Banque Belge Pour L'étranger* v *Hambrouck* ([1921] 1 KB 321 at p. 334) H fraudulently obtained a number of cheques from his employer, which he paid into his own account, and his bank collected the amounts from his employer's bank. H then withdrew these sums by cheques in favour of his mistress, D, who paid the cheques into her own account. The bank sought to recover the amount from the mistress and further sought a declaration that the amount placed to her credit was the bank's property in equity. It was argued that the mistress, D, took the money without notice of H's wrongdoing and she acquired a valid title. The court rejected this argument since the mistress was a volunteer, and said that the only person acquiring the property sought to be traced who is immune from the payer's claim is one who has given value. Lord Atkin in giving judgment reviewed the law and cited *Taylor* v *Plummer* (3 M & S 562) as setting out the position at common law:

> 'The plaintiff', he says [Lord Ellenborough], ' ... is not entitled to recover if the defendant has succeeded in maintaining these propositions in point of law – viz., that the property of a principal entrusted by him to his factor for any special purpose belongs to the principal, notwithstanding any change which that property may have undergone in point of form, so long as such property is capable of being identified, and distinguished from all other property ... It makes no difference in reason or law into what other form, different from the original, the change may have been made ... for the product of or substitute for the original thing still follows the nature of the thing itself, as long as it can be ascertained to be such, and the right only ceases when the means of ascertainment fail, which is the case when the subject is turned into money, and mixed and confounded in a general mass of the same description.'

Atkin LJ in *Banque Belge* then goes on to discuss *Sinclair* v *Brougham* where he notes that Lord Haldane LC, in dealing with Lord Ellenborough's judgment in *Taylor* v *Plummer,* said:

> 'Lord Ellenborough laid down, as a limit to this proposition, that if the money had become incapable of being traced, as, for instance, when it had been paid into the broker's general account with his banker, the principal had no remedy excepting to prove as a creditor for money had and received,' and proceeds to say 'you can, even at law, follow, but only so long as the relation of the debtor and creditor has not superseded the right *in rem*.'

Atkin LJ in *Banque Belge* then goes on to say:

> 'But if in 1815 the common law halted outside the banker's door, by 1879 equity had had the courage to lift the latch, walk in and examine the books: in *Re Hallett's Estate*. I see no reason why the means of ascertainment so provided should not now be available both for common law and equity proceedings. If, following the principles laid down in *Re Hallett's Estate*, it can be ascertained either that the money in the bank, or the commodity which it has bought, is "the product of, or substitute for, the original thing" then it still follows "the nature of the thing itself". On these principles it would follow that as the money paid into the bank can be identified as the product of the original money, the plaintiffs have the

common law right to claim it, and can sue for money had and received. In the present case less difficulty than usual is experienced in tracing the descent of the money, for substantially no other money has ever been mixed with the proceeds of the fraud.'

In *AGIP (Africa) Ltd* v *Jackson* ([1991] 3 WLR 116) Fox LJ distinguished the *Banque Belge* v *Hambrouck* case on the grounds that in the latter case no further funds had at any time been paid into the mistress's account and that each amount was credited only after the clearance of the cheque used for the transfer involved. Fox LJ concluded in the *AGIP (Africa) Ltd* case that the funds could not be traced at common law because the amount involved went through a mixed fund. The money could, however, be traced in equity, which would 'follow money into a mixed fund and charge the fund'.

However, Fox LJ said that equity would grant a tracing order only where there was a 'fiduciary relationship, which called the equitable jurisdiction into operation'.

The courts have examined the nature of the fiduciary requirement in a number of cases. In *Sinclair* v *Brougham* ([1914] AC 398) the Birkbeck Building Society operated a banking business which was held to be *ultra vires*. In the winding-up of the Society, conflicting claims arose between the interests of the shareholders and the customers (called depositors). One of the questions which had to be decided was whether the depositors had the right to trace into the general assets of the Society. The House of Lords held that there was a fiduciary relation between the depositors and the directors; the directors had mixed the funds and the depositors had the right to trace them into the hands of the Society.

In *Re Diplock* ([1948] Ch 465) the mixing resulted not as a result of the conduct of the fiduciary agent but from the conduct of an innocent volunteer to whom the agent handed the money. The Court of Appeal held 'equity may operate on the conscience not merely of those who acquire a legal title in breach of some trust, express or constructive, or of some other fiduciary obligation, but of volunteers provided that as a result of what has gone before some equitable proprietary interest has been created and attaches to the property in the hands of the volunteer.'

In *Chase Manhattan Bank NA* v *Israel-British Bank (London) Ltd* ([1981] Ch 105) the action concerned a sum of money paid by mistake of fact. In July 1974 the plaintiff, Chase Manhattan Bank NA (in New York), and the defendant, Israel-British Bank (London) Ltd (in London), were carrying on business as bankers. On, or before, 2 July an Italian bank instructed the plaintiff to pay US $2,000,687.50 to Mellon Bank International, another bank in New York, for the defendant's account. The plaintiff duly made payment through the New York clearing house system on 3 July. Later on the same day, the plaintiff made a further payment of the same amount and to the same account, through the New York clearing. The second payment purported to be made on the instructions of a bank in Hong Kong but no such payment instruction had been given and it was a pure mistake. The cause of the second payment was a clerical error made by an employee of the plaintiff on 3 July. That error was discovered in good time but only corrected in part and caused the mistaken payment. The claim was for a declaration that the defendant became a trustee for the plaintiff in the sum paid by mistake, although there had been no previous fiduciary relationship between them before the mistaken payment was made. The plaintiff, therefore, argued that they were entitled in equity to trace the amount into the defendant's assets despite the defendant's insolvency. Counsel for the defendant (following *Re Hallett's Estate* and *Re Diplock* ([1948] Ch 465)) argued that there was no right to trace in equity unless some initial fiduciary relationship existed between the parties. Goulding J rejected the argument that in order to recover money paid under a mistake of fact, the plaintiff needs to establish a fiduciary relationship prior to the mistaken payment. The fact there was a mistaken payment was in itself enough to give rise to a fiduciary relationship (*Sinclair* v *Brougham* [1914] AC 398). In the course of his judgment Goulding J said:

'(a) If one party P transfers property to another party D by reason of a mistake of fact, P has in general a right to recover it and D a duty to restore it. (b) P in general has a right to sue in equity for an order that D return the property, or its traceable proceeds, to P. Sometimes this requires actual retransfer by D, sometimes the court can use the alternative remedy of reformation, i.e. rectification of instruments, to produce the same result. P is said to retain an equitable title to the property notwithstanding it may have been legally transferred to D, and D is treated as a constructive trustee thereof. (c) In many cases P has also a common law right of action in quasi-contract to recover damages in respect of his loss. (d) The court will not, in its equitable jurisdiction, order specific restitution under (b) above where common law damages under (c) furnish adequate relief. (e) Accordingly where the property in question is money, equitable relief is not available to restore the sum paid by mistake if the payee D is solvent. But when D is insolvent P is entitled to a decree in equity for the purpose of tracing the money paid and recovering it or the property representing it. (f) Modern analysis concentrates attention less on the protection of P than on preventing the unjust enrichment of D, thus bringing the law of mistake into a broad jurisdiction of restitutionary rights and remedies.'

Goulding J clearly extended the rule in *Sinclair* v *Brougham* that where the purpose for which a payment is made cannot be fulfilled, a fiduciary relationship arises between the payer and the payee, and the payer retains the equitable ownership of the funds in question to the situation where money is paid under a mistake of fact.

The tracing remedy was examined recently by the House of Lords in *Lipkin Gorman* v *Karpnale Ltd* ([1991] 3 WLR 10). This action was based on the fact that Cass, the solicitors' dishonest partner, used money obtained by fraud from the firm's client account in order to gamble at the club, where he lost a considerable amount of money. The House of Lords, reversing the Court of Appeal, held that the solicitors were entitled to recover from the club the net amount lost by Cass. Their Lordships held that the effect of s. 18 of the Gaming Act 1845 was that the club could not be regarded as having given valuable consideration. The exchange of money into chips did not constitute a separate transaction, involving the furnishing of valuable consideration; it merely involved the provision of the medium used for gambling in lieu of the cash itself. Since no consideration was furnished for the amount involved, the money was recoverable in an action in restitution. The question the House had to decide was whether the solicitors could institute such an action to recover the money or did the money belong to the bank (i.e. was it the bank's own money). Lord Goff of Chieveley held that the solicitors had title to the money which could be traced at common law. He said:

'Before Cass drew upon the solicitors' client account at the bank, there was of course no question of the solicitors having any legal property in any cash lying at the bank. The relationship of the bank with the solicitors was essentially that of debtor and creditor; and since the client account was at all material times in credit, the bank was the debtor and the solicitors the creditors. Such a debt constitutes a chose in action, which is a species of property; and since the debt was enforceable at common law, the chose in action was legal property belonging to the solicitors at common law.

There is in my opinion no reason why the solicitors should not be able to trace their property at common law in that chose in action, or any part of it, into its product, i.e. cash drawn by Cass from their client account at the bank. Such a claim is consistent with their assertion that the money so obtained by Cass was their property at common law.'

A similar conclusion with regard to the right to trace misappropriated funds was reached in the *AGIP* case. However, the funds in respect of which the tracing order was granted in *Lipkin Gorman* had not lost their identity at any time by becoming part of a mixed fund.

LIABILITY OF THE PAYING AND COLLECTING BANKS IN NEGLIGENCE

At common law when a bank pays, collects or transmits a cheque bearing a forged or unauthorised indorsement it is guilty of a conversion and is liable to the true owner of the cheque for the amount for which it was drawn. This liability still exists although it is now subject to statutory defences.

Statutory protection conferred on the paying bank

Section 60 of the Bills of Exchange Act 1882 protects a paying bank if it pays a cheque in good faith and in the ordinary course of business to a person other than the true owner where the defect in the title of the person who receives payment is the forgery of the indorsement on the cheque.

Carpenters' Company v *British Mutual Banking Company Ltd* [1938] 1 KB 511

The plaintiffs were trustees of a home and kept an account with the defendant bank through which they paid the expenses of the home. The plaintiffs' clerk, Blackborow, was the assistant clerk and the secretary of the committee which looked after the home. He regularly obtained cheques in order to pay tradesmen who supplied goods to the home. Blackborow also maintained a private account with the defendant bank. In 1920, he commenced to misappropriate cheques, drawn in favour of tradesmen, by fraudulently indorsing the payee's name on the cheques and paying them to the credit of his personal account. When the frauds were discovered the plaintiffs brought an action against the bank for the amount of the forged cheques. Branson J held that the bank did not act without negligence and therefore could not rely on s. 82 of the

Bills of Exchange Act 1882 (superseded by s. 4 of the Cheques Act 1957) (as the collecting bank) but that the bank had paid the cheques in good faith and in the ordinary course of business despite the negligence which deprived it of the protection under s. 82. The plaintiffs appealed.

The Court of Appeal, by a majority, held that the bank by receiving the cheques for payment and crediting Blackborow's account with the amounts of such cheques was guilty of conversion and liable under s. 82 of the 1882 Act. Greer LJ in discussing the *EB Savory & Co.* v *Lloyds Bank Ltd* ([1932] 2 KB 122) said (p. 529):

'The decision seems to involve that if the bank acts both in the capacity of the collecting bank and of the customer's bank, it must be held guilty of conversion and liable for the face value of the cheques unless it can bring itself within the protection of s. 82. In the present case what happened was that when the cheques were presented to the defendant bank they had never ceased to be the property of the drawers, the Carpenters' Company, as they had never in fact been indorsed by the payees. The defendant bank was then asked by Blackborow to receive the cheques, and to place the amounts to the credit of his private account with it. This the bank did, and by so doing it in my judgment converted the cheques to its own use and became liable to the Carpenters' Company, the drawers of the cheques, for the face value of the cheques.'

With regard to the scope of s. 60 of the Bills of Exchange Act 1882, Greer LJ continued (p. 529):

'In my judgment s. 60 ... only protects a bank when that bank is merely a paying bank, and is not a bank which receives the cheque for collection.'

Good faith and without negligence under s. 60

Section 60 of the Bills of Exchange Act 1882 provides:

'A thing is deemed to be done in good faith within the meaning of this Act, where it is in fact done honestly, whether it is done negligently or not.'

Negligence itself does not imply the absence of good faith. In the *Carpenters* case the Court of Appeal was divided on the issue whether negligence by the paying bank precludes the protection conferred by s. 60. Mackinnon LJ took the view (p. 536):

'A thing that is done not in the ordinary course of business may be done negligently; but I do not think the converse is necessarily true. A thing may be done negligently and yet be in the ordinary course of business.'

This view was also accepted by Slesser LJ who said (p. 534):

'... negligence does not necessarily preclude the protection of section 60 ...'

However, Greer LJ did not agree with the view that a bank could be protected by s. 60 where it had been guilty of negligence. He took the view that a bank could not argue:

'when acting negligently, that it was acting in the ordinary course of business.'

The good faith requirement has already been dealt with in connection with s. 29 of the Bills of Exchange Act 1882. It must be remembered that in *Raphael and Another* v *Bank of England* ((1855) 17 CB 161) Cresswell J said:

'A person who takes a negotiable instrument bona fide for value has undoubtedly a good title ...'

The courts have not defined what will amount to obviously suspicious circumstances so that the paying bank will lose the protection of s. 60. In *Auchteroni & Co. v Midland Bank Ltd* ([1928] 2 KB 294) the court held that the bank was justified in paying over the counter a bill for £876 9s, although it was suggested that a different course might have been adopted if a bill for a larger amount had been presented by a tramp or office boy.

Payment in the ordinary course of business under s. 60

Baines v *National Provincial Bank Ltd* (1927) 96 LJKB 801

The plaintiff was a bookmaker carrying on business at York. He had an account with the branch of the National Provincial Bank at Harrogate. The advertised closing hour of the branch was 3 p.m. The plaintiff drew a cheque on his account in favour of Wood for £200 and gave it to him shortly before 3 p.m. Wood cashed the cheque shortly after 3 p.m. on the same day. The following morning the plaintiff sent a countermand to the bank at 9 a.m., when the bank opened. The bank debited the plaintiff's account and he brought an action against the bank for a declaration that it was not entitled to debit the account.

The court held that the bank was justified in debiting the customer's account with the amount of the cheque, payment having been made in the ordinary course of business although outside normal advertised business hours. Lord Hewart CJ said (p. 802):

'In my opinion there is no substance at all in the plaintiff's contention. What precisely are the limits of time within which a bank may conduct business, having prescribed – largely for its own convenience – particular times at which the doors of the building will be closed, is a large question which is not raised here. What is contended on behalf of the defendants is that they are entitled, within a reasonable business margin of their advertised time for closing, to deal with a cheque, not of course in the sense of dishonouring it, but in the sense of doing that which the cheque asks them to do, namely, to pay it.'

In the *Joachimson* case Atkin LJ said that it was part of the banker's obligation to pay cheques in normal business hours and banking business necessarily continues after the close of the advertised opening hours with customers being dealt with after the advertised banking hours.

Section 80 of the Bills of Exchange Act 1882 provides that where a bank on which a crossed cheque is drawn pays it in good faith and without negligence, the paying bank is placed in the same position and has the same rights as if payment of the cheque had been made to the true owner. It should be noted that s. 80 expressly requires that payment is made without negligence and a bank which loses the protection of s. 60 will of necessity lose its protection under s. 80.

The Cheques Act 1992, s. 1(1), provides that a bank will not be negligent if it deals with a cheque crossed 'account payee' contrary to an indorsement. In such a case the bank is protected by s. 80 of the Bills of Exchange Act 1882.

Additionally, s. 1 of the Cheques Act 1957 confers protection on the paying bank if it pays a cheque in good faith and in the ordinary course of business when the cheque is not indorsed or irregularly indorsed.

Problems caused by ss. 60, 80 and 1

The Jack Committee on Banking Services accepted that protection for the paying bank along the lines of the statutory provisions is still required. The existing statutory provisions, however, are not entirely clear or wholly consistent. There is considerable overlap between the sections and the ambit and their relationship is unclear. Even the prerequisites of ss. 60 and 80 of the Bills of Exchange Act 1882, and s. 1 of the Cheques Act 1957, are not consistent. Sections 60 and 1 require the bank to act in 'good faith' and in the 'ordinary course of business', whilst s. 80 requires the bank to act in 'good faith' and 'without negligence'. Moreover, ss. 60 and 80 only apply to cheques whilst s. 1 applies to cheques and other analogous instruments. The scope of the protection under ss. 60 and 1 is made unclear by the requirement that the bank must act in the 'ordinary course of business'.

The Committee accepted that although requirements such as the paying bank must act in 'good faith' (defined in s. 90 of the Bills of Exchange Act 1882) and 'without negligence' are reasonably clear, the requirement of 'ordinary course of business' (in s. 60 of the Bills of Exchange Act 1882 and s.1 of the Cheques Act 1957) is more difficult to define. Although the traditional view has been that the term 'ordinary course of business' extends to transactions undertaken during normal business hours, it would probably also extend to carrying out and completing the customer's instructions after closing hours.

The Jack Committee, therefore, recommended that:

(a) the concept of 'ordinary course of business' should be removed from the statutory provisions in question; and

(b) the protection available under the various statutes should be brought together in a single legislative provision. The new provisions should be made uniform to the extent that each requires the bank to act in 'good faith' and 'without negligence'.

Consequently, the existing provisions under the Bills of Exchange Act 1882 and the Cheques Act 1957 should be repealed.

Protection conferred on the collecting bank

A collecting bank may find that it has collected payment on a cheque for a customer who has no title or a defective title to it. At common law, the bank can, therefore, be made liable in conversion to the true owner although it has acted in good faith and with care. However, in order to escape the rigours of the common law the bank may claim (a) that it is the holder in due course of the cheque; or (b) that it is protected by s. 4 of the Cheques Act 1957 (as amended by the Cheques Act 1992).

Collecting bank as the holder in due course

Section 2 of the Cheques Act 1957 provides:

'A banker who gives value for, or has a lien on, a cheque payable to order which the holder delivers to him for collection without indorsing it, has such (if any) rights as he would have had if, upon delivery, the holder had indorsed it in blank.'

Westminster Bank Ltd v *Zang* [1966] AC 182

The defendant having lost heavily at cards borrowed £1,000 from a friend, Tilley, and gave him a cheque in return. The loan was made out of money belonging to a company which Tilley controlled. Tilley, subsequently, paid the unindorsed cheque to the credit of the company's account. Tilley did not indorse the cheque in favour of the company although the clearing rules required cheques paid into the account for someone other than the named payee had to be indorsed. On the day the cheque was paid in the company's account was overdrawn by over £1,000 in excess of the agreed overdraft limit.

The cheque was dishonoured and the collecting bank surrendered it to Tilley for the purpose of enabling him to bring an action against the drawer. The action was not proceeded with and the bank took redelivery of the cheque from Tilley. The bank eventually commenced its own action claiming to be a holder in due course under s. 2 of the Cheques Act 1957. The defence unsuccessfully pleaded the Gaming Act and raised the following defences:

(a) the cheque was delivered by the bank, not as holder under s. 2, but as an agent of the company;
(b) the words of the section 'which the holder delivers for collection' could not apply to an unindorsed cheque paid into an account which was not that of the payee;
(c) that the bank had not given value for the cheque; and
(d) that the bank had ceased to be a 'holder' of the cheque when it surrendered it to Tilley in order to enable him to sue on it.

Roskill J found for the bank. The Court of Appeal allowed the defendant's appeal. The bank appealed to the House of Lords.

The House of Lords dismissed the appeal and held that the bank had failed to establish that it gave value for the cheque as it could not be shown that it had agreed to allow or had in fact allowed the company to draw against the cheque.

Lord Denning MR and Danckwerts LJ held that in order to plead s. 2 of the Act it was necessary to show that the cheque was delivered to the bank for the credit of the payee unless it was indorsed. The bank therefore lost its lien when it returned the cheque to Tilley for the purposes of pursuing a legal action and when it retook delivery it could not be a holder in due course because the bank had notice of dishonour.

Lord Denning MR in the Court of Appeal said that it was possible for a bank to become a holder for value of a cheque (pp. 202–203):

'In order to make this good, it is sufficient for them to show that they credited the account of the company at once before it was cleared. They must show that there was an express or implied agreement between banker and customer that the customer could draw against the cheques before they were cleared ...'

This rule was established in *A.L. Underwood Ltd* v *Bank of Liverpool* ([1924] 1 KB 775) where Scrutton LJ said (p. 805):

'I think it sufficient to say that the mere fact that the bank in their books enter the value of the cheques on the credit side of the account on the day on which they receive the cheques for collection does not without more constitute the bank a holder for value. To constitute value there must be in such a case a contract between banker and customer, expressed or implied, that the bank will before receipt of the proceeds honour cheques of the customer drawn against cheques. Such a contract can be established by entry in the customer's pass book, communicated to the customer and acted upon by him. Here there is no evidence of any such contract. No cheque paid in was ever drawn upon until cleared; and the form of paying-in slip in respect of some of the later cheques indicates that the bank assumed that they had not entered into any such contract.'

In the House of Lords Viscount Dilhorne held that (a) the reduction of the overdraft by crediting the cheque to the account amounted to value; (b) no implied agreement to pay against uncleared effects would be read into the circumstances of the case; (c) the printed words in the paying-in slip negatived any such agreement; and (d) no evidence was presented to show cheques drawn by the company and presented between 'April 27 and May 2' were only honoured in consequence of the uncleared cheques.

In B*arclays Bank Ltd* v *Harding* ([1963] 1 WLR 1021) the bank paid against uncleared effects and advanced money to the payee of a cheque which was later dishonoured. The bank claimed to be a holder in due course and the drawer was held liable to pay the amount of the cheque. The fact that the cheque was unindorsed did not adversely affect the position of the bank because of s. 2 of the Cheques Act 1957 (see note on the *Harding* case in 1962, *Journal of Business Law*, p. 283). Megaw J held that in respect of an unindorsed cheque s. 2 gives the 'banker the same rights as he would have had if upon delivery the holder ... had indorsed the cheque in blank'. Megaw J said that the bank had at all times remained in possession of the cheques and had therefore not lost or abandoned any rights it might have had as holder in due course.

More recently, in *Barclays Bank Ltd* v *Astley Industrial Trust Ltd* ([1970] 2 QB 527) the plaintiff bank maintained a current account for Mabon's Garage Ltd which was substantially overdrawn. The bank received five cheques for £2,850 drawn by the defendant company and payable to Mabon's Garage Ltd. As a result of receiving these cheques, to the credit of the customer's account, the bank decided to pay two cheques amounting to £345 drawn by Mabon Garage Ltd which it would otherwise have dishonoured. The five cheques for £2,850 were dishonoured and the bank brought an action against the defendants claiming the value of the cheques, plus interest. The bank's action was based on the grounds that they were the holders of the cheques in due course. It was alleged that, on behalf of the defendants, the bank received the cheques merely as agents for collection. The court held that the bank took the cheques within the meaning of s. 29(1)(b) of the Bills of Exchange Act 1882, to the extent of the customer's overdraft the bank acquired a lien over the cheques, and although the cheques were delivered for collection, the bank under s. 27(3) of the Act became a holder in due course.

Milmo J (p. 539) distinguished the *Westminster Bank Ltd* v *Zang* case and held:

'In my judgment the holder of a cheque who has a lien on it is by virtue of s. 27(3) deemed to have taken that cheque for value within the meaning of s. 29(1)(b) to the extent of the sum for which he has a lien ... and although the cheques were delivered, *inter alia*, for collection, the plaintiffs were holders of the cheques and by reason of s. 27(3) are deemed to have become holders for value ... The plaintiffs took the cheques in good faith and without notice of any defect in Mabon's title and the conditions in s. 29(1) to make them holders in due course have been satisfied.'

The learned judge cited (with approval) *obiter dicta* of Lord Atkin in *Midland Bank Ltd* v *Reckitt* ([1933] AC 1) where it was said:

'... the bank claim to be holders in due course to the extent of the overdraft existing when they were paid in. That they were holders for value to that extent is, I think, true whether the value is said to be the payment of the antecedent debt (the overdraft), or to be the lien to the extent of the overdraft ...'

Milmo J rejected the argument that the bank could not be a holder for value for the unpaid cheques because it charged interest on the amount of the overdraft.

Protection under s. 4 of the Cheques Act 1957

The collecting bank may be liable in conversion and lose the protection of s. 4 of the Cheques Act 1957. The courts have examined the standard of care owed to the true owner of a cheque or other instrument to which s. 4 applies in numerous cases. Recently, in *Marfani* v *Midland Bank Ltd* ([1968] 1 WLR 956) Diplock LJ said:

'What the court has to do is to look at all the circumstances at the time of the acts complained of, and to ask itself: were those circumstances such as would cause a reasonable banker, possessed of such information about his customer as a reasonable banker would possess, to suspect that his customer was not the true owner of the cheque.'

The question whether the bank has breached this duty of care has been examined in many cases as discussed below.

In opening the account

Although the wording of s. 4(1) of the Cheques Act 1957 appears to make the bank liable in relation to the collection of the cheques the courts have held that the obligation imposed on the collecting bank, to take care, exists from the beginning of the banker–customer relationship. The bank is not only concerned with the apparent respectability of the customer but with all matters relating to him which may be relevant to the use of his account.

Lloyds Bank Ltd v Savory & Co. [1933] AC 201

The respondents were a firm of stockbrokers, who had in their employ two clerks, Perkins and Smith. In accordance with rules of the London Stock Exchange, the respondents were in the habit of issuing cheques, payable to jobbers, crossed and made payable to bearer. During a period of around six years both Perkins and Smith misappropriated a number of cheques and paid them into the appellant bank for the credit of an account Perkins had with the Wallington branch, and in the case of Smith for the credit of his wife's account at Redhill and subsequently at Weybridge. Neither branch inquired as to their respective customer's employment, although it was known by the branch manager where Perkins maintained his account that he was a stockbroker's clerk. Whilst the stolen cheques were, in each instance, deposited with a London branch of the bank and sent to the Clearing House for payment, the paying-in slips were sent to the country branch for credit with no mention being made of the names of the drawers.

When the frauds were discovered the respondents brought an action for conversion against the bank for money had and received. The bank raised s. 82 of the Bills of Exchange Act 1882 and alleged that it had acted in good faith and without negligence in receiving payment on the cheques. Judgment was given for the bank and Savory & Co. appealed to the Court of Appeal which allowed the appeal. The bank appealed to the House of Lords.

The House of Lords held that the bank had failed to undertake a full inquiry into the circumstances of the customer as laid down in the bank rule book and therefore the bank had acted negligently. The bank had failed to inquire on opening the wife's account (to which stolen cheques were transferred) as to her husband's occupation or his employers. This failure to inquire, coupled with the City branch's failure to inquire how the husband came to have possession of the cheques before instructing a transfer to the wife's account, collectively amounted to negligence. Lord Wright giving judgment said (p. 231):

> '... where the new customer is employed in some position which involves his handling, and having the opportunity of stealing, his employers' cheques, the bankers fail in taking adequate precautions if they do not ask the name of his employers ... This is specially true of a stockbroker's clerk; it may be different in the case of an employee whose work does not involve such opportunities, as, for instance, a technical employee in a factory. But in the case of a stockbroker's clerk or other similar employment, the bank are dealing with something which involves a risk fully known to them ...'

Lord Russell of Killowen (dissenting), however, was cautious about the significance which should be placed on information relating to the customer's employment or that of the customer's spouse and said (p. 225):

> 'I know of no authority before the present case justifying that proposition, and can conceive no logical basis on which one can rest an obligation on A to make an inquiry for the purpose of regulating and guiding his future action during an indefinite period of time the answer to which may cease to be correct immediately after it is given.'

Marfani & Co. v *Midland Bank Ltd* [1968] 1 WLR 956

One Kureshy, an employee of the plaintiff company, obtained from his employers a cheque for £3,000 drawn in favour of Eliaszade. Kureshy, by pretending to be the payee, opened a current account at a branch of the Midland Bank. The bank obtained a favourable reference in respect of Kureshy under the name of Eliaszade from another long-standing customer of the bank but the reference was only received after the bank had made available banking facilities to Kureshy. The bank collected the cheque for Kureshy who within a few weeks had drawn out the proceeds of the cheque and absconded.

The plaintiffs brought an action in conversion, it being argued that the bank received payment on the cheque at a time when it had not made inquiries about the customer. The bank refuted the allegation of negligence on the grounds that it would not have let the customer withdraw the proceeds of the cheque until references had been received and that a satisfactory reference is more reliable than inquiries of the customer himself. Neild J held in favour of the bank and the plaintiffs appealed.

The Court of Appeal dismissed the appeal and accepted that the bank had acted according to current banking practice since it had obtained and relied on a reference (given by another customer) as to Kureshy's respectability. The Court of Appeal established a new standard of care relating to inquiries which a bank must make and Lord Diplock said (p. 973):

> 'What the court has to do is to look at all the circumstances at the time of the acts complained of, and to ask itself were those circumstances such as would cause a reasonable banker, possessed of such information about his customer as a reasonable banker would possess, to suspect that his customer was not the true owner of the cheque.'

The problem raised in the *Savory* case relates to the extent of the collecting bank's inquiries. Lord Buckmaster (at p. 216) held that in similar circumstances it may be reasonable to make inquiries in relation to a daughter or housekeeper of the customer in order reasonably to prevent misappropriation.

The *Savory* case marks an extreme limit of the duty of care. In subsequent cases the courts appear to have taken a more flexible approach and in *Orbit Mining and Trading Co. Ltd* v *Westminster Bank Ltd* Harman LJ, referring to the Savory case, said:

> '... it cannot at any rate be the duty of the bank continually to keep itself up to date as to the identity of a customer's employer.'

Lord Diplock LJ in the *Marfani* case referred to the *Savory* case and said that it was decided in the light of social conditions of the 1920s when banking facilities were less commonly used and suspicion might more commonly be aroused. It was decided according to the expert evidence available at that time and is an illustration of the general principle:

> 'that a banker must exercise reasonable care in all the circumstances of the case.'

The court in *Marfani* also took the view that it did not constitute any lack of reasonable care if before opening an account for an applicant the bank refrained from making inquiries which would probably fail to lead to the detection of the customer's dishonest purpose, if he were dishonest, and which would only offend him if he were not. The *Marfani* case is not to be treated as removing all the burdens placed on the banks by the *Savory* case. It recognises that negligence is to be measured by varying, current professional banking standards and every case must be considered on its merits.

More recently in *Lumsdon and Co.* v *London Trustee Savings Bank* ([1971] 1 Lloyd's Rep 114) Donaldson J held that the bank was negligent in not fully establishing the customer's credentials when the account was opened, although damages were reduced due to the contributory negligence of the plaintiffs. The plaintiffs, stockbrokers, employed one Blake as a temporary accountant. Their practice was to draw cheques in the abbreviated form, e.g. 'Brown' instead of 'Brown Mills & Co.' Blake opened an account in the name of J.A.G. Brown with a cash deposit of £1 at the branch of the defendant bank. Blake than gave a reference for the fictitious 'Brown' to the effect that 'Brown' was of good character and probity. Blake signed the reference 'J. Blake, DSc, PhD', but failed to provide the name of his own bankers, as requested by the manager. The manager concluded that he was dealing with two professional men and failed to make any further inquiries. The plaintiffs drew a number of cheques in favour of Brown Mills & Co. but made them payable to 'Brown' with a gap in front of the payee's name. Blake inserted the initials 'J.A.G.' in the gap and paid them into his own account.

The plaintiffs claimed the value of the cheques from the defendants on the grounds of conversion. The defendants claimed that they had acted in good faith and without negligence and were protected by s. 4 of the Cheques Act 1957, and, in any event, the plaintiffs were liable of contributory negligence.

The duty to inquire is a continuous one and arises every time a transaction occurs which is apparently out of harmony with the description of the customer's business or occupation or otherwise inconsistent with the normal manner of conducting business. In *Nu-Stilo Footwear Ltd* v *Lloyds Bank Ltd* ((1956) 77 JIB 239) the bank was held liable when cheques inconsistent with a newly established business were presented to the credit of the customer's account and payment received. The implication of the decision is that a bank must at all times be cognisant of the customer's affairs. The strict attitude of the courts was illustrated in *Baker* v *Barclays Bank Ltd* ([1955] 1 WLR 822) in which case one Bainbridge misappropriated cheques belonging to 'Modern Confections', a business in which he was a partner. The cheques were indorsed and handed over to one Jeffcott who paid them to the credit of his account at Barclays Bank. The bank manager was assured by Jeffcott that the cheques were being cashed for a friend who was the sole proprietor of 'Modern Confections'. The manager was satisfied with the explanations and never asked to see Bainbridge personally. In an action by the other partner the bank was held to have been negligent in not making further inquiries. Devlin J said:

'I do not think that in this case I need go as far as to hold that every failure to make proper inquiries, whether or not they appear to be material, is fatal to a defence under s. 82 ... In my judgment, however, if a bank manager fails to make inquiries which he should have made, there is, at the very least, a heavy burden on him to show that such inquiries could not have led to any action which could have protected the interests of the true owner; and that burden the bank has, in my judgment, failed to discharge ...'

The banker's duty of care and inquiry operates when the first large cheque which is indorsed in favour of a customer is presented for collection. This duty is less stringent where a number of small cheques are presented indorsed in favour of the customer over a considerable time (see *Crumplin* v *London Joint Stock Bank Ltd* ((1913) 30 TLR 99).

Cheques drawn payable 'to A for B'

Bute (Marquess) v *Barclays Bank Ltd* [1955] 1 QB 202

The plaintiff employed one McGaw as manager of certain sheep farms on the Island of Bute. His duties included making applications to the Department of Agriculture for Scotland for hill farm subsidies in respect of the farms and in January 1949, he submitted three such applications. In April 1949 McGaw resigned his employment but in September 1949, the Department of Agriculture, according to their usual practice, sent to McGaw three warrants crossed 'not negotiable' for a total of £546. The warrants were payable to Mr D. McGaw and immediately after were added the words 'for the Marquess of Bute'. The Marquess had not notified the Department of Agriculture that McGaw's employment had been terminated.

On 29 September, McGaw applied to a bank in Yorkshire for permission to open a personal account with the warrants, and the bank credited the warrants to an account in his name and forwarded them for collection. The proceeds of the warrants were credited to the bank and it, having received references, permitted McGaw to draw on the account. In an action for conversion against the bank the following defences were raised:

(a) the warrants were not the property of the plaintiff, or alternatively they bore no indication that McGaw was not entitled to receive the proceeds of the warrants personally;

(b) the plaintiff was estopped from denying that he had intended the warrants to be received by McGaw; and

(c) that the bank was protected by s. 82 of the Bills of Exchange Act.

McNair J rejected the defences raised by the bank and held that in an action in conversion the claimant need only establish that at the material time he was entitled to immediate possession of the subject-matter, that in any event the test of true ownership was the intention of the drawer and that the Department of Agriculture had indicated its intention by inserting the words 'for the Marquess of Bute' after the name Mr D. McGaw.

The argument that the plaintiff was estopped from denying that payment could be made to McGaw personally was rejected and McNair J (p. 213) held:

'On this state of facts it was argued that an estoppel against the plaintiff was established by the application of the principles (1) that an estoppel by representation may arise from A putting into possession of B, or allowing B to obtain possession of, a document which itself contains a representation that the payment may be made to B personally; and (2) that, if the document contains such a representation or is reasonably understood by the person to whom it is presented it contains such a representation, the person to whom it is presented can safely pay B and is under no obligation to make investigation or inquiry to ascertain whether the representation is true ... But the representation must be clear and unequivocal or at least reasonably understood to be clear or unequivocal ... as a matter of construction, the warrants do not contain a representation that payments may be made to McGaw personally; but for the purpose of the principles above stated, the crucial question on the facts of this case is whether they could reasonably be understood to contain a representation.'

Prior to the *Marquess of Bute* case it was possible to argue that a cheque drawn 'Pay A for B' entitled A to receive the proceeds although he would be personally accountable to B. Moreover, it could be argued that it was the drawer's intention that A should receive the money and that A alone was entitled to the immediate possession of the instrument. In the light of the *Marquess of Bute* case this argument can no longer be supported. The case was compared with *Slingsby* v *District Bank Ltd* ([1932] 1 KB 544) and McNair J held payment directed to 'Pay B through A' must necessarily be different from 'Pay A to B'. Considering the large number of cheques with which banks have to deal every day, they could not be expected to scrutinise each cheque with the skill and care of detectives.

Cheques drawn by an agent

The duty on the bank to inquire is not removed by the fact that an agent who draws cheques on his principal's account payable to himself acts under a power of attorney.

Midland Bank Ltd v *Reckitt and Others* [1933] AC 1

One Terrington carried on practice as a solicitor. He was authorised under a power of attorney, given by Sir Harold Reckitt, to draw cheques on the latter's bank account which was maintained with Barclays Bank in Hull. The solicitor fraudulently drew a number of cheques totalling approximately £18,000 in favour of himself. The cheques were signed by using a rubber stamp with the client's name and the word 'by' and on the lower line 'his attorney' and placing his own signature between the lines. The solicitor then placed the cheques to the credit of his personal account on which he was overdrawn. The client brought an action against the defendants for damages in conversion of the cheques. The defendants alleged that the cheques were crossed cheques and that they had received payment in good faith and without negligence.

The House of Lords (affirming the Court of Appeal) held that the bank, in presenting and receiving the cheques, was liable in conversion. Moreover, from the manner in which the cheques were drawn the bank had knowledge that the money did not belong to the solicitor. The bank should have made inquiries regarding his authority to draw the cheques for himself. Lord Atkin in giving judgment (p. 15) said:

> 'It seems to me clear that in an omission of an ordinary business precaution, in breach of a plain duty imposed upon a creditor to take reasonable care to see that a known agent paying his own debt to his creditor out of his principal's money is acting within his authority, the bank were negligent in making no inquiry as to their customer's authority to make these payments.'

Although the *Reckitt* case imposes a duty to check the authority of an agent where he draws on his principal's bank account in favour of himself this duty is not an absolute rule to make inquiry. In *Penmount Estates Ltd* v *National Provincial Bank Ltd* ((1945) 89 Sol Jo 566) the bank succeeded in its defence that it had not been negligent. In that case cheques payable to the principal were fraudulently indorsed and paid into the solicitor's client account. The court held that the collecting bank was not guilty of negligence in crediting the cheque to the solicitor's account as it was normal for a solicitor to pay into an account money belonging to his clients.

Negligence in connection with crossed cheques

The question arises whether a collecting bank can claim the protection of s. 4 of the Cheques Act 1957 if it can show that it made reasonable inquiries or acted without negligence in collecting the cheque. In *Great Western Railway Co. Ltd v London and County Banking Co. Ltd* ([1899] 2 QB 172)) (see p. 162) it was suggested by Lord Brampton that s. 82 of the Bills of Exchange Act 1882 'might not give the same protection to the banker collecting cheques drawn "not negotiable" as it does where the crossing is simple.' The point was discussed for the first time in the *Crumplin* case.

Crumplin v London Joint Stock Bank Ltd (1913) 30 TLR 99

The plaintiff was a stockbroker, who employed as manager, book-keeper and cashier one Rands. Occasionally, Rands introduced business, receiving commission for the introductions. In 1909, he introduced a Mr Davies for whom a transaction was properly carried out. Subsequently, and for a considerable time afterwards, Rands, speculating on his own behalf, used the name of Davies as cover. When a profit was made he drew cheques payable to Davies which were signed by the plaintiff and crossed 'not negotiable'. Two such cheques were signed 'per pro'. Rands then forged Davies' indorsement on the cheques and paid them into his account with the Fenwick branch of the defendant bank.

When the fraud was discovered the plaintiff brought an action claiming that the bank had been negligent in accepting cheques for payment marked 'not negotiable' drawn for one person to the credit of another person.

The court held that the 'not negotiable' crossing is merely one factor amongst many to be considered in deciding whether the collecting bank has been negligent. In the circumstances the bank had not been negligent and Pickford J said:

> 'In the present case evidence was given by persons of importance in the banking world, who said that transactions of this kind were not uncommon ... it was quite clear from that evidence that the practice for cheques of this description to be paid in was so common so as not to raise suspicion. It came down to a mere question whether, looking at the total number of payments in, the number of these cheques that were paid in, their amount, and the period over which they were paid in, those circumstances were sufficient to put the defendants on inquiry ...'

The *Crumplin* case was important because it clearly established that merely collecting a cheque marked 'not negotiable' for someone other than the named payee does not make the collecting bank liable in negligence. This was followed by the *Morison* case (in 1914) where the court said that it is not conclusive evidence of negligence against a collecting bank that it collects a cheque marked 'not negotiable' without special inquiry. More recently, in the *Penmount* case where the court examined the effect of 'not negotiable' crossings, it was said that the bank does not have to be abnormally suspicious in order to prove it exercised due care, although it did not contest liability in relation to the 'Account Payee only' crossing.

It should be remembered that the Law Reform (Contributory Negligence) Act 1945 has been held to apply not only to actions for negligence but also to other torts such as conversion, so that if the plaintiffs can be held to have contributed to the loss the amount of damages recoverable will be reduced (see *Lumsden & Co.* v *London Trustee Savings Bank* [1971] 1 Lloyd's Rep 114).

Recommendations of the Jack Committee

The Jack Committee examined the nature of the statutory protection conferred on the collecting bank. It was of the opinion that the bank is in a highly favoured position. The intended payee will find himself without a remedy against the bank which collects payment if the bank acts in good faith and without negligence. In Scots law, the collecting bank is actually protected against the true owner unless bad faith can be shown. The Committee, therefore, reinforced its proposals relating to verification of a customer's identity on opening an account.

The Committee recommended that, in Scotland, the protection conferred to the collecting bank should be similar to that applied in the rest of the UK.

FURTHER RECOMMENDATIONS OF THE JACK COMMITTEE

The Jack Committee also examined a number of other issues relating to cheques and payment orders.

Cheque truncation

Although the present system of cheque clearing is considerably mechanised, it still involves the daily movement between banks and their branches of millions of cheques each day. To some extent, banks have already reduced the flow of paper by a system of cheque truncation. The system involves the capture of relevant data to enable payment of each cheque to the payee's account, and simultaneously for the debtor's account to be debited, without the physical presentation of the cheque itself. The system of cheque presentations, however, faces several problems, for example the law requires bills (including cheques) to be duly presented for payment. At present, that requires the physical presentation of the instrument through the clearing system. A further problem which results from a system of electronic transmission of data is that the paying bank does not have the opportunity to examine cheques and therefore to detect possible forgeries.

The Jack Committee recommended that banks adopt and extend the system of cheque truncation. The Committee recommended that banks obtain the written consent of customers to truncate cheques and where a customer insists on the physical presentation of cheques the full costs of such an exercise be passed on to the customer.

The White Paper on Banking Services provides that the government will introduce legislation to facilitate the truncation of cheques. In case of a disputed transaction the government paper recommended that the Code of Banking Practice provide that in case of dispute the customer's account should be recredited within a number of working days unless the truncated cheque can be produced by the bank within a certain time period.

The Banking Code does not specifically deal with cheque truncation.

Amount in words and figures

A proposal before the Jack Committee that where there is a discrepancy between the words and figures that the amount in figures should be paid attracted no support. At present, the bank may pay the amount in words, or at its own risk the lower figure. Although the amount in words is only scrutinised when the cheque is examined before being paid, the use of the words, nevertheless, provides a valuable protection to the drawer. To remove the requirement that the amount of the cheque should be written in words, in addition to figures, or to reduce their importance would only facilitate fraud. The Committee, therefore, concluded that the existing rule which gives precedence to words should remain.

Out-of-date cheques

The Committee came to the conclusion that a rule is required for the payment of cheques which have been in circulation for an undue period of time. It proposed a standard of best practice should establish a minimum of six months from the date of issue within which a bank should be willing to pay a cheque or bank payment order. In fact most banks will not pay a cheque which has been in circulation for more than six months.

Assignment and attachment of funds

In England, although not in Scotland, a bill (including a cheque) does not operate as an assignment of funds, and the holder of an unpaid cheque has no equitable claim on the drawee (bank). The assignment will occur from the time the bill or cheque is presented to the drawee. The bill of exchange operates simultaneously as an assignment of funds. The practical effect of the rule is that, if the drawee holds funds owing to the drawer, then the payee as assignee may sue the drawee not on the bill but on the character of the instrument effecting the assignment. It was represented to the Jack Committee that the funds attached rule which applies in Scotland is unsatisfactory not merely for banks but also for their customers. For a business customer, the effect of the operation of the rule can be serious since where the customer has an insufficient credit balance to meet a cheque for a large amount, not only would that cheque have to be returned but any small cheques presented at the same time would also be returned unpaid.

The Jack Committee, therefore, recommended the repeal of s. 53(2) of the Bills of Exchange Act 1882 and the abolition of the 'funds attached principle.'

Cheque cards

It was submitted to the Jack Committee that the £50 limit on cheque cards should be increased to keep pace with inflation. The Committee made no recommendations regarding the limit and considered it purely a commercial matter for banks to decide upon. Since the publication of the report, APACS – which runs the cheque card scheme – has announced that cheque cards with a limit of £100 and £250 respectively will be made available to certain customers. The £50 limit is also retained.

9 Bank finance

There are several forms of bank finance available to a customer. This may range from the simple overdraft to the finance of trade through letters of credit to the provision of guarantees, especially in construction contracts where the guarantee may take the form of a performance bond.

BANK OVERDRAFT AND TERM LOANS

An overdraft is repayable by the customer immediately upon a demand being made by the bank, unless the bank has otherwise agreed.

Williams & Glyn's Bank Ltd v *Barnes* [1981] Com LR 205

The defendant was the founder, chairman and majority shareholder of Northern Developments Holdings Ltd, a property development company which from 1965 banked mainly with the plaintiff bank. In 1972, when NDH's overdraft with the bank was £6.5 million, the bank lent £1 million to the defendant personally to enable him to purchase more shares in the company. It was anticipated that this loan would be repaid by the defendant out of money owed to him by the company or other companies controlled by him.

In 1973 the property market collapsed and the bank after several attempts to rescue the business appointed a receiver. An action was brought to recover the £1 million owed personally by the defendant, who admitted the debt but raised various defences and counter-claims involving the manner in which the bank had dealt with the company.

Gibson J held that the defendant had no defence to the personal claim based on the bank's conduct towards the company. He, however, examined the claims made by the defendant and held:

(a) it was not an express term of the loan that it should be repaid out of money owed to the defendant by the company and there was no implied term in the contract that the bank would not damage the company so as to make payment impossible;

(b) the bank did not owe to the defendant, as a shareholder in the company, a duty not to breach any duties owed to it or did not owe any duty to the defendant, as shareholder, not to reduce the value of his shareholding by breaches of duties owed to the company;

(c) the bank owed no duty to advise the defendant as to the prudence of buying shares in the company when it ought to have realised that the company was at risk;

(d) an overdraft is repayable on demand, unless it is expressly or impliedly agreed otherwise;

(e) the bank was under no obligation to comply with any requests to raise the overdraft limit.

An overdraft arises when the customer, either with the express or implied consent of the bank overdraws on a current account. In *Foley* v *Hill* ((1848) 2 HLC 28) it was established that normally the banker–customer relationship is that of debtor–creditor but when the current account is overdrawn that relationship is reversed and the customer becomes the debtor of the bank for the amount overdrawn. The reversal of the debtor–creditor relationship may take place without the express agreement of the parties. A term loan usually provides that the borrowing company will be given a facility to borrow up to a stated amount.

In legal terms there is little difference between the overdraft and the term loan and the *Barnes* case is applicable to both. Both the overdraft and the term loan are advances to the customer made at the discretion of the bank, although there has been an increase in unauthorised borrowing – this is facilitated by the undertaking to honour cheques backed by cheque guarantee cards.

On the question of repayment of an overdraft Gibson J held that:

'Bankers ... regard repayability on the demand as a universal or normal attribute of overdrafts, but there is nothing to suggest that they regard that attribute as overriding an agreement to the contrary. If a usage to that effect existed it would not, in my judgment, be lawful or reasonable ... In truth, this custom or usage is no more than recognition of the rule of law which results from the nature of lending money: money lent is repayable without demand, or at latest on demand, unless the lender expressly or impliedly agrees otherwise ...'

Where an overdraft or other loan facility is granted for a fixed duration, the courts will hold that the amount is not repayable on demand. In *Titford Property Co. Ltd* v *Cannon Street Acceptances Ltd* (unreported) Goff J held that a provision that a loan should be repayable on demand was repugnant to an overdraft facility expressed to be for a term of 12 months.

Interest is calculated on overdrafts at the agreed rate, or if there is no agreement, at the bank's currently published lending rate. If an account is continuously overdrawn the interest element can be a substantial component of the debit balance of the account at any time. The right to compound interest is not lost when demand for repayment is made: *National Bank of Greece SA* v *Pinios Shipping Co. No. 2* (*The Times*, 1 December 1989).

As with other debts, the creditor may obtain summary judgment for an amount unpaid on the overdraft or loan account after payment has become due.

COMMERCIAL DOCUMENTARY CREDITS

Apart from the financing of companies for agreed purposes there are different kinds of transactions entered into by banks in order to provide companies with finance in connection with certain classes of business dealings. Probably, the most significant facility made available by banks in connection with import and export sales is the letter of credit.

Professor Pennington has defined a commercial letter of credit (see *Commercial Banking Law* by Pennington, Hudson and Mann, Macdonald & Evans, 1978, p. 309) as:

> '... an undertaking by a bank to pay a sum of money to the person to whom the credit is addressed, or to accept or purchase a bill of exchange drawn or held by that person, and the undertaking is either absolute, or, more usually, is given on condition that the person fulfils the requirements set out in the credit, for example the presentation to the bank of documents showing that goods have been shipped or despatched by sea, land or air and will be available for collection by the bank or someone nominated by it.'

And in *Re Equitable Trust Company of New York* v *Dawson Partners Ltd* ((1925) 25 LlLR 90 at 93) the system of commercial letters of credit was explained as intended:

> 'to allow the seller to obtain money as soon as he ships the goods by discounting bills drawn on the purchaser, while the purchaser has not to pay for the goods until some time after he has sold them. To do this the discounting bank must be furnished with some security satisfactory to it that if the shipment complies with certain conditions it will be paid for. This is obtained by the promise of the bank giving the ... credit to accept bills for the price if the shipment complies with the specified conditions ...'

Uniform Customs and Practice (UCP) for Documentary Credits

For many years the practice relating to commercial documentary credits has been subject to a body of rules formulated by the International Chamber of Commerce. The rules are now observed in almost every country in the world. In *Forestal Mimosa Ltd* v *Oriental Credit Ltd* ([1986] 2 All ER 400) the Court of Appeal had to consider the effect of a marginal insertion in the credit which incorporated the UCP 'except so far as expressly stated'. On the facts of the case, if the relevant provision of the UCP (Art. 10(b)(iii)) had not been inserted the confirming bank may have had a defence on the ground that the applicant had refused to accept 90-day drafts which were required under the credit and duly presented by the beneficiary. The court held that it was wrong to approach the question of construction by looking at the credit without the UCP. The credit contained no express provision excluding the UCP and the Court of Appeal held the bank's undertaking as set out in the credit to be subject to the UCP. Where, therefore, the UCP are incorporated in a letter of credit they become an express part of the facility. They are to be read together, and given the same prominence as, the express terms of the credit. Any departure or exclusion of the UCP should be clearly agreed and set out in writing on the credit.

The question of construction of the UCP was discussed again in *Co-operative Centrale Raiffeisen-Boerenleenbank BA* v *Sumitomo Bank Ltd* (*The Royan*) ([1988] 2 Lloyd's Rep 250). In that case a bank that had confirmed a letter of credit raised objections to the documents when these were initially tendered by a negotiating bank. It, further, advised the negotiating bank: 'Please consider these documents at your disposal until we receive our Principal's instructions concerning the discrepancies mentioned ...' It was argued for the negotiating bank that these words did not comply with the procedure for rejection, laid down at the relevant time in article 8(e) of the 1974 Revision, under which the notice of rejection had to state that the documents were held at the tenderer's disposal or were being returned to him. Gatehouse J said that the words used by the confirming bank did not bring the matter to an end by a conclusive rejection of the documents but disclosed an intention to await the issuing bank's instructions. The Court of Appeal, reversing the judgment of Gatehouse J held that the formula involved indicated in clear terms that the documents had not been accepted. Lloyd LJ said that 'it was not necessary for [the confirming bank] to say, in so many words, that they were holding the documents at the [issuing bank's] disposal.' Article 8(e) did not require the use of a precise formula and it was sufficient for the confirming bank to indicate, in clear language, that it was not accepting the documents. It is unlikely that the Court of Appeal would have reached the same conclusion if article 8(e) had to be construed as a statutory, and thereby a mandatory, provision. Both in the USA and Europe the view seems to be that the UCP should not be subjected to the rigorous construction of statute but should be treated as a set of standard contractual provisions.

Legal relationship between the debtor and beneficiary

The payment obligation
The opening of the letter of credit is a condition precedent to the seller's obligation under the contract of sale to supply the goods. In *H. & J.M. Bennett Europe Ltd* v *Angrexco Co. Ltd* (unreported, decision 6 April 1990) the court reiterated the principle that the buyer's duty under a contract of sale providing for payment by a letter of credit is to provide a credit which complies with the terms set out in the contract. An attempt to modify the contract of sale by using the credit as an opportunity to impose additional duties on the seller amounts to a breach of the contract of sale.

Trans Trust SPRL v *Danubian Trading Co. Ltd* [1952] 1 Lloyd's Rep 348

The defendants entered into a contract to buy from the plaintiffs a quantity of steel which the plaintiffs themselves were to purchase from Azur SA, a Belgian company which itself was buying the steel under an option from the suppliers. It was a term of the contract that the defendants were to make payment by a confirmed letter of credit to be opened immediately in favour of Azur SA, at a Belgian bank, by an American company to whom the defendants had in turn contracted to sell the steel. The defendants failed to procure the opening of the credit and eventually repudiated the contract.

The plaintiffs claimed from the defendants, as for breach of contract, the profit which they would have made if the transaction had been carried through. The plaintiffs also claimed to be indemnified by the defendants against any damages which Azur SA, might subsequently claim and recover against them.

The Court of Appeal upheld the judgment of McNair J and said that the defendants were in breach of the obligation to procure the opening of the letter of credit and that it was within the contemplation of the parties that a failure to obtain the credit in favour of Azur SA would result in the plaintiffs being unable to complete the purchase of steel from Azur SA and that accordingly the plaintiffs were entitled to recover their loss on the resale.

Denning LJ said that the duty of the seller to carry out the transaction is dependent on the buyer providing the letter of credit. The learned judge looked at the effect of a stipulation requiring a credit to be opened in advance and said (p. 355):

'Sometimes it is a condition precedent to the formation of a contract, that is, it is a condition which must be fulfilled before any contract is concluded at all. In those cases the stipulation "subject to the opening of a letter of credit" is rather like a stipulation "subject to contract". In other cases a contract is concluded and the stipulation for a credit is a condition which is an essential term of the contract. In these cases the provision of the credit is a condition precedent not to the formation of a contract, but to the obligation of the seller to deliver the goods. If the buyer fails to provide the credit, the seller can treat himself as discharged from any further performance of the contract and can sue the buyer for damages.'

Where, in the underlying contract of sale, it is agreed that payment is to be by a letter of credit it is paramount that the credit is opened before the supplier of the goods comes under any obligation to perform his part of the contract by shipping the goods. In *Dix* v *Grainger* ((1922) 10 LILR 496) the plaintiff was an export merchant who brought an action against the defendant claiming damages for an alleged breach of contract. It was a term of the underlying contract that an irrevocable letter of credit should be opened. On a failure to open this credit it was held that there was a fundamental breach by the plaintiff which excused the seller from performing his part of the contract (see also *Garcia* v *Page & Co.* (1936) 55 LILR 391).

Time for opening the credit

Etablissements Chainbaux v *Harbormaster Ltd* [155] 1 Lloyd's Rep 303

A contract for the sale of engine units by the defendants to the plaintiffs, a French company, was entered into. Payment was to be made by an irrevocable letter of credit in sterling payable against shipping documents. The credit was to be opened in London within a 'few weeks'. There was a delay in opening the credit because of an exceptionally long delay in obtaining exchange control permission from the French government, during which time an extension of the time for opening the credit was granted by the sellers. Subsequently, the sellers purported to repudiate the contract before the extended time period had expired and without giving advance notice to the buyers.

The buyers brought an action alleging wrongful repudiation of the contract of sale on the ground that they were entitled to obtain the opening of the credit within a reasonable time which had not yet expired. Alternatively, if such time period had expired, the sellers had granted an extension of the time during which the credit could be opened and they could not repudiate the contract of sale without giving reasonable notice.

Devlin J held that the buyers were in breach of their obligation to obtain the opening of the letter of credit 'within a few weeks' which was a condition precedent to the delivery of the goods but that the breach had been waived by the subsequent conduct of the sellers. Although the sellers had not re-imposed any term relating to the opening of the letter of credit and thereby made it an essence of the contract, they had shown that the buyers could not have complied with their obligation to provide a letter of credit within any reasonable extension of time and, therefore, the sellers were entitled to repudiate the contract. Devlin J in giving judgment held (p. 310):

'It is quite plain that a contract is performed or it is not performed. These provisions have to be complied with according to their terms, and it is therefore no answer for a party to say "I cannot provide you with a letter of credit for the full amount but I can provide you with a letter of credit for 90% of the amount" – 90% is as irrelevant as zero for that purpose – and similarly it is no use saying "I cannot provide you with a letter of credit but I can provide you with some other way which is just as good" ... the defendants are entitled to insist on the contract being performed in the way in which those terms are prescribed.'

Devlin J in the *Etablissements* case had three questions to consider, namely:

(a) *What was originally a reasonable time for opening the credit?* What is considered a reasonable time is to be assessed in the light of circumstances which prevailed when the contract was concluded. Devlin J cited Lord Watson in *Hick v Raymond & Reid* ([1893] AC 22) who said reasonable time:

'has invariably been held to mean that the party upon whom it is incumbent duly fulfils his obligation, notwithstanding protracted delay, so long as such delay is attributable to causes beyond his control, and he has neither acted negligently nor unreasonably.'

And in deciding what is a reasonable time in the *Etablissements* case Devlin J said (p. 312):

'The plaintiff cannot say that in fact the few weeks do not begin to run until he has got the exchange control permission to buy the necessary sterling so long as he can show that during the period he was trying his best to get the sterling – that is not an admissible argument. He must have the sterling during that time and he cannot show he exercised due diligence to get the sterling – that is irrelevant to the computation of reasonable time, which is intended to be a time for arranging the letter of credit.'

(b) *Whether having extended the time for the opening of the letter of credit the plaintiffs have made the provision of the credit within the extension an essence of the contract.* Devlin J said that although an extension of time for the opening of the credit had been granted, performance within that time was of the essence and that the defendants could only terminate the contract after giving reasonable notice. However, citing *Richards v Oppenheim* ([1950] 1 KB 616) the judge said that reasonable notice is not always essential if:

'... the seller, or the defendant, fails to give it [notice], it is open to him to prove that if he had given a reasonable notice it would have been of no use to the plaintiff ...'

Similarly, in *A.E. Lindsay & Co. v Cook* ([1953] 1 Lloyd's Rep 328) it was held that it is no excuse for the debtor to say that he has done everything possible to ensure that the credit was issued within the time permitted and even for him to show that the delay in the issue of the credit was due to the negligence of the bank or its agent.

(c) *Where the credit provides for a date by which the payment facility is to be pro-vided.* The cases so far have looked at situations which required the credit to be opened within a reasonable time and the court had to determine what was rea-sonable time. In other cases the underlying contract may itself provide a date by which the credit is to be opened.

Garcia v *Page & Co. Ltd* (1936) 55 LILR 391

A contract of sale, dated 27 May 1935, was entered into by an English company to supply certain goods to a buyer in Spain. It was a term of the contract that the buyer should arrange for the opening of a 'confirmed credit in London immediately' in favour of the sellers. There was a delay in providing the credit and the sellers notified the buyers that if the credit was not received in London by 24 August, they would cancel the contract. The credit was opened by 24 August but not notified to the sellers until 27 August. The sellers notified the buyer that as the credit had not been notified to them according to the terms of the contract they were entitled to repudiate the contract.

There was a referral to Porter J on the question whether the opening of the credit was a condition precedent to the sellers' obligations under the contract.

The court held that a confirmed credit had to be opened immediately after the contract of sale was entered into, that is, within such a time as the buyer would need (as a person of reasonable diligence) to get the credit established. The buyer had failed to establish the credit within the agreed time and the sellers were consequently entitled to repudiate the contract.

If the contract provides for the shipment of the goods by the seller at any time during a stated period, the buyer in the absence of an express stipulation must arrange for the credit to be made available to the seller at the beginning of the shipment period.

Pavia & Co. v *Thurmann-Neilsen* [1952] 2 QB 84

By a contract in writing dated 20 January 1949, the sellers, Thurmann-Neilsen, agreed to sell to the buyers, Pavia & Co, SPA about 1,500 tons of shelled Brazilian groundnuts. Shipment was agreed over a long period in February and/or March and/or April at the sellers' option, c.i.f. Genoa. The contract provided that payment was to be by means of a 'confirmed, irrevocable, divisible, ... credit'. The buyers were repeatedly pressed to provide the credit facilities but these did not become available until 22 April 1949. The sellers' bank in Brazil refused to agree to the goods being sent to the port of shipment unless and until the credit had been opened in the sellers' favour. The sellers despatched about 675 tons after 22 April, but failed to ship the rest of the agreed goods under the contract. They subsequently brought arbitration pro-ceedings, claiming damages for breach of contract by the buyers in failing to open the credit.

At the hearing by the board of an appeal from the umpire's award giving damages to the sellers, it was argued for the buyers that their obligation under the contract was confined to providing the credit only in time for presentation of the documents.

For the sellers it was argued that the credit required under the contract had to be available to them throughout the whole of the shipment period, or as soon as possible from the beginning of the shipment period or within a reasonable time from the beginning. This question was submitted to the court. McNair J held that the credit should have been opened at the latest by such a time as it would take a reasonably diligent person to open the credit. The buyers appealed.

The court dismissed the appeal and held that in a contract for the sale of goods c.i.f., where the seller could ship the goods at any time during a prolonged period, the buyer must, in the absence of an express stipulation, open the credit and make it available to the seller at the beginning of the shipment period. Lord Denning (p. 88) said:

'In the absence of express stipulation, I think the credit must be made available to the seller at the beginning of the shipment period. The reason is because the seller is entitled, before he ships the goods, to be assured that, on shipment, he will get paid. The seller is not bound to tell the buyer the precise date when he is going to ship; and whenever he does ship the goods, he must be able to draw on the credit. If, therefore, the buyer is to fulfil his obligations he must make the credit available to the seller at the very first date when the goods may be lawfully shipped in compliance with the contract.'

It is clearly established that the seller is entitled to withdraw from the contract of sale unless the credit facility is established by the very first day of a designated shipping period or where a specific loading date is specified. The question has been looked at again in recent cases. In *Sohio Supply Co.* v *Gatoil (USA) Inc.* ([1989] 1 Lloyd's Rep 588) the contract of sale required the buyer to furnish a documentary credit '10 days prior to estimated load date'. The seller argued that he was entitled to receive the letter of credit 10 days prior to the commencement of the stipulated shipping period. The buyer argued that the 10 days involved were to be calculated as from either the last day of the shipping period or from the day on which the buyer 'would properly estimate that the ship would arrive'. Although the Court of Appeal found it unnecessary to decide on the point, Staughton LJ indicated that he preferred the seller's construction and that the letter of credit should have been opened 10 days before the first day of the loading period.

Another recent case which examined the issue of the time for opening the credit is *Transpetrol Ltd* v *Transol Olieprodukten Nederland BV* ([1989] 1 Lloyd's Rep 309) where the contract required the buyer to furnish a letter of credit within one day following his receipt of the seller's nomination of the ship. The contract, however, provided that the seller will give the buyer three days' notice of his intention to nominate. In fact, the seller nominated the ship, without first serving a notice of intention. The buyer claimed that the seller's failure to comply with this requirement excused the delay in the actual furnishing of the letter of credit. Phillips J held that the only stipulation respecting the credit was that it be furnished within one day of the date of nomination and as the buyer had failed to comply with that requirement the seller was within his rights to repudiate the contract of sale. As regards the requirement that the seller give three days' notice of intention to nominate the ship, the court said that the true meaning of the clause was to impose on the seller a duty to nominate a vessel which would deliver the oil at least three days before the vessel's ETA at the designated port of delivery. Otherwise, the notice would be of no use to the buyer and was 'nonsensical'.

The requirement of an irrevocable credit

Giddens v Anglo-African Produce Co. Ltd (1923)14 LILR 230

The sellers agreed to sell South African yellow maize under two separate contracts which required the buyers to establish a credit with the National Bank of South Africa. The document issued in favour of the sellers stated 'Negotiation of drafts under this credit is subject to the bank's convenience. All drafts negotiated hereunder are negotiated with recourse against yourself.'

The buyers sued for damages for breach of contract. It was argued for the sellers that the buyers had failed to establish the credit as required under the contract.

The court held that if the underlying contract merely requires payment to be made by a 'banker's credit', the obligation is to ensure that an irrevocable letter of credit is made available because the whole purpose of financing the transaction by a credit is to assure the creditor that he will be paid by a reliable institution willing to commit itself irrevocably to make payment against proper shipping documents. The documents presented did not amount to an established credit and consequently there was no obligation on the sellers to carry out their obligations under the underlying contract.

If the contract provides for a particular form of contract and such a contract is not made available by the beginning of the shipment period, the seller is discharged from liability under the contract of sale. Where by mistake the wrong type of credit is opened in favour of the beneficiary, the issuing bank and the applicant of the credit may rectify the credit provided it is done before the commencement of the shipment period. The UCP on Documentary Credits requires that the debtor's obligation is to open an irrevocable credit unless the underlying contract of sale specifically allows a revocable credit. Article 10 of the UCP provides that an irrevocable credit constitutes a definite undertaking of the issuing bank, provided that the stipulated documents are presented and that the terms and conditions of the credit are complied with.

The requirement of a confirmed credit
The word 'confirmed' has a meaning distinct from 'irrevocable' and so if the underlying contract calls for a 'confirmed' credit to be made available in favour of the seller then that requirement must be satisfied.

Panoutsos v Raymond Hadley Corp. of New York [1917] 2 KB 473

A contract for the sale and shipment of a cargo of flour to be shipped to Greece not later than 7 November, provided that 'each shipment shall be deemed to be a separate contract' and that payment should be by a 'confirmed banker's credit'. The buyer opened a banker's credit which was not in fact a 'confirmed' credit. The seller, with notice of the fact, made some shipments and received payment by means of the credit and also agreed to give the buyer an extension of time for shipment of the goods.

Subsequently, the seller purported to cancel the contract on the ground that the credit was not in accordance with the contract. The buyer refused to accept the cancellation and the dispute was referred to arbitration. The arbitrators found that the credit was not a confirmed credit as required under the contract but that the sellers had waived strict compliance under the contract. The question referred to the court was whether the arbitrators could properly find that the seller had waived the term of the contract requiring payment to be by a confirmed letter of credit.

The court held that the seller was entitled to insist on strict compliance with the terms of the contract of sale which required a 'confirmed credit' to be made available. That right had, however, been waived by the seller's conduct.

The legal effect of a confirmed credit is stated in the UCP which provides that: 'When an issuing bank authorises or requests another bank to confirm its irrevocable credit and the latter has added its confirmation, such confirmation constitutes a definite undertaking of such bank (the confirming bank), in addition to that of the issuing bank, provided that the stipulated documents are presented and that the terms and conditions of the credit are complied with.'

It should be noted that only an irrevocable credit will be confirmed by a confirming bank. Moreover, the requirement that the credit be an irrevocable confirmed credit imposes two independent obligations, and both must be complied with. With an irrevocable credit the obligation is on the issuing bank to ensure that the credit issued is irrevocable, i.e the issuing bank gives a binding and definite undertaking to honour the credit, whereas confirmation of the credit is usually given by an intermediate bank who undertakes to honour the credit in its own right. Neither bank is, however, under an obligation to honour the credit if non-complying documents are presented.

Where the buyer is in breach of a term of the underlying contract of sale, the seller may waive strict compliance. This does not mean that the seller can never avail himself of the condition in the future but in order to revert to the original terms of the contract the seller must give reasonable notice (see *Etablissements Chainbaux* v *Harbormaster Ltd* and *Richards* v *Oppenheim*). The waiver may be express or by conduct but may also be the result of inaction (see *Plasticmoda SpA* v *Davidson (Manchester) Ltd* [1952] 1 Lloyd's Rep 527).

Legal relationship between the beneficiary and the issuing bank

The seller (beneficiary) under a commercial letter of credit is under no obligation to conform to the terms of the credit but if he wishes to be paid under the credit he must conform to the terms. The law requires that the documents presented by the beneficiary conform strictly to the terms of the credit.

Equitable Trust Company of New York v *Dawson Partners Ltd* (1927) 27 LILR 49

The respondents, Dawson Partners Ltd, were importers and merchants, and they entered into a contract with one Rogge (trading under the name J.H. Rogge & Co.) for the purchase of a consignment of vanilla beans. The contract required a credit to be opened with a bank in Batavia. The respondents wrote to the appellants (the Equitable Trust Company of New York) requesting them to open, by cable, a confirmed credit with a certain bank in Batavia. The credit was payable against certain documents including a Dutch government certificate evidencing the goods to be sound and sweet and of prime quality.

The credit was opened through a correspondent bank, the Hong Kong & Shanghai Banking Corporation in London, which communicated the credit by cable to their branch in Batavia. The respondents were informed by Rogge that it was not the practice of the Dutch East Indian government to give certificates of quality and it was arranged for a certificate of quality to be issued by experts who were sworn brokers and signed by the Chamber of Commerce.

The appellants agreed to the change in the letter of credit and notified by letter the Hong Kong & Shanghai Bank in London, which notified the bank in Batavia of the change in the terms of the credit. The Hong Kong & Shanghai Bank despatched in their secret cypher code to their office in Batavia an instruction that the credit was to be honoured against documents including a 'certificate of quality issued by experts who are sworn brokers, signed by the Chamber of Commerce'. Unfortunately, they made use of a code in which the words 'experts who are sworn brokers' denoted either the plural or singular and when the message was received by the bank in Batavia it was decoded in the singular.

The bank in Batavia made payment against documents which included a certificate of quality signed by only one expert. By the time the documents arrived in London it was known that Rogge had fraudulently shipped a quantity of wood and iron instead of the goods required under the contract.

The respondents objected to the certificate of quality on the ground that it was signed by only one broker and that his signature was countersigned by an official of a commercial association and not by the Chamber of Commerce, as required. The respondents commenced an action out of which this appeal arose.

Viscount Sumner (in the House of Lords) with reference to the documents said (p. 52):

> 'It is both common ground and common sense that in such a transaction the accepting bank can only claim indemnity if the conditions on which it is authorised to accept are in the matter of accompanying documents strictly observed. There is no room for documents which are almost the same, or which will do just as well. Business could not proceed securely on any other lines. The bank's branch abroad, which knows nothing officially of the details of the transaction thus financed, cannot take it upon itself to decide what will do well and what will not. If it does as it is told, it is safe; if it departs from the conditions laid down, it acts at its own risk. The documents tendered were not exactly the documents which the defendants had promised to take up, and prima facie they were right in refusing to take them.'

H

The issuing and confirming banks are under a duty to the beneficiary of the credit to honour the credit on the fulfilment of certain conditions set out in the letter of credit. This duty to honour the credit is unilateral and the bank is bound to honour the credit only if its terms are strictly observed. In *English, Scottish and Australian Bank* v *The Bank of South of Africa* ((1922) 13 LlLR 21 at 24) Bailhache J said:

> 'It is elementary to say that a person who ships in reliance on a letter of credit must do so in exact compliance with its terms. It is also elementary to say that a bank is not bound to honour drafts presented to it under a letter of credit unless those drafts with the accompanying documents are in strict accord with the credit as opened.'

In *Kwei Tek Chao* v *British Traders & Shippers Ltd* ([1954] 1 All ER 779) Devlin J said that the seller of goods has two distinct obligations:

(a) to deliver the proper documents of title;
(b) to ship the proper goods.

Against that the buyer has two distinct rights:

(a) to reject the documents;
(b) to reject the goods.

The documents must, therefore, comply with the strict terms of the letter of credit for two reasons:

(a) if the issuing bank is to be entitled to reimbursement from its customer for the sum paid to the beneficiary under the credit the documents must comply;
(b) if the goods are lost at sea or destroyed or damaged and the customer has to bring an action against the responsible parties he must again have valid documents of title.

In *Kwei Tek Chao* the court was concerned with a forged bill of lading but as a document of title it must conform to the description of the goods.

In *Bank Melli Iran* v *Barclays Bank DCO Ltd* ([1951] 1 Lloyd's Rep 367) a letter of credit was issued which described the contract goods as '100 new Chevrolet trucks'. The documents required to be presented under the credit included a US government certificate which described the goods as 'new, good Chevrolet ... trucks'. Moreover, the invoice described the goods as 'in new condition'. The court held that the documents tendered and accepted by the issuing bank were defective. McNair J said that the invoice which described the goods as 'in new condition' was not synonymous with an invoice which described the goods as 'new'. Moreover, the description in the US government certificate as 'new (comma) good' might clearly denote goods which were different from 'new' trucks. Similarly, in *Rayner & Co.* v *Hambros Bank Ltd* ([1942] 2 All ER 649) a bank received instructions to open a credit in favour of the plaintiffs for a cargo of 'coromandel groundnuts'. The credit was properly opened and notified to the beneficiary who presented documents which included a bill of lading which described the goods as 'machine shelled groundnut kernels' although the accompanying invoice referred to the goods as 'coromandel groundnuts'. The Court of Appeal held that the documents were non-conforming although evidence was introduced to show that 'coromandel groundnuts' were commonly known in the trade as 'machine shelled groundnut kernels'. In *Kydon Compania Naviera SA* v *National Westminster Bank Ltd* ([1981] 1 Lloyd's Rep 68) the credit required a sight draft on Euroasia Carriers and the provision of a sight draft on the Janata Bank was grounds for rejecting the documents although the draft served no specific useful purpose.

Unless, however, the credit calls for a full description of the goods on the bill of lading it is sufficient that the documents collectively give a full description of the goods. In *Guaranty Trust Co.* v *Van den Berghs Ltd* ((1926) 22 LlLR 447) the defendants pleaded that the documents accepted by the plaintiffs (the issuing bank under the credit) were non-conforming because the bill of lading described the goods as 'coco-nut oil' instead of 'Manila coco-nut oil' as required under the credit, although a certificate of origin did so describe the goods. There was not a requirement in the credit that the bill of lading should give a full description of the goods.

The Court of Appeal held that assuming the documents required the goods to be described as 'Manila coco-nut oil' the certificate of origin made it clear that the goods were of that nature and the documents were complying documents. Sargant LJ said:

> 'The objection that the oil was not described in the bill of lading as 'Manila oil' was, I think, sufficiently cured by the indications in the certificate of origin that it was Manila oil ...'

Similarly, in *Midland Bank Ltd* v *Seymour* ([1955] 2 Lloyd's Rep 147) Devlin J held that it is sufficient if the set of documents contain all the particulars called for in the letter of request and the defendant was obliged to reimburse the bank. The learned judge continued:

> '... if each document contains all, it would produce a state of affairs that would be unusual. For instance I suppose rarely if ever does one find the price of goods set out in the bill of lading. It is a piece of information which is wholly irrelevant to any of the purposes of the bill of lading, and one does not find it there. Similarly, I suppose one would not find it in the insurance certificate. But I cannot say upon what principle of construction you can say that the bill of lading need not contain the quantity and the full description, except by saying that each of the documents must contain all ...'

In *London and Foreign Trading Corporation* v *British and North European Bank* ((1921) 9 LlLR 11) the plaintiff sought to recover from the defendant bank money which the defendant bank had paid in compliance with a letter of credit. The plaintiffs contended that the bank had paid out on an insufficient bill which stated the number of bags of maize shipped under the contract but not the weight as required under the credit. Rowlatt J said:

> 'The authority given to the bank was limited to payment against a bill of lading showing shipment of 500 tons and the invoice could not be used to interpret the bill of lading and satisfy the terms of the credit.'

In *Astro Exito Navegacion SC* v *Chase Manhattan Bank NA (The Messiniaki Tolmi)* ([1988] 2 Lloyd's Rep 217) the letter of credit required a notice of readiness and a gas-free certificate in relation to a contract of sale for a ship. The documents were rejected on the grounds that the documents were non-conforming. The court held that it is for the beneficiary under the credit to provide conforming documents and insofar as the gas-free certificate did not show the necessary approval it was defective.

Examining the documents

The insistence of the courts that documents presented under a letter of credit comply strictly with the terms of the credit produces the legal consequence that if the documents do not comply exactly with the credit the bank is entitled to reject the documents as a whole. If the documents do not appear to comply with the terms of the credit the bank must not delay unreasonably in rejecting them or it will lose its right of rejection by implied waiver. Similarly, if the issuing bank employs an intermediatory bank to confirm or advise the credit, the confirming bank acts as an agent of the issuing bank and it must reject documents which do not conform with the terms of credit with reasonable despatch if the issuing bank is to be able to reject them as against the beneficiary. The question of payment under reserve is provided for under Art. 16(f) of the UCP:

> 'If the remitting bank draws the attention of the issuing bank to any discrepancies in the documents or advises the issuing bank that it has paid, incurred a deferred payment undertaking, accepted or negotiated under reserve or against an indemnity in respect of such discrepancies, the issuing bank shall not be thereby relieved from any of its obligations under any provision of this article. Such reserve or indemnity concerns only the relations between the remitting bank and the party towards whom the reserve was made, or from whom, or on whose behalf, the indemnity was obtained.'

In *Banque de l'Indochine et de Suez SA* v *J.H. Rayner (Mincing Lane) Ltd* ([1983] 1 All ER 468) it was held that a confirming or issuing bank may take up documents which appear to contain discrepancies or which do not conform to the terms of the credit but which make the acceptance 'subject to reserve' so as to entitle it subsequently to reject the documents and claim repayment of any amount paid under reserve if it turns out that its objections to the documents are justified.

Banque de l'Indochine et de Suez SA v J.H. Rayner (Mincing Lane) Ltd [1983] 1 All ER 468

The defendants agreed that payment for goods supplied by them to the purchasers was to be by means of an irrevocable letter of credit to be issued by a bank in Djibouti and confirmed by the plaintiff bank. The plaintiff bank objected to the documents presented for alleged discrepancies but were, nevertheless, willing to make payment subject to the reservation of their right to object to them. The defendants accepted that payment under the credit was to be under reserve. The issuing bank refused to accept the documents taken up by the plaintiffs because of the alleged discrepancies, and the plaintiff bank consequently sought reimbursement from the defendants on the grounds that it was entitled to repayment, upon the issuing bank rejecting the documents. The defendants contended that they were under no obligation to repay the money unless the alleged discrepancies were established as being valid.

Parker J held that the payment 'under reserve' did not entitle the plaintiffs to demand repayment of the money paid under the credit simply because the issuing bank had rejected the documents. By making payment 'under reserve' the plaintiff bank had merely reserved the right to repayment of money if it could, subsequently, show that at the time it made payment the bank was not under any contractual liability to pay under the credit and could properly have rejected the shipping documents. Since the bank was not contractually bound to make payment because of the discrepancies to which it had objected (which was a valid reason for rejection) it was entitled to repayment. Parker J said that a payment under a reserve is normally made in the following circumstances:

(a) that the remitting bank genuinely believes that there are discrepancies justifying non-payment;
(b) that the beneficiary believes that the bank is wrong and that he is entitled to payment; and
(c) that the paying bank believes that the issuing bank will, despite the irregularities, take up the documents and reimburse the remitting bank.

The words payment 'under reserve' protect the paying bank from being unable to reclaim the payment made to the beneficiary if the discrepancies pointed out by the paying bank provide valid grounds for rejection of the shipping documents; but if the beneficiary is in fact entitled to payment under the terms of the credit despite the objections expressed by the paying bank, he can retain the money paid subject to reserve even though the paying bank could have rejected the shipping documents on other, unexpressed grounds.

The Court of Appeal ([1983] 1 All ER 1137) upheld the judge at first instance, and said that although the term 'payment under reserve' is not defined either by the ICC or the law, banks will often accept documents which are not strictly in compliance with the terms of the letter of credit and make payment under reserve. The Court of Appeal observed that 'payment under reserve' will normally relate to circumstances in which the beneficiary can be called upon to repay the money which has been paid under a letter of credit. However, the Court said that 'payment under reserve' may have one of two meanings:

(a) that the money paid under the letter of credit is repayable on demand if the issuing bank in reliance on some or all the defects alleged by the non-conforming bank declines to reimburse the confirming bank or to ratify the payment; or
(b) once again the issuing bank relying on all or some of the defects alleged by the confirming bank declines to reimburse the confirming bank or to ratify the payment, but in this instance the money is recoverable only by an action being brought by the confirming bank against the beneficiary.

The Court of Appeal rejected the submission that a bank agrees, either expressly or implicitly, that if it makes 'payment under reserve', (because the documents presented by the beneficiary under the letter of credit appear not to comply with the terms of the credit) it will only be able to recover the amount if it subsequently discovers that the documents do not in fact comply with the credit by bringing an action against the beneficiary. Kerr LJ said that what the parties intend when payment is made under reserve is that the beneficiary will be bound to repay the money on demand if the documents are rejected by the issuing bank, whether on its own initiative, or on the buyer's instructions. Kerr LJ was also of the opinion that since the confirming bank will normally specify the grounds for rejecting the documents, it should be implied that the issuing bank can subsequently only rely on those grounds to reject the documents, even though there are other grounds on which the bank could legitimately have rejected the documents.

The notice of rejection need only identify the discrepancies in respect of which the documents are rejected on that particular occasion. There is no duty to identify each and every discrepancy. Therefore, the statement of a particular reason or reasons for rejecting documents is not enough to found a representation, waiver or estoppel in respect of other discrepancies. In *Kydon Compania Naviera* v *National Westminster Bank Ltd* ([1981] 1 Lloyd's Rep 68) Parker J said:

> 'it cannot, as a matter of general principle, be right that a bank can never be estopped any more than it can that a bank by stating one reason impliedly represents that the documents are otherwise in order or impliedly promises that if the stated defect is rectified it will pay.'

Circumstances founding an agreement or estoppel were held to exist in *Floating Dock Ltd* v *Hong Kong and Shanghai Banking Corp.* ([1986] 1 Lloyd's Rep 65) where the employees of the issuing bank reached an agreement with the beneficiary regarding amendment of two credits in such circumstances that the beneficiary could reasonably assume that the bank would not rely upon a particular ground of rejection.

In *Bankers Trust Co.* v *State Bank of India* (*The Times*, 25 June 1991) the Court of Appeal held that the issuing bank under a letter of credit which is subject to the Uniform Customs and Practice must examine the documents presented and decide within a reasonable time whether or not to reject them for discrepancies. The term 'reasonable time' includes time necessary in the circumstances for consultation with experts or with the applicant of the credit himself, to enable the bank to make its decision. In that case the issuing bank released a set of documents, comprising 900 documents, to the applicant so as to enable him to examine the documents for the purpose of deciding whether to reject them or to waive the discrepancies discovered in them. The applicant took approximately three days to examine the set, which was a period comparable to that spent by the issuing bank's own staff on their initial examination. Relying on expert evidence and disagreeing with Gatehouse J in *Co-operative Centrale Raiffaisen-Boerenleenbank BA* v *Sumitomo Bank 'The Royan'* ([1987] 1 Lloyd's Rep 345) Hirst J held that the documents should not be released to the customer for a prolonged examination but only for the short period of time required to enable the applicant of the credit to consider the points referred to him by the bank. He held a period of three days for the applicant of the credit to examine the documents to be excessive. Hirst J also indicated that a period of eight days would be unreasonable time for the bank's own examination of the documents.

In *Harlow and Jones* v *American Express Bank and Creditanstalt-Bankerein* ((Third Party) [1990] 2 Lloyd's Rep 343) Gatehouse J held that where documents under a letter of credit were sent 'on collection terms only' because the letter of credit had expired, the letter is still governed by the terms of the credit, and the bank owes a duty to the seller either to reject the documents or to accept them in accordance with the terms of the credit. The bank was held liable to the seller when it released documents to the sub-purchaser against acceptance. Relying on expert evidence Gatehouse J examined the meaning of release of documents on a collection basis and said:

'... the expert witnesses for all parties were agreed that the words "on a collection basis" or "for collection" are equivalent and must take their meaning from their context. The experts were also agreed that it is common practice that documents which are discrepant, including documents which are presented after the expiry date of the letter of credit, are sent to the issuing bank for collection or on a collection basis under the Letter of Credit which will be expressly or impliedly extended if, after inspection, the opener and his bank decided to accept the documents and thus waive the discrepancies. In this event, in the strict analysis, it is probably a re-negotiation of the credit in which the opener may, but not necessarily, require allowances.'

Gatehouse J concluded on this basis that the discrepant documents despatched to the issuing bank on a collection basis were still tendered under the documentary credit. Consequently, a decision to accept them invoked the bank's duty to make payment under the documentary credit. Moreover, the judge concluded that payment could alternatively be recovered under the Uniform Rules for Collection because article 10 provides that documents tendered on a genuine collection basis were to be released against payment and not against the mere acceptance of the draft. Gatehouse J rejected the argument that the Uniform Rules for Collection were inapplicable because they had not expressly been incorporated in the remittance letter.

The Supreme Court of Singapore in *United Bank Ltd* v *Banque Nationale de Paris* (unreported, decision of 7 June 1991 – see *JBL,* January 1992) had to construe article 8(e) of the 1974 UCP (now superseded by article 16(d)). The court held that the issuing bank's notice in which it listed certain discrepancies and stated that it was holding the documents on a 'collection basis' did not constitute a valid rejection under article 8(e) of the 1974 UCP. However, on the construction of 'reasonable time' during which to reject the documents the judge was less stringent but held that once the issuing bank reached its decision, it had to notify it forthwith to the negotiating bank and that the appropriate formula had to be used in that notice.

Forged documents

The issuing bank must reject non-conforming documents (e.g. where a certificate is signed by only one authorised expert instead of the necessary two experts). However, what is the position if the reason for the non-conformity is that the documents are forged or affected by the fraud of the beneficiary?

United City Merchants (Investments) Ltd v *Royal Bank of Canada and Others* [1983] 1 AC 168

Glass Fibres and Equipment Ltd sold manufacturing equipment to a Peruvian company, the second defendants, and agreed to invoice for twice the agreed contractual price so that the Peruvian company might exchange Peruvian currency (to the total of the excess for US dollars) in breach of Peruvian exchange control regulations. Payment was to be made by an irrevocable letter of credit. This was issued by the Banco Continental SA (the third defendants) and confirmed by the Royal Bank of Canada. Fibre Glass assigned their rights under the contract to the plaintiffs as security for advances.

The goods were shipped on board a day after the last agreed shipment date and the carriers' agent issued a received for shipment bill of lading dated on the last date of shipment. On presentation of the documents the confirming bank refused to accept the documents on the ground that they had information which indicated that the bill of lading was not as represented.

At first instance Mocatta J held that the fraud of the agent was not known to the plaintiff when the documents were presented and the Royal Bank was not entitled to refuse payment against documents which prima facie appeared to be in order. In a separate hearing concerning the breach of exchange control it was held that the refusal to make payment was justified because the agreement to pay the inflated price was in breach of the Bretton Woods agreement and therefore the payment under the credit was justified.

The Court of Appeal reversed the judgment and held that the bank was entitled to refuse payment when the documents included one which contained a material mis-representation of fact. With regard to that part of the credit that related to the excess of the purchase price the court held that the credit was divisible so payment could have been paid to the extent that it did not infringe the exchange control regulations but because of the misrepresentation the action failed. The plaintiffs appealed.

The House of Lords held that the bank was not entitled to refuse payment against documents which on their face were in order and the unknown (to the beneficiary) fraud of the third party was not a justification for refusing payment. The court should not enforce that part of the transaction which was in breach of the Bretton Woods agreement. Lord Diplock giving judgment said (p. 182):

'It is trite law that there are four autonomous though interconnected contractual relationships involved. (1) The underlying contract for the sale of goods, to which the only parties are the buyer and the seller; (2) the contract between the buyer and the issuing bank under which the latter agrees to issue the credit and either itself or through a confirming bank to notify the credit to the seller and to make payments to or to the order of the seller (or to pay, accept or negotiate bills of exchange drawn by the seller) against presentation of stipulated documents; and the buyer agrees to reimburse the issuing bank for payments made under the credit. For such reimbursement the stipulated documents, if they include a document of title such as a bill of lading, constitute a security available to the issuing bank; (3) if payment is to be made through a confirming bank the contract between the issuing bank and the confirming bank authorising and requiring the latter to make such payments made under the credit; (4) the contract between the confirming bank and the seller (or to accept or negotiate without recourse to drawer bills of exchange drawn by him) up to the amount of the credit against presentation of the stipulated documents ... It is trite law that in contract, ... the parties to it, the seller and the confirming bank, "deal in documents and not in goods", as article 8 of the Uniform Customs puts it. If, on their face, the documents presented to the confirming bank by the seller conform with the requirements of the credit as notified to him by the confirming bank, that bank is under a contractual obligation to the seller to honour the credit, notwith-standing that the bank has knowledge that the seller at the time of the presentation of the conforming documents is alleged by the buyer to have, and in fact has already, committed a breach of his contract with the buyer for the sale of the goods to which the documents appear on their face to relate, that would have entitled the buyer to treat the contract of sale as rescinded and to reject the goods and refuse to pay the seller the purchase price ...'

The duty to examine the documents was examined by Lord Diplock (p. 184) where he said:

'... as between the confirming bank and the issuing bank and the buyer the contractual duty of each bank under a confirmed irrevocable credit is to examine with reasonable care all documents presented in order to ascertain that they appear on their face to be in accordance with the terms and conditions of the credit, and, if do so appear, to pay to the seller/beneficiary if the credit so provides. It is so stated in the latest edition of the Uniform Customs. It is equally clear law, and is so provided by article 9 of the Uniform Customs, that confirming banks assume no liability or responsibility to one another or to the buyer "for the form, sufficiency, accuracy, genuineness, falsification or legal effect of any documents".'

The application of article 9 of the Uniform Customs was illustrated in *Gian Singh & Co Ltd* v *Banque de I'Indochine* ([1974] 1 WLR 1234) where the customer was held liable to reimburse the issuing bank for honouring a documentary credit on the presentation of an apparently conforming document which was an ingenious forgery and which the bank had not been negligent in failing to detect.

Lord Diplock rejected the reasoning of the Court of Appeal which held (p. 187):

'... from the premiss that a confirming bank could refuse to pay against a document that it knew to be forged, even though the seller/beneficiary had no knowledge of that fact. From this premiss they reasoned that if forgery by a third party relieves the confirming bank of liability to the seller/beneficiary, fraud by a third party ought to have the same consequence ...'

He then continued (p. 188):

'But even assuming the correctness of the Court of Appeal's premiss as respects forgery by a third party of a kind that makes a document a nullity for which at least a rational case can be made out, to say that this leads to the conclusion that fraud by a third party which does not render the document a nullity has the same consequence appears to me, with respect, to be a *non sequitur* ...'

The House of Lords distinguished the *United City Merchants* case from earlier authorities which had established that the bank was entitled to reject forged documents where the forgery was that of the beneficiary under the credit. In the *United City Merchants* case the forgery (which was unknown to the beneficiary) was committed by a third party.

Lord Diplock on page 183:

'There is one established exception: that is, where the seller, for the purpose of drawing on the credit, fraudulently presents to the confirming bank documents that contain, expressly or by implication, material representations of fact that to his knowledge are untrue. Although there does not appear among the English authorities any case in which this exception has been applied, it is well established in the American cases of which the leading or "landmark" case is *Szteyn* v *Henry Schroder Banking Corporation* ((1941) 31 NYS 2d 631) ...'

In the *Szteyn* case the seller's fraud had been brought to the attention of the bank before the shipping documents were presented for payment. The case was approved by the Court of Appeal in *Edward Owen Engineering Ltd* v *Barclays Bank International Ltd* ([1978] QB 159), a case involving performance bonds but to which the courts applied the rules of letters of credit.

In *Korea Industry Co.* v *Andoll* ([1990] 2 Lloyd's Rep 183) the Singapore Court of Appeal held that the court will not restrain the payment of funds due under an irrevocable letter of credit, unless there is clear evidence that there has been or is likely to be a fraudulent demand under the credit, and the bank is aware that the demand made, or about to be made, is fraudulent.

In *Tukan Timber* v *Barclays Bank plc* ([1987] 1 FTLR 154) Hirst J held that the plaintiffs were not entitled to an injunction to restrain a bank making payments under an irrecoverable letter of credit on the ground of fraud where they could not show that a further fraudulent demand would be made notwithstanding that fraudulent demands had already been made. The plaintiffs were engaged in the timber trade with a Brazilian company. At the plaintiffs' request the defendants issued a letter of credit in favour of the Brazilian company that included provision for advance payment upon receipt by the defendant of a simple receipt from the Brazilian company countersigned by a director of the plaintiffs. The letter of credit was issued in substitution for earlier letters of credit. The Brazilian company had threatened to issue receipts to obtain advance payments using receipts countersigned by a director of the plaintiffs in its original form as opposed to the new form. The defendants refused to pay the Brazilian company and the plaintiffs commenced proceedings against the defendants and sought an interlocutory injunction to restrain the defendants from making any advance payments under the letter of credit. Hirst J held that only where a bank has notice of fraud committed by the beneficiary can the court interfere, and there is a heavy burden of proof on the plaintiff. The plaintiffs argued that the bank did have notice of fraud because of the previous attempts of the beneficiary to claim under fraudulent demands. The judge declared that what was at issue was whether the plaintiffs had proved that a further demand would be made on the strength of another fraudulent receipt bearing the purported signature of one of the authorised signatories. The judge concluded that the plaintiffs had not satisfied the burden of proof, particularly as the beneficiary of the credit would realise that he was alerted to possible fraud.

Bretton Woods point

The Bretton Woods Agreements Order in Council 1946, made under the Bretton Woods Agreements Act 1945, gives effect in the UK to article VIII, section 2(b), of the Bretton Woods Agreement, which is in the following terms:

> 'Exchange contracts which involve the currency of any member and which are contrary to the exchange control regulations of that member maintained or imposed consistently with this agreement shall be unenforceable in the territories of any member ...'

The House of Lords affirmed the Court of Appeal's decision in *Wilson, Smithett & Cope Ltd* v *Teruzzi* ([1976] QB 683) where the court held that it should 'look at the substance of the contracts and at the form. It should not enforce a contract that is a mere "monetary transaction in disguise".'

The effect of the word 'unenforceable' was examined in *Batra* v *Ebrahim* (unreported but cited by Ackner LJ in [1982] QB 208) as follows:

'If in the course of the hearing of an action the court becomes aware that the contract on which a party is suing is one that this country has accepted an international obligation to treat as unenforceable, the court must take the point itself, even though the defendant has not pleaded it, and must refuse to lend its aid to enforce the contract. But this does not have the effect of making an exchange contract that is contrary to the exchange control regulations of a member state other than the United Kingdom into a contract that is 'illegal' under English law or render acts undertaken in this country in performance of such a contract unlawful. Like a contract of guarantee of which there is no note or memorandum in writing it is unenforceable by the courts and nothing more.'

Restraining the bank from making payment

In *Bolivinter Oil SA* v *Chase Manhattan Bank NA* ([1984] 1 Lloyd's Rep 251) the Court of Appeal made a number of observations regarding the grant of *ex parte* injunctions restraining payment under letters of credit, performance bonds and guarantees:

'Before leaving this appeal, we should like to a add a word about the circumstances in which an *ex parte* injunction should be issued which prohibits a bank from paying under an irrevocable letter of credit or a purchase bond or guarantee. The unique value of such a letter, bond or guarantee is that the beneficiary can be completely satisfied that whatever disputes may thereafter arise between him and the bank's customer in relation to the performance or indeed existence of the underlying contract, the bank is personally undertaking to pay him provided specified conditions are met. In requesting his bank to issue such a letter, bond or guarantee, the customer is seeking to take advantage of this unique characteristic. If, save in the most exceptional cases, he is to be allowed to derogate from the bank's personal and irrevocable undertaking, given be it again noted at his request, by obtaining an injunction restraining the bank from honouring that undertaking, he will undermine what is the bank's greatest asset, however large and rich it may be, namely by its reputation for financial and contractual probity. Furthermore, if this happens at all frequently, the value of all irrevocable letters of credit and performance bonds and guarantees will be undermined.'

Judges who are asked, often at short notice and *ex parte*, to issue an injunction restraining payment by a bank under an irrevocable letter of credit or performance bond or guarantee should ask whether there is any challenge to the validity of the letter, bond or guarantee itself. If there is not or if the challenge is not substantial, prima facie no injunction should be granted and the bank should be left free to honour its contractual obligation, although restrictions may well be imposed upon the freedom of the beneficiary to deal with the money after he has received. The wholly exceptional case where an injunction may be granted is where it is proved that the bank knows that any demand for payment already made or which may be made, is tainted by fraud to the bank's knowledge. It would certainly not normally be sufficient that this rests upon an uncorroborated statement of the customer, for irreparable damage can be done to a bank's credit in the relatively brief time which must elapse between the granting of such an injunction and an application by the bank to have it discharged.

Sir John Donaldson MR, therefore, said that three propositions had been established as law by successive courts on the question whether or not to grant an injunction:

(a) that the issuing or confirming bank is not concerned with disputes between its customer and the beneficiary relating to or arising in connection with the underlying contract. The issuing or confirming banks are under an independent personal duty to the beneficiary to honour the credit or bond or guarantee and to make payment under the credit on presentation of the proper shipping documents;

(b) that a court which is requested to grant an *ex parte* injunction which restrains the bank from making payment under the letter of credit, performance bond or guarantee must itself decide whether the validity of the bank's undertaking may be challenged. An injunction should not prima facie be granted unless the bank can show that its obligations under the credit are invalid or unenforceable; and

(c) that the courts may grant an injunction only in exceptional circumstances, namely where it is known to the bank that payment is being sought by the beneficiary acting fraudulently as regards the bank's customer. There must be evidence of fraud committed or sought to be committed by the beneficiary, and an uncorroborated allegation of fraud by the issuing bank's customer will be insufficient to induce the courts to grant an injunction restraining the bank from honouring its obligations. Further the fraud must be that of the beneficiary personally.

The relationship between the buyer and the issuing and confirming banks

The obligation of the applicant to put the bank in funds is the counterpart of the bank's obligation to honour the credit.

Sales Continuation Ltd v *Austin Taylor & Co Ltd* [1967] 2 All ER 1092

The defendants (selling agents in London) entered into a contract on 14 May 1965 on behalf of exporters in Malaysia (the Nesasi Sawmill Company) to sell timber to importers in Belgium. Under the contract property in the goods was to pass on shipment subject to an unpaid sellers' lien for the unpaid purchase price. The defendants applied for and obtained, on 19 May, from the plaintiff bankers an irrevocable credit, in favour of the Nesasi Sawmill Company, to be honoured against the presentation of a draft (to be accompanied by the usual shipping documents), drawn on the plaintiff bankers by the Nesasi company. The defendants' application to open the credit contained an undertaking to provide the bank with funds to meet any disbursements and the bank had authority to debit the customer's account without giving any previous notice.

The plaintiffs, having received the application, sent a letter to the manager of the Eastern Bank Ltd in London, asking the bank to advise Nesasi Sawmill Company that an irrevocable credit had been opened in their favour. The letter to Nesasi Sawmill Company informed them of the opening of the credit and gave an undertaking to 'place the value of such documents at your disposal ninety days after sight D/A'.

On 15 July, a draft under the letter of credit was drawn on the plaintiffs. The draft was accompanied by the necessary documents of title and under the terms of the letter of credit this draft would become payable by the plaintiffs on 28 October. The plaintiffs accepted the draft and handed the documents of title to the defendants on 30 July, in order to enable the defendants to present the documents to the Belgian bank and collect the purchase price. The plaintiffs obtained from the defendants a receipt headed 'Trust Receipt' under which the defendants undertook to hold the documents of title and the goods when received as trustees for the plaintiffs and to pay the proceeds of sale to the plaintiffs.

The documents of title were delivered by the defendants to the buyers and the defendants received payment in respect of the goods sold under the contract. The money was received after a receiver and manager of the plaintiffs was appointed by the holders of a mortgage and debenture. The receiver gave notice of his appointment to the defendants. On 12 August, the defendants received payment of the timber but did not pay to the plaintiff bankers. The plaintiff bank went into voluntary liquidation and its assets were insufficient to discharge its liabilities. On 28 October, the draft drawn by Nesasi Sawmill Company was presented to the plaintiffs and returned dishonoured. The defendants paid to Nesasi Sawmill Company the sum collected by them from the purchasers as the purchase price of the dishonoured draft and sent the dishonoured draft to the liquidator of the plaintiffs. The plaintiffs sued the defendants for the money that they had received from the Belgian buyers.

Paull J held that the receiver could not insist on the buyer paying the amount of the credit to him, since it was an essential element of the contract between the plaintiffs and the buyer that if the buyer put the plaintiffs in funds to meet the drafts, the plaintiffs would honour the drafts accepted by them. The appointment of a receiver was evidence of an intention not to complete their side of the contract because the whole of its assets would be appropriated in paying the debenture debt. The learned judge said (p. 1096):

> 'In my judgment it is an essential element in the contract between the plaintiffs and the defendants that there was an implied term that, provided the defendants put the plaintiffs in funds to meet any accepted draft, the plaintiffs would in fact honour the accepted draft. That term is necessary to give business efficiency to the contract.'

In *Greenhough* v *Munroe* ((1931) 53 F 2d 362) an American court held that the buyer's obligation to put the bank in funds could not be enforced after the bank had ceased to carry on business and stopped payment of its debts as they fell due.

The issuing bank's right to be reimbursed was examined by Lord Sumner in *Equitable Trust Co. of New York* v *Dawson Partners Ltd* ((1926) 25 LlLR 90) where he said:

> 'There is really no question here of waiver or of estoppel or of negligence or of breach of contract of employment to use reasonable care and skill. The case rests entirely on performance of the conditions precedent to the right of indemnity, which is provided for in the letter of credit.'

The Uniform Customs absolve the issuing bank from responsibility for the consequences arising out of delay, or the loss of messages, letters or documents, or for delay, mutilation or errors arising in the transmission of cables, telegrams or telex, or for errors in the transmission of technical terms. If the Uniform Customs were applied strictly then the bank in the *Equitable Trust* case would not be held liable.

Where the issuing bank uses an intermediate bank (to advise or confirm the credit) the banks are in an agency relationship (although the confirming bank gives its own undertaking to make payment) and the right of reimbursement between the banks depends on the intermediate bank taking up complying documents and performing its part of the bargain under the letter of credit. In *Equitable Trust Co.* v *Dawson & Partners Ltd* the court said there is no agency relationship between the buyer (the applicant of the credit) and the confirming bank. The issuing bank cannot escape liability by alleging that the error in accepting non-complying documents was committed by the confirming bank. On the contrary the confirming bank acts as an agent of the issuing bank and it is the latter bank which is responsible to the applicant of the credit. However the American courts have held that the confirming bank may be liable to the buyer if it is guilty of fraud (see *Oelbermann* v *National City Bank of New York* (1935) 79 F 2d 354).

PERFORMANCE GUARANTEES AND PERFORMANCE BONDS

Lord Diplock in *United City Merchants (Investments) Ltd* v *Royal Bank of Canada* ([1983] 1 AC 168 at 184) said that the issuing of a performance guarantee or performance bond imposes on the bank obligations analogous to those imposed by a confirming bank to the seller under a documentary credit. The UCP are expressed to apply to 'all documentary credit, including, to the extent to which they may be applicable, standby letters of credit'. In *Paget's Law of Banking* (10th edition) it is stated: 'There appears to be no material difference between a standby letter of credit, a performance bond and a performance guarantee; all three expressions describe an instrument which is intended to protect the beneficiary in the event of the applicant's default in performance.'

A performance bond constitutes an unconditional obligation to pay the beneficiary upon demand and upon presentation of such additional documents (if any) as may be specified. Lord Denning in *Edward Owen Engineering Ltd* described performance bonds as 'virtually promissory notes payable on demand'.

Edward Owen Engineering Ltd v *Barclays Bank International Ltd* [1978] 1 All ER 976

The plaintiff company entered into a contract with Libyan buyers to supply and erect a glasshouse installation covering five acres, at a cost of £500,000. The buyers called for a performance bond for 10 per cent of the contract price to be issued in their favour. The plaintiffs instructed their bank, the defendants, to provide the bond against their counter guarantee. The defendants requested the Umma Bank in Libya to issue the required bond and gave an undertaking to the Libyan Bank to pay on 'first demand, without any conditions or proof'.

The buyers had agreed under the contract of sale to supply a confirmed irrevocable letter of credit, but instead supplied a letter of credit which was not confirmed and the plaintiffs repudiated the contract. The Libyan buyers claimed under the performance bond from the Umma Bank which in turn claimed payment from the defendants.

The plaintiffs sought an injunction to restrain the defendants from paying under the guarantee. An interim injunction was granted but it was discharged by Kerr J. The plaintiffs appealed.

The Court of Appeal dismissed the appeal and held that a bank which issues a performance guarantee is bound to honour it. The bank is not concerned with disputes between the parties unless there is clear evidence of established fraud to the underlying contract. Lord Denning said (p. 983):

> 'A bank which gives a performance guarantee must honour that guarantee according to its terms. It is not concerned in the least with the relations between the supplier and the customer; nor with the question whether the supplier has performed his contracted obligation or not; nor with the question whether the supplier is in default or not. The bank must pay according to its guarantee, on demand if so stipulated, without proof or conditions. The only exception is when there is a clear fraud of which the bank has notice.'

Lord Denning adopted a passage from the judgment of Kerr J in *R.D. Harbottle (Mercantile) Ltd* v *National Westminster Bank Ltd* ([1977] 2 All ER 862 at p. 870) where the learned judge said:

> 'It is only in exceptional circumstances that the courts will interfere with the machinery of irrevocable obligations assumed by the banks. They are the life-blood of international commerce. Such obligations are as collateral to the underlying rights and obligations between the merchants at either end of the banking chain. Except possibly in clear cases of fraud of which the banks have notice, the courts will leave the merchants to settle their disputes under the contracts by litigation or arbitration as available to them or stipulated in the contracts. The courts are not concerned with their difficulties to enforce such claims; these are risks which the merchants take. In this case the plaintiffs took the risk of the unconditional wording of the guarantees. The machinery and commitments of banks are on a different level. They must be allowed to be honoured, free from interference by the courts. Otherwise, trust in international commerce could be irreparably damaged.'

It was argued that the document between the two banks was expressed to be a guarantee and as such the bank could not be liable on the guarantee unless there was a principal debtor and some default by him in his obligations under the court. On this point Geoffrey Lane LJ said (p. 986):

> 'Although this agreement is expressed to be a guarantee, it is not in truth such a contract. It has much more of the characteristics of a promissory note than the characteristics of a guarantee.'

The courts treat performance bonds much like letters of credit in that a bank which gives a performance guarantee payable on demand is not concerned with the relations between the buyer and seller under the underlying contract of sale or with the question of default under the underlying contract. The bank must therefore make payment under the performance guarantee without proof of default. In *Howe Richardson Scale Co. Ltd* v *Polimex-Cekop & National Westminster Bank Ltd* ([1978] 1 Lloyd's Rep 161) the court held that it would be wrong to interfere with the right of the buyers under an on demand performance guarantee to receive payment. To give the bank the right to inquire into an alleged breach of the underlying contract would be against the irrevocable nature of obligations undertaken by the bank (see also *Intraco Ltd* v *Notis Shipping Corp. (The Bhoja Trader)* [1981] 1 Lloyd's Rep 256).

In *Siporex Trade SA* v *Banque Indosuez* ([1985] 2 Lloyd's Rep 546) under a contract dated 19 October 1984, Siporex (the plaintiffs) sold to Comdel Commodities a quantity of tallow c. & f. Alexandria, Egypt. The price was payable by a confirmed irrevocable transferable letter of credit to be opened by the end of November/first week of December 1984. A provision was inserted that a performance bond for 10 per cent of the total c. & f. value should be opened by Banque Scandinave in favour of Siporex. On 23 October 1985, Banque Indosuez issued a performance bond and undertook to pay on first written demand in the event that no letter of credit was issued by Comdel in favour of Siporex. On 28 November 1985, a letter of credit was notified by Banque Indosuez acting as issuing bankers on behalf of Comdel to Siporex via Banque Scandinave. Siporex corresponded with Comdel and indicated that the letter of credit did not accord with the contract and specified all the discrepancies in detail. On 10 December, Siporex notified Comdel that the documents were non-complying and they were in default. At the same time Siporex issued a demand on Banque Indosuez. Hirst J reaffirmed that the whole basis of performance bonds was to provide a complete security realisable when the stated event of default occurred. Moreover, there is no real hardship on the bank in imposing strict liability to pay, especially as the bank can protect itself with cross indemnities. The judge held that the bank guarantor is not and should not be concerned in any way with the rights and obligations of the underlying contract between the parties.

Difficulties on the construction of the bond tend to arise where the instrument contains references to the event upon the occurrence of which the bond may be drawn on. In *Esal (Commodities) Ltd* v *Oriental Credit Ltd* ([1985] 2 Lloyd's Rep 546) an instrument was described as a performance bond provided:

'We undertake to pay the said amount of your written demand in the event that the supplier fails to execute the contract in perfect performance.'

It was submitted on behalf of the applicant that on the true construction of the bond (a) there was no liability save in the event of an established breach of the contract referred to in it; alternatively (b) the bond required the beneficiary to assert in his demand that the supplier had failed properly to execute the contract. The Court of Appeal rejected the first submission but on the second submission Ackner LJ held that such an assertion was required. He observed that the requirement that the beneficiary must when making his demand for payment also commit himself to claiming that the contract has not been complied with, may prevent some of the many abuses that have occurred.

In *I.E. Contractors Ltd* v *Lloyds Bank plc* (unreported, 14 March 1989) the terms of a construction contract required the contractor to furnish to the Iraqi employer a performance bond issued by the R bank in Iraq. Such a bond was in due course provided by the R bank against three counter-indemnities executed at the contractor's request by Lloyds Bank. The performance bond issued by the R bank was expressed to cover 'damages which you [viz., the employers] claim are duly and properly owing to your organisation by [the contractor] under the terms' of the respective construction contract. The R bank undertook 'to pay you, unconditionally, the said amount on demand, being your claim for damages brought about by [the contractor].' In two counter-indemnities Lloyds Bank undertook to pay on their receipt of a demand; only under the third facility was R bank obliged to state in its demand that it had been required to make payment under the performance bond. The demand under the performance bond eventually made by the employer merely stated that the contractor had not 'fulfilled the contractual obligations in respect of' the project involved. No reference was, apparently, made to the demand being made a claim for damages. The R bank's claim under all the counter-indemnities read 'At beneficiaries' demand please credit full guarantee amount equivalent to ... due to shortages not yet finished.' No statement was made about the R bank's liability to make payment under the performance bond. The Court of Appeal held that the first two demands indicated that they were made on the basis provided in the respective facility. The beneficiaries' demand stated that the demand involved a failure to perform contractual obligations and this implied that the demand involved a claim for damages. As regards the first two counter-indemnities, their wording indicated that a bare demand was adequate. Such a demand was inadequate under the third facility furnished by Lloyds Bank. The difference between the judgment at first instance and the Court of Appeal judgment depends on the construction of the documents. There is no difference of opinion regarding the rule that a demand can be met only if the beneficiary asserts that payment is due on the basis provided in the performance bond.

Fraud in performance bonds

There is, however, one exception to the bank's undertaking to make payment without proof of default, namely the established fraud of the beneficiary of the credit or performance guarantee. In *Szteyn* v *J. Henry Schroder Banking Corporation* ((1941) 31 NY Supp 2d 531) the American court held that where the seller's fraud has been called to the bank's attention before shipping documents are presented the bank may reject the documents and refuse payment. The same rule will be applied to a clear case of fraud in performance guarantee cases. In *R.D. Harbottle (Mercantile) Ltd* v *National Westminster Bank Ltd* ([1977] 2 All ER 862) an English seller entered into three contracts with Egyptian buyers for the sale of horse tic beans and coal. Each contract required the sellers to establish performance guarantees in favour of the buyers with Egyptian banks, and confirmed by the National Westminster Bank in England where the sellers had an account. The terms of the guarantees were extensive and payment was expressed to be 'on demand' by the buyers 'without any reference to or any necessity for confirmation or verification. The buyers demanded payment and the sellers attempted to prevent the National Westminster Bank and the Egyptian banks from making payment to the buyers. Interlocutory injunctions were obtained by the sellers but these were discharged on the application of National Westminster Bank. Kerr J said that except in a clear case of fraud of which the bank has notice, the courts will not interfere with the irrevocable and unconditional terms of the guarantee. The banks are only concerned to ensure that the terms of their mandate have been complied with and in the case of performance guarantees to be fulfilled on demand, that the demand has in fact been made by the customer.

Similarly, in *Bolivinter Oil SA* v *Chase Manhattan Bank & Others* ([1984] 1 WLR 392) the court said that only in a 'wholly exceptional case', where fraud can be clearly proved, would an injunction be granted preventing payment.

In *Stroberg-Carlson Corporation* v *Bank Melli Iran* ((1979) 467 F Supp 530) an action was brought by the plaintiffs to prevent the Bank Melli of Iran from making payment against two bank guarantees issued in favour of the government of Iran without first notifying the plaintiffs in writing of the demand and giving them ten days to establish the unjustified or fraudulent nature of a demand. The American court held that because of political instability in Iran an injunction would be granted. Although the grant of an injunction would involve reading into the terms of the guarantee a requirement that the bank should give notice of the demand for payment, this was justified because the plaintiff would find it virtually impossible to bring an action in the Iranian courts. Nevertheless, it is clear that the courts will only relax the rule that the performance guarantee is payable immediately on demand in exceptional cases.

In *The State Trading Corporation of India* v *E.D. & F. Man (Sugar) Ltd & Another* ([1981] Com LR 235) a contract for the purchase of sugar was only partly performed when the Indian government prohibited the export of sugar. The buyers proposed to give notice of default to the State Bank of India but the plaintiffs obtained an interim injunction to prevent notice being given. The Court of Appeal refused to imply a term into the contract that notice of default could only be given on reasonable cause or evidence of default. Such a term would mean that the bank could be prevented from paying by the mere assertion of the plaintiff that he was not in default.

In *Potton Homes Ltd* v *Coleman Contractors (Overseas) Ltd* ((1984) 128 SJ 282) the plaintiffs sought to prevent payment of a performance bond by the Midland Bank alleging disputes with the defendant. The Court of Appeal questioned the extent to which the performance guarantee or bond is independent of the underlying contract of sale. Eveleigh LJ said:

'I would wish at least to leave it open for consideration how far the bond is to be treated as cash in hand as between the buyer and seller.'

However, Eveleigh LJ continued:

'The facts of each case must be considered. If the contract is avoided or if there is a failure of consideration between the buyer and seller for which the seller undertook to procure the issue of the performance bond, I do not see why, as between seller and buyer, the seller should not be unable to prevent a call upon the bond by the mere assertion that the bond is to be treated as cash in hand.'

In *United Trading Corporation SA and Murray Clayton* v *Allied Arab Bank Ltd* ([1985] 2 Lloyd's Rep 554) an English seller contracted to provide over one billion eggs and other foodstuffs to an Iraqi state body known as 'Agromark'. Agromark required the seller to secure performance of its obligations under the contract of sale. A performance bond was issued by Agromark's bank, Rafidain, and counter-guaranteed by the seller's bank. Trade between the parties was affected by the Iran–Iraq war after September 1980 and so successive extensions of the performance bond were requested and agreed. Demands were made on the performance bonds by Agromark in 1984 and the seller sought injunctions to prevent payment by its bank on the basis that the claims were 'manifestly fraudulent'. The Court of Appeal held that although it was seriously arguable that Agromark could not have honestly believed in the probity of its demands, the seller could not establish that that was the only inference to be drawn from the facts. Ackner LJ considered the standard of proof and said:

> 'We would expect the Court to require strong corroborative evidence of the allegation, usually in the form of contemporary documents ... In general for the evidence of fraud to be clear, we would also expect the buyer to have been given an opportunity to answer the allegation and to have failed to provide any, or any adequate answer, in circumstances where one could properly be expected. If the court considers that on the material before it the only realistic inference to draw is that of fraud, then the sellers would have made out a sufficient case of fraud.'

Moreover, the judge indicated that where a person fails to answer a charge of fraud, having been given a fair and adequate opportunity to do so, the court is entitled to draw from his silence an inference of guilt.

Proper law of performance bond

In *Attock Cement Co. Ltd* v *Romanian Bank for Foreign Trade* ([1989] 1 All ER 1189) a performance bond was issued by a Romanian bank in Bucharest at the request of a Romanian contractor who had agreed to construct a cement plant in Pakistan. The building contract was made expressly subject to English law but the performance bond, which was available on demand being made in Bucharest failed to include an express stipulation. The court rejected the argument that by implication the proper law which governed the performance bond was the proper law of the construction contract. Staughton LJ held 'Seeing that the letter of credit or performance bond is intended to be a separate transaction, I would hold that it is not so affected, and is ordinarily governed by the law of the place where payment is to be made under it.'

The question of the proper law of contract may now be governed by the Contracts (Applicable Law) Act 1991.

10 Security for bankers' advances and enforcing the security

FACTORS AFFECTING THE VALIDITY OF A SECURITY CONTRACT

Undue influence

The principle justifying the court setting aside a transaction for undue influence is based on the victimisation of one party by another. In *National Westminster Bank plc v Morgan* ([1985] AC 686) the House of Lords held that in order for the presumption of undue influence to operate, it must be shown that the transaction was wrongful and operated to the manifest disadvantage of the person influenced.

National Westminster Bank plc v Morgan [1985] AC 686

The plaintiff bank agreed to lend Mr and Mrs Morgan £14,500 to refinance a building society loan which was in arrears and for which the building society was pressing for repayment. The bank loan was secured by a legal charge on the matrimonial home. The branch manager took the mortgage form to Mrs Morgan to sign, and she expressed concern that the loan might be used by her husband in the course of his business. The manager assured Mrs Morgan that it would not be so used. Although the loan was unlimited the bank only sought to enforce the security when the loan was not used for refinancing the mortgage on the matrimonial home.

Mrs Morgan resisted the bank's action, alleging that the bank manager had obtained her consent to the loan transaction by undue influence.

The bank argued that undue influence could only be raised if the transaction had been manifestly disadvantageous to the wife. The trial judge rejected the wife's defence and held that the bank manager had not placed pressure on the wife to sign the mortgage application form and the circumstances were not such that required the manager to advise her to take independent legal advice. Moreover, there was not a confidential relationship between the wife and the bank so as to raise a presumption of undue influence. The Court of Appeal overruled the trial judge. The bank appealed to the House of Lords.

The House of Lords held that the principle that justified the setting aside of a transaction on the ground of undue influence was the victimisation of one party by the other, and before a transaction could be set aside for undue influence, whether in reliance on the evidence or on the presumption or the exercise of undue influence, it had to be shown that the transaction had been wrongful in that it constituted a manifest and unfair disadvantage to the person seeking to avoid it. The evidence of the mere relationship of the parties was not sufficient to raise the presumption of undue influence without also evidence that the transaction itself had been wrongful in that it enabled an advantage to be taken of the person subjected to the influence.

The principle justifying the court setting aside a transaction for undue influence was established by Lindley LJ in *Allcard* v *Skinner* ((1887) 36 Ch D 145) where he said (pp. 182–183):

> 'The principle must be examined. What then is the principle? Is it that it is right and expedient to save persons from the consequences of their own folly? Or is it that it is right and expedient to save them from being victimised by other people? In my opinion the doctrine of undue influence is founded upon the second of these two principles. Courts of equity have never set aside gifts on the ground of the folly, imprudence, or want of foresight on the part of donors. The courts have always repudiated any such jurisdiction ... On the other hand, to protect people from being forced, tricked or misled in any way by others into parting with their property is one of the most legitimate objects of all laws; and the equitable doctrine of undue influence has grown out of and been developed by the necessity of grappling with the insidious forms of spiritual tyranny and with the infinite varieties of fraud.'

Lindley LJ continued (p. 183):

> 'The undue influence the courts of equity endeavour to defeat is the undue influence of one person over another; not the influence of enthusiasm on the enthusiast who is carried away by it, unless indeed such enthusiasm is itself the result of external undue influence ...'

The nature of undue influence alluded to by Lindley LJ in *Allcard* v *Skinner* was asserted in *Bank of Montreal* v *Stuart* ([1911] AC 20) where Mrs Stuart had guaranteed loans made to a company of which her husband was the president. The guarantee was arranged by a director of the company, who acted as solicitor to the company and also acted as Mr Stuart's legal adviser. When the company went into liquidation Mrs Stuart sought to set aside the guarantees on the ground that she had acted under the influence of her husband, who was the bank's agent, and that she received no independent advice. The Privy Council dismissed the appeal from a finding of the Supreme Court of Canada that the bank had failed to advise Mrs Stuart of the risks of the guarantee transaction. The Privy Council concluded that unfair advantage was taken of Mrs Stuart's confidence in her husband by her husband and the bank.

The *Bank of Montreal* v *Stuart* case is one in which the undue influence of a third party was relied on to set aside a transaction entered into with the bank. In *National Westminster Bank* v *Morgan* and *Lloyds Bank Ltd* v *Bundy* ([1975] QB 326) the undue influence was that of the bank. In the *Bundy* case the undue influence arose from the nature of the relationship between the bank and its elderly customer who guaranteed his son's overdraft and gave a charge over his farm. Although the majority of the court based its decision on the view of undue influence as explained in *Allcard* v *Skinner,* Lord Denning MR based his judgment on the principle of 'inequality of bargaining power'. The *Morgan* case reaffirms the traditional view of the doctrine of undue influence and not the principle of inequality of bargaining power. The mere inequality of bargaining power between the bank and its customer does not in itself place the bank under a fiduciary duty of care or in a position in which responsibility for the undue influence exercised by another is readily imputed to him. Nevertheless, the *Bundy* case has not been overruled.

The *Morgan* case shows that a bank would not be held subject to a fiduciary duty of care merely because it failed to advise a customer, who was about to execute a mortgage, to seek legal advice or because some information supplied by the bank was inaccurate on a specific technical matter.

In *Midland Bank Ltd* v *Shephard* ([1988] 3 All ER 17) a customer, whose account with the bank was overdrawn, arranged to transfer the liability to a new account opened jointly by himself and his wife. Under the standard terms and conditions applicable to the account, the spouses became jointly and severally liable for any loan or overdraft debited to their account. Subsequently, and without the knowledge of the wife, the husband obtained an overdraft of £10,000 on the joint account. When the husband defaulted, the bank obtained summary judgment against the wife. The wife appealed alleging undue influence on the part of her husband in respect of the joint account mandate and that he had acted as the agent of the bank for this purpose. The Court of Appeal dismissed the appeal. Neill LJ said that for the wife to succeed she had to prove:

'(a) that she was induced or must be presumed to have been induced to sign [the document] by the undue influence of [the husband], or by his fraudulent misrepresentation or fraudulent concealment of material facts; (b) that the contract into which she was induced to enter was manifestly disadvantageous to her; and (c) that in the circumstances the acts of [the husband] are to be attributed to the bank.'

The same reasoning was applied in *Bank of Baroda* v *Shah* ([1988] 3 All ER 24) in which case the defendants granted the bank a legal charge over their property to secure an overdraft granted to S Ltd. They had been induced to do so by the fraud and misrepresentation of a relative, who was one of S Ltd's directors. The defendant did not obtain independent legal advice as the solicitors of S Ltd took charge, although the defendants had not instructed them. The Court of Appeal, reversing the trial court, held that the relative's undue influence and misrepresentation could not be imputed to the bank. Dillon LJ concluded that the bank was not under a duty to ensure that a mortgagor actually obtained independent legal advice. There was nothing to indicate that the bank was aware of the unusual relationship between S Ltd's solicitors and the defendants.

In *Bank of Credit and Commerce International SA* v *Aboody* ([1989] 2 WLR 759) the Court of Appeal established that not only must the party pleading undue influence show that the undue influence was exercised and caused the transaction to be entered into but that the transaction resulted in a manifest disadvantage. In the *Aboody* case Mrs Aboody, on moving to the UK with her family, became a co-director and secretary of a company established by her husband although she took no part in the management of the business. She eventually signed three guarantees which were secured by separate charges over her house. The company collapsed and the bank claimed under the joint and several guarantees given by Mr and Mrs Aboody. Mrs Aboody alleged that her consent had been obtained by the undue influence of her husband. The court held that although there had been undue influence, there was no manifest disadvantage to Mrs Aboody since at the time of giving the guarantees the company was supporting the family in considerable comfort and there was a reasonable prospect that the company would succeed. Slade LJ described undue influence as:

> 'an equitable doctrine developed so as to cover what would otherwise be a gap in our law, by enabling the court to give relief in the case where a "disadvantageous transaction" is the product of the undue influence of another and the court considers it unconscionable, but it would be otherwise unimpeachable at law'.

Therefore, a party seeking to set aside a transaction on the grounds of undue influence must establish that undue influence was exercised over him and that the transaction was disadvantageous.

Misrepresentation and mistake

A contract of security is likely to be avoided not only if it is entered as a result of the undue influence but also if it is induced by a material misrepresentation of fact made by the bank or its agent.

Mackenzie v *Royal Bank of Canada* [1934] AC 468

The plaintiff, Mrs MacKenzie, in 1920 signed a letter of hypothecation over certain shares she owned. The security was given to secure an advance to MacKenzie Ltd, a company in which her husband was a major shareholder, or to her husband, for the benefit of the company. The company later became bankrupt and the bank took over such of the company's property as was secured to it under the charge. The bank also obtained a letter signed by the plaintiff and her husband which stated '... we hereby agree that your so doing shall not in any way release us from our obligation under the guarantees to the bank, nor shall our personal securities be in any way affected until the amount due to the bank by MacKenzie Ltd has been actually paid.'

The company's business continued to deteriorate and the bank entered into negotiations for the reconstruction of the company. The bank again required the plaintiff to guarantee the borrowing of the new company and the bank manager and her husband assured her that her shares were still bound to the bank but that this was a way of regaining them. After the plaintiff had signed the guarantee and the accompanying form of hypothecation she was asked to take the form to a solicitor for him to sign stating that she had been independently advised. This advice had not in fact been received.

An action was brought by the plaintiff alleging that she had been induced to hypothecate the shares due to misrepresentation. The trial judge gave judgment for the plaintiff. This was reversed on appeal. The plaintiff appealed to the Privy Council.

The Privy Council allowed the appeal. Lord Atkin held (p. 475):

'... the contract cannot be allowed to stand ... A contract of guarantee, like any other contract, is liable to be avoided if induced by material misrepresentation of an existing fact, even if made innocently ... even at common law, such an innocent misrepresentation would afford an action on the contract ...'

A contract, including one of guarantee, may be vitiated due to a mistake or misrepresentation. Where the bank chooses to explain the nature and effect of a guarantee it must ensure that it does not misstate the purpose or effect of the undertaking. In *Cornish* v *Midland Bank plc* ([1985] 3 All ER 513) the plaintiff, a customer of the defendant bank, signed a second mortgage in favour of the defendant bank without appreciating, and being informed by the bank, that it was not merely to secure a loan for £2,000 for renovations to a farmhouse jointly owned by the plaintiff and her husband, but also for unlimited advances made to her husband. The bank in fact made further advances to the husband under the mortgage and when the farmhouse was eventually sold, the proceeds barely covered the first and second mortgages and the expenses of the sale. In an action by the plaintiff against the bank the court held that the bank had been negligent in explaining the effect of the mortgage to the plaintiff and that the bank's mortgage should be set aside for undue influence. The husband was also ordered to indemnify the bank in respect of damages awarded in favour of the plaintiff. The husband and the bank appealed. The Court of Appeal held that where a bank chooses to advise a customer as to the nature and effect of a mortgage in favour of the bank prior to the customer executing the mortgage, the bank is under a duty not to negligently misstate the effect of the mortgage. However, the mortgage would not be set aside unless the customer could show that the bank had taken unfair advantage so that the presumption of undue influence applied. Kerr LJ (pp. 522–523) suggested that in certain circumstances a bank may owe a duty to the giver of the security, particularly if he is a customer, to offer some explanation as to the nature and effect of the security document to be executed.

However, in *O'Hara* v *Allied Irish Banks Ltd* ([1985] BCLC 52) Harman J held that a bank is not under any duty to explain the terms and legal effect of a guarantee to a potential guarantor who is not a customer. It should, however, be remembered that liability might arise under *Hedley Byrne & Co. Ltd* v *Heller & Partners Ltd* ([1964] AC 465).

More recently, the bank's duty in respect of a guarantee obtained by it was examined in *Lloyds Bank plc* v *Waterhouse* (unreported, Court of Appeal decision, 1 February 1990). In that case the bank agreed to grant a loan facility, intended primarily to enable a new customer to acquire a farm, provided his father, who was not a customer of the bank, executed a guarantee. In the course of negotiations, the bank's employee advised the father that the guarantee covered only the loan granted to the son for the acquisition of the property in question. On this understanding the father, who was illiterate, executed the guarantee. The bank was unaware of this disability, but was aware that the father had not read the document before he executed it. The guarantee given by the father was an 'all monies guarantee', under which the father became liable for all the son's liabilities. The Court of Appeal, reversing Leggatt, held that the father was not liable. Purchas LJ based his decision on the ground of *non est factum* and after a review of *Saunders* v *Anglia Building Society* ([1971] AC 1004) the learned judge concluded:

> 'that in order for this defence to succeed the father must establish three things: (a) that he was under a disability, in this case illiteracy. There is no challenge to this as an existing fact. For this purpose it is irrelevant that the bank were not aware of this disability; (b) that the document which the father signed was 'fundamentally different' or 'totally different' from the document he thought he was signing; and (c) that he was not careless...or did not fail to take precautions which he ought to have taken in the circumstances to ascertain the contents or significance of the documents he was signing.'

Purchas LJ concluded that the father had not been careless. He also held that an 'all monies guarantee' was fundamentally different from a guarantee backing a specific transaction as it exposed the guarantor to considerably wider liability. Although the father was not a customer, the bank had committed a breach of a duty of care owed to him when it failed to give him an accurate answer to the question respecting the nature of the guarantee.

Sir Edward Eveleigh, however, took the view that the guarantee should be set aside on the ground of its having been executed by the father on the basis of a unilateral mistake of fact of which the bank was aware at the relevant time.

Other grounds for setting aside security

Standard Chartered Bank Ltd v *Walker* [1982] 1 WLR 1410

A company issued to the plaintiff bank a debenture giving the bank a charge over the company's assets in respect of any existing or future indebtedness. The debenture empowered the bank to appoint a receiver, with a proviso that any such person would be the company's agent and that the company alone would be responsible for his acts or omissions. The defendants, directors of the company, had also guaranteed the indebtedness of the company up to £75,000.

In November 1980, the bank appointed a receiver who engaged auctioneers to auction the company's assets. The auctioneers estimated the sale of the stock to realise approximately £90,000. The auction was held on a cold day in February 1981 and it realised only £42,864. The entire amount was absorbed in the expenses of the realisation and paying the preferential debts. The bank then brought an action against the defendants for the amount of the guarantee and applied for summary judgment.

The defendants resisted the claim alleging that the stock had been sold at a gross undervalue because the sale had been at the wrong time of the year and had been insufficiently advertised. They also alleged that the bank had instructed the receiver to dispose of the stock as soon as possible.

From an appeal from the registrar Bristow J gave judgment for the bank. The defendants appealed to the Court of Appeal.

The Court of Appeal held that a receiver realising assets under a debenture owed a duty both to the borrower and to a guarantor of the debt to take reasonable care to obtain the best price possible and he also owed a duty to exercise reasonable care in choosing the time of sale. Moreover, the bank, although deemed to be the company's agent, might be liable if it can be shown that it interfered in the course of the receivership. The court therefore gave leave to defend. Lord Denning MR following *Cuckmere Brick Co. Ltd* v *Mutual Finance Ltd* ([1971] Ch 949) said (p. 1415):

> 'If a mortgagee enters into possession and realises a mortgaged property, it is his duty to use reasonable care to obtain the best possible price which the circumstances of the case permit. He owes this duty not only to himself, to clear off as much of the debt as he can, but also to the mortgagor so as to reduce the balance owing as much as possible, and also to the guarantor so that he is made liable for as little as possible on the guarantee. This duty is only a particular application of the general duty of care to your neighbour ...'

The same duty is owed by a receiver. Lord Denning followed the principle established by Rigby LJ in his dissenting judgment in *Gaskell* v *Gosling* ([1896] AC 575) where the learned judge said:

> 'The receiver is the agent of the company, not of the debenture-holder, the bank. He owes a duty to use reasonable care to obtain the best possible price which the circumstances of the case permit. He owes this duty not only to the company, of which he is the agent, to clear off as much of its indebtedness to the bank as possible, but he also owes a duty to the guarantor, because the guarantor is liable only to the same extent as the company ... It could be that the receiver can choose the time of sale within a considerable margin, but he should, I think, exercise a reasonable degree of care about it.'

The *Standard Chartered Bank* case overruled *Barclays Bank Ltd* v *Thienel* ((1978) 122 SJ 472) and *Latchford* v *Beirne* ([1981] 3 All ER 705). The Court of Appeal in the *Standard Chartered Bank* case examined the development of the duty of care owed by a mortgagee in exercising his rights and realising the secured property. In *Cuckmere Brick Co. Ltd* v *Mutual Finance Ltd* it was accepted that a mortgagee who takes possession of the mortgaged property and personally takes steps to realise it must act with due care, and if by his negligent conduct he realises the property at an undervalue, he will be liable to the mortgagor in damages. In the *Cuckmere* case the plaintiffs created a security in favour of the defendants over land which they owned and on which they obtained planning permission to construct flats and houses. The defendants subsequently took possession of the property and appointed auctioneers to sell the land. The advertisements relating to the land failed to mention that planning permission to construct flats had been granted although the advertisement did refer to planning permission having been granted in respect of the houses. The plaintiffs brought this omission to the attention of the defendants and requested that the sale of the property be postponed. The auctioneers, however, in accordance with their instructions went ahead with the sale and the land was sold at an undervalue. The plaintiffs brought an action claiming an account from the defendants for the difference between the market value of the land and the price for which it had been sold. The Court of Appeal held that a mortgagee when exercising his power of sale owes a duty to the mortgagor to take reasonable care to obtain the best price possible and the defendants were in breach of that duty in proceeding with the sale without adequately publicising the planning permission obtained to construct the flats. The authorities prior to the *Cuckmere* case had held that a mortgagee would only be liable to the mortgagor if he acted in bad faith and the mortgagee was, therefore, merely under an obligation not to deliberately cheat or defraud the mortgagor.

In the *Barclays Bank Ltd* v *Thienel* case the question was whether a duty of care owed under the law of tort to a mortgagee, or by a receiver appointed, either by a debenture-holder or the court, should be extended to protect a third party who guarantees a loan or overdraft granted to a mortgagor. In that case the guarantor alleged that the sale of certain mortgaged property was at a gross undervalue and there had been a want of care in realising the asset. Thesiger J held that the guarantor could not rely on the want of care because of a widely worded clause in the guarantee which authorised the bank 'to realise any securities in such a manner as you think expedient'. The court considered the *Cuckmere* case and refused to extend the duty of care owed by the mortgagee (or receiver) to protect anyone other than the mortgagor, including a guarantor of the loan who would become liable to pay under the guarantee if the mortgagor failed to discharge the debt.

In *Latchford* v *Beirne* ([1981] 3 All ER 705) the guarantor again sought to allege that there had been a want of reasonable care in the disposal of the mortgaged assets. Milmo J held that no duty of care was owed to a guarantor and he equated a guarantor with a creditor, towards whom duty of care is not owed.

The Unfair Contract Terms Act 1977 would now apply to render any term which purported to make the guarantor liable for a larger sum than that outstanding under the guarantee void (see *Gillespie Bros. & Co. Ltd* v *Roy Bowles Transport Ltd* ([1973] QB 400).

In *American Express Banking Corp.* v *Hurley* ([1985] 3 All ER) on the insolvency of a company the bank appointed a receiver to realise the security. The sale of the secured assets failed to realise an amount to cover the indebtedness to the bank and the bank therefore sued on a personal guarantee given by a director of the insolvent company. The guarantor claimed that the bank and the receiver had been negligent in realising the secured assets. The court held that the receiver had acted as an agent of the mortgagor until the company was put into liquidation. While the receiver was the mortgagor's agent, the mortgagee was not responsible for the conduct of the receiver unless the mortgagee directed or interfered with the receiver's activities. On the facts, the court held that the bank had not in any way interfered or directed the receiver's activities at any time prior to the liquidation of the company. However, the mortgagee or receiver was under a duty to a guarantor of the mortgagor's debt to take reasonable care to obtain the true market value of the mortgaged property when either of them realised the property in the exercise of a power of sale. In the circumstances the receiver had not taken reasonable care to obtain the true market value of the secured assets which he knew was specialised equipment but in respect of which he had failed to take either specialist advice or to advertise in specialist publications.

The bank's right to select the time for the enforcement of the security was examined recently in *China and South Sea Bank Ltd* v *Tan* ([1990] 1 Lloyd's Rep 113) where F Ltd charged and delivered to the bank a parcel of shares to secure F Ltd's undertaking as a guarantor of amounts advanced to one of the bank's customers. The bank brought an action, in summary procedure under Order 14 of the RSC, to enforce the guarantee and L Ltd sought leave to defend the action on the ground that the shares had become worthless and that by failing to sell them before this had happened, the bank had committed a breach of a duty of care owed by a creditor to a guarantor. Reversing the decision of the Court of Appeal of Hong Kong, the Privy Council held that the bank could exercise the rights acquired by it upon the debtor's default 'at any time or times simultaneously or contemporaneously or successively or not at all'. Lord Templeman explained the position as follows (p. 115):

> 'The creditor is not obliged to do anything. If the creditor does nothing and the debtor declines into bankruptcy the mortgaged securities become valueless and the surety decamps abroad, the creditor loses his money. If disaster strikes the debtor and the mortgaged securities but the surety remains capable of repaying the debt then the creditor loses nothing. The surety contracts to pay if the debtor does not pay and the surety is bound by his contract. If the surety, perhaps less indolent or less well protected than the creditor, is worried that the mortgaged securities might decline in value then the surety may request the creditor to sell and if the creditor remains idle then the surety may bustle about, pay off the debt, take over the benefit of the securities and sell them. No creditor could carry on the business of lending if he could become liable to a mortgagee and to a surety or to either of them for a decline in value of mortgaged property, unless the creditor was personally liable for the decline.'

It might be arguable that the bank's failure to comply with a request to sell the security (and to recover the debt) at the time of the request constitutes an unconscionable exercise of its contractual rights.

In *Parker-Tweedle* v *Dunbar Bank plc* (*The Times*, 29 December 1989) the court expressly rejected the idea that the duty of care owed by a receiver in selling mortgaged property is tortious. The case suggested that the duty of care owed by a receiver to a third party is of an equitable nature. The law has, therefore, established:

(a) a receiver will be personally liable for his own negligence which causes injury to a mortgagor or a company which has issued the debentures under which the receiver was appointed or to a guarantor of the mortgage of the debenture debt;

(b) debenture-holders will not be ipso facto liable to the company which issued debentures for the negligent conduct of a receiver appointed under them;

(c) but if the debenture-holders intervene in the conduct of the receivership, and the company or the guarantor of the debenture debt suffers a loss then the debenture-holder becomes a joint tortfeasor and may be vicariously liable for any loss.

TYPES OF SECURITY

Banker's lien

Brandao v *Barnett* (1846) 12 Cl & Fin 787

The plaintiff was a Portuguese merchant whose London agent, Burn, regularly purchased exchequer bills, received interest on them on his behalf, and when required traded them in exchange for other bills. Burn maintained an account with the defendant bank and deposited several tin boxes with them in which he deposited the exchequer bills and to which he had the keys.

On 1 December 1836, he handed some exchequer bills to the defendant bank with a request that they receive the interest due on them and to exchange the bills for others, which the defendants duly did. Before Burn had the opportunity to collect the bills, acceptances were presented and paid against his account which were in excess of the credit balance. Burn became bankrupt and the defendant bank claimed a lien on the bills it held.

The Court of Common Pleas found for the plaintiff. On appeal the Court of Exchequer Chamber reversed the decision. The plaintiff appealed.

The House of Lords held for the plaintiff. Lord Campbell in the course of his judgment said (p. 1629):

'... I am of the opinion that the general lien of bankers is part of the law merchant, and is to be judicially noticed – like the negotiability of bills of exchange, or the days of grace allowed for their payment.'

He continued on p. 1630:

'Bankers most undoubtedly have a general lien on all securities deposited with them, as bankers, by a customer, unless there be an express contract, or circumstances that show an implied contract inconsistent with a lien.'

However, he then went on to say:

'Now, it seems to me, that, in the present case, there was an implied agreement on the part of the defendants, inconsistent with the right of lien which they claim ...'

The banker's lien was recognised as early as 1794 in *Davis v Bowsher* ((1795) 5 Term Rep 488). Enforcing the banker's lien Lord Campbell said that the general lien is an implied pledge and the lien exists, provided the bank acts in good faith, even if the subject of the lien turns out to be the property of a stranger. The lien confers a mere right to retain the goods until the debt is paid off but the pledge confers a power of sale.

In *Brandao v Barnett* it was said that 'all securities' may be the subject of a lien – this includes both negotiable and non-negotiable securities. In *Misa v Currie* ((1876) 1 App Cas 554) an order to pay money to a particular person was an instrument over which a lien could be created. Lord Hatherly said:

'I do not see, regard being had to the lien which bankers have upon all documents which are placed in their hands by customers who are indebted to them in the course of their banking transactions, that it would make any important difference whether it should be held to be an authority or a bill of exchange.'

Similarly, in *Jeffrys v Agra and Masterman's Bank* ((1866) LR 2 Eq 674) a form of deposit receipt was held to be the subject of a lien.

In *Re Keever* ([1966] 3 All ER 631) and in *Barclays Bank Ltd* v *Astley Industrial Trust Ltd* ([1970] 2 QB 527) negotiable instruments in the form of cheques were held subject to a lien.

In *Re Keever* the debtor, on 5 October 1962, committed an act of bankruptcy by failing to comply with a bankruptcy notice. On 15 November a cheque for £3,000 in favour of the debtor was presented by her to her bank for collection. She had two accounts with her bank both of which were in debit. A receiving order was made against the debtor on 16 November and on that day the cheque was cleared and the debtor's bank received £3,000. The question which arose was whether the bank was entitled to set off the £3,000 against the amounts of the debits on the debtor's two accounts. The court held that on the day the cheques were paid in for collection (15 November) the bank obtained a lien on the cheque for the amount of the debtor's overdraft. The creation of the lien by the delivery of the cheque was a 'contract, dealing or transaction' within s. 45(d) of the Bankruptcy Act 1914 and was one for which the existence and continuation of the overdrafts constituted valuable consideration. The bank was therefore entitled to a set-off. Ungoed-Thomas J held (p. 633):

'It is established law that a banker has a lien for his general balance on securities deposited with him ... A cheque can be the proper subject of a lien ... Such a lien "is not merely over the paper on which the order to pay is written but over the chose in action." ... It may be in respect of an overdraft not yet due for payment but constituting a contingent liability ... And the lien is applicable in respect of the balance on all accounts between the bank and the customer, including a loan account.

On the other hand, it seems clear that when a person hands a cheque to a bank for collection merely, and there is no overdraft or other form of indebtedness to the bank on the part of that person, then no lien (except perhaps for bank charges for collection) can arise, since there is no indebtedness or other obligation to the bank in respect of which the lien can operate. If the bank credits the bank account of a customer with the amount of the cheque before collecting the money payable in accordance with it, but without informing the customer of that credit, and enabling him to draw on it, then such crediting is a mere book entry without obligation by the bank to the customer and no lien can arise by reason of it. However, if the bank informs the customer of the credit in circumstances which enable him to draw on it before payment on the cheque is received, then there arises before payment an obligation on the part of the bank to the customer to honour such drawings, and the bank would have a lien on the cheque for any amount so drawn ...'

More recently, in *BCCI* v *Dawson and Wright* ([1987] FLR 342) Drake J said:

'The effect of this provision of the Act [s. 27(3) of the Bills of Exchange Act 1882] is that a bank has a lien on any cheques delivered into its possession by a customer, provided that the customer is indebted to the bank and that the bank has not agreed, expressly or impliedly, that its right shall be excluded.'

Until *Halesowen Presswork and Assemblies Ltd* v *Westminster Bank Ltd* ([1971] 1 QB 1) it was unsettled whether money paid into a bank account was subject to a lien. Buckley LJ said:

'The money or credit which the bank obtained as the result of clearing the cheque became the property of the company. No man can have a lien on his own property and consequently no lien can have arisen affecting that money or that credit ...'

This dictum was approved by the House of Lords hearing the case on appeal.

A lien does not extend to items held for safe keeping by the bank. A simple handling of cheques for collection does subject them to a lien.

Pledge

The essence of a pledge is that the security vested in the pledgee consists exclusively of the possession of the goods in question and not any derivative proprietary interest in them. A pledge is not complete unless and until there has been actual or constructive delivery.

Madras Official Assignee v *Mercantile Bank of India Ltd* [1935] AC 53

Merchants who purchased goods from a distant seller obtained from the railway company which carried the goods to them a railway receipt in respect of each wagon load. In return for a loan from the respondent bank these receipts were deposited with the bank, together with a letter of hypothecation and a promissory note. In order to enable the merchants to obtain delivery of the goods it was the practice of the bank to hand over the railway receipts to them. The goods were then unloaded into a warehouse under the control of the respondent bank, so the bank had actual possession of them.

The merchants became insolvent and at the time of bankruptcy some 46 railway receipts had been pledged to the respondent bank but some 14 of these were in the hands of the merchants who had received them back for the purposes of unloading the wagons.

The proceeds of sale of the goods covered by the 46 receipts were claimed by the official assignee in the bankruptcy. It was argued that even if letters of hypothecation gave the respondents a valid charge on the goods represented by the 14 receipts in the hands of the merchants at the date of their insolvency, the Official Assignee could still claim the goods because the respondents had terminated their pledge in respect of those goods by giving back possession of the railway receipts to the merchants.

Waller J granted the motion. The High Court allowed the appeal of the bank. The Official Assignee of Madras appealed to the Privy Council.

The Privy Council dismissed the appeal and held that the receipts were documents of title under the Indian Contract Act 1872, that their delivery constituted a pledge of the goods and that pledge was effective even though the bank handed the documents back to the pledgor as trustee. Lord Wright dealt with the law on pledges and said (p. 58):

'At the common law a pledge could not be created except by a delivery of possession of the thing pledged, either actual or constructive. It involved a bailment. If the pledgor had the actual goods in his physical possession, he could effect the pledge by actual delivery; in other cases he could give possession by some symbolic act, such as handing over the key of the store in which they were. If, however, the goods were in the custody of a third person who held for the bailor, so that in law his possession was that of the bailor, the pledge could be effected by a change of the possession of the third party, that is by an order to him from the pledgor to hold for the pledgee, the change being perfected by the third party attorning to the pledgee, that is acknowledging that he thereupon held for him; there was thus a change of possession and a constructive delivery: the goods in the hands of the third party became by this process in the possession constructively of the pledgee. But where goods were represented by documents the transfer of the documents did not change the possession of the goods, save for one exception, unless the custodier (carrier, warehouseman or such) was notified of the transfer and agreed to hold in future as bailee for the pledgee. The one exception was the case of bills of lading, the transfer of which by the law merchant operated as a transfer of the possession of, as well as the property in, the goods ...'

The redelivery of documents to the pledgor for a limited purpose was illustrated in *North Western Bank Ltd* v *Poynter* and *Re David Allester Ltd*. In both cases it was said that the release of the documents of security was for a limited purpose, i.e in order that the goods could be handled and sold by businessmen who were experts in the field and not by bankers. In *Re David Allester Ltd* Astbury J said:

'The bank as pledgee had a right to realise the goods in question from time to time, and it was more convenient to them, as is common practice throughout the country, to allow the realisation to be made by experts, in this case by the pledgors. They were clearly entitled to do this by handing over the bills of lading ... for realisation on their [i.e. the bank's] behalf without in any way affecting their pledge rights: see *North Western Bank* v *Poynter*.'

Guarantees

A guarantee is a promise to answer for the debt, obligation or liability of another made to a person to whom that other is already, or about to become, liable. A guarantee undertaking makes the guarantor secondarily liable. A contract of guarantee is not a contract *uberrimae fidei*.

Hamilton v *Watson* (1845) 12 Cl & Fin 109

In 1835 Ellis obtained a bank loan of £750 against a bond by himself, his father and two sureties. On the death of one of the sureties, the bank pressed for payment or for fresh security but neither was made available. In 1837 a new bond was eventually signed, in which the appellant joined as surety. The appellant knew nothing of the previous history of the loan. When Ellis died, the appellant was called upon by the bank to pay the loan under the guarantee. The appellant contended, *inter alia*, that he was not liable because he had not been informed of the full history of the loan at the time he signed as surety.

The House of Lords held for the respondent (the public officer of the bank). Lord Campbell said (p. 1343):

'Now the question is, what, upon entering into such a contract, ought to be disclosed? and I will venture to say, if your Lordships were to adopt the principles laid down, and contended for by the appellant's counsel here, that you would entirely knock up those transactions in Scotland of giving security upon a cash account, because no bankers would rest satisfied that they had a security for the advance they made, if, as it is contended, it is essentially necessary that every thing should be disclosed by the creditor that is material for the surety to know. If such was the rule, it would be indispensably necessary for the bankers to whom the security is to be given, to state how the account has been kept: whether the debtor was in the habit of overdrawing; whether he was punctual in his dealings; whether he performed his promises in an honourable manner; for all these things are material for the surety to know. But unless the questions be particularly put by the surety to gain this information, I hold that it is quite unnecessary for the creditors, to whom the surety-ship is to be given, to make any such disclosure; and I should think that this might be considered as the criterion whether the disclosure ought to be made voluntarily, namely, whether there is anything that might not naturally be expected to take place between the parties who are concerned in the transaction, that is, whether there be a contract between the debtor and the creditor, to the effect that his position shall be different from that which the surety might naturally expect; and, if so, the surety is to see whether that is disclosed to him. But if there be nothing which might not naturally take place between the parties, then, if the surety would guard against particular perils, he must put the question, and he must gain the information he requires.'

A contract of guarantee is not a contract *uberrimae fidei*, requiring full disclosure of all material facts by one or both of the parties. The bank is not bound to volunteer to a proposing guarantor information as to the customer's financial position or banking habits. The bank is not under an obligation to disclose to the guarantor that the customer's account is overdrawn or the fact that the customer was suspected of defrauding the guarantor. In *Cooper* v *National Provincial Bank Ltd* ([1945] 2 All ER 641) Mrs Rolfe had an account with the National Provincial Bank, Lancaster Gate branch, in the name of 'The Vale Farms Co.' on which her husband, an undischarged bankrupt, had authority to sign. The bank agreed to grant an overdraft in return for guarantee undertakings. The plaintiff agreed to guarantee the overdraft but before he signed the forms he was told by the branch manager that the account had been 'overdrawn some hundred pounds for some time'. The bank called in the guarantees but the plaintiff brought an action claiming that the guarantee should be declared void because certain material facts had not been disclosed, namely that Mr Rolfe, who was an undischarged bankrupt, was allowed to draw on the account and that cheques had on occasion been drawn on the account which had subsequently been countermanded. The bank maintained that there was no obligation to make disclosure and counter-claimed for £1,386 5s 11d under the guarantees. The Court of Appeal held that the plaintiff's action failed and there was no obligation on the bank to make the disclosures alleged. Lawrence LJ said: 'In my opinion, there was no duty on the bank to disclose any of these facts, since there was nothing in the contract between the bank and their customer, Mrs Rolfe, which was unusual or which might not reasonably have been anticipated by the plaintiff, the surety.' In *National Provincial Bank of England* v *Glanusk* ([1913] 3 KB 335) Lord Glanusk had guaranteed the overdraft of his brother-in-law. The guarantee was on the face of it for all moneys which might be owing to the plaintiffs, but the guarantor contended that there was an antecedent agreement that it should cover only the estate account, and that the bank knew, and should have informed him that his brother-in-law was using the account for unauthorised purposes. The court held that even if it could have been proved that the bank had been suspicious of the unauthorised transaction, it owed no duty to communicate its suspicions to the guarantor.

J

In *Westminster Bank Ltd* v *Cond* ([1940] 46 Com Cas 60) the customer had an overdraft guaranteed by two sureties. He wished to increase his overdraft limit and was asked by the bank for additional security. The defendant agreed to guarantee the account but in an interview with the bank manager enquired about the customer's prospects. The bank manager replied that he did not think he would have any difficulty in paying off the overdraft. The bank manager, not being specifically asked about the state of the customer's account, did not volunteer that the account was overdrawn. On the customer's insolvency, the defendant refused to pay on the guarantee alleging that the manager owed him a duty to disclose that there was a previous overdraft even when no specific enquiry had been made. The court held that there was no such duty of disclosure.

A guarantor can terminate his liability by notice. In *Offord* v *Davies and Another* ((1862) 12 CB (NS) 748) the guarantee was expressed to be for a period of 12 months. Before the end of the 12 months the guarantor countermanded the guarantee and when the bank claimed on it, the defendants were held not liable.

A surety for repayment of money borrowed may be liable under the guarantee if the contract was entered in good faith and in the belief that it was legal. In *Garrard* v *James* ([1925] Ch 616) the plaintiff provided £1,500 for the purchase of preference shares in a company and the company agreed to repurchase the shares under certain circumstances. Two of the company's directors had guaranteed the due performance of the undertaking. The company later refused to buy back its shares on the ground that it was contrary to the law. The bank claimed against the directors under the guarantee and the court held that the bank was entitled to sue on the guarantee.

Joint and several guarantees

National Provincial Bank of England v Brackenbury (1906) 22 TLR 797

The plaintiff bank required a guarantee for £100 for the account of Brewers and Maltsters Machinery Manufacturing Co. Ltd and arrangements were made for Mr Brackenbury, Mr Hazelhurst, Mr Brown and Mr Johnson to sign a joint and several guarantee. The guarantee was signed on 26 November 1904 by the first three named guarantors but Mr Johnson became ill and died before his signature could be obtained.

The bank made an advance, relying on the three guarantors who had signed the form, and on default of the principal debtor claimed on the guarantee. Payment not being made, the bank brought an action against Mr Brackenbury claiming £102 12s 10d, including interest. The defendant pleaded that he was released from any liability by the plaintiffs having, without his consent, agreed to accept three sureties instead of four.

Walton J held that where a number of people have agreed to execute a joint and several guarantee they are entitled to look towards each other for contribution should the bank make demand under the guarantee. The fact that the guarantee had not been signed by one of the agreed guarantors rendered it incomplete and void.

The *Brackenbury* case was applied in somewhat more complicated circumstances in *Ford & Carter Ltd* v *Midland Bank Ltd* ((1979) 129 New LJ 543). In that case Wilson Lovett & Sons with four associated companies gave a mutual guarantee to the bank and all five companies executed a memorandum indorsed on the guarantee. Another member of the group, Ford & Carter Ltd, purported to join the guarantee and its name was added to the memorandum, with the signatures of two of its officers. No fresh signatures were obtained from the original five guarantors. Ford & Carter executed a floating charge in favour of the bank in support of its guarantee undertaking. In 1971 all the guarantors were called to pay under the guarantee. Ford & Carter asked the bank to appoint a receiver under the floating charge and went into liquidation. The liquidator then challenged the company's liability under the guarantee. The House of Lords upheld the decision of the trial court, and said that the wording of the memorandum did not envisage the addition of further members of the group to the guarantee undertaking. Lord Salmon said:

> 'Had it been intended to cater for such an event so that any new wholly-owned subsidiary should automatically become a party to the guarantee merely by signing it, nothing would have been easier than to have written that guarantee in language which would clearly have had that effect.'

In *Amalgamated Investments & Property Co. Ltd* v *Texas Commerce International Bank Ltd* ([1982] 1 Lloyd's Rep 27) the court held that if parties to a contract of guarantee show an intention to introduce terms which were not literally within the contract they signed, their intention prior to signing the contract may be taken into account in interpreting those terms. Similarly, the conduct of the parties can be taken into account in order to vary the terms set out in any contract they sign and if the parties can show that they intended to place a different meaning to certain terms other than their literal meaning they are bound by the meaning intended.

In *Bank of Scotland* v *Wright* (Queen's Bench Division, 13 July 1990), Mr Wright, who had been declared redundant, decided to invest his redundancy money in a butchery and freezing business, Dinewell Holdings, and a subsidiary, Dinewell Frozen Foods Ltd. The capital base proved too small for the development of an expanding freezer centre and home delivery business. The Royal Bank of Scotland was willing to provide the extra capital but required a personal guarantee from the directors and a second charge over their homes. The facility was extended to £200,000 but the group collapsed. Mr Wright denied personal liability for the large overdraft of the subsidiary freezer company claiming his guarantee was limited to the holding company's ultimate debit balance. The guarantee clauses in question provided that Mr Wright guaranteed full and final payment of sums 'due to you by your customer whether solely or jointly with any other obligant or by any other firm ... or in any other manner or way whatsoever'. The final clause provided that the sum recoverable should not exceed 'the ultimate balance that may become due'. The holding company had guaranteed the subsidiary's liability and he had guaranteed the holding company's liability. The court held that guarantees are to be construed strictly but where capable of more than one meaning the surrounding circumstances can be taken into account. Applying *Coghlan & Amalgamated Investments* ([1982]

1 QB 84) Mr Wright was held liable for the group debts under his guarantee. He was aware that his guarantee was to be part of an 'interlinked mesh of securities' and the facility extended to the holding company included the grant of a facility on which both the parent and subsidiary company could draw.

In *M.S. Fashions Ltd & Others* v *Bank of Credit and Commerce International SA & Another* (*The Times,* 23 June 1992) the Court of Appeal held that a surety for two companies who were principal debtors of BCCI could use the set-off effect of rule 4.90 of the Insolvency Rules, to reduce the debt which the surety and the companies owed BCCI by the amount standing to the credit of the surety in his deposit account with BCCI on the date BCCI went into liquidation.

Letters of comfort

Where no security is provided for a loan, and a contract of guarantee or indemnity is inappropriate, a letter of comfort may be provided instead. Such letters may be given by a parent company in relation to the debts incurred by a subsidiary company or by a government agency which is unable to provide guarantees. The purpose of such an undertaking is that the parent company (or other entity) will give an undertaking to support the subsidiary's business ventures and confirm that the latter will be in a position to meet its liabilities to the lender. A question of considerable interest is whether the letter of comfort is a legally binding contract.

Chemco Leasing SpA v *Rediffusion plc* [1987] 1 FTLR 201

The defendants wrote to the plaintiffs thanking them for the confidence reposed in a subsidiary of the defendants, and for the provision of lease financing facilities to be used by the subsidiary for the purchase of equipment. The defendants 'confirmed' that the share capital of the subsidiary was owned 99.91 per cent by Computer Machinery Corporation France SA which was in turn owned 100 per cent by the defendants. The letter continued with an assurance that:

'... [the defendants] will be in a position to exercise sufficient control over the administration and management of [the subsidiary] to ensure that its obligations to Chemco are maintained.'

The letter continued:

'... we are not contemplating the disposal of our interests in [the subsidiary] and undertake to give Chemco prior notification should we dispose of our interest during the life of the lease. If we dispose of our interest we undertake to take over the remaining liabilities to Chemco [the subsidiary] should the new shareholders be unacceptable to Chemco.'

Over a period of time, Chemco and the subsidiary entered into various contracts for the leasing of equipment. The defendants decided to dispose of their interest in the subsidiary and Chemco received only three days' notice of the proposed sale. The subsidiary eventually went into liquidation and payments of the rental to the plaintiffs ceased. Chemco then attempted to enforce the defendants' letter of comfort. During a period of about nine months after the sale of the subsidiary the plaintiffs expressed no dissatisfaction regarding the new shareholders of the subsidiary.

Staughton J held that the comfort letters were contractual undertakings possessing both intention to create legal relations and sufficiency of terms. The judge, therefore, dismissed the plaintiff's claim holding that the defendant's obligation to 'take over' the remaining liabilities of the subsidiary could not arise until the plaintiffs had given reasonable notice of the unacceptability of the new shareholders. The plaintiffs appealed.

The Court of Appeal dismissed the plaintiff's appeal. The court preferred an analysis of the letter of comfort in terms of offer and acceptance and the defendants' offer to take over the remaining liabilities had lapsed in the absence of an acceptance within a reasonable time. The requirement of reasonable notice was implied into the agreement.

The *Chemco* case should be compared with *Kleinwort Benson Ltd* v *Malaysia Mining Corporation Berhad* ([1988] 1 All ER 714). In the *Kleinwort* case the Malaysia Mining Corp. Bhd formed MMC Metals Ltd as a wholly owned subsidiary to trade in tin on the London Metal Exchange. In order to carry out this function, the subsidiary needed substantial extra funding and, consequently, the defendants commenced negotiations with the plaintiffs. The plaintiffs, initially, granted the defendants and the subsidiary jointly a facility of £5 million, on terms that the defendants were to be jointly and severally liable with the subsidiary for the loan. Under this arrangement, commission of $3/_8$ per cent was payable annually. The defendants refused to accept such liability and refused to give the guarantee. The plaintiffs, therefore, furnished a revised facility on terms of $1/_2$ per cent commission and indicated a letter of comfort would be acceptable. The terms of the letter of comfort were eventually agreed. Following the collapse of the tin market in 1985, the subsidiary went into liquidation. The plaintiffs terminated the facility and claimed the amount of the loan from the defendants who denied liability on the ground that the letter of comfort was intended to be binding. Hirst J held that the plaintiff bankers were entitled to succeed in their claim for damages. He reiterated the basic principles of contractual intention and concluded that the defendants had failed to rebut the presumption of intention to create legal relations in commercial transactions. Hirst J said the task of the court was to ascertain the intention of the parties and that depended on:

'... the proper construction of the written words themselves, set in their surrounding circumstances or matrix, and without paying any regard in this task of interpretation to any evidence from the parties or anyone else as to what they thought the contract meant or intended it to mean. Extrinsic evidence may, however, be admissible to show that what appears to be a valid and binding contract is in fact no contract at all.'

The Court of Appeal reversed Hirst J, and although it accepted that in commercial transactions there is a presumption of intention to be legally bound, the court said that the presumption is of no assistance in deciding whether the words were intended as a binding promise or not. Ralph Gibson LJ held that the words used in the letter of comfort did not amount to a promise by the defendants which was contractual in nature. The letter of comfort was therefore evidence of a certain yet unenforceable and purely moral obligation.

The Australian courts have recently examined the binding effect of letters of comfort. In *Paulger* v *Butland Industries Ltd* (unreported, decision of 25 October 1989 – see JBL May 1991, p. 281) the managing director of a company which was in financial difficulties wrote to the creditors of the company asking for tolerance whilst negotiations were in hand for the sale of a part of the business. He gave an undertaking to make good all outstanding matters within 90 days and gave a personal guarantee to the effect that all amounts outstanding would be paid. The company was placed in receivership and one of the creditors brought an action against the general manager. The court gave judgment for the creditor and this was affirmed by the Court of Appeal. It was pointed out that the guarantee came into existence by means of an offer and acceptance and required consideration, and the personal guarantee of the manager made him personally liable.

In *Banque Brussels Lambert SA* v *Australian National Industries* (unreported, Sup Ct of NSW, 12 December 1989 – see JBL, May 1991, p. 282) S Ltd, which was a fully owned subsidiary of SH Ltd, wished to obtain a loan facility from the B Bank of Brussels. A Ltd, which owned 45 per cent of the capital of SH Ltd, issued a letter of comfort and confirmed that 'it would not be our intention to reduce our shareholding in [SH Ltd] from the current level for the duration of the loan facility'. The company also gave an undertaking to notify the bank of any decision to dispose of its shareholding in SH Ltd. A Ltd eventually sold its shares in SH Ltd without giving the required notice. S Ltd went into liquidation and the bank brought an action to recover its loss from A Ltd. The court held that the letter of comfort did not constitute a guarantee and A Ltd was not liable in debt for S Ltd's default. However, A Ltd could still be liable for breach of contract provided the letter of comfort created a binding undertaking. Rogers J said:

'There should be no room in the proper flow of commerce for some purgatory where statements made by businessmen, after hard bargaining and made to induce another business person to enter into a business transaction would, without any express statement to that effect, reside in a twilight zone of merely honourable agreement. The whole thrust of the law today is to attempt to give proper effect to commercial transactions.'

Garnishee orders

If a judgment creditor knows that the judgment debtor is owed money by a third party the creditor can obtain an order of the court directing the third party to pay the money owed to the judgment creditor instead of the judgment debtor.

Choice Investments Ltd v *Jeromnimon* (*Midland Bank Ltd, garnishee*) [1981] 1 All ER 225

Mr Jeromnimon owed the plaintiff company the sum of £982.16 in sterling. The plaintiff company successfully obtained judgment against him for the amount of the debt and costs. The plaintiff company discovered that Mr Jeromnimon had a bank account at the Midland Bank in Wigmore Street in which sums were held to his credit. The bank obtained a garnishee order nisi against the bank by which the sums standing to the credit of the bank were attached to the judgment. It was then discovered that Mr Jeromnimon had three accounts with the bank. Two accounts in sterling had minimal credit balances but the third account was a United States dollars seven-day notice deposit with a credit balance of $2,358.55 with $166.04 accrued interest.

No difficulty arose with the two sterling accounts but the question was whether the account in US dollars could be attached.

Lord Denning MR held that the English courts could not only attach the credit balances with the banks expressed to be in sterling (whether in the form of a current or deposit account) but also any credit balances expressed in foreign currencies. The amount held in the third account was in US dollars and therefore a debt payable on demand. The judgment debtor could therefore require payment in dollars and not merely its sterling equivalent.

There is no reason why an amount expressed in a foreign currency standing to the credit of a judgment debtor in the jurisdiction cannot be attached. A refusal by the courts to attach such amounts would enable a judgment debtor to avoid a judgment creditor enforcing his judgment by merely converting any credit balance in his bank account into a foreign currency.

Where a garnishee order nisi is served on a bank, it operates to freeze the amount attached under the order and the bank must pay the amount to the judgment creditor or into the court. Similarly, where an order is made which attaches a credit balance expressed in a foreign currency the bank must put a 'stop' on such amount of the foreign currency as is necessary to satisfy the judgment in sterling.

A current account balance may be regarded as a debt 'owing or accruing' to the customer when a garnishee order nisi is served because the service of such an order is said to constitute a sufficient demand by operation of law to satisfy any right a banker may have as between himself and his customer to a demand before payment of money standing to the credit of a current account can be enforced.

In *Rogers* v *Whiteley* ([1898] AC 118) a customer had a credit balance of over £6,800 on his current and deposit accounts. The customer had given notice to transfer his credit balance from the deposit account to his current account. A creditor of the customer obtained a judgment against him for £6,000 and obtained a garnishee order nisi which ordered 'all debts owing or accruing' from the bank to the customer be attached to answer the judgment recovered against him. That order was served on the bank, and thereafter the bank refused to honour any cheques drawn by the customer. The House of Lords held that the bank had acted correctly. Lord Watson said:

> 'The effect of an order attaching "all debts" owing or accruing due by him to the judgment debtor is to make the garnishee custodier for the court for the whole funds attached; and he cannot, except at his own peril, part with any of those funds without the sanction of the court.'

The *Rogers* v *Whiteley* case was decided at a time when a credit balance on a deposit account could not be attached by a garnishee order. Now this can usually be done under s. 38 of the Administration of Justice Act 1956, which provides that a sum standing to the credit of a person in a deposit account with a bank is deemed to be a sum 'due or accruing' to that person and may be attached if certain conditions are satisfied. However, credit balances on the following accounts still cannot be attached by a garnishee order:

(a) accounts in the National Savings Bank;
(b) accounts in the Trustee Savings Bank;
(c) accounts in any savings bank maintained in pursuance of any enactment by any local authority; or
(d) any account in any bank with two or more places of business if the terms applicable on that account permit withdrawals on demand, on production of a deposit book, at more than one of those places of business, with or without restrictions as to the amount which may be withdrawn.

A joint account cannot be attached in respect of a debt owed by one of the parties. The same rule applies to a partnership account. In *Hirschorn v Evans, Barclays Bank Ltd, garnishee* ([1938] 2 KB 801) the husband and wife had a joint account at a bank. A garnishee summons was served on the bank that named the husband alone as the judgment debtor. The Court of Appeal accepted the view of the bank that the summons did not attach to the joint account and the bank could not dishonour cheques drawn on the joint account.

However, money standing to the customer's balance may be attached by service of a garnishee order nisi although the money is trust money. In *Plunkett v Barclays Bank Ltd* ([1936] 2 KB 107) the plaintiff, a solicitor, had opened two accounts with Barclays Bank, one being a client account. On 7 September 1935, £48 5s in cash was paid into the client account, the sum representing rent and costs payable by a client to a third party. On 9 September an application was made for a garnishee order nisi by the plaintiff's former wife, in respect of costs in her successful divorce proceedings against him. The order was made, and served on the defendant's bank. The bank informed the plaintiff that it must regard both his accounts as being attached by the order. On 11 September the bank dishonoured the cheque for £48 5s drawn on the client account, with the answer 'Refer to Drawer'. The plaintiff brought an action against the bank for alleged breach of contract by the dishonour of the cheque and for alleged libel in writing 'Refer to Drawer' on the back of the cheque. The court held that the money standing to the credit of the client account was a debt owing from the bank to the plaintiff, and therefore the garnishee order nisi attached that debt in the hands of the bank. The bank was justified in returning the cheque unpaid.

Mortgages

In *Santley v Wilde* ((1899) 2 Ch 474) Lindley MR said 'A mortgage is a conveyance of land or an assignment of chattels as a security for the payment of a debt or the discharge of some other obligation for which it is given.'

A mortgage has two essential features, namely (a) it provides security for the performance of an obligation which is usually the repayment of a loan and interest therein; and (b) the security purpose is attained by transferring to the creditor or mortgagee certain rights in property.

Lloyds Bank plc v Margolis and Others [1954] 1 WLR 644

In September 1936 the plaintiff bank took security over a farm to secure an overdraft in favour of George Lyster, its owner. In December 1938 the customer being in the process of selling the farm received a written demand for repayment. The farm was sold to the first and then the second defendants respectively, in both cases subject to the mortgage. On 29 November 1950 the bank brought an action and sought to enforce the mortgage. The defendants claimed that the charge was unenforceable and the bank was barred by the Statute of Limitations.

Upjohn J held that the time began to run from the date of the demand and not from the date of the various advances and the bank could pursue its claim. Upjohn J said (p. 649):

> '... at all events where there is the relationship of banker and customer and the banker permits his customer to overdraw on the terms of entering into a legal charge, which provides that the money then due or thereafter to become due is to be paid on demand, that means what it says. As between the customer and the banker, who are dealing on a running account, it seems to me impossible to assume that the bank were to be entitled to sue on the deed the very day after it was executed without making a demand and giving the customer a reasonable time to pay.'

The Statute of Limitations 1980 provides that the period for which a valid cause of action subsists is six years from the date the action is acquired. In the case of specialty debts that period is extended to twelve years. Before a bank can bring a valid cause of action it must make a demand for repayment of the debt. In *Joachimson* v *Swiss Bank Corporation* ([1921] 3 KB 110) it was held that where money is standing to the credit of a customer on a current account with the banker, in the absence of an arrangement to the contrary, a demand for repayment is necessary before a cause of action arises. In the *Margolis* case the agreement expressly provided for a demand before a cause of action could be brought. The conditions for a sale or foreclosure were examined in *Hunter* v *Hunter and Others* ([1936] AC 222) and the court said that it is essential for the due protection of the borrowers that the conditions of its exercise should be strictly complied with.

The court examined *Barclays Bank Ltd* v *Beck* ([1952] 1 All ER 549) where the defendants, who were overdrawn with the plaintiff bank, executed a charge in favour of the bank. Clause 1 of the charge read:

> 'The farmer hereby covenants with Barclays Bank Ltd ... that the farmer will on demand or upon the death of the farmer without demand pay to the bank the balance of all moneys now or hereafter owing by the farmer under any account current ... and all other moneys and liabilities now or hereafter due or to become due ... to the bank in respect of any advance made or to be made by the bank ...'

In 1950 the bank appointed a receiver to realise the security but the proceeds of sale did not release sufficient moneys to discharge the debt to the bank and £600 remained outstanding. An action was brought by the bank to recover this amount. The defendants argued that where a security is given for a simple contract debt the two claims are merged and only the security can be enforced. The bank having recovered on the security it could not then sue on the debt created by the overdraft. The Court of Appeal held in favour of the bank. Somerville LJ said:

'The question here, as it seems to me, is whether the ordinary contractual position as between banker and customer, which would be usual in respect of advances apart from this clause, is merged in and destroyed by being replaced by what appears in clause 1. In my opinion that clause, so far from doing that, indicated that the position is contrary.'

Cuckmere Brick Co. Ltd and Another v Mutual Finance Ltd [1971] 1 Ch 949

The plaintiffs owned some land with planning permission to erect 100 flats. They charged the land to the defendants by way of a legal mortgage with the payment of £50,000. They subsequently obtained permission to build 35 houses on the land instead. No construction took place for five years and the defendants called in the mortgage and advertised the site for sale. The estate agents advertised the land for sale and advertisements included mention of the planning permission to build houses. The plaintiffs protested that the advertisements should also refer to the permission for the flats. The sale went ahead and realised £44,000. The plaintiffs brought an action claiming that the land was worth £75,000 and more would have been realised if the defendants had properly advertised the planning permission for the flats. The defendants claimed the balance of the advance.

The Court of Appeal held that, when exercising a power of sale, the mortgagee owes a duty to exercise reasonable care to obtain the proper price. Salmon LJ said (p. 966):

'It is impossible to pretend that the state of the authorities on this branch of the law is entirely satisfactory. There are some *dicta* which suggest that unless a mortgagee acts in bad faith he is safe. His only obligation to the mortgagor is not to cheat him. There are other *dicta* which suggest that in addition to the duty of acting in good faith, the mortgagee is under a duty to take reasonable care to obtain whatever is the true market value of the mortgaged property at the moment he chooses to sell it ...'

He then continued:

'The proposition that the mortgagee owes both duties, in my judgment, represents the true view of the law ... The mortgagor is vitally affected by the result of the sale but its preparation and conduct is left entirely in the hands of the mortgagee. The "proximity" between them could scarcely be closer. Surely they are "neighbours".'

In *Bank of Cyprus (London)* v *Gill* ([1980] 2 Lloyd's Rep 51) the Court of Appeal held that the mortgagee's duty to get the best price did not require that they should wait for a depressed market to rise. The bank had taken independent advice and the mortgagor himself had been given the opportunity to sell the property.

The *Cuckmere* case was applied in *American Express* v *Hurley* ([1985] 3 All ER 564 (see p. 225)) where a loan was secured against a charge against the company's property. The defendant, a director of the company, also gave a personal guarantee. Eventually a receiver was appointed to realise the security. The sale realising an inadequate amount to repay the bank loan, the bank claimed on the personal guarantee of the defendant. The defendant cross-claimed that the receiver had been negligent in obtaining the true value of the assets realised. The court applied *dicta* of Salmon LJ and held that the mortgagee owes a duty to obtain the best price possible. The *Cuckmere* case has also been applied in *Re Potters Oils Ltd (No. 2)* ([1986] 1 All ER 890).

Williams & Glyn's Bank Ltd v Boland and Another

Williams & Glyn's Bank Ltd v Brown [1980] 2 All ER 408

The bank agreed to make two separate loans to the two defendants for business purposes and required the defendant in each case to mortgage his matrimonial home by way of security. The houses were registered in the name of each defendant and in each case the wife's consent or signature was not required on the mortgage forms. The two defendants defaulted and the bank brought proceedings for, and was granted, possession. On appeal the possession order was discharged on the grounds, *inter alia*, that the wife was in actual possession of the land within s. 70 of the Land Registration Act 1925 and therefore had an overriding interest in the land. The bank appealed.

The House of Lords confirmed the decision of the Court of Appeal. The wife's actual possession was a minor interest but when protected by actual possession was capable of being an overriding interest. The House took the view that the fact that the vendor or mortgagor was in occupation did not exclude the possibility of occupation by others; nor was the occupation of the wife inconsistent with the title of her husband since she had independent rights of her own. The wife's interest was capable of being an overriding interest. Lord Scarman said (p. 416):

> 'The courts may not put aside, as irrelevant, the undoubted fact that if two wives succeed, the protection of the beneficial interest which English law now recognises that a married woman has in the matrimonial home will be strengthened, whereas, if they lose, this interest can be weakened, and even destroyed by an unscrupulous husband. The difficulties are, I believe, exaggerated; but bankers, and solicitors, exist to provide the service which the public needs. They can, as they have successfully done in the past, adjust their practice, if it be socially required. Nevertheless, the judicial responsibility remains, to interpret the statute truly according to its tenor.'

It should be remembered that the decision protects the rights of occupiers in possession. It does not protect all occupiers even if they are spouses in matrimonial homes. In *National Provincial Bank Ltd* v *Ainsworth* ([1965] AC 1175) the Court of Appeal found in favour of the deserted wife and it was held that she had an overriding interest under s. 70 of the Land Registration Act 1925. The House of Lords, however, overruled the Court of Appeal. In *Barclays Bank plc* v *Khaira and Another (The*

Times, 19 December 1991) Mrs Khaira, who with her husband had created a charge over their house as a security in order to secure a loan, alleged that the bank's claim for possession was invalid because of her husband's fraudulent misrepresentation to her and undue influence, and that he acted as the bank's agent at the time the security was given. The court held that in the normal course of events a bank owed no duty of care in tort or contract to explain or to advise the taking of independent advice to those who came to its premises to sign securities. The Matrimonial Homes Act 1967 now gives a spouse who lacks a legal title to the house a statutory right of occupation but this binds the mortgagee or purchaser only if it has been registered.

The *Boland* case applies to registered land. In the case of unregistered land an equitable interest can affect a purchaser or mortgagee only if he has actual or constructive notice of it.

Hopkinson v *Rolt* (1861) 9 HL Cas 514

The appellant was an officer of the Commercial Bank of London. A customer of the bank had mortgaged to it certain property as security for a loan of £20,000. The bank's mortgage was expressed to be for the 'sums and sum of money which then were or was, or at any time and from time to time thereafter, should or might become due or owing'. The respondent made a loan to the bank's customer against a second mortgage of the property. The bank was notified of the second mortgage. The bank continued to make advances. On the customer's bankruptcy the second mortgagee claimed the bank's advances were postponed to his own claim.

The court held that further advances made by the bank under the first mortgage were postponed to the second mortgage. Lord Campbell said (p. 535):

'Although the mortgagor has parted with the legal interest in the hereditaments mortgaged, he remains the equitable owner of all his interest not transferred beneficially to the mortgagee, and he may still deal with his property in any way consistent with the rights of the mortgagee. How is the first mortgagee injured by the second mortgage being executed, although the first mortgagee having notice of the mortgage, the second mortgagee should be preferred to him as to subsequent advances? The first mortgagee is secure as to past advances, and he is not under any obligation to make any further advances. He has only to hold his hand when asked for further loans. Knowing the extent of the second mortgage, he may calculate that the hereditaments mortgaged are ample security to the mortgagees; and if he doubts this, he closes his account with the mortgagor. Thus far the mortgagor is entitled to do what he pleases with his own.'

If a subsequent mortgagee has given notice of his charge to the first mortgagee before further advances are made, the first mortgagee cannot tack further advances to the first mortgage. If the mortgage secures an overdraft the rule in *Clayton's* case will apply as regards subsequent payments into the account so as to reduce the debit balance at the date the bank receives notice of the subsequent mortgage. If therefore the overdraft is reduced by the bank after notice of the subsequent mortgage there will be a corresponding debit balance at that date for which the bank has priority. If further advances are then made by the bank increasing the overdraft, the bank cannot tack them to the original loan and will be deferred to the second mortgagee. In order to avoid the operation of the rule in *Clayton's* case the bank should close the mortgagor's account once notice of a subsequent mortgage is given and any future payments in or drawings out by the mortgagor should be through a separate account. The leading case in which the bank suffered by its failure to close the original account on notice of the second mortgage was *Deeley* v *Lloyds Bank Ltd* ([1912] AC 756).

Section 94 of the Law of Property Act 1925, however, permits further advances to be made and provides:

'(c) whether or not [the mortgagee] had such notice as foresaid [i.e. notice of an intervening mortgage] where the mortgage imposes an obligation on [the first mortgagee] to make such further advances.'

Under s. 94 if the bank or other mortgagee has placed himself under an obligation to make further advances, whether it has notice of further advances or not, the first mortgagee has priority over all advances made in fulfilment of its obligation. Section 94 reverses the decision in *West* v *Williams* ([1899] 1 Ch 132).

Fixed and floating charges

There are a number of reasons for a creditor to obtain security in the form of a charge and not rely solely against a debtor company. First, in the event of the insolvency of a company a secured creditor will have priority at least over unsecured creditors, and according to the seniority of his claim have priority over other less senior security holders. This is a direct consequence of the fact that a security interest confers some type of proprietary interest on its holder. Secondly, the secured creditor may have a right to pursue property subject to a charge unless it is acquired by a bona fide purchaser for value. Thirdly, the security interest gives its holder the right of enforcement. Finally, a charge affords a degree of measure of control over the business of the debtor company.

Re Castell & Brown [1898] 1 Ch 315

In 1885 the company issued a series of debentures secured by a floating charge. It was expressly provided by each debenture that the company was 'not at liberty to create any mortgage or charge upon its freehold and leasehold hereditaments, in priority thereto'. The title deeds of various properties, which had been left in the possession of the company, were later deposited with the company's bank to secure an overdraft. A dispute arose as to the question of priority.

The bank's charge was held to have priority over the earlier debentures. Romer J said:

'In the first place, I cannot hold that there was any negligence on the part of the bank. When making its advances to Castell & Brown Ltd (which I will hereafter call the company), it found the company in possession of the deeds in question, and apparently able, as unincumbered owner, to charge the property. The company purported as such unincumbered owner to give a charge to the bank, and I think the bank was, under the circumstances, entitled to rely upon obtaining a charge free from incumbrance ... as the bank had no reason to suppose that the company was not fully able to give a valid first charge, and found the company in possession of the deeds, which showed no incumbrance, I think the bank was not bound to make any special inquiry ...'

The question of priority of a charge will depend on a number of factors, i.e. the nature of a charge, the date of registration, and crystallisation of a floating charge. The most significant feature in identifying a floating charge is that the company retains autonomy in respect of the assets subject to the charge. The essence of the charge is determined by the degree of freedom enjoyed by the company to deal with those assets. In *Siebe Gorman & Co. Ltd* v *Barclays Bank Ltd* ([1979] 2 Lloyd's Rep 142) the court held that a fixed charge had been created in favour of a bank over book debts (in this case bills of exchange) when the charge provided that the company could not assign or charge these debts and had to pay the proceeds into an account with the chargee bank which the company could not operate without the consent of the bank. This case is in contrast with *Re Brightlife Ltd* ([1987] Ch 200) where the court held that a floating charge had been created when the company could pay the charged proceeds into its bank account and use them in the normal course could business. However, the mere fact that there is some restriction in the power of the company to use the charged asset does not preclude it from a subsequent floating charge; the restriction must substantially deprive the company of its power to deal with the assets in the normal course of business.

A floating charge may, however, be vulnerable because it may be deferred to any subsequent fixed or equitable charge created by a company over its assets. To firm up their security against subsequent security interests created by the company, and which may otherwise have priority, it is possible for the debenture-holder to prevent the company creating subsequent charges that have priority or rank equally with their charge. Such restrictions, although common, are strictly construed.

In *Re Castell & Brown Ltd* the court held that a fixed charge may be created having priority over an earlier floating charge. This is so even where the creation of charges having priority is expressly prohibited by the terms of the instrument which establishes the floating charge provided the person taking the later security has no notice of the prohibition. Registering the charge in accordance with the companies legislation does not constitute notice of such a prohibition (*Wilson* v *Kelland* [1910] 2 Ch 306).

Crystallisation is a term used to describe a process by which the floating charge is converted to a fixed charge.

There has been some debate whether an automatic crystallisation clause is effective on the occurrence of certain events, e.g where the company attempts to create a charge which ranks equally or *pari passu* with an existing charge. It is undoubtedly settled law that such clauses are effective. In *Re Woodroffes (Musical Instruments) Ltd* ([1986] Ch 366) Nourse J commented:

'Although the general body of informed opinion is of the view that automatic crystallisation is undesirable I have not been referred to any case in which the assumption in favour of automatic crystallisation on cessation of business has been questioned.'

Similarly, in *Re Brightlife Ltd* ([1987] Ch 200) Hoffman J (*obiter*) remarked:

'... a provision for automatic crystallisation might take effect without the knowledge of either the company or the debenture-holder. The result might be prejudice to third parties who gave credit to the company ... I do not think that it is open to the courts to restrict the contractual freedom of the parties to a floating charge on such grounds ... These arguments for and against the floating are matter for Parliament rather than the courts ...'

CAN A BANK BE HELD LIABLE IN THE INSOLVENCY OF A COMPANY?

Banks as shadow directors

Where a company gives security the bank may seek to protect its investment by reserving certain rights. Section 251 of the Insolvency Act 1986 provides that a person may be liable as a shadow director if he is someone 'in accordance with whose directions or instructions the directors are accustomed to act'. However, the definition goes on to provide that a person will not be a shadow director by means only of the fact that the directors act on advice given by him in a professional capacity. Whether a person acts as a shadow director depends on whether he merely gives advice or whether he gives directions or instructions. This will depend on the facts of each individual case and the degree of intervention.

Re A Company (No. 005009 of 1987) ex p Copp [1989] BCLC 13

In 1986 the financial position of the company began to deteriorate due to the loss of a major customer. The company reached its permitted overdraft limit and the bank then commissioned a report into the company's affairs and exerted pressure for security for the overdraft. In May 1987, the company granted the bank a debenture by way of a specific charge over all the book and other debts from time to time owing. The debenture provided that the company was to pay all monies received in respect of the debts into the company's account. The company also agreed not to sell, factor, discount or otherwise charge or assign the same without the written consent of the bank. The company agreed to assign from time to time such book debts or other debts to the bank. The company took steps to implement the recommendations in the bank's report. A receiver was appointed by the bank under the debenture and in August 1987 the company went into a creditor's voluntary liquidation.

The liquidator sought, *inter alia*, declarations that the debenture created a floating charge and not a fixed charge, that the debenture was invalid under s. 239 of the Insolvency Act 1986 as a preference in favour of the bank and that the bank had wrongfully traded under s. 214 of the Act on the basis that the bank was a shadow director.

The receiver and the bank sought an order that the claims should be struck out as disclosing no cause of action.

Knox J refused to strike out the claims for preferences and for wrongful trading against the bank, both of which depended on a finding that the bank was a shadow director. The facts which Knox J held could result in the bank being found to have been a shadow director were that when the bank discovered that the company was experiencing financial problems it started to exert pressure on the company; obtained a debenture from the company; and commissioned a report which made several recommendations, which the directors of the company, under pressure from the bank, had followed.

A bank will often appoint one of its officers as a director to a company in return for the provision of finance or a loan. This is usually done for the purpose of monitoring the company's ongoing financial position and the appointment of such a nominee director will not *per se* impose liability on the bank as a shadow director. However, the nominee director may facilitate communications or direct instructions between the bank and the company; if that communication becomes interference in the company's business the bank may be liable. It should also be remembered that any directors appointed by the bank will owe fiduciary duties to the company.

Section 214 of the Insolvency Act 1986

Section 214 of the Insolvency Act empowers the court to declare a director or shadow director of a company liable to contribute to the assets of the company if the director knew, or ought to have concluded, that the company had no reasonable prospect of not going into insolvent liquidation and did not take reasonable steps to minimise potential loss to the company's creditors. The section will come into operation if, at the time the company goes into liquidation, its assets are insufficient to pay its debts and liabilities. It must be proved to the court that a director or shadow director against whom a declaration is sought 'knew or ought to have concluded that' insolvent liquidation was unavoidable. However, the director or shadow director may prove in his defence that he 'took every step ... he ought to have taken' to minimise creditors' losses.

Re Produce Marketing Consortium Ltd (No. 2) [1989] BCLC 520

The liquidator of a company sought an order under s. 214 of the Insolvency Act 1986 declaring that two directors were liable to contribute to the assets of the company. The company acted as an agent in relation to the import of fruit and although it had traded successfully for several years, gradually its turnover and profitability was reduced until it went into a creditor's voluntary liquidation, with a deficit of approximately £317,694. The gradual decline of the business was obvious over a number of years from the company's audited accounts. One of the directors admitted in February 1987 that the liquidation of the company was inevitable but said that it continued to trade because it enabled an advantageous realisation of the company's stock of perishable fruit in cold store. This was said to be an attempt to minimise loss to the creditors within s. 214(3) of the Insolvency Act 1986.

Knox J held the two directors liable to contribute £75,0000 to the company's assets. The court said that they ought to have concluded in July 1986 that there was no reasonable prospect of avoiding insolvent liquidation because they had an intimate knowledge of the business and must have known that the turnover was well below previous years, and would lead to a considerable deficit.

Section 212 of the Insolvency Act 1986

Section 212 allows a liquidator to recover property that has been misapplied by persons who formed the company or managed the company. The persons who may be made liable in misfeasance proceedings in the winding-up of a company are:

(a) any person who is or has been an officer of the company;
(b) any person who has acted as liquidator, administrator or administrative receiver of the company;
(c) any person who is, or has been, concerned, or taken part, in the promotion, formation or management of the company.

Any such person may be liable if he has 'misapplied or retained, or become accountable for any money or other property of the company, or been guilty of any misfeasance or breach of any fiduciary or other duty in relation to the company.'

Misfeasance proceedings may be taken against a director of a company in relation to a breach of his duty to consider the interests of creditors when the company is insolvent. In *West Mercia Safetywear Ltd* v *Dodd* ([1988] BCLC 250), Dodd was a director of A.J. Dodd & Co. Ltd and its wholly owned subsidiary, West Mercia Safetywear Ltd. The parent company was owed £30,000 by the subsidiary and the parent company had a large overdraft at the bank which Dodd had personally guaranteed. Both companies got into financial difficulties and Dodd was advised by an accountant that they should go into a creditors' voluntary liquidation. West Mercia was then paid £4,000 by one of its debtors and Dodd transferred that from the account of the subsidiary to the overdrawn account of the parent company apparently in part payment of the £30,000 debt but in reality to reduce his liability under the guarantee. The transfer was a preference but the money could not be recovered because of the insolvency of the parent company. The liquidator brought proceedings against Dodd personally who was ordered to pay £4,000 to West Mercia Safetywear Ltd.

It should be noted that s. 212 of the Insolvency Act 1986 allows an action to be brought against a director (including a shadow director) under s. 741(1) of the Companies Act 1985. Moreover, the wording of s.212 is such that any person who is, or has been, concerned or has taken part in the management or formation or promotion of the company may be held liable and that includes a shadow director who is in breach of his fiduciary duties.

RETENTION OF TITLE CLAUSES

Aluminium Industrie Vaasen BV v *Romalpa Aluminium Ltd* [1976] 2 All ER 552

The plaintiffs, a Dutch manufacturer of aluminium foil, sold quantities of foil to the defendants, an English company carrying on business in England. A clause in the contract of sale provided that the ownership in the foil delivered by the plaintiffs would only be transferred to the defendants when the purchase price was paid in full. Until the purchase price was paid the buyers were required to store the foil in such a way so as not to impair the plaintiffs' title and to keep the foil separate from other goods. The clause further provided that if the foil was mixed with other materials in the manufacturing process the ownership of the resulting goods was to be vested in the plaintiffs. The defendants were given the power to resell the manufactured goods but subject to the condition that until all indebtedness to the plaintiffs was discharged they were to assign to the plaintiffs any claims they had against the sub-purchasers.

The defendant company got into financial difficulties and a receiver was appointed by the debenture-holders at a time when the company owed the plaintiffs £122,000 for the foil supplied.

The receiver conceded that £35,152 was held by him as representing the proceeds of sale of the aluminium foil but contended that this money was subject to the debenture-holders' security. The plaintiffs claimed that they were entitled to that sum in priority to the secured and unsecured creditors of the defendant company. Mocatta J gave judgment for the plaintiffs and the defendants appealed.

The Court of Appeal affirmed the decision of Mocatta J, at first instance. Roskill LJ said:

'I see no difficulty in the contractual concept that, as between the defendants and their sub-purchasers, the defendants sold as principals, but that, as between themselves and the plaintiffs, those goods which they were selling as principals within their implied authority from the plaintiffs were the plaintiffs' to whom they remained fully accountable.'

Roskill LJ continued:

'If an agent lawfully sells his principal's goods, he stands in a fiduciary relationship to his principal and remains accountable to his principal for those goods and their proceeds.'

The Sale of Goods Act 1979 (s. 19) allows the seller of goods to sell them subject to a reservation of title clause. Consequently, property never passes to the buyer of the goods (whether a company or an individual) and that person is not in a position to give security over it. A supplier of goods sold subject to a reservation clause will have precedence to secured creditors and preferential creditors in the company's liquidation.

The *Romalpa* case was followed by *Borden (UK) Ltd v Scottish Timber Products Ltd* ([1979] 2 Lloyd's Rep 168) and involved the sale of resin which was used to manufacture chipboard. The Court of Appeal held that the effect of the reservation of title clause was to reserve property in the suppliers of the resin until it was used in the manufacturing process. Once it was used in the manufacturing process the resin lost its identity and there was nothing to trace. There was no right to trace the proceeds of sale and even if the suppliers had acquired an interest in the chipboard it would have been by way of a charge which was void for want of registration under the Companies Act 1985. Bridge LJ questioned whether there could ever be a right to trace over heterogeneous goods which are mixed as opposed to homogeneous goods envisaged in *Re Hallett's Estate* ((1880) 13 Ch D 696).

It often becomes difficult for the courts to determine the intention of the parties and unless it is clear that the seller was intended to have an absolute interest in the manufactured goods he must be treated as having lost ownership in the goods supplied. In

Re Bond Worth ([1979] 3 All ER 919) there was a clause in the contract under which the sellers claimed to have beneficial and equitable ownership in the goods or manufactured products or proceeds of resale. The court held that the clause created an equitable charge. Slade J said:

'In my judgment, any contract which, by way of security for the payment of a debt, confers an interest in property defeasible or destructible upon payment of such debt, ... must necessarily be regarded as creating a mortgage or charge, as the case may be. The existence of the equity of redemption is quite inconsistent with the existence of a bare trustee–beneficiary relationship.'

In *Clough Mill Ltd v Martin* ([1985] 1 WLR 111) Goff LJ emphasised that the court will give effect to the intention of the parties and said:

'... concepts such as bailment and fiduciary duty must not be allowed to be our masters, but must be regarded as the tools of our trade. I for my part can see nothing objectionable in an agreement between parties under which A, the owner of the goods, gives possession of those goods to B, at the same time conferring on B a power of sale and a power to consume the goods in manufacture ... if that is what the parties have agreed should happen, I can see no reason why the law should not give effect to that intention.'

Although, in theory, the parties can enter into a bargain on any terms they wish, it is unlikely that the supplier of the original goods will be intended to have absolute ownership of goods which have been manufactured by the buyer by using in part goods supplied by the supplier. Goff LJ said:

'... and I find it impossible to believe that it was the intention of the parties that the seller would thereby gain the windfall of the full value of the new product, deriving as it may well do not merely from the labour of the buyer but also from materials that were his, without any duty to account to him for any surplus or the proceeds of sale above the outstanding balance of the price due by him to the seller. It follows that ... must be read as creating either a trust or a charge.'

Goff LJ then went on to express the view that in such a situation he did not take the agreement as creating a trust.

In *Tatung (UK) Ltd v Galex Telesure Ltd* ([1989] 5 BCC 25) a supplier of electrical equipment claimed to be entitled to both the proceeds of sale and the rental from the hire of goods supplied under a contract. A reservation of title clause permitted the buyer to sell or to hire out the goods. The court held that the intention of the parties was clear and the supplier's interest in the property remained. However, his interest did not amount to the whole of such sums received but was limited by express agreement to any sums outstanding. Phillips J said (p. 335):

'If I am correct in my conclusion that the interest that the plaintiffs acquired in *Romalpa* was an interest by way of security, not an absolute interest, then I see no reason why it should not be categorised as a charge, albeit that it was held to be an interest acquired under the principle in *Re Hallett's Estate*.'

Similarly, in *E. Pfeiffer Weinkellerei-Weineinkauf GmbH v Arbuthnot Factors Ltd* ((1987) 3 BCC 608) a German wine exporter supplied wine to an English importer on terms that ownership of the wine was to remain with the supplier until paid for. The buyer, however, had the power to sub-sell. In the insolvency of the buyers the suppliers argued that they were beneficially entitled to all the proceeds of the sub-sales with a contractual duty to repay any surplus. The court held that not merely would such an arrangement be uncommercial but it could not be reconciled with the express intention of the parties. Any interest of the suppliers in the proceeds of resale was limited and must therefore create a charge.

A similar approach was adopted in *Specialist Plant Services Ltd and Another* v *Braithwaite Ltd* ((1987) 3 BCC 119) in which case a company supplied materials to be used in repairing machinery on terms of trade which provided that property in the repaired goods would vest in them until they received payment. Balcombe LJ held that this was clearly '... a clause which creates a charge, over the goods into which the items which the plaintiffs have used in the repairs have been incorporated, as security for payment of the costs of repair.'

In *Accurist Watches Ltd* v *King* ([1992] FSR 80) a Swiss concern, the plaintiff, was the registered owner of the trade mark Bueche-Girod which was used in relation to watches. The first defendant was the managing director of an English company, BG, which had entered into a distribution agreement with the plaintiff in August 1972 under a licence to sell watches, supplied to it by the plaintiff, under the plaintiff's trade mark. The agreement was varied to allow BG to use the mark to sell certain watches supplied by third parties. In 1986 and 1987 three German companies (the second, third and fourth defendants) supplied quantities of watches to BG for resale in England. It was assumed by the court that the contracts of supply were made in accordance with the terms of the distribution agreement, so that BG was entitled to use the plaintiff's trade mark on the goods. Accordingly, the German suppliers affixed the trade mark to the watches prior to supplying them to BG, in anticipation of the resale by BG. Each of the contracts between BG and the German companies required payment within 30 days, and contained reservation of title clauses under which the property in the watches did not pass to BG, and the German supplier was granted the right to take possession if any sums were owing to the supplier, even if the resale took place within the 30-day credit period. BG subsequently became insolvent and defaulted on its payments to the German suppliers. The distribution agreement was cancelled and the suppliers retook possession of the unsold watches. The suppliers then tried to resell the watches using the first defendant as their selling agent. The problem was that the watches had the plaintiff's trade mark. Mallett J held that despite the trade mark the original suppliers could resell the goods which were subject to a reservation of title clause. The learned judge said that to hold the contrary would:

> 'have a serious effect on commercial life, destroying the value of title clauses and other forms of security such as a fixed charge over branded goods ...'

The Companies Act 1989

The Companies Act 1989 made substantial changes to the rules on registration of company charges. Section 396 of the Companies Act 1989 which amends s. 93 of the Companies Act 1985 deals with the type of charges which need registration:

'(b) a charge on goods or any interest in goods, other than a charge under which the chargee is entitled to possession either of the goods or of a document of title to them.'

In the *Borden* case it would have been impossible to have a document of title to the resin which had been used to manufacture the chipboard but in *Armour* v *Thyssen* the German supplier would have been entitled to a document of title.

The other question which arises is whether the charge is created under the contract of sale or by operation. This is significant because s. 395 of the Companies Act 1985 provides:

'Charge means any form of security interest (fixed or floating) over property, other than an interest arising by operation of law.'

In the *Tatung* case Phillips J said that the seller's rights were:

'the creature of contract and not of law. The charge was directly created by the agreement, to which the defendants were party, that the plaintiffs should have the interest specified in the proceeds of dealing with the property.'

Appendix
The Recommendations of the Bingham Report

The Bank of Credit and Commerce grew up before banking supervision, in the UK or on an international level, had become the watchword. The effect of its collapse has focused attention not only on the shortcomings in law but also on the shortcomings of those carrying out the supervisory function. Bingham J in his report on the "Inquiry into the Supervision of the Bank of Credit and Commerce International", published in October 1992, said:

> 'I do not recommend any radical recasting of the system of banking supervision which has grown up in the UK and internationally over the last 20 years. I have not identified any crucial deficiencies in the arrangements now in force and due to come into force. I make a number of suggestions which should, if accepted, strengthen those arrangements, but ultimately supervisory arrangements can be no more effective than those who operate them: it is on the skill, alertness, experience and vigour of the supervisors, in the UK and abroad, that all ultimately depends.'

The Bingham Report made a number of recommendations which are outlined in this appendix.

UK BANKING SUPERVISION

(a) The Bingham Committee felt that the Bank of England's Board of Banking Supervision lacked, in the BCCI collapse, important information needed to fulfil its role. The Board's members should be alerted 'to any fact which even might cause their antennae to twitch.' This should be done by ensuring that meetings should not be so frequent that able and experienced independent members with other interests cannot attend them, and the volume of papers provided for meetings should not be so large as to be unassimilable.

(b) Although the Bank of England's traditional techniques of supervision based on trust, frankness and a willingness to co-operate 'on the whole have served the community well', the Bank needs to be alert to the possibility of fraud, astute in recognising it, and active in investigating it. With that in mind, the Bingham Report recommended that the Bank should establish a trained and qualified special investigations unit within the supervision division to consider all warnings and suspicions of malpractice and to ensure all warnings are investigated effectively.

(c) The Bank should take steps to strengthen its internal communications, which were exposed by the inquiry as a serious weakness. Guidelines are to be issued on communication with the Treasury and other public bodies.

(d) The Bank should strengthen its legal unit following BCCI. The main value of such a unit is not to warn supervisors of what they cannot lawfully do, but to ensure they are aware of the full extent of their powers under the law. The unit will also give sound and practical legal advice on supervisory questions.

(e) The Bank has powers to refuse or revoke authorisation on the grounds that a bank cannot be effectively supervised, and to make banks locate their head-offices in the country of authorisation. If the Bank feels that it needs further powers in this area, these should be enacted. The Bingham Report said that the one clear lesson of the BCCI affair is that 'banking group structures which deny supervisors a clear view of how business is conducted should be outlawed. If there is any continuing doubt about the Bank's power to prevent that situation recurring, such power should be expressly conferred.' The Bingham Committee took the view that the Bank of England, in authorising overseas banks, may not only rely on the overseas supervisors but the Bank must be satisfied that s.9(3) of the Banking Act 1987 has been satisfied. Moreover, the Basle Concordat provides for the sharing of supervisory responsibility on an agreed basis. The Bingham Committee did not feel that a statutory formula on the authorisation of non-EC banks and the extent of the reliance which the Bank of England should place on information supplied by overseas supervisors would provide a satisfactory solution.

EUROPEAN COMMUNITY

Within the EC the Bingham Report recommended that the Second Banking Co-Ordination Directive should contain provisions:

(a) Which prevent member states from supervisory 'forum shopping'.

(b) That a bank's place of incorporation is treated as its home, and that head-offices should be in the same state as its registered offices. Thus an institution should not be permitted to incorporate and subject itself to supervision in a member state where it thinks supervisory standards to be the most lax while effectively running its business from another member state where the regulation is more erroneous.

(c) The Directive should confer on EC Member States the right to refuse or withdraw banking supervision in the case of bank structures considered inappropriate for bodies carrying on banking activities.

(d) An EC Directive should establish banking deposit guarantee schemes in all member states and impose the guarantee obligation in Member States other than the bank's home state. Consequently, depositors in EC states other than the home state will be protected in the event of the insolvency of the bank.

INTERNATIONAL SUPERVISION

The Bingham Committee had two main recommendations relating to international supervision. The Committee:

(a) Took the view that, adopting the view of the Treasury and Civil Service Select Committee, the role of Bank for International Settlements should be expanded to encompass the monitoring of supervisory standards. The Bingham Report said that:

> 'It makes very good sense that supervision should be primarily conducted by the home supervisor who is closest to the bank and best placed to monitor but if host supervisors are increasingly to rely on the home supervisor they must be reassured by some form of independent verification that the home supervisor is really doing his job.'

(b) The Committee recognised that banking supervisors have until now tolerated the use of financial centres which offer 'impenetrable secrecy' and which for that reason tend to be favoured by those with 'something to hide'. The Committee recommended that the involvement of such a centre in the affairs of a bank should be sufficient to revoke or refuse recognition as an authorised institution.

DISCLOSURE AND CONFIDENTIAL INFORMATION

The Bingham Committee then made a number of recommendations on the question of disclosure of confidential information. The Committee took the view that:

(a) The principle that international supervisors should exchange information relevant to each other's supervisory concerns is clearly stated and well understood both within the Community and outside. However, it appears there is less agreement on the details of the information to be disclosed and the use to which that information may be put. The position is made more complicated by the First Co-Ordination Directive under which information may be exchanged with third countries only if the information is subject to obligations of professional secrecy as stringent as those imposed upon the member state. It is undesirable that there should be uncertainty in this area and an international agreement on what information should be disclosed and to whom and when. The Bingham Report recommends that if an international consensus cannot be achieved then it would be desirable for the European Commission to negotiate agreements outside the Community and for supervisors to enter into bilateral memoranda of understanding.

(b) An international database should be established listing those whom any supervisor has found to be nor fit nor proper to be a director, manager or controller of a bank.

APPOINTMENT OF AUDITORS

The Bingham Committee considered the question of the auditor's duty to report directly to the Bank of England. It concluded that a statutory clarification of s. 47 of the Banking Act 1987 would be advantageous for a number of reasons:

(a) It would strengthen the position of the auditor, and clarify his duty, if it were specified in a clear and explicit statutory provision.

(b) It would establish the correct relationship between client, auditor and supervisor and these are issues which should be determined by Parliament.

(c) It is desirable that the duty should be:
(i) to report to the Bank any information or opinion which the auditor knows or should reasonably know to be relevant to the Bank's fulfilment of the criteria in Schedule 3 of the 1987 Act;
(ii) to provide information reasonably requested by the Bank for the purposes of its supervisory duties.

(d) The statutory duty would clarify the position of foreign auditors of UK branches not subject to the disciplinary jurisdiction of the Institute of Chartered Accountants.

(e) All companies in a banking group should have the same accounting dates.

(f) A report covering all aspects of accounting and annual control should be commissioned annually from the reporting accountant of a bank incorporated outside the UK, rather than every four or five years.

(g) The Bank of England should consider introducing checks and remedies to prevent organisations under the common control of banking groups from having opportunities for fraud and manipulation.

(h) The Bank should have the power to require a separate audit of banks domiciled outside the EC.